DIVIDING THE LAND

University of Chicago Geography Research Paper no. 238

Series Editors
Michael P. Conzen
Chauncy D. Harris
Neil Harris
Marvin W. Mikesell
Gerald D. Suttles

Titles published in the Geography Research Papers series prior to 1992 and still in print are now distributed by the University of Chicago Press. For a list of available titles, see the end of the book. The University of Chicago Press commenced publication of the Geography Research Papers series in 1992 with no. 233.

DIVIDING THE LAND

*Early American Beginnings of
Our Private Property Mosaic*

Edward T. Price

THE UNIVERSITY OF CHICAGO PRESS
Chicago and London

Edward T. Price is professor emeritus in the Department of Geography, University of Oregon.

The University of Chicago Press, Chicago 60637
The University of Chicago Press, Ltd., London
© 1995 by the University of Chicago
All rights reserved. Published 1995
Printed in the United States of America

04 03 02 01 00 99 98 97   2 3 4 5

ISBN: 0-226-68065-7 (paper)

Library of Congress Cataloging-in-Publication Data

Price, Edward T.
    Dividing the land   :   early American beginnings of our private
property mosaic   /   Edward T. Price
        p. cm. – (University of Chicago geography research paper ; no. 238)
        Includes bibliographical references and index.
    1. Real property–United States–Maps–History. I. Title. II. Series.
GA109.5.P75   1995   94-39568
333.3′0973–dc20   CIP

♾ The paper used in this publication meets the minimum requirements of the American National Standards for Information Sciences–Permanence of Paper for Printed Library Materials, ANSI Z39.48-1984.

For Margaret

Contents

Figures

Note: Where it was suitable, maps and aerial photographs were framed to represent 3 x 3-mile squares. Such maps and photographs are presented at a scale of 1 1/2 inches to the mile. Other areas less than seven miles wide are presented at scales of 2/3, 1, and 2 1/4 inches to the mile, thus forming a series of four scales stepping up at 50 percent increments. Maps of larger areas vary greatly in the sizes of areas they represent, and are scaled to fit the space. Whenever appropriate, maps and aerial photographs are identified with the 1:24,000 or 1:25,000 USGS quadrangles representing the same areas, by naming the quadrangles in the figure captions.

Tables

Preface

Patterns of land division are important among the many features of regions that geographers study in trying to describe and find meaning in the lives of the people in those regions. The land division of the greater part of the United States was laid out in the framework of the rectangular surveys of the U.S. Land Office. My interest in these surveys was enhanced by a few years of residence in Ohio, a virtual museum of early efforts toward a uniform system. But later, in trying to prepare a class lecture on the irregular land division found in parts of the country opened up earlier as colonies, I ran into a great shortage of information.

The frustration of that experience was the point of departure for research leading to preparation of this volume dealing with the land division patterns of the major parts of the United States that were surveyed under the auspices of early colonies and states rather than by the federal government as part of its public domain. The study focuses on the variety of geometric patterns in which the lands of the present United States were originally laid out by their European settlers, on the processes that turned the land into those parcels of private property, on the variables that controlled those processes, and on comparison of both the patterns and processes that were characteristic of the various colonies and states. Later conditions and events that throw perspective on the original land division include the continuing redivision of the land, the fashioning of a new federal land system, and the persistence of the role of land parcels in the lives of their occupants.

The information on land division that had proved so difficult to find in a university library turned out to be abundant, albeit mostly in crude form, in state and local archives. The grants of most of the land in the original colonies are still intact and available, but they present another problem. Processing a million or two individual land grants for their norms and their meanings is beyond the scope of most studies; I have relied heavily on the occasional availability of land grant maps (Appendix B) compiled from the archival records and showing the original grants of all the land in a county or a township.

The land grant maps are numerous enough to give a good idea of the range of land geometries found within the whole area of this study. The number of land grant maps in many of the individual states, however, is relatively small and often insufficient for the generalizations that might most efficiently describe what happened in each of those states. The presentation of a number of individual cases from the land grant maps helps provide the reader the contact with basic data needed for a sense of the reality sought in the study.

Division of the land is a topic that falls in the meeting ground of several fields, notably including history and geography. Among the contributions of historians, general works dealing with periods during which settlement occurred give special attention to the policies and processes that governed the passage of the public land into private hands. A variety of works have also treated the land question in particular aspects or in particular regions. A specialized historical treatment of the subject under the heading of land tenure, however, is the work of an agricultural economist, Marshall Harris. Historians have also selected small areas for more detailed study of the distribution of land among settlers or followed the later cadastral changes effected by citizens trying to make the best use of the land for their purposes and capabilities.

Comparative accounts of the different American land division systems by geographers have mostly been of the nature of summaries in either comprehensive works or in shorter studies. More detailed studies of smaller areas are fairly numerous, variously considering policy background, rules for and conduct of grants, analysis of results, subsequent cadastral changes, and comparison among different areas, commonly including land grant maps of specific areas and occasionally distribution maps of resulting survey patterns. But intensive state-by-state studies of land division that might have made the preparation of this volume relatively easy have, for the most part, not been carried out. The one exhaustive state study, that of William Wallace on New Hampshire, mostly presented as a series of oral papers, has not been published. Two states have been the subject of studies characterizing the varied survey patterns of their parts: Louisiana through the work of John W. Hall, and Texas through the work of Terry Jordan. Peter Wacker has also made a notable contribution to the study of early land division in New Jersey.

Originally I set out to put together an overview of all land surveys in the United States other than the federal system. When this proved too much, it seemed logical to limit the study to the nineteen states with no territory under the federal survey (the original thirteen, five states derived from their territory, and Texas). Louisiana was added to include its display of French longlots, whose fascinating geometry was created in part by processes not significant in other areas of the study.

Dividing the Land differs from preceding studies in its combination of two characteristics: first, its broad scope in treating comparatively the variety of land patterns in the twenty colonies and states with which it deals; and second, its empirical base, insofar as was possible, in the specifics of actual land patterns. I hope it will provide context and meaning for other land division inquiries.

Acknowledgments

I am grateful for the help of more people than I can name here who gave me or directed me to the information on which this study is based. Great dependence was placed on the resources of state land archives, under whatever agencies or names they fell, of Alabama, Connecticut, Florida, Georgia, Kentucky, Louisiana, Maine, Maryland, Massachusetts, New Hampshire, New York, Pennsylvania, South Carolina, Tennessee, Texas, and Virginia. The Delaware Historic Preservation Section played a similar role for that state. Pat Bryant and Marion Hemperley of the Georgia Surveyor General Department typified the eagerness of many archive staffs to see the stories in their records told. A scattering of county offices—registries of deeds, tax assessment, surveyors, and engineers—also yielded valuable information, mostly on cadastral changes after the original division.

Al Urquhart, Sam Hilliard, David Lowenthal, David Marentette, and Don Holtgrieve read different versions of the manuscript, and many of their suggestions have been incorporated in the final text. Several geography colleagues have helped with suggestions on particular chapters. David Marentette's work on my writing should be appreciated by every reader, although David is not responsible for surviving difficulties. The suggestions of two anonymous readers for the publisher were much appreciated and considerably followed.

Susan Trevitt-Clark, Ed Thatcher, and Peter Stark of the University of Oregon Map Library have patiently searched for obscure or nonexistent maps I wanted, and refrained from complaining about the number of topographic maps I have left for refiling. Terri Benedict, Wanda Weber, and Diana Ash are the most recent members of the University of Oregon Department of Geography secretarial staff who repeatedly typed manuscript chapters of this book before computerization finally simplified (but did not eliminate) their work.

My sketch maps (and sometimes sketchy ideas) have been made readable through the valuable help of David Kuhn and Jane Sinclair. Leslie Loney has also contributed her talents on three maps. Bill Loy gave helpful advice in this connection.

xvii

I am grateful for the help of the staffs of the University of Chicago Geography Research Paper series and of the University of Chicago Press in bringing the study to publication. Michael Conzen and Penelope Kaiserlian submitted it for publication. Carol Saller, whose skilled hand touched every page, edited the manuscript, and Martin Hertzel was responsible for the book design.

The backing of all members of my family has been important and appreciated. Peggy and Susan were on hand, as they have been at many critical times during the past two years, to help with both assembling the manuscript and reading proof. Sandy, Larry, Ken, and Jeffrey put in further hours on the proof. And Liz Keeler saw the proofreading finished after our family had gone home. Finally, my heartfelt thanks, as ever, go to Margaret for her support, encouragement, patience, suggestions, and companionship.

Part I

Introduction

1

Framework of the Land

COLONIAL settlement advanced in waves over the pristine American land, greatly varied in its nature, but little divided or improved by its aboriginal inhabitants. As the waves moved on, they left new landscapes in their wake, land more intensively used, and, to that end, fragmented among myriad owners, tenants, and managers. The farms we sometimes see being subdivided today are the heritage of older divisions in which more than two-thirds of the present United States was parceled out in private holdings.[1]

Huge land grants launched most of the American colonies under their various sponsors. Allotting that land became a principal business of the colonies, for land was long their principal wealth and they could prosper only as they put it in the hands of people who would use it productively. First, land was the bait to attract farmers into the colonies; it was used also to attract artisans and investors, develop industry, and settle frontier defenders. Tracts of public land were set aside for the support of schools, churches, and colonial governments. Land was given to officials, soldiers, and others in reward for their services. Less accountably, officials granted land to friends, relatives, people of influence, and, not least, to themselves. Quitrents[2] and the sale and rental of land benefited sponsors and governments of colonies.

Land division practices had a quality of ongoing experimentation that was separately worked out in the individual colonies for furthering settlement along the lines desired. The evolving practices became integral parts of the colonies' differing ways of life. Foreign

---

[1]Marion Clawson, *America's Land and Its Uses* (Baltimore: Johns Hopkins Press for Resources for the Future, 1972), 10.

[2]The quitrent survived as the last tangible obligation of feudalism, an annual fee to be paid in lieu of any other dues. The quitrent also signified fealty to the proprietor or ruler under whom the land was held.

Most italicized terms are defined in a glossary, p. 364.

3

visitors to the United States who marvel at the regularity and uniformity of the land survey in the Middle West are often unaware of the irregularity and variety of its colonial antecedents.

The Land Divided

The patterns of property lines drawn on the land are projections of the societies that create them, and they both facilitate and constrain those societies in their daily working. The spatial order of *cadastral* maps[3] may be read for clues about the social order: the distribution of landed wealth, the types of land that are and were valued, spatial patterns of residence, whether and how settlements were planned, and changes in ownership occasioned by individual interest and social change. The identities of particular societies are often encoded in the geometry of their landownership.

The divided land defines a multitude of jurisdictions managed by owners and their delegates in accordance with their goals and abilities, subject to society's laws. The sum of these land management actions includes much of the activity occurring in the territory embraced by political units at whatever level. As the size, shape, nature, and surroundings of a holding affect its suitability for different uses, so the land in a larger area constitutes a productive plant, the utility of which may be limited in accordance with the particular net of properties formed by its division. Thus the division of the land is of concern not only to each property owner individually, but also to all members of the community and to the society as a whole. The values affected by the land division are not only commodities of commerce, including land itself, but also consumer aspects of the land as living space for residents and community application of zoning and conservation measures.

The original division of the land, which usually initiated a long sequence of gradual historical changes, is the primary focus of this book. This was the setting of the stage and our beginning point for understanding the later cadastral map. State archives containing the original grants from European crowns form the ultimate underpinning for titles and boundaries of most land alienated before the Revolution, although most states have reduced the period through which titles must be traced. These original grants record traces of settler struggles with their new environments. Properly interpreted, they

---

[3]Maps showing landownership.

reflect both individual and community goals of the time. They mark the beginning of experiences with particular pieces of land that led to continuation, modification, or abandonment. And the attitudes that accompanied ownership were sometimes passed on with the land parcels.

A society's division of the land may increase the natural intricacy resulting from variations in slope, vegetation, drainage, soil, and water bodies. When land is divided, every boundary becomes a legal barrier. A wall, fence, or hedge may make it also a physical barrier. Parts of properties may become centers of activity as residences and headquarters, while other parts remain peripheral. Roads and paths add a variety of accessibility. Some features of the property mosaic will still reflect aspects of nature: streams form property boundaries; land of poorer quality may have been excluded by oddly drawn lines. The land division geometry, like the geometry of nature, affects the distribution of people over the land, their access to productive facilities and markets, and their interaction with one another.

Land as property reveals nature and culture inextricably entangled. A parcel of land has an indubitably physical existence, biological too with its vegetation and soils. Property boundaries and location are in part bare mathematical entities. That the land is property means that it is also imbued with human perceptions based on territorial instincts and culture, drawing on both sentimental and utilitarian roots. Land, like other aspects of culture, exhibits a frequently arbitrary diversity from place to place, in the manner in which it might be treated, in rights of use, in types of tenure, and in laws governing these customs. Indeed the meanings of their property to two owners may be so disparate that a single line separates values as incommensurate as the proverbial apples and oranges, even if the parcels are identical in physical quality.

Land may be examined too as a carrier of attitudes: a potential keeper of the social and economic milieu that went with its original granting and a conservative force as a vested interest that keeps its owner-occupant in one place. Land division, as a shaper of the landscape, is one among the plethora of artifacts that reveal a manner of living and guide the young along its path.[4] A forbidding fence along a property line, a driveway leading through a gate to a well-kept farmstead, or a set of complementary land uses adapted to the soils

[4]Philip L. Wagner, "Cultural Landscapes and Regions: Aspects of Communication," *Geoscience and Man* 5 (1974): 135–36, 141.

and slopes within a farm's bounds—such guides may be instructive far beyond their immediate application on a farm.

Whatever their form, landownership (cadastral) patterns are among the most persistent features of the human landscape. Rooted in both the land and the possessive attitudes of owners, parcels are troublesome to reshape. General patterns may persist even after consolidation of properties has erased earlier boundaries or subdivision has created new boundaries. Vacated property lines may survive as visible features in field boundaries, vegetation boundaries, fence and hedge lines, or roads. The original division of most American areas left imprints that still mark them today. Land patterns and ownership commonly survived transfers in governmental jurisdiction among Britain, the Netherlands, France, Spain, Mexico, Texas, and the United States.

The divided land resembles a great game board on which property may be traded or rented, subdivided or consolidated, improved or neglected. The acquisitive play of some aggressive participants suggests the game of Monopoly, whereas the cautious play of neighbors with different goals is better described by a game title such as the Farming Game. Although the players are governed by the same cadastral rules, their values and goals may be highly disparate.

Patterns of Parcel Layout

No shape of farm was generally preferred over other shapes in early North American settlement. Although fields have traditionally been designed to accommodate the plowing method used, most American farms have been large enough to contain fields in almost any shape. Compact shapes of farms, in the absence of conditions to the contrary, frequently have an advantage of minimizing travel between farmsteads and outlying portions of the farms. The early New England farm was exceptional in having its holdings fragmented in a number of separate parcels.

Almost universal characteristics of American rural property are boundaries that are either straight lines[5] or the edges (or courses) of streams, lakes, swamps, bays, or ocean. Thus most holdings are polygons, although many have a natural water boundary on one side, and a few are mostly or even entirely surrounded by water.

---

[5]The lines are straight in the surveyors' descriptions and maps. As the lines survive on the ground, they may be a little crooked.

The occurrence of several distinguishable patterns of land survey is shown in figure 1.1. The large area classified as "irregular" covers surveys often described as "metes and bounds" (Appendix A). That these surveys seem such a mass of chaos probably explains why most analyses of them have been only local. Irregular surveys show few right angles, sets of lines square with the compass or parallel with one another, single lines long enough to bound several different pieces of property, or other systematic repetition. The irregular classification conceals occasional regularity in areas too small to identify on this map. A second category of irregular shapes is mapped in eastern New York, where, much more than in any other colony, the land was granted in large estates. Most of New England is distinguished for its township-by-township settlement and subdivision, which gave it a unique mixture of regular and less regular survey patterns.

The other survey patterns on the map are defined by the nature and degree of their geometric regularity. Three of the types involve rectangularity: the grids surveyed by the U.S. Land Office, other grids surveyed by states or land companies, and less regular surveys in which most corners are nonetheless right angles. The final type is division into longlots: elongated strips, usually laid out side by side and fronting on a waterway or road.[6]

The area mapped in irregular land divisions extends along the Atlantic coast from New York City to Florida, running inland as far as the Kentucky-Illinois border. Between one place and another, jumbles of irregular parcels are often describably different in shapes, sizes, and collective patterns, which is to say that they are not completely chaotic. A rather typical survey is found in Rapho Township, Lancaster County, on the Pennsylvania Piedmont (fig. 14.5), where most of the original land grants were compact polygons of moderate, but somewhat varied size. The polygons averaged eight sides, helter-skelter in direction, with relatively few reentrant angles. Visually much simpler were the valley land patterns near Martinsburg, West Virginia (fig. 8.3), where grants elongated on average about 2:1 tended to line up with the Appalachian ridge to the northwest; many parcels had four sides, a number of them actually rectangles, but the average number of sides was still nearly seven. Otherwise irregular surveys on the Piedmont of South Carolina (fig. 8.2) include a scattering of square parcels of varying size and orientation, which were among the first holdings laid out by

---

[6]Longlots are arbitrarily defined for this study as being at least three times as long as wide.

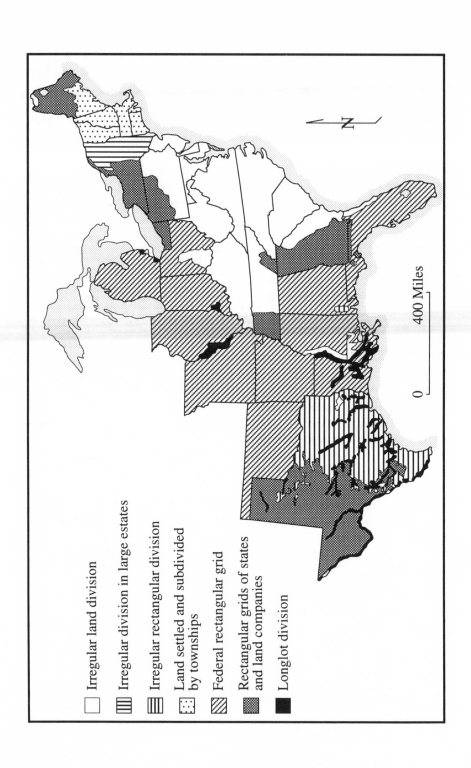

N

400 Miles

0

Irregular land division

Irregular division in large estates

Irregular rectangular division

Land settled and subdivided by townships

Federal rectangular grid

Rectangular grids of states and land companies

Longlot division

early pioneers. The surveys of Fairfax County, Virginia (fig. 7.5), were notable for the spread of parcel sizes: ranging from less than fifty acres to more than twenty thousand acres. Certainly the most contorted of all assemblages of parcels was that found in Howard County on the Maryland Piedmont (fig. 8.1). A sample of twenty-nine contiguous properties showed an average of thirty-nine sides and fifteen reentrant angles, enclosing many extended and ungainly shapes. Evidently the land traditions produced by the interaction of laws, grantees, surveyors, and terrain vary. Appendix C summarizes the distribution of parcel sizes for many localities, and Appendix D summarizes some quantitative measures of land division geometry.

Township surveys in colonial New England tended to become more regular as time progressed (e.g., compare the plats of figs. 2.2, 2.3, 3.1, and 3.2 with fig. 4.1). Even the seventeenth-century patterns, however, were usually more orderly than most of the surveys elsewhere. The early township layout actually resembled traditional manors or farming villages of England, their land in blocks of house lots facing a common green, in open fields and meadows divided into strips, and in common pastures and woods.[7]

The regularity of gridded land division was uncommon in most parts of colonial North America. Such division reached its greatest frequency in eighteenth-century New England towns,[8] where the parcels of the grids were more often compact than markedly elongated. An elaborate grid system had been projected for Carolina counties, with their baronies and colonies (fig. 5.3), but very little of the plan was ever inscribed on the land itself. South Carolina's eighteenth-century township scheme offered a new opportunity for platting grids, which materialized at least in the Swiss township of Purrysburg. Following the Revolution, as the checkerboard survey was being instituted for the federal lands, rectangular grids were

---

[7]Ironically there is little, if any, evidence that the manors in early America adhered to the land patterns of their European predecessors. Certainly they left no such lasting imprint on the land.

[8]The terms "town" and "township" are virtually synonymous in New England and New York. As I will use the terms, the town is the community, including its people and government, whereas the township is the sharply bounded land area within which its people live and its government has jurisdiction.

Fig. 1.1 (*facing page*). Land survey types. Modified from "Land Division Types," map published as frontispiece in Francis J. Marschner, *Boundaries and Records* (Washington: USDA, 1960); and modified with the use of: USGS topographic quadrangles; Jordan, "Division of the Land"; Hall, "Louisiana Survey Systems"; Hilliard, "An Introduction to Land Survey Systems in the Southeast."

adopted for new areas of Georgia (fig. 10.2), Pennsylvania (figs. 14.8, 14.9), and New York, and in some of the land laid out for veterans in western Maryland. Also, some New York estates were eventually divided into grids. Later great parts of western Texas were laid out in square grids, most notably lands given to railroads (fig. 16.6). Grids had characterized the plans for many towns and cities by late in the seventeenth century, before they were used much for rural lands.

Tendencies toward rectangularity in land patterns were almost completely absent in many surveys, but appeared with characteristic frequency in others. Rectangularity dominated in some New England towns of otherwise irregular geometry. It was strongly favored in the three original counties of Pennsylvania (figs. 14.1 and 14.2), as in Amelia (fig. 8.7) and probably other townships of South Carolina. Most Texas grants were rectangular (fig. 16.7), whether under Spanish, Mexican, Texas Republic, or Texas State regimes, and the rectangularity was usually preserved on later subdivision. Some New York estates and Carolina baronies acquired their quota of right angles and parallel lines when they were subdivided.

The spectacular arrays of longlots on the river levees of Louisiana (figs. 15.3, 15.4) are unmatched elsewhere in the area of this study, although longlots characterized most areas of French settlement. Longlots were common also on Texas's major rivers, from the giant Spanish grants along the Rio Grande to the modest farms laid out by German colonization companies on the Concho (fig. 16.6). Smallholdings of Dutch colonies also featured longlots, possibly following traditional forms for dividing drained areas in Europe. In the English colonies longlots sprang from two different roots: one was the widespread policy that property on navigable streams have a depth three to six times the frontage; the other, modeled on the field strips of the medieval village, was common where township settlement was attempted. Longlots often appeared in ladder-like frames,[9] sometimes running between parallel or near-parallel straight lines.

Sources of Variety in Land Division Patterns

This variety in American land patterns evolved from models in the European homelands modified in accordance with the purposes of

---

[9]Ladder patterns of division comprise lots separated by parallel transverse lines drawn between longer pairs of lines. The lots so marked off are not necessarily of uniform width.

the colonies as defined by their charters, implemented under their differing sponsors, and influenced by the desires of the settlers. The actual distribution, selection, and surveying of land depended on decisions that were opportune under frontier conditions. Colonists drew their property lines on what they considered a blank slate, with little regard to those who had occupied the land before.

North American settlement came at a time when land in Western Europe, including Britain, France, the Netherlands, Spain, Sweden, and Germany, was in the midst of a long transition from the fragmented farms and *open-field* systems of the medieval manor to the *enclosed* farms held in individual ownership common today.[10] The early New England farms comprising scattered longlots resembled the older open-field patterns. Most American farms in other colonies comprised a single, usually irregular parcel of land, and resembled the enclosed properties of Europe. Such American farms, however, had been surveyed afresh in a new land, whereas the European enclosures were usually superimposed on old open-field layouts.

Most European farmers had very small landholdings, often not more than ten or twenty acres; even those holdings were often lost when enclosure took place. Farmers looking to the New World for new opportunities wanted, and usually were able to arrange, independent ownership and larger holdings. Some of the colonies also permitted large feudal manors with land held under overlords, even after new establishments of the same type had been outlawed in England. The American land was shaped to accommodate people in a variety of estates, but freehold and feudal tenures were not likely to coexist in contentment. The trend of the times and the need for immigrants both favored freer tenures.

The mix of purposes that went into the plans for English colonies included extension of the English domain, Christianization of the native population, profits from land and trade, freedom of religion for members of the sponsors' particular Christian denominations, and new opportunities for settlers. Although the crown claimed both governmental jurisdiction and ownership of the land, no English colony in America was originally settled under direct management of the royal government. The investments and risks of starting colonies were largely borne by individuals or private organizations under royal charters that specified territories and conditions for settle-

---

[10]In open-field farming, a number of farmers own strips in a single field and farm it cooperatively. Under enclosure, a farmer-owner has sole control of his land, which is commonly all in a single parcel.

ment, government, landownership, and trade. In the present United States, only some Spanish colonies might be said to have begun as governmental projects.

The sequence of British colony sponsors began with corporations, recently reformed from older-style trading companies, as founders of the first successful colonies.[11] Shortly after 1620 the style of English charters shifted toward seigniorial grants to one or several individual proprietors.[12] Both the corporations and the proprietors founded their colonies in the hope of profit from skimpy investment, with most of the leaders pursuing their primary interests in England rather than becoming colonists themselves.

In New England, however, the early settlers, under the corporations, were largely religious dissenters who soon transformed their colonies into self-governing or, *corporate*,[13] bodies with close ties to their churches. Expansion from these early cores eventually took over unsettled claims of several seigniorial interests. The last colonial charter, for Georgia, was a reversion to control by a corporation, one dedicated, however, to charity rather than profit. Thus colonies could be described variously as commercial trading venture, religious refuge, feudal *palatinate*,[14] real-estate promotion, and haven for the worthy poor. Dutch, Swedish, and French colonization depended on trading company enterprise.

A slight majority of the English colonies eventually came directly under the crown because their charter plans failed, they were separated from other colonies, or (in New York) the proprietor succeeded

[11]Virginia, Plymouth, and Massachusetts were founded under such charters. The nature of the charters and of their tenure provisions is presented in Viola Florence Barnes, "Land Tenure in English Colonial Charters of the Seventeenth Century," in *Essays in Colonial History Presented to Charles McLean Andrews by His Students* (New Haven: Yale University Press, 1931), 4–40. The evolution of English colonial charters can be seen to have occurred in fairly logical sequence when the original thirteen American colonies are considered alongside settlements in Ireland, Canada, Bermuda, the Bahamas, and the West Indies as well as several abortive charters and grants in the present United States.

[12]Colonies of proprietary origin included Maryland, Carolina, and Pennsylvania.

[13]Marshall Harris, *Origin of the Land Tenure System in the United States* (1953; reprinted Westport, Conn.: Greenwood Press, 1970), 98–116. "Corporate" here denotes self-government rather than private corporations. Its roots lay in action that did not wait for charters, such as the Mayflower Compact and the independent settlements of Connecticut and Rhode Island, as well as the transfer of governance under the Massachusetts Bay charter from England to Massachusetts.

[14]Palatine powers derived from the "Bishop of Durham" clauses in the charters of Maryland and Carolina. The Bishops of Durham had for a time been given the powers of the palace to rule their unsettled frontier.

to the throne.[15] Land administration, however, was not made uniform in these royal colonies. Rather they continued their own meandering courses. In addition large blocks of land in four of them were held and distributed by private proprietors independently of the colonial governments. Maryland and Pennsylvania-Delaware remained as proprietary colonies until the Revolution, while Massachusetts, Connecticut, and Rhode Island continued their corporate status, at least in substance.

A ubiquitous theme in the division of the land is the tension between the interest of the individual seeking land and the perceptions of authorities regarding which land division and settlement patterns would be most conducive to the proper development of the colony. Individuals wanted freedom to pick out the choicest land and often more than they needed. The interest of the colony often lay in maintaining compact settlement without intervening vacancies, dividing the poor land along with the good, and limiting ownership to the amount of land that would be productively worked. The colonial bureaucracy in England favored landholdings of moderate size, whereas the officials of the colonies, more responsive to powerful local interests, often connived in grants of large tracts.

The first parcels of land in several colonies were marked off in accord with systems planned by their sponsors, but the colonies were too busy with survival and new settlers to maintain such niceties. In most of the colonies, the desire of individuals for land soon came to drive the process of selection and division. Only in New England did the interest of the colonial society long keep the independent thrusts of individuals effectively in check.

In two-tier actions, the New England colony granted townships to proprietors who in their turn surveyed the land and assigned it to settlers in accordance with their perceptions of equity among families, even *sizing* the parcels according to quality. Townships remained the units of land division even after they later became more commercial in their initiation.

Outside New England most of the land was marked off one parcel at a time, regardless of the nature of sponsorship. Most land was distributed on the issue of a *warrant* authorizing survey of the acreage to which the colonist was entitled under the colony's laws. The colonist could then show the surveyor what vacant land he wished

---

[15]Virginia in 1625 was the first colony to come under the royal government, to be followed by New Hampshire, New York, New Jersey, the Carolinas, and finally Georgia in 1752.

marked off. Legal limits on the location and shape of the parcel were relatively minor. We can imagine that the surveyors themselves exerted some influence on their clients' choices, objecting to parcels bounded by too many survey courses or by traverses over the most difficult terrain, or favoring lots adjoining previous surveys or likely to simplify later surveys. In any case, the freedom of choice was sufficient to produce parcels of highly varying shape, the first ones often widely scattered, as each individual tried to enclose the land best suited by quality and location and leave a safe berth against possibly conflicting claims. This individual choice of parcels came to be termed *indiscriminate location.* The resulting irregularity in shape of parcels was often, but not always, accompanied by wide disparity in size of parcels.

The most distinctive formula for land entitlement in the English colonies was the *headright.*[16] A headright offered a certain amount of land, most typically fifty acres, for each new colonist. The land was awarded to the person paying the colonist's passage. Expenses of acquiring land included fees for filing the claim and paying the surveyor. The land had to be settled and cultivated—that is, *seated and planted*—before ownership was finally secured. The headright system was highly adaptable. The land allocated to a small farmer would be in proportion to the size of the family that he brought in, but a wealthy person importing many servants (or sometimes slaves) could receive a large tract to work with their labor. Additional headrights were sometimes awarded to indentured servants at the end of their terms or, later on, to other landless residents. Headrights, in a crude way, measured out the land in proportion to the number of colonists who were ready to work it and were in need of its products.

Headright grants were offered in Virginia within ten years of the founding of the colony. But the idea of luring colonists by promises of land was older, for each participant in Raleigh's Lost Colony of 1587 had been promised 500 acres "onely for the adventure of his person,"[17] (a disastrous adventure measured by either cost or reward). Headrights were offered later in several other colonies, primarily in the South.

---

[16]Commonly called "immigration" rights in the colonies. The earliest use of "headright" I have found was in a 1783 Georgia act for opening a land office.

[17]Statement by Thomas Heriot, 1587, in Richard Hakluyt, *The Principal Navigations, Voyages, Traffiques, and Discoveries of the English Nation,* 12 vols. (Glasgow: James MacLehose Sons, 1904)(originally published 1589), 8: 385.

The practice of *squatting*[18] eventually became the folk equivalent of the headright. People whose lore was of field and woods rather than of such abstract matters as authorization, survey, and filing, simply built a house, cleared some land, planted crops, and marked their corners: seating and planting and crude surveys first, authorization later.[19] Some squatted for lack of any legal entitlement, others because they were far from the capitals where the transactions might be formalized.

The history of squatting is not well recorded, but some of the colonies responded by according land rights to those who had occupied it for several years. If the land was being sold, the squatters might have to pay the standard price to gain title. Squatting was unusual in New England and early Georgia, places where land was closely controlled in the local community.

Late in the seventeenth century the sale of land was replacing grants by headrights in both Maryland and Virginia. Pennsylvania, founded about this time, depended mainly on selling land. The private proprietors who owned large tracts of Virginia, North Carolina, New Jersey, and later New Hampshire sold their land for their own profit. Even in Massachusetts and Connecticut a number of townships were sold at auction, and the winners in turn sold lots to individuals.

Many of the larger tracts into which the land was divided ended up being sold off in smaller parcels by their owners. These larger tracts included: the great private proprietaries just mentioned; surveyed tracts or unlocated quantities of western land granted wholesale by Virginia on condition of their owners recruiting settlers at a rate such as a family to 1,000 acres; manor grants, mostly in Maryland, Carolina, New York, and Pennsylvania, few of which ever functioned as manors, but which became plantations or were divided into tenancies and eventually sold to farmer-owners. In the division of large tracts of land, the sellers sometimes mapped out more regularity in the parceling than was likely to occur from warrants for survey specifying only the acreage.

---

[18]This term, like "headright," seems to be of U.S. origin, and to have been unrecorded during most of the colonial period.

[19]These three assertions of claims were known on the frontiers as "cabin rights," "corn rights," and tomahawk rights" (blazing trees), respectively.

Social Aspects of Land Division

Tenures

Most colonial land was assigned to colonists in *free and common socage*. This tenure differed in practice from our modern ownership in *fee simple* only in the obligation of a quitrent. The land of ten colonies was technically connected with the crown, like thousands of farms in various parts of England, through the king's Manor of East Greenwich in the County of Kent. The tenures of Kent were relatively liberal among English tenures, and helped point the American communities in the direction of freer landholding. Although Maryland and Pennsylvania land was *held as of* the Castle of Windsor, and Georgia land as of the Manor of Hampton Court, these distinctions seem to have had little significance.

Free and common socage was also the tenure under which most of the charters had assigned land to the colony sponsors. Some proprietors, however, had more freedom to assign parcels in other tenures than the king himself enjoyed in England after 1620. Even so, most of the land they granted was also in free and common socage, which was almost the only tenure of grants made in colonies after they came under the crown.

The exceptions to free and common socage included the land of manors, which were clearly forbidden only in Virginia and Georgia.[20] Virginia and Georgia were also the only English colonies whose original sponsors (like the Dutch company in New Netherland) had not actually been granted the land they were assigned to administer. The Georgia trustees for most of their regime granted the land to individuals in *tail male*,[21] a tenure suited only to a tightly managed society. Community approval of land transfers was also required in early New England, in that buyers had to be acceptable to the local town. Tenures, however, were virtually fee simple in New England, where landholders considered themselves tenants of God rather than of the king, and quitrents were mostly ignored.

Land granted to farmers in areas controlled by the Netherlands, France, and Spain was usually also in a free tenure (*allodial*). The Dutch *patroonships* were the equivalent of manors. The similar French *seigneuries* were mostly confined to the St. Lawrence Valley, and the Spanish seem to have granted no feudal holdings in Florida,

[20]Harris, 149.

[21]Land held in tail male could change ownership only by passage to male heirs or reversion to the crown. In Georgia exceptions could be granted by the trustees.

Louisiana, or Texas. Tenure in the Swedish grants in Delaware and Pennsylvania had likely been allodial also, although little is known about it.

Distribution of Land among Populations

The settlement of a new land is a ready opportunity to use land assignment as a tool of social goals, as colonial sponsors were well aware. In actuality land assignment was probably governed as much by expediency as by social ends, but the sharing of land among the people was much more uneven in some colonies than in others.

The most even distribution of land occurred in Georgia's first settlement, where every charity colonist received fifty acres, and in New England, where most people who wanted to farm could have at least enough land for subsistence. The limit on grants in Georgia was 500 acres for independent colonists with several servants, and holdings much larger than that in New England were so rare as not to be part of the system.

At the other extreme lay the great estates of New York. Although a large part of the settlers under the Dutch had received family farms, the English responded rather to the cue of patroonships, most of the area granted by the English having been in fewer than 200 tracts of from 5,000 to well over a million acres.

The colonies between New York and Georgia mixed grants of both large and small tracts from early in their settlement. Both headrights and land sales systems lent themselves to such variety. Georgia too soon picked up the ways of other colonies to grant large tracts along with the small.

Following the Revolution, the states that the colonies became still showed no uniformity in the further distribution of their land. Most continued to make land available to farmers, more often by sale than by headrights. Georgia resumed the democratic ways of its early distribution policy, first with headrights no longer tied to immigration, then with a string of land lotteries offering chances to all. Vermont sold its remaining townships in a fashion similar to older New England colonies in the eighteenth century. Several states distributed free land to veterans, most granting acreages steeply graded with rank. Speculators bought tremendous tracts in New York and part of Maine. Elsewhere—Pennsylvania, western Virginia, Kentucky, and Tennessee—they amassed tracts by buying rights from veterans and other claimants. Most of these large tracts, however, were put on the market and ended up in the hands of farmers.

Family Farms

Small farms were included in the first known grants of land made near the end of Virginia's first decade, and the policy for headrights continuing such grants, with special concessions for the "ancient planters," was formulated in 1618. The small farm became an important part of the ownership pattern throughout the South as Maryland, Carolina, and Georgia provided for headrights in their original plans. Small farms could also be created by sale of part of a larger parcel, by an owner's gift to a servant on completion of the term of service, and by special individual grants.

Small farms were losing ground to large estates through much of the South in the eighteenth century. Many were consolidated into the slave-worked plantations. Where small farmers declined in number, it was probably more because of the monopoly slaveholders had on low-cost labor than because of any monopoly on land. Family holdings continued to be mixed in with the larger ones in most areas.

In New England individuality among townships meant that typical family property ran from as little as twenty-five or thirty acres to up to 500 acres; the larger holdings were usually planned for division among the next generation. Consolidation of fragmented farms moved rapidly before the seventeenth century was over. In the eighteenth century farms in new townships were increasingly laid off in single parcels. Paradoxically, many of these commercially initiated townships sold all their land in equal acreages to their first owners.

Pennsylvania's original land plans hardly proclaimed the open door that would bring in farmers in such numbers. Land was to be sold, and the first sales favored those ready to buy from 500 up to 5,000 or 10,000 acres. Penn's plan for some townships plainly did include small farmers, and the headright for the freed servant was another way for the farmer to acquire land. The early eighteenth-century immigration forced a more rapid conveyance of land through purchase of or squatting on colony land and subdivision of large tracts, making Pennsylvania the "best poor man's country."[22]

---

[22] A contemporary characterization of Pennsylvania incorporated in the title of James T. Lemon's book, *The Best Poor Man's Country* (Baltimore: Johns Hopkins Press, 1972).

The other middle colonies developed family farm traditions early from their Dutch, Swedish, and New England settlement. The family farm remained important in Delaware under Penn and in New Jersey as the land filtered down from its proprietors. The English in New York, however, focused for more than a century on the formation of large estates, which were relatively slow to be broken up.

The Revolution found family farms well established in all the colonies except New York. Following the Revolution, there was no doubt that the family farm was to be favored in the new republic. Southern plantations, however, were the most serious of the challenges to family farms.

Large Estates

Among large holdings, I distinguish proprietary grants, feudal and other pretentious estates, and commercial property. The last includes land in productive uses as well as land held for sale, usually with plans for subdivision. Many estates may have served more than one of these roles, in response to the opportunism of their owners.

The largest holdings, of course, were the great proprietorships granted by the crown, all of which were founded with view to profit. The feudal trappings of Maryland and Carolina led to marking off large manors in their early years. The religious motives linked to the founding of Maryland had little effect on the manner in which that colony managed its land. In the case of Pennsylvania, however, Penn's beliefs may account for both the lack of feudal designs connected with his manors and the ready granting of family farms. In any case these proprietary colonies, like the great private proprietorships, can be seen in retrospect as realms leading to further division of the land rather than as products of that process. On a smaller scale, the New England towns were also proprietorships, explicitly for dividing the land among farmers.

The holdings planned as feudal estates were to have been distinguished by the special relation between the lord of the manor and his more or less permanent tenants, and the landed lords were to enjoy favored influence in their colony governments. The feudal estates were unable to compete for the labor they needed because cheap land offered workers a preferable alternative. When slave labor gave all large holdings in the South an economic advantage, the special jurisdiction of manors offered them no special benefit. Most proprietary manors in Maryland and Pennsylvania, like Lord Fairfax's so-called manors in the Northern Neck, were divided into commercial tenancies before they were sold off. In New York unpopular vestiges of feudalism survived well into the nineteenth century on some estates in the form of such arrangements as *perpetual leases* and *quarter sales.*

The first genre of large estate in British North America comprised the *particular plantations*[23] of Virginia, virtual subcolonies that fall in the line of descent of the later slave-worked plantations. Other productive commercial estates included those of the Narragansett planters in Rhode Island and large tracts held for timber production, which first achieved prominence in interior Maine after 1800.

Some of the largest commercial holdings were for the merchandising of land, to take advantage of the advance of prices with further settlement. Such was the real gain from many of the manors too. Big western tracts taken over by private parties for settling included Virginia's grants to individuals such as Morgan Bryan and William Beverley and the huge grant to the Loyal Land Company, purchases of rights by the Philadelphia speculators after the Revolution, and the sales of giant tracts in western and northern New York.

Huge private estates were also amassed from multiple grants and purchases. Examples from eighteenth-century Virginia included those of the Byrd and Carter families. Some of their land was primarily for resale; some was rented to tenants, including newly settled immigrants; some was used for production of iron and other commodities; and much of it was held as estates reinforcing the sense of family substance. Some of these great holdings persisted through a generation or two, but total acreages usually declined as tracts were divided among heirs or sold off to meet expenses.

Some Circumstances Linked with Land Division

Land Division and Ethnic Groups

Many tracts of land within colonies were set aside before further division for particular ethnic groups to establish their communities. Tracts for the Welsh, Dutch, and Germans in Pennsylvania's original surveys were of this nature. Townships specifically planned for ethnic groups were laid out in New Netherland and later in New York, South Carolina, and Georgia. Private land was donated for a settle-

---

[23]Any new core of settlement was described as a plantation.

ment of Huguenots on the James River, and Moravians purchased a tract in North Carolina for their community.

As for ethnic influences on parceling the land, only the New England settlements seem clearly distinctive among the English colonies. A Scottish pattern of tenanted estates put its stamp on East Jersey for a time. The French showed their strong preference for riverine longlots, as the Dutch and Spanish did in lesser degree. Some square *sitios* for grazing enterprises were laid off in Spanish Texas and Louisiana, and the Mexicans crystallized the distinction between grazing and farming land with their huge leagues (*leguas*) and modest farms (*labores*) in Texas.

Land Division and Land Quality

An important question for any evaluation of land division is whether that division or system of division facilitated effective use of the varied surface and soil of the area. The federal survey, for example, has been criticized on the ground that its arbitrary grid provided only a haphazard relation between the ownership parcels available under its rules and the terrains on which the farms might be set.[24] Solutions to the problem can be only local, for areal configurations of varying land qualities are unique, while available farm technologies and economic conditions are changeable. Improving use of natural terrain receives consideration as properties are rearranged through sales and exchanges. The scale of the present study permits only limited observation on aspects of the relation of land division to land quality.

The doctrine of indiscriminate location had the rationale of permitting a grantee to optimize his selection of a tract of land. But a boundary good for one selection was not necessarily good for the next tract, and the selections of earlier settlers might leave large areas of undesirable land in awkward shapes for later comers. Some colonies tried to combat these problems with rules forbidding narrow strips between properties, forbidding undue elongation of property, requiring inclusion of some poor land with the good, and sometimes calling for square or rectangular shapes.

Land along streams was sought by settlers, but might be avoided where the good farmland was on the uplands and the streams were in

[24]Hildegard Binder Johnson, "Rational and Ecological Aspects of the Quarter Section," *Geographical Review* 47 (1957): 330–48.

deep troughs. The first settlers' preference for extended stream frontage was usually inhibited along navigable streams by laws limiting frontage and forbidding the straddling of streams by holdings. These laws not only gave more owners access to streams, but tended to divide up the bottomland, slope, and upland too.

The greatest attention to dividing land of differing qualities among all settlers of a community occurred in seventeenth-century New England, where each person might receive a parcel in each field or meadow. It was easier to divide the land equitably when the family holding was in small separate parcels than when it was all in one piece.

Mexican policies in Texas were also followed with logical recognition of land quality in laying out large areas for grazing and smaller areas for farming. Irrigable land with workable and productive soils, of course, tended to be chosen for the latter.

Land Division and Communities

In early New England, where the resident of a town was assigned a lot or lots from presurveyed tracts of land, ownership of land bound its occupant closely to the township community. In the South, by contrast, where the settler had more choice in defining his own parcel of land, ownership of it placed him in a much looser matrix of county, parish, and neighborhood.[25]

Colonial planning often anticipated a closer tie between residence and community than most typically developed. Although the early New England towns usually grouped house lots in a central village, the farmers did not necessarily place their houses on those lots or remain on them even if they lived there at first. Townships in other colonies, whether or not of New England genesis, were likely to be similarly conceived. The baronies and smallholder "precincts" of Carolina were also planned to have village nuclei surrounded by farmland. Other townships, manors, and plantations, even if they lacked plans for a clear nucleus-farmland separation, still functioned as community units, embracing both the residence and farm activity of numerous people. Townships usually deeded their land to residents, manors rented it, and plantations operated it undivided.

[25]See Robert D. Mitchell, "American Origins and Regional Institutions: The Seventeenth Century Chesapeake," *Annals of the Association of American Geographers* 73 (1983): 412.

The land plans of several colonies incorporated an inlot-outlot tie between urban centers and adjoining farm or garden areas. On the Chesapeake some early grants included a lot in Jamestown or St. Mary's and a farm outside. Farm lots were grouped around New Haven and Savannah in accordance with the grouping of lots in the towns. City lots in Philadelphia and Charleston were granted to owners whose farms were too far away to be called outlots.

Two other communities closely connected with the division of the land were the line villages of the Louisiana levees, where the narrowness of the longlots brought the farmhouses at their ends close together, and the extensive empresario colonies of Mexican Texas.

The cases in which land division defined or was defined by a nascent local community were in the minority among the English colonies. Counties were first created in Virginia in 1634, after-the-fact containers for the scatter of individual farms and plantations. Colonial counties, like districts and parishes that served in their stead, were neither creatures nor creators of the original land division, although county surveyors in several colonies were soon laying out the land, and county recorders were keeping records of all land transfers after the original patents. The *hundreds* and townships outside New England that were merely subdivisions of counties also had little to do with land division. Land parcels often straddled the boundaries between them. Except for New England, the business of land division was mostly a function of the colonies and the succeeding states.

Competition and Conflict among Land Systems

The variety of land systems was a factor in the competition among the several colonies for settlers and land, sometimes leading to conflict, especially near the boundaries or in territory disputed between colonies. The simplest sorts of competition sprang from differences in the costs of acquiring and holding land. Maryland was recognized as being at such a disadvantage compared with either Virginia or Pennsylvania; Maryland's greater efficiency in collecting quitrents may have further discouraged settlement there.[26] Virginians filtering into the tidewater areas around Albemarle Sound established

[26]Beverley W. Bond, Jr., *The Quitrent System in the American Colonies* (New Haven: Yale University Press, 1919): 217–18. Collection of quitrents in Maryland was also a deterrent to land speculation.

the first settlements in North Carolina, and the Carolina proprietors found it necessary to abate their quitrents in that one district to keep the colonists there satisfied. While the Pennsylvania-Maryland border was in dispute, both colonies offered land near the border on more favorable terms than elsewhere. New York's concentration on large land grants discouraged settlement by farmers. The Georgia trustees finally were unable to hold to the restrictions they planned on holdings, tenure, and slavery, in part because people familiar with plantations in adjoining South Carolina found the Georgia rules obstacles to their ideas of success. In general, competition for settlers seems to have kept land prices and quitrents modest and to have discouraged repressive practices on the part of colonial administrations.

The most contended clashes on land systems, however, occurred around the borders of New England. As New England villages gained a foothold in southern New Netherland, Dutch villagers were quick to demand the same rights they found their neighbors enjoying. Connecticut's and Massachusetts's freehold grants on land also claimed by New York manors were tempting to some of the manor tenants, and disrupted orderly life on border estates for some years. New Hampshire and New York both granted land in the present area of Vermont, but the settlers, mostly New Englanders with New Hampshire grants, made possession count over the crown's ruling in New York's favor. New England settlers were welcomed in New Jersey, and they invaded Pennsylvania under auspices of the Susquehannah Company, but trouble ensued in both places before New Englanders' land claims and the local land laws were reconciled. In all these cases liberal land tenure and local community government were rights the New England settlers sought to keep and their neighbors were sometimes tempted to seek.

The trouble stemming from New Englanders' moves into other colonies was not paralleled in the great interior migration from Pennsylvania into Maryland, Virginia, and the Carolinas. Even though the Pennsylvanians were family farmers settling in colonies where plantations were common, they had little ideological trouble taking land on the host colonies' terms, based variously on purchase, grants, and a frontier tolerance of squatting. Virginia's large grants to those who contracted to bring in settlers represented one accommodation to these moves along the western frontier.

American settlers moved into areas now in states on the Gulf of Mexico and the Mississippi River while they were still held by Spain or Britain. They planted irregular land patterns beyond the national boundaries even while areas within the national domain were being regimented in the square grid. These Americans were numerous, spreading fast, and often carrying the Southern taste for indiscriminate location.

Land Division and Roads

Anyone casually familiar with roads in areas of even terrain surveyed by the United States Land Office is likely to assume that property lines and roads are commonly laid out together. In fact, the roads that so frequently ran along the section lines were located subsequent to the survey on the basis of local decisions. But the evidence of the present study suggests that roads, in areas of irregular surveys, developed with surprisingly little attention to the original property lines. The reasons for such discordance were that property lines would neither afford suitable terrain nor approximate the most direct routes to destinations. When property is divided after roads are built, however, the roads offer convenient courses for the new property lines, and are frequently followed for that purpose.

Part II

New England: Dividing Land by Townships

THE COLONIES and states of New England during the settlement period formed a region more coherent culturally than the other regions in this study. This coherence included their land division practices, especially in their adherence to townships as the units of planning and implementation. Charters actually were issued granting parts of New England to both commercial corporations and seigniorial proprietors. Although the two most critical implantations of colonists fell legally under the charters of corporations, by coincidences the Plymouth and Massachusetts Bay colonies were close together, and the members of both emphasized their own communal ends rather than those of their official sponsors.

So Massachusetts not only developed ahead of other colonies, but it played vital roles in the population and development of other parts of New England. Settlement in Connecticut and Rhode Island was initiated by dissidents seeking more independence than Massachusetts offered. New Hampshire and Maine not only received emigrants from Massachusetts, but both came under the government of Massachusetts during part of their early settlement periods. New Hampshire and Connecticut, in their turn, played the most direct roles in the development of Vermont.

2

Beginnings: Communal Land Division

THE LAND of New England was divided township by township,[1] no matter how a township had been granted or under what sort of administration it fell. With only limited exceptions, actions of the local communities are the keys to understanding land division in New England. In the middle and southern colonies, by contrast, both land policy and its administration lay with the colonial governments, and people seeking land usually had to deal individually with the proper offices in their colonial capitals.

More fully, land division in New England occurred in two stages corresponding to the two tiers of corporate government: the colony and the town. First the *general court*[2] of a colony approved the grant of a new township, often after its sponsors had purchased it from local Indians; then the *proprietors* of that township assigned the land to its inhabitants. Colonies usually did not grant land directly to individuals, and townships seldom permitted individuals free choice of their land. Grants that were individually located, however, were called *pitches*.[3]

The proprietors comprised the body of people to whom a township was granted by a general court, most commonly following a petition or purchase agreement. As owners of the new township, the proprietors then had the responsibility of allocating land to people who

---

[1]Melville Egleston, *The Land System of the New England Colonies*, Johns Hopkins University Studies in Historical and Political Science, ser. 4 (Baltimore: Johns Hopkins, 1886): 27–32.

[2]The general court was the governing body of the colony. Royally appointed governors with genuine power were exceptional in colonial New England.

[3]Amelia Clewley Ford, *Colonial Precedents of Our National Land System as It Existed in 1800*, Bulletin of the University of Wisconsin, no. 352 (Madison: University of Wisconsin History Series, vol. 2, no. 2, 1910), 13; William Haller, Jr., *The Puritan Frontier: Town-Planting in New England Colonial Development, 1630–1660* (New York: AMS Press, 1968), 34–35.

29

came to live there. Custom, experience, and the demands of other townsmen influenced the proprietors in their actions, and sometimes they were also constrained by conditions imposed by the general court or governor. One authority described the proprietorship as essentially a business institution for settling the land and initiating operation of a new town. Occasionally leaders of an older town might be appointed as trustees for dividing the land of a new town.[4]

The place of proprietors among the many classes of townspeople must be explained. The *freemen*, whom we might think of as the typical citizens of a town, were nearly always landholders and were at least supposed to have taken an oath of loyalty to the colony.[5] The freemen governed the town through the town meeting and through the *selectmen* chosen as an executive committee for carrying out the policies of the freemen. *Commoners*, or *freeholders*, held rights to use and share in the ongoing division of the common land, whether or not they were also proprietors. Other landholders held no such hereditary rights in the common, and even some freemen might be neither commoners nor landholders at all. Still other residents possessed neither land nor any of the foregoing rights. But the privileged and the less privileged alike might come to live in the community only if they had been accepted by the town. Finally, membership in the local church might be required for the exercise of any of the privileges mentioned above. These qualifications and privileges of townsmen varied somewhat with colonial laws and local customs.

Once settlement of a town was under way and the town had incorporated, the proprietors turned the government of the town over to the freemen and confined their work as a separate body to the further assignment of land. In the seventeenth century the number of proprietors founding a town was usually small, typically not more than five or six. Later towns that were offered as bounties to soldiers or sold on the open market often had all their fifty or more grantees as proprietors. The body of proprietors might be enlarged as a town developed, even on occasion to include all the landowners or all

---

[4]Roy H. Akagi, *The Town Proprietors of the New England Colonies: A Study of Their Development, Organization, Activities, and Controversies, 1620–1770* (Philadelphia: University of Pennsylvania Press, 1924).

[5]Katherine M. Brown, "Freemanship in Puritan Massachusetts," *American Historical Review* 54 (1954): 865–83; Richard C. Simmons, "Freemanship in Early Massachusetts: Some Suggestions and a Case Study," *William and Mary Quarterly*, ser. 3, no. 19 (1962): 422–28; Bruce C. Daniels, "Connecticut's Villages Become Mature Towns: The Complexity of Local Institutions, 1676 to 1776," *William and Mary Quarterly*, ser. 3, no. 34 (1977): 83–103.

those eligible to vote in the town meeting. In other words, the body of proprietors sometimes merged with the town meeting.

The public trust borne by proprietors did not always override their interests as individuals. A substantial mix of commercial enterprise for profit has been recently revealed[6] in the founding and operation of even the seventeenth-century New England towns. The founding of a town required capital not only for a variety of start-up costs but also the time of well-connected people to negotiate with Indians and the general court.[7] A number of towns were founded by individuals or groups who, not planning to live in them, recruited settlers to buy their land or at least to validate their land titles and make their land productive. A few resident landlords were powerful enough to dominate the societies in their towns. More than a hundred absentee landlords operated farms in townships in which they were not resident; a number of such individuals each held land in several townships.

In dividing the land the early proprietors proceeded by assigning lots in successive tracts to those accepted as landholders in the township. The first tract was usually set aside for house lots, others as meadowland for hay and grazing and as upland for cultivation. These tracts were seldom divided equally, but rather were allocated on formulas determined by the proprietors and taking into account such matters as standing in the community, wealth, occupation, size of family, number of cattle, residence or birth in the town, and participation in purchase of the land. Allocations in Massachusetts usually emphasized the recipient's potential for using the land, whereas, in Connecticut, his investment in buying the land from the Indians was more often recognized.[8] Lot sizes were sometimes further adjusted to compensate for variations in quality or location of the land (sizing).[9] Sometimes proprietors made separate *gratulation* grants to reward individuals who had been of particular service to the town. The different land allocation formulas reflected a variety of traditions and purposes among the towns and their promoters.

[6]John Frederick Martin, *Profits in the Wilderness: Entrepreneurship and the Founding of New England Towns in the Seventeenth Century* (Chapel Hill: University of North Carolina Press for the Institute of Early American History and Culture, 1991).

[7]Martin, 9–10.

[8]Joseph Sutherland Wood, "The Origin of the New England Village" (Ph.D. diss., Pennsylvania State University, 1978), 25.

[9]Leonard W. Labaree, *The Early Development of a Town as Shown in Its Land Records*, Connecticut Tercentenary Commission Pamphlet no. 13 (New Haven: Yale University Press, 1933), 4–5.

Ownership of land usually tied the ordinary individual or family closely to the religious, social, and economic life of the town. Newcomers might have to move a time or two before they found the right town for putting down their roots.[10] Once established as landowners, they were less likely to move. New Englanders jealously guarded the free tenures (mostly without quitrents) under which most of them held their land. Although the town was a strongly communal society, landownership was a firmly established individual right.

The successive divisions of land in a township often spread over a period of a generation, or sometimes even a century. Some proprietors granted out the land as fast as settlers arrived and surveyors could mark off the parcels. Others granted only what they thought was immediately needed. In either case the common land remaining under control of the proprietors shrank as parts of it were granted. Inhabitants who had established their ownership of land could sell it, although in early years the town had first option to buy it. After the common land had been distributed or declared the permanent property of its proprietors, newcomers could acquire land only by purchase. Village greens or forest reserves sometimes remain today as permanent common land.

The English open-field village was the most common model for the layout of the early New England town. The English village embraced a concentration of houses set around the edge of an open green, each house usually on an elongated lot providing some space for gardens and farm buildings. Beyond the village lay a group of large arable fields and common pastures and woodlands. The open fields were divided into long narrow strips, each assigned to a villager, but all the strips in a field were devoted to the same use in a particular year. Each farmer held a scattered group of land parcels, and had rights of using the common grazing lands and collecting wood in the forest. Prominent buildings of the village were the mansion of the lord, the church, and probably a grain mill.

The land layout of many early New England villages virtually duplicated the English model, except that the scale of house lots and farm strips was likely to be larger in New England.[11] The allocation of land by successive divisions fitted readily with grouping the

[10]Virginia DeJohn Anderson, *New England's Generation: The Great Migration and the Formation of Society and Culture in the Seventeenth Century* (Cambridge: Cambridge University Press, 1991), 106ff.

[11]Anthony N. B. Garvan, *Architecture and Town Planning in Colonial Connecticut* (New Haven: Yale University Press, 1951), 56.

house lots in a central location and scattering the individual's holdings in separate fields and meadows.

In social organization the New England town differed radically from its English ancestors. With no feudal lord, local government in New England was less aristocratic and more democratic and theocratic. The town was the "organization to cope with the temporal problems of a Puritan church congregation,"[12] just as the first colonies had represented the temporal extension of the larger religious movement. Appropriately, the church building also served as the meetinghouse where the citizens assembled to make decisions on town affairs.

In spite of these systematic organizational differences between villages in Old England and in New England, much of the diversity among New England villages sprang from diversity among their ancestor villages in England. Recent studies have shown surprisingly close parallels between specific New England townships and the English villages or districts from which their settlers came. These parallels include sizes of landholdings, shapes and orderly arrangement of parcels, equality or inequality in land assignments, open-field or enclosed farming, regulation of the common, propensity to buy and sell land, choice of crops, diversity of economic activities, and government.[13]

Most important in the changes occurring in New England after the first settlement were the early disappearance of open-field farming and the abandonment of the village as the farmers' residence in favor of dispersed dwellings on consolidated or enclosed farms.[14] Both

[12]Haller, 108.

[13]David Grayson Allen, *In English Ways* (Chapel Hill: University of North Carolina Press for Institute of Early American History and Culture, 1981), deals with five Massachusetts towns, Rowley, Hingham, Ipswich, Newbury, and Watertown. Rowley settlers came from Yorkshire, where they had known the most conservative open-field manors. Settlers of the other towns came from areas of more change in East Anglia and Wiltshire-Hampshire. Sumner Chilton Powell, *Puritan Village: The Formation of a New England Town* (Middletown, Conn.: Wesleyan University Press, 1963), deals primarily with Sudbury, Mass., and the differing attitudes of settlers from an open-field village in Hampshire, a borough in Hertfordshire where farmers had been rapidly adding to their holdings, a more urbanized borough in Suffolk, and rural parishes of East Anglia.

[14]Philip J. Greven, Jr., *Four Generations: Population, Land, and Family in Colonial Andover, Massachusetts* (Ithaca: Cornell University Press, 1970), 50–59, describes the manner in which dispersion occurred in one New England town. Although the first two divisions of upland in Andover occurred in clearly defined fields, the next such division gave the inhabitants larger parcels that were scattered about the township. The fourth division of upland in 1662 outdid all others, giving each original family more

changes may have originated with the granting of farms in remote parts of townships, as apparently happened in Andover.[15] Joseph Wood, in a recent study, has presented evidence from a large number of examples that concentration of farmers' residences in a village was not a feature of many early New England towns.[16] Wood suggests that the conventional view that the farmers all lived in the central village developed from misreading the settlers' concept of their town as a close community (therefore a village) and from assuming incorrectly that the commercial village ultimately appearing at the town center grew from an earlier agricultural village.[17] New England towns, both early and late, were often laid out as if settlement would be in nucleated villages. The design simply proved more persistent than the practice.

Two of the several reasons for concentrating residence in villages were explicitly pursued in early New England. The first was defense. As long as Indian attacks were likely, concentration of settlers had evident advantages. The other reason was the insistence on attendance at church and town meetings. A Massachusetts law of 1635 forbade residence more than half a mile from the meetinghouse.[18] When a number of families had nonetheless collected at a distance from the meetinghouse, they often established their own church, society, or parish, forming a second community within the township. The next step was often a petition to separate the new community as an independent township.

As an introduction to New England land division, the story of early settlement in Massachusetts shows how land division by township got its start.[19] Massachusetts stemmed principally from the Plymouth settlement of 1620 and the Massachusetts Bay settlement of 1628–30. Plymouth and Massachusetts developed as separate colonies, and were not united until 1691. Land division in later colonial towns will be treated in sections dealing separately with the seventeenth and eighteenth centuries. The date of 1700 roughly separates

than three times the land it had received before. Movement of farmers from the village onto their dispersed holdings was only a matter of time.

[15]Edna Scofield, "The Origin of Settlement Patterns in Rural New England," *Geographical Review* 28 (1938): 657.

[16]Joseph Wood.

[17]Ibid., 3, 5, 7, 10.

[18]Ibid., 35.

[19]Discussion of the beginning of land division in New England suffers from the fact that very few of the histories of the early towns include property maps of more than the rows of house lots laid out to be the central villages of the townships.

an earlier period of communal township founding from a later period of more commercial township founding. After the Revolution most of the undivided land of New England lay in the present areas of Maine and Vermont, which will be the subjects of the final section.

Early Massachusetts Towns

Plymouth Colony

The band of English dissenters who would settle at Plymouth (fig. 2.1) found sponsors who were organized as a particular plantation under the London branch of the Virginia Company,[20] which had rights as far north as the forty-first parallel of latitude.[21] After the Pilgrims landed and settled at Plymouth just north of the forty-second parallel, the sponsors in England obtained a new patent from the Council for New England,[22] successor to the Plymouth branch of the Virginia Company.

The plans for distributing land in the new colony were essentially those projected earlier in Virginia. Land and houses and any profits were to be common property under the sponsors for the first seven years.[23] Fifteen hundred acres were promised each stockholder in the particular plantation. Hundred-acre headrights were to go to settlers paying their own way, otherwise to the stockholders.[24] A tract of 1,500 acres was to be set aside for public use.[25]

Temporary allotments of house and garden plots were laid out on both sides of what is now Leyden street, running perpendicular to the shore in Plymouth. The nineteen lots, three rods deep with half a rod width for each member of a family, could hardly have covered an acre all together. Seven dwellings and four company houses were built the first year, and building progressed as the colony grew.[26]

In Massachusetts, as much as in Virginia, the settlers grew restive under the communal arrangements, and in 1623 each family was as-

---

[20]Manning Curlee Voorhis, "The Land Grant Policy of Colonial Virginia, 1607–1644" (Ph.D. diss., University of Virginia, 1940), 17.

[21]George D. Langdon, Jr., *Pilgrim Colony* (New Haven: Yale University Press, 1966), 2, 8–9, 17.

[22]Ibid., 16–17.

[23]Ibid., 9.

[24]Ibid., 17.

[25]Marshall Harris, 104.

[26]William T. Davis, *Ancient Landmarks of Plymouth* (Boston: Damrell and Upham, 1899), 53, 156–57.

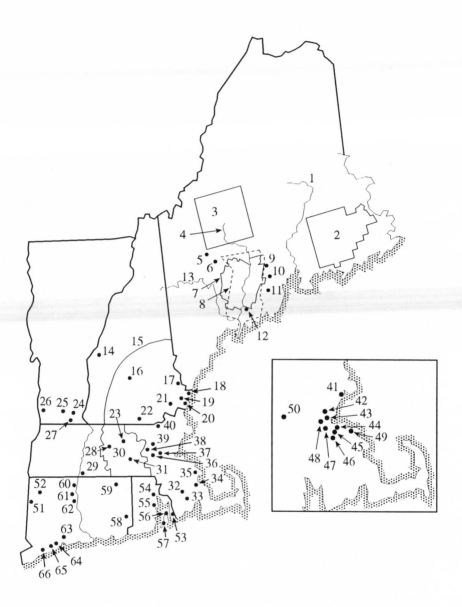

signed a plot of land "for present use."[27] Then "much more corne was planted than other waise would have bene," reported Bradford, the colony's leader.[28] The next year family plots were reassigned at the rate of an acre a person—a total of 197 acres in 94 parcels ranging from one to ten acres each. The parcels, which we assume were on good upland sites, were laid out in clusters, each cluster assigned to the settlers who had arrived on one of the immigrant ships.[29]

In 1627 the colony contracted to buy up the company that had sponsored it, assigning shares of both the assets and debt among the fifty-eight "Purchasers" according to the sizes of their families.[30] Livestock were apportioned among the colonists, houses were appraised for equalizing the wealth, and a new land division of twenty acres per person was ordered:

> They should only lay out settable or tillable land . . . And they were first to agree of the goodnes and fitnes of it before the lott was drawne, and so it might well prove some of their owne, as an other mans . . . But yet seekeing to keepe the people together, as much as might be, they allso agreed . . . that whose lotts soever should fall next the towne, or most conveninte for nearnes, they should take to them a neighbore or tow [sic], whom they best liked; and should suffer them to plant corne with them for 4. years; and afterwards they might use as much of theirs for as long time, if they would. Allso every share of 20. acers was to be laid out 5. acres in breadth by the water side and 4. acres in lenght, excepting

[27]William T. Davis, ed., *Bradford's History of Plymouth Plantation* (New York: Charles Scribner's Sons, 1920), 146.
[28]Davis, *Ancient Landmarks of Plymouth*, 49–50.
[29]Ibid., 50–52, 162.
[30]Langdon, 28–31.

Fig. 2.1 *(facing page)*. New England locations: 1. Penobscot R. 2, 3. Bingham Purchases 4. Kennebec R. 5. Avon 6. Farmington 7. Kennebec County 8. Kennebeck Proprietors Claim 9. Unity 10. Freedom 11. Liberty 12. Dresden 13. Androscoggin R. 14. Lebanon 15. Inland limit of Masonian claims 16. Salisbury 17. Dover 18. Portsmouth 19. Exeter 20. Hampton 21. Kingston 22. Nashua 23. Princeton 24. Marlboro 25. Wilmington 26. Bennington 27. Halifax 28. Barre 29. Springfield 30. Worcester County 31. Leicester 32. Taunton 33. Freetown 34. Plymouth 35. Duxbury 36. Framingham 37. Watertown 38. Marlborough 39. Sudbury 40. Andover 41. Saugus 42. Medford 43. Charlestown 44. Roxbury 45. Dorchester 46. Milton 47. Brookline 48. Cambridge 49. Hingham 50. Wayland 51. Kent 52. Cornwall 53. Little Compton 54. Providence 55. Warwick 56. Portsmouth 57. Newport 58. Voluntown 59. Woodstock 60. Windsor 61. Hartford 62. Wethersfield 63. New Haven 64. Milford 65. Bridgeport 66. Fairfield.

nooks and corners, which were to be measured as they would bear to best advantage. But no meadows were to be laid out at all . . . because they were but streight of meadow grounds . . . but every season all were appoynted wher they should mowe, according to the proportion of catle they had.[31]

Thus, earliest Plymouth was a compact settlement, actually palisaded for a time. Land distribution was carefully planned for equal treatment of all. The twenty-acre parcels were compact in shape rather than elongated. Allotments were made well before the citizens were ready to venture beyond the village. Within a few years, however, the population dispersed onto separate farms, and the population of Plymouth village itself declined.[32]

The Massachusetts Bay settlement, beginning in 1630, offered Plymouth a period of prosperity, a stimulus for broader dispersal of settlement, and additional colonists. Plymouth was well enough established to provide the newer colony with food and other supplies during its first decade. The need for more pastureland may have been the first incentive for dispersal.[33] Some of the "great lots" granted in 1627, which were located several miles from Plymouth village, suddenly became valuable. Many Plymouth farmers found it advantageous to move their residences to their land, and other parts of Plymouth colony were taken up by settlers coming in from Massachusetts Bay.[34]

At least seven new townships were established in Plymouth between 1636 and 1642. Duxbury, across the bay from Plymouth village, was the first concentration of transplanted Plymouth farmers. Finding the church at Plymouth inconveniently distant, they had organized their own in 1632.[35] Five years later Duxbury became a separate town. Taunton and other towns in Plymouth colony were first settled by groups of Massachusetts families.

The spread of townships over the colony was accompanied by dispersion of farmers within the townships. No early town developed a village core long inhabited by farmers. To be sure there were occasional neighborhoods with more farmers than others, and such neighborhoods were formed into new parishes and later into new

[31]Davis, *Bradford's History of Plymouth Plantation*, 217–18.
[32]Langdon, 39.
[33]Anderson, 155–56.
[34]Darrett B. Rutman, *Husbandmen of Plymouth: Farms and Villages in the Old Colony, 1620–1692* (Boston: Beacon Press for Plimouth Plantation, 1967), 13–15.
[35]Ibid.

towns. Even in towns settled by organized groups of migrants, the farmers sooner or later spread out to make use of the land they needed.[36]

The granting of land in Plymouth colony was centralized in the hands of a court of assistants until about 1640. In the spirit of the Pilgrim settlement, landholdings were at first limited to settlers' immediate needs, surplus land being saved for those who might come later. As towns came to be granted to groups of settlers, control of town lands passed largely to the towns and their inhabitants. The settlers in a few new towns were represented by commissioners who were charged with dividing the land under the eye of the general court, which ordered that grants be made according to the "seuall estates, rankes, and quallities" of the settlers.[37] Unlike the proprietors in most later New England towns, these commissioners had not been granted the land themselves. The court overruled the commissioners in one case after considering protests that arose from the commissioners' first division of meadowland.

In addition to granting land to towns, the general court eventually made some generous grants to individuals. The most prominent among these were in recognition of early service in the colony: dividends granted to original purchasers of 1627 in three tracts on Cape Cod and in the southwest of the colony, and later grants to "old freemen" who had been in the colony by 1640. Towns were formed on these grants, but the land was available to newcomers only by purchase from the grantees. Freetown, for example, was formed on a dividend to twenty-six old freemen, who received half a square mile each. Children born to first settlers, and "old servants" from before 1640 also were given preference in buying land there. By 1675 the colony land available for distribution was nearly gone, and the opportunity for speculative profits consequently much enhanced.[38]

The towns were more generous in dividing up their land than the general court had been. They accepted newcomers in some number, and, as long as land was plentiful, often permitted most of the freemen to become proprietors. Allocation of the land in successive divisions was seldom on the basis of equality.

Plymouth township did not complete division of its common lands until a few years after 1700. In this respect it was neither especially fast nor especially slow. All the land outside the village tract went

[36]Joseph Wood, 137–41.
[37]Langdon, 48–52.
[38]Ibid., 39–48, 53–57.

to 201 freeholders in a series of divisions. A family that depended only on grants from the town over this period would have found its land in several parcels,[39] but it is unlikely that many settlers long operated farms so fragmented.

The land within Plymouth village, save the cemetery, the green, and space for public buildings, was soon in private hands. The original one-acre parcels left by farmers who moved to other towns were withdrawn from control of these nonresidents to make room for newcomers. A 1701 map of Plymouth shows sixty-seven properties in the "mile and a half" tract allocated to the municipality, half of them concentrated in the few blocks where Plymouth's first houses had risen.[40] Thus the village grew again after its decline, but it was no longer to be occupied primarily by farmers.

Massachusetts Bay

The Massachusetts Bay colony of Puritans was a later, separate, and largely independent root of New England settlement. It blossomed in 1630 with the arrival of a thousand settlers in an unusually large colonization expedition. The Puritans, like the Pilgrims, had planned to concentrate settlement in or immediately about a single center, but disease and a threat of foreign attack led them to break up quickly into several groups, most of which chose sites along the shores and estuaries of the present Boston area—Charlestown, Watertown, Roxbury, Medford, Saugus, and the Shawmut Peninsula (soon to be named Boston). Salem to the north had been established as a commercial center shortly before, and Dorchester was quickly settled by a separate group.[41]

Although the company court of assistants in England had proclaimed a headright plan in 1630,[42] the Massachusetts Bay colony

---

[39]Davis, *Ancient Landmarks of Plymouth,* 161–62.

[40] Ibid., 160.

[41]The company had developed a land allocation plan in 1629. Adventurers were to have land at the rate of 200 acres for each fifty pounds invested. Adventurers and others were also to receive headrights of 50 acres for each person transported to the colony. An integral part of the plan involved the idea of a town plat with small house lots. Egleston, 18–20; William I. Davisson and Dennis J. Dugan, "Land Precedents in Essex County, Massachusetts," *Essex Institute Historical Collections* 106 (1970): 258–59.

[42]Nathaniel B. Shurtleff, ed., *Records of the Governor and Company of the Massachusetts Bay in New England,* 5 vols. (Boston: Press of William White, Printer to the Commonwealth, 1853), 1: 50.

itself was virtually divided into towns before its leaders even had a chance to consider the matter,[43] and these towns parceled out their own lands in the name of their inhabitants.[44] Cambridge (Newtown) was soon planned and laid out to be the central community, but the separate towns continued their own development,[45] and Boston with its seaward position actually became the center of government, commerce, and population growth.

The small peninsula offered Boston limited resources for feeding itself, however. Much of it was hilly or wet, and it lacked adjoining land for ready expansion. Settlers planted gardens and orchards on their house lots, which were usually no more than half an acre. Family farms of up to four acres[46] were set aside in Fort Field on the slopes of Fort Hill south of the settlement nucleus, in Mill Field on the North End, in New Field on the northwest, and in Colborne's Field leading into the isthmus connecting Boston with the mainland. The town purchased a tract for use as a common pasture and training field from a lone squatter who had arrived before the fleet.

As more settlers came, pressure on the land increased. Boston responded in two ways: appropriating land around the margins of the bay not occupied by other towns,[47] and further restricting grants of the scarce land in Boston proper. In their town meetings Bostonians argued over how land should be allocated, and how much should be saved for newcomers.[48] Specific decisions were left to the selectmen. Home lots were soon all that nonresidents were allowed to hold on the peninsula and, as land became even scarcer, the only use for which the town would grant land. In 1641 the town ordered all the remaining land except the commons divided among "the present inhabitants." Newcomers would have to buy their land from owners willing to sell.

The outlying lands were divided unequally. Allotments to members of the gentry ran as high as 700 acres and averaged 200 acres. Most of the shore to the north and south of Boston, and some of the nearby islands, went in large holdings. Some land went to farmers

---

[43]Darrett B. Rutman, *Winthrop's Boston: Portrait of a Puritan Town, 1630–1649* (Chapel Hill: University of North Carolina Press for Institute of Early American History and Culture, 1965), 26–30.

[44]Ibid., 44–46. The Massachusetts general court gave chartered towns official control of their land as early as 1636 (Davisson and Dugan, 255).

[45]Rutman, *Winthrop's Boston*, 31.

[46]Ibid., 39.

[47]Ibid., 44, 69–70.

[48]Haller, 61–62.

who would work it themselves, some to merchants or officials whose servants would work it, some to absentee shareholders who might rent it. As few as thirty families received nearly half the land at the town's disposal, and some of them obtained additional land from the colony. The half dozen holdings of John Winthrop were scattered far and wide. His wife had a grant of 3,000 acres, its location deferred, presumably for the benefit of her heirs. An ordinary resident was likely to have only one or two parcels aside from his house and small allotment in Boston, but some acquired more by purchase.[49]

A selection of other early Massachusetts towns will illustrate the individuality of their origins and their land systems. Dorchester and Hingham originated in settlement by groups who came directly from England. Watertown began as one of the towns formed on the breakup of the main Puritan settlement in 1630. Sudbury was a new community formed by immigrants dissatisfied with the land situation they found in Watertown, whereas Marlborough was settled some years later by dissidents of Sudbury who opposed that town's land policies. Three other towns were settled as parts of older towns: Brookline as additional pastureland for Boston, Milton as part of Dorchester, and Framingham as an expansion of Sudbury. Not surprisingly, the settlement patterns of these towns ranged from dispersed farms of variable size and shape to central residential villages surrounded by open fields divided into longlots.

The congregation that settled Dorchester came from the town of the same name in Dorsetshire, England; they probably planned a separate settlement from the beginning,[50] for their ship came separately from the main Puritan fleet. Although the first parcels of land were only a few acres and larger parcels were passed out in later divisions,[51] the compact settlement thus implied did not develop.[52] A contemporary observer describing it as "the greatest town in New England" spoke of its woods, arable land, hay grounds, and gardens.[53] That Dorchester settlers were relatively prosperous and expected generous farms may help explain why the population spread

[49]Rutman, *Winthrop's Boston*, 76–97.

[50] Ibid., 26; Committee of Dorchester Antiquarian and Historical Society, *History of the Town of Dorchester, Massachusetts* (Boston: Ebenezer Clapp, Jr., 1859), 14–18.

[51]Anne Bush MacLear, *Early New England Towns: A Comparative Study of Their Development*, Studies in History, Economics, and Public Law 29, no. 1 (New York: Columbia University, 1908): 82–83, 87–88, 95.

[52]Joseph Wood, 63.

[53]William Wood, *New England's Prospect*, ed. Alden T. Vaughan (Amherst: University of Massachusetts Press, 1977) (originally published 1634), 58.

over the township. Thus dispersed settlement in a township, even though it was settled as a close-knit community, is nearly as old as the Puritan beginnings in New England.

Watertown (fig. 2.2) was settled in 1630 on the north side of the Charles River, upstream from the original Puritan settlement core at Charlestown, by East Anglians who followed one of their leaders to the site.[54] From an initial settlement at its eastern edge,[55] Watertown grew westward, and residences were rapidly dispersed. The "Great Dividents" comprised lots of twenty to 100 acres granted to more than 100 residents, who were soon practicing the enclosed farming they had known in East Anglia. An obsession for buying and selling land helped farmers consolidate holdings.[56] As the original village center was replaced by farms, a new Meeting House Common was reserved closer to the center of the township. Still many of the townspeople were living some distance from the meetinghouse. The new "Town Plot" near the western edge of the township was laid out in 1638 explicitly for drawing together those dwelling farthest from the meetinghouse.[57] Few of the grantees, however, moved to their new Town Plot lots.[58]

Sudbury was founded in 1638 or 1639 by residents of Watertown, several of whom had lived there only a year or two and some of whom had known open-field farming in England and were uncomfortable with the independence of Watertown landowners.[59] Others of those who moved to Sudbury had been unable to get any land in Watertown. In Sudbury they concentrated their dwellings on four-acre lots on the edges of a large grazing common and laid out arrays of elongated parcels in several fields and meadows (fig. 2.3). In contrast with Dorchester and Watertown, Sudbury was probably as similar to an English open-field village as any town in New England.

After a decade or so some of Sudbury's residents, especially East Anglians and younger citizens, grew dissatisfied with the tight traditional rule of the selectmen. When time came to divide the 6,400

[54]Allen, 125.

[55]Ibid., 126; MacLear, 36.

[56]Allen, 127.

[57]MacLear, 85. The material on the internal arrangement of Watertown is based on the map "The Original Allotments of Land and the Ancient Topography of Watertown," in Henry Bond, *Genealogies of the Families and Descendants of the Early Settlers of Watertown, Massachusetts* (Boston: Little Brown and Co., 1855), app. 4, 1082–94. A simplified version of the map appears in figure 2.2.

[58]Joseph Wood, 67–68.

[59]Powell, 75–79.

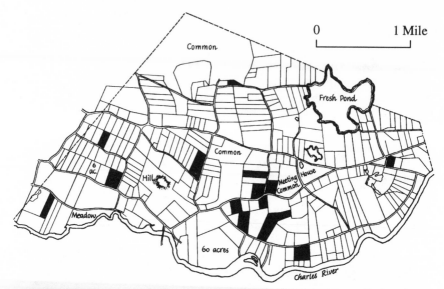

Fig. 2.2. Watertown, Mass. The Watertown lots are inferred from records identifying residents along streets. The shaded lots belonged to men who subsequently moved to Sudbury. Figure 6 from Sumner Chilton Powell, *Puritan Village*, copyright 1963 by Wesleyan University, reprinted by permission of the University Press of New England. Lexington (south center) and Newton (north center) quadrangles.

acres of a new two-mile tract on the western edge of the township, the dissident group demanded equal acreage for every man. Their immediate challenge failed. The land was divided in uniform parcels of 130 acres, but not for every man. Some citizens moved onto their farms in the new tract, thus beginning to disperse the settlement, and in 1656 the dissident group obtained a new grant for what came to be Marlborough.[60]

Sudbury's swim against the current of enclosure would not advance further. The first division of Marlborough land was in parcels of sixteen to fifty acres intended as both house lots and farms; parcels in subsequent divisions, the first of which was meadow, were granted in proportion to first division parcel sizes.[61] Framingham, another offshoot from Sudbury, was settled in a dispersed farm pattern in the 1660s. Framingham farmers retained membership in the Sudbury church until they separated in 1675 because of their remoteness.[62] By

[60]Ibid., 118–34, passim.
[61]Ibid., 136; see also Charles Hudson, *History of the Town of Marlborough* (Boston: T. R. Marvin and Son, 1862), 35–38.
[62]Joseph Wood, 80–83.

1700 Sudbury's own population was widely dispersed. In 1723 the township was divided along the Sudbury River.[63] Wayland on the east side retains today a few retail establishments facing the original village green. Sudbury on the west side, where there was no early village, has a more rural aspect with only its town buildings, two churches, and a school focused on a crossroads. Both have become bedroom suburbs of Boston.

Hingham is included in the sample of towns because it was "distributed in a haphazard pattern of small parcels,"[64] lacking large fields in which most of the inhabitants would hold strips. Landholdings up to 1670, thirty-seven years after its settlement, averaged only twenty-two and a half acres.[65] Hingham's population came from a village of the same name in Norfolk, England, located between the open fields of the Midlands and the enclosed farms of Suffolk and Essex.[66] The Norfolk village's land parcels are described as blocks rather than strips. Its subsistence economy emphasized dairying with animal rearing, grains, and small home industries. The dairymen of Hingham, Massachusetts, also produced their animals and grains and home textiles, and followed old Hingham in their disinclination to trade their land as the Watertown settlers did. But small groups of adjoining owners frequently pooled their land for the purpose of enclosure.[67] A 1635 effort to form a village center by laying out house lots along a street was too late, for those already settled were reluctant to move.[68]

The new townships that were first divided as outlying parts of earlier townships usually lacked an original core of house lots and were unlikely to form village nuclei. Framingham has already been discussed as an extension of Sudbury. The land that became Milton was nearly all allocated by Dorchester for grazing purposes in generous holdings ranging to more than 200 acres. Part of Milton was laid out in strips and part in irregular blocks.[69] Milton became a separate town in 1667. Muddy River, later Brookline, was one of the outlying areas divided among residents of Boston long before it was sepa-

[63]Ibid., 84.
[64]Allen, 63–64.
[65]Ibid., 65.
[66]Ibid., 58–62.
[67]Ibid., 65, 76.
[68]Joseph Wood, 64, 67.
[69]Edward Pierce Hamilton, *A History of Milton* (Milton, Mass.: Milton Historical Society, 1957), 17, 19–20, 30; Joseph Wood, 64–66.

Fig. 2.3. Sudbury, Mass., central part. Figure 9 from Sumner Chilton Powell, *Puritan Village*, copyright 1963 by Wesleyan University, reprinted by permission of the University Press of New England. Maynard (southeast), Concord (southwest), Natick (northwest), and Framingham (northeast) quadrangles.

rately incorporated in 1711. Brookline is unique in being the subject of a series of published maps showing landownership at intervals of twenty to forty years between 1641 and 1822.[70] Although its village of two dozen families is reported as having adjoined a 300-acre common set aside by Boston in 1639,[71] the maps offer no evidence of such a nucleus. In 1641 most of the holdings in Brookline comprised less than fifty acres, forming irregular ladder patterns made up of strips, but

[70]Theodore F. Jones, *Land Ownership in Brookline from the First Settlement*, with genealogical additions by Charles F. White, Publication no. 5 of the Brookline Historical Society (Brookline, Mass.: Riverdale Press, 1923).

[71]Rutman, *Winthrop's Boston*, 94.

half the area was taken up by a few irregular parcels of up to 600 acres. Successive maps show gradually increasing numbers of holdings as the family names of original owners slowly disappeared. By 1822 there were twice as many parcels as in 1641, not counting additional parcels formed from the subdivision of a marsh and a common. Right angles in boundaries were fairly common, but the overall impression is of irregularity. Less than a tenth of the 1641 property lines were still property lines in 1822. The net of curving roads bore little relation to the early property lines, but formed the frame for the subsequent urban layout of Brookline.

Among the eight towns in the Boston area just considered, only Sudbury seems to have maintained a village settlement pattern and open-field farming for even a generation. Sudbury's choice reflected its English antecedents and the deliberate promotion of conservative features by its founding leaders. Other townships began with grouped house lots, but the English experience of their settlers or the economic convenience of enclosed land management led them to disperse almost immediately, even when their settlers had come from England in cohesive groups. Townships first settled as the outlying parts of earlier townships made little if any effort to form villages or to pursue open-field farming. Marlborough had enclosed farming as its very rationale, just as Sudbury had chosen the open-field way. Unfortunately we do not have complete and reliable land division maps for the earliest towns in Massachusetts. The evidence we do have supports the belief that the farm and meadowland was usually divided in elongated strips.

The Plymouth and Massachusetts Bay colonies broke up quickly and easily into self-governing towns, even though each had originally planned a single compact residential settlement surrounded by farmlands. Farmers in Plymouth were soon granted land several miles from the original settlement. Many moved their residences to the farmland, and established separate towns under their own local governance. In Massachusetts Bay the larger number of initial colonists split into several groups even before any central nucleus had been established. This dispersion into smaller towns may well have provided for both subsistence and community better than the original plan could have. Dorchester was the first town settled by a group migrating from England with the intent of establishing a separate community within the Puritan colony. Soon the general courts of both colonies began to approve the formation of new towns as well as the division of towns already settled. At times the general courts even initiated the formation of new towns.

Most of the towns in both colonies divided their land unevenly by formulas recognizing different combinations of leadership, contributions, ability, and need. With experience in the new land, most of the people lived on dispersed farms, with only the meetinghouse and perhaps a tavern to keep the town core at the main road junction in focus.

3
Diffusion of Townships

Early Towns outside Eastern Massachusetts

The Connecticut Valley and Connecticut

WITHIN a few years of the Puritan arrival in Massachusetts, new settlements appeared in the Connecticut Valley of Massachusetts and Connecticut, along the Connecticut coast, in Rhode Island, and in southeastern New Hampshire. Although most of the settlers of these communities came from Massachusetts, the trading possibilities of a few coastal harbors attracted immigrants directly from England also.

The land of greatest attraction was the wide belt of alluvium and terrace that floored the Connecticut Valley, farmland of quality and quantity not found elsewhere in New England. Springfield, Massachusetts, and Windsor, Hartford, and Wethersfield in Connecticut were settled in the 1630s, seventy-five miles west of the nearest Massachusetts settlements. The settlement form most common in these townships is described as the "broad-street village," with its house lots strung out on both sides of a single street and farmland divided into strips that were typically long and perpendicular to the river (fig. 3.1).[1] Broad-street villages were laid out through the rest of the seventeenth century in the Connecticut Valley and to the southwest in Connecticut.

The physical nature of the Connecticut Valley lent itself to the layout of these towns. The expanse of fertile land meant that farmers could live in compact villages and still find adequate farmland close by. Hartford was laid out with a compact core,[2] but most of the towns had thirty or forty houses stretched along a mile of street.

---

[1]Joseph Wood, 48, 54–57, 102–15, 149; Charles M. Andrews, *The River Towns of Connecticut,* Johns Hopkins University Studies in Historical and Political Science, ser. 7, nos. 7–9 (Baltimore: Johns Hopkins, 1889), 56–63.

[2]Joseph Wood, 104; John W. Reps, *The Making of Urban America* (Princeton: Princeton University Press, 1965), 131.

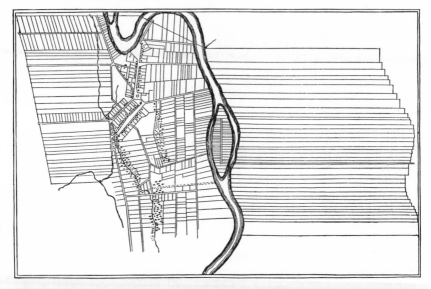

Fig. 3.1. Wethersfield, Conn. The longlots east of the river were nearly three miles long. From Andrews, *The River Towns of Connecticut*. Hartford South (east) and Glastonbury (west) quadrangles.

The wide terraces permitted long farm strips, which could be narrow enough to bring residents fairly close together. The earlier towns usually assigned a resident several strips in fields separated by commons, whereas later towns on the east side of the river often included a farmer's entire holding of meadow, cultivable terrace, and woodland in a single strip that might be as long as three miles.[3]

Strip division in Connecticut, however, was not limited to broad-street villages. The township of Milford, ten miles southwest of New Haven, showed the most elaborate development of *shots*, or ladders, to be found (fig. 3.2). Leonard W. Labaree, in his intriguing account, saw Milford's growth and eventual fission as "fundamentally the result of the land system . . . the central link in the chain, binding together the history of the older and newer towns."[4] Church and government were both manipulated by the land system they had created.

Milford was founded by a group of Puritans under their minister, who left the town of New Haven in 1639. They laid out narrow house lots of two and three-quarters to seven acres on both sides of two

[3]Haller, 109.
[4]Labaree, 27.

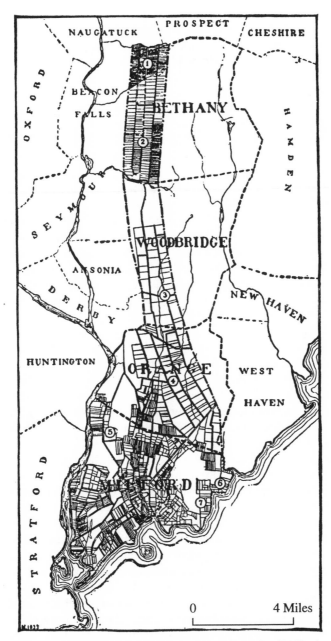

Fig. 3.2. Milford, Conn. The map identifies the present bounds of Milford, as well as adjoining towns that include parts of Milford's northern expansion. From Labaree, *Early Development of a Town*. Milford (north center), Woodmont (northwest), Ansonia (east), and Naugatuck (southeast) quadrangles.

streams flowing into Long Island Sound. Seven general divisions of farmland and two of meadowland were completed by 1687, with an attendant fragmentation of individual holdings. In the early divisions fields of strips running in various directions clustered around the original house lots. In the first four divisions of farmland, the town meeting ordered land assigned by the "rule of persons and estates," that is, by size of family and personal wealth, but always with some special concessions for personal status or leadership. The last three divisions considered estates only. The allocations were also adjusted by sizing.

The later expansion of Milford was entirely to the north in a narrowing neck of land between adjoining towns that finally reached twenty miles inland from Long Island Sound. Here were ladders bounded by sides parallel to the bounds of the township, with transverse strips sometimes even in width. After 1687 lands were no longer distributed by the town meeting, but by four separate groups of proprietors. One tract was reserved by town vote for a group of old residents (or their heirs) and certain approved new ones, who then became the body of proprietors for that tract. The "One-Bit" and "Two-Bit" purchases from the Indians were named for the cost of shares to the purchasers, who became the proprietors for those tracts. The proprietors of these various tracts held them in cautious reserve for a generation or two; one was not divided until 1769. Even then a few odd parcels survived. Lacking the power to sell them, and considering the fragments too few for general distributions, the proprietors devised the idea of leasing them for 999 years in transactions completed shortly after 1800.

The extended laying out of Milford epitomized much New England history. The town's central green remained as the last of the common lands. The *haufendorf*-like jumble of blocks of strips about the original center was typical of the field-by-field expansion of early towns. The neck to the north with its parallel ladders or ranges was more typical of eighteenth-century patterns in Connecticut and central New Hampshire. Its length revealed the drive of many individuals for ever more land, its width successive negotiations with growing communities on each side. Milford also made a number of special land grants—for support of the church and ferry, for the planting of hops and tobacco, and for facilitating selected industries and commerce. The community at times made concessions to individual needs of residents, and the separate bodies of proprietors in later days offered support to the community, the last one in 1806 dedicating the proceeds of its sales of 999-year leases to the school fund to yield interest "forever."

But Milford's fragmentation of ownership and elongation to the north could not last. The northern lands might at first serve only as woodlots or future reserves for families in the old core. Later these families or their sons would move to new parcels in favored areas, trading, if needed, to consolidate their farms. The new clusters of people demanded their own churches in their own neighborhoods, and separate towns ultimately followed. Milford's area was reduced from sixty square miles at its greatest extent to about twenty-five square miles today.

The longest strips anywhere northeast of Texas probably belonged to the township of Fairfield lying to the west of Milford and settled about the same time by people from the Connecticut Valley towns.[5] The northern part of what used to be Fairfield has a series of parallel roads that, except for their irregular spacing, resembled the range roads of many later towns (fig. 3.3). Here the longlots, however, ran parallel to the roads, reaching northwest to the former limits of the township, nine or ten miles long. The widths of the lots ran from three rods (sixty acres if ten miles long) up to fifty-nine rods (1,180 acres).[6] Although Fairfield had many divisions, these longlots laid out in 1682 constituted the greatest part of its land, and gave many of its citizens abundant land to hold for later subdivision.[7] Much of the subdivision appears to have been effected by lines across the longlots, which were thereby converted into ladders.

New Haven deserves special notice for its unusual town center and the manner in which the outlying farm divisions focused on the center. Its founding in 1638 by well-to-do Puritan merchants from England may account for the layout of its core as a square divided into nine large square blocks, each more than 800 feet on a side and containing more than fifteen acres.[8] The first town with a square grid in English North America, its core was more regular than other compactly shaped cores such as Hartford and Fairfield. The central block of New Haven's grid has remained an open green to this day.

---

[5]Bruce C. Daniels, *The Connecticut Town: Growth and Development, 1635–1790* (Middletown, Conn.: Wesleyan University Press, 1979), 13.

[6]Garvan, 54–58. An earlier report gives the range of lot widths as from little more than a rod up to seventy rods; Elizabeth Hubbell Schenck, *History of Fairfield*, vol. 1 (New York: Author, 1889), 335–36.

[7]Garvan, 57–58. A few of Fairfield's residents held significantly more than 1,000 acres.

[8]Reps, 128.

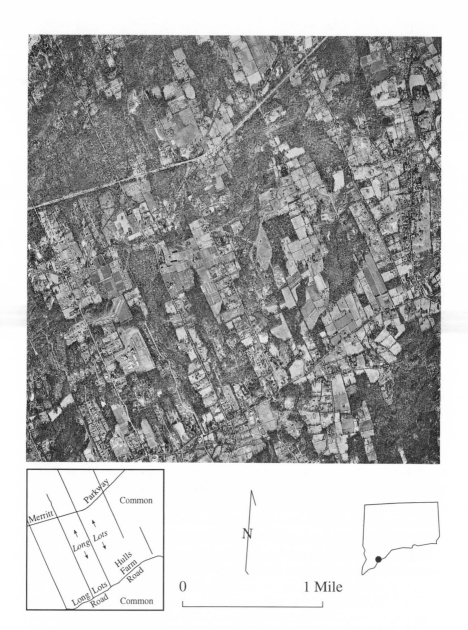

Merritt Parkway Common

Long Lots

Long Lots Road Hulls Farm Road Common

N

0   1 Mile

The eight blocks surrounding it, which were originally divided into house lots ranging from less than half an acre to more than three acres,[9] are now occupied by New Haven's downtown and Yale University.

Additional land extending a mile beyond the grid and known as the "two-miles-square" provided the farmland that early settlers soon learned they would need. The two-miles-square was divided into several "quarters" in the form of irregular sectors that were sooner or later separated by oblique streets radiating out from the center.[10] Most of these outland quarters were assigned to holders of land in the adjoining residence blocks or quarters of the town center. The present urbanized area of the two-miles-square shows a striking pattern of both minor and major radial streets with circumferential connecting streets that probably mark the direction of the old farm strips (fig. 3.4). After two divisions by "persons and estates" and separate allotments in the meadow and neck of land between two streams, individual holdings ranged from eight and a half acres up to nearly a thousand acres. New Haven became the core of a colony that embraced a few other towns until it was incorporated in Connecticut in 1662.

By 1675 the townships founded in Connecticut had claimed all the Connecticut Valley as well as the coastal strip in the south, leaving most of the less desirable hilly interior unoccupied by Europeans.[11] In 1653, however, John Winthrop, Jr., had bought a large, ill-defined portion of the eastern hills from the Indians, and in 1680 and 1684 James Fitch similarly obtained another large portion of the eastern hills, which partially overlapped the claims of Winthrop. The Connecticut government's confirmation of these and other smaller claims produced the largest block of land in New England south of New Hampshire that was private immediately before its townships were set off. A great deal of acrimony and litigation ensued in the

[9]Map, "New Haven in 1641," in Edward E. Atwater, *History of the Colony of New Haven to Its Absorption into Connecticut* (New Haven: Author, 1881).

[10]Ibid., 103–11.

[11]Daniels, *Connecticut Town*, 16–18.

Fig. 3.3 (*facing page*). Fairfield and Westport, Conn., west of Bridgeport. The parallel north northwest–south southeast roads and strips of Fairfield from the latter half of the seventeenth century provide the base for current suburbanization. The evidence of the photograph favors the report that individuals' strips were parallel to rather than perpendicular to the parallel roads. The "half mile" common in the southeast and the "mile" common in the northeast were eventually divided irregularly (Schenck, map opp. 1:1). USGS, 1960. Westport (south of center) quadrangle.

division of eastern Connecticut into townships between 1686 and 1734.[12]

Rhode Island

Rhode Island began like Connecticut with separate settlements stemming from Massachusetts, but took longer to develop any effective coordinating authority. Even after Rhode Island received a charter in 1662, much of its territory remained in dispute and beyond control of the colony. Although the tradition of town units repeatedly appeared in Rhode Island, much of the original settlement was simply rural without any town organization.[13]

Rhode Island's first four towns, Providence, Portsmouth, Newport, and Warwick, were all founded on land obtained from the Narragansett Indians by dissidents who found the religious orthodoxy of Massachusetts restrictive and downright hostile. The founders of Newport and Warwick had also met hostility in other Rhode Island towns. The freedom of conscience favored by the leaders of all four towns led, not surprisingly, to different policies of land division. The people of Providence and Warwick leaned toward more equality than they had known in Massachusetts, the people of Portsmouth and Newport toward more individual enterprise.[14]

The first settlers of Providence, beginning in 1638, received equal shares of different types of land totaling 100 acres each, and became proprietors of the undivided land.[15] The first assignments were in a single row of fifty-two elongated strips (averaging about 120 x 2,300 feet, or six acres) fronting on a street that paralleled the shallow tidal channel a few hundred feet distant to the west.[16] A number of

[12]Ibid., 17–27; Richard L. Bushman, *From Puritan to Yankee: Character and the Social Order in Connecticut, 1690–1765* (Cambridge: Harvard University Press, 1967), 84–103.

[13]William E. Foster, *Town Government in Rhode Island,* Johns Hopkins University Studies in Historical and Political Science, 4th ser., no. 2 (Baltimore: Johns Hopkins, 1886), 7–12; Joseph Wood, 141.

[14]William G. McLoughlin, *Rhode Island* (New York: W. W. Norton Co., 1978), 21.

[15]Irving Berdine Richman, *Rhode Island: Its Making and Its Meaning* (New York: G. P. Putnam's Sons, 1908), 92, 154.

[16]John Hutchins Cady, *The Civic and Architectural Development of Providence* (Providence: Book Shop, 1957), 7, 10. The hundred acres included the home lot, a six-acre planting lot, meadow or pasture, and woodland. Charles M. Andrews, in *The Colonial Period of American History,* 4 vols. (New Haven, Conn.: Yale University Press, 1934–38), 2: 6, apparently referring to the long uncentralized row of "straggling" house lots, said the settlement "differed as strikingly in appearance from the lay-out of a Massachusetts

"quarter rights" were sold in 1645 to additional settlers who received twenty-five acres and quarter shares in the undivided land.[17] The extensive common lands became the subject of controversies, when nonproprietor inhabitants asserted their own interest in these lands. The business center of the city of Providence[18] expanded from the original settlement to the west as the Great Salt River was filled in.

The town of Warwick faced the same conflict between equality and proprietorship that Providence did, and, by also recognizing two different classes of proprietors, it maintained relative peace for a generation until increasing population created land pressures.[19] Seventeen "purchasers" received shares in the entire township about 1650 upon contribution of ten pounds to the common fund.[20] Another fifty-one persons who were accepted as "inhabitants" received six-acre house lots and equal shares in the "four-mile common" of the eastern part of the large township for the payment of twelve shillings.

The four-mile common was divided slowly in a series of twelve or more divisions that gave 200–350 acres to each proprietor, with occasional individual grants. Most of the dividing came after 1700. In 1750 nearly half the four-mile proprietorships belonged to holders with the same surnames as those who had been original proprietors a century before. The persistence of proprietary families suggests that Warwick had remained a rural community in contrast with Providence's increasing commercial role.

Some of the founders of Portsmouth (ca. 1638) were wealthy people who expected freedom to pursue their business interests. The original plan was to settle everyone together in the central village, but a different pattern soon emerged—small farm grants near the village for people of modest means and large grants for the wealthier at a distance greater than would be compatible with living in the village. After six years the common people gained a greater voice in land allocation, and many received supplementary grants sufficient for their family subsistence. Grants of common land were suspended

town as the shapelessness of the Rhode Island religious organization differed from the orderliness of the Massachusetts system."

[17]Richman, 242–43.

[18]Reps, 138–39.

[19]Bruce C. Daniels, *Dissent and Conformity on Narragansett Bay: The Colonial Rhode Island Town* (Middletown, Conn.: Wesleyan University Press, 1983), 18, 26.

[20]Harold R. Curtis, "Warwick Proprietors' Divisions," *Rhode Island Historical Society Collections* 20 (1927): 33–34.

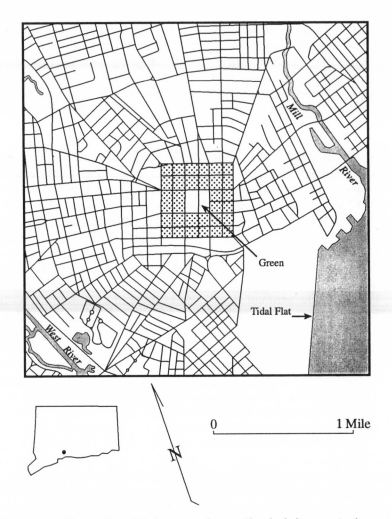

Fig. 3.4. New Haven, Conn. Modern street layout. The shaded square in the center represents the original nine blocks of New Haven with the open green (unshaded) at its core, all these blocks long since divided by more streets. The streets radiating out from the center are thought to have originated as paths for the citizens to go out to their farmland. Many of the streets connecting the radial streets, which probably follow the long boundaries of former strips of farmland, make for difficult traffic connections. Compare with Newtown, Pa. (fig. 14.3), where the early farm land is still farmed. From New Haven quadrangle, USGS.

for a generation after 1657, a measure that would virtually freeze the status quo.[21]

Portsmouth had hardly been settled when a schism led some of its wealthiest citizens to resettle at Newport, which developed as a prosperous center for commercial agriculture and trade, and rapidly outgrew other Rhode Island towns. A sample of landholdings at Newport and Portsmouth in 1639–40 shows a range from nine to 730 acres,[22] with small farmers concentrating on crops and large farmers on livestock.[23]

None of these first four towns of Rhode Island actually gave everyone equal rights in the land. With the possible exception of Newport, however, the common people gained more voice in distribution of the land as time went on. As in Massachusetts, the populations of Rhode Island towns tended to disperse onto the farmlands except where the villages grew as commercial centers.

Most of the other Rhode Island towns that were founded to be towns lay along the eastern fringe of Narragansett Bay and were developed under the authority of Plymouth colony. Among these, Little Compton is of interest for the fact that its house lots were laid out near the center of the township in 1677 only after three earlier divisions had been made. Little Compton had been purchased in 1673 by proprietors living in Duxbury. The house lots were not used for the purpose intended because of the removal of the Indian threat about the time they were laid out. All together about 180 acres of land were drawn by each of the thirty-two proprietors in a series of divisions between 1674 and 1794.[24]

Other parts of Rhode Island were settled as farmland without any town organization. The southwestern part of the colony (present Washington County) was mostly taken up by the large holdings of well-to-do livestock raisers, who became known as Narragansett Planters. Two land companies had purchased tracts of land from the Indians about 1660 and sold it in parcels that ran as large as 12,000 acres.[25] The large estates were slowly divided after colonial days.

---

[21]Dennis A. O'Toole, "Democratic Balance: Ideals of Community in Early Portsmouth," *Rhode Island History* 32 (1973): 3–17.

[22]Carl Bridenbaugh, *Fat Mutton and Liberty of Conscience: Society in Rhode Island, 1636–1690* (Providence: Brown University Press, 1974), 133–34.

[23]Ibid., 18–22, 129–30.

[24]Henry I. Richmond, "The Plat of Little Compton," *Rhode Island Historical Society Collections* 21 (1928): 93–94, and map opp. p. 93.

[25]Edward Channing, *The Narragansett Planters,* Johns Hopkins University Studies in Historical and Political Science, ser. 4, no. 3 (Baltimore: Johns Hopkins, 1886). Part of the

Westconnaug, falling in the southern half of the present town of Foster and the southwestern third of Scituate to the west of Providence, is another example of a group land purchase that may never have even been intended as a town. The minutes of the Westconnaug proprietors, extending from 1662 to 1779, have survived as a record of the purchase. Division of the land and settlement occurred only around 1717. There is no mention of house lots, only larger tracts in about four divisions. The area is sparsely settled even to the present, and the largest nucleated center has no more than thirty houses. Most of the presettlement meetings of the proprietors were held outside Westconnaug, but later meetings were often held at some home within the purchase.[26]

New Hampshire

In New Hampshire the first settlements were tidewater communities along the Piscataqua River that depended heavily on fishing and trade. Exeter and Hampton, both offshoots of Massachusetts in the late 1630s, were a few miles inland and more dependent on farming.[27] Hampton resembled the classical Puritan village, and was singled out by Wood as a lasting compact agricultural village in early eastern New England.[28] Its centrally located village remained as the core of settlement long after farming declined. Today the village has expanded with suburban settlement, while a second concentration of people occupies the shoreline to the east.

Kingston and Dunstable (Nashua) were new inland frontier settlements in the latter half of the seventeenth century, laid out with villages of house lots, detached farmlands, and commons. But New Hampshire farmers were beginning to show a preference for unitary farms. New *plantations*[29] often developed without village centers. Most of the towns of southeastern New Hampshire formed by split-

land was technically acquired on foreclosure of a mortgage, which the Indians had no chance of redeeming.

[26]Theodore G. Foster, transcriber, "The Minutes of the Westconnaug Purchase," *Rhode Island Historical Society Collections* 25 (1932): 121–28; 26 (1933): 26–36, 94–98; 27(1934): 24–32, 57–61, 127–28.

[27]William H. Wallace, "Some Aspects of Colonial Settlement in New Hampshire," *Proceedings,* New England–St. Lawrence Valley Geographical Society 7 (1977): 16–23.

[28]Joseph Wood, 72–73, 149; Wallace, "Colonial Settlement," 4.

[29]"Plantation" in New England commonly designated a new settlement not yet incorporated as a town.

ting off from Dover, Portsmouth, Exeter, and Hampton as settlement expanded, without having been planned as independent towns.[30]

Summary

Massachusetts, Connecticut, Rhode Island, and New Hampshire all laid out their settlements as townships, at least roughly following the English model, but showing a growing tendency of the farmers to reside on their own land outside the villages. The layout of new towns was progressively adjusted through the seventeenth century by enlarging the house lots that typically made up the first divisions.[31] This enlargement apparently was an effort to minimize the dispersion of farmers by making their house lots large enough to farm. From as little as half an acre in Boston to a few acres in many other early towns, house lots were commonly twenty to sixty acres in the latter part of the seventeenth century. A loose concentration of residences seemed preferable to no concentration at all. Even twenty acres of usable land would suffice most farmers for a few years. But the township's good farmland was not likely to be limited to the central area. Either some of the farmers would move to more distant sites, or such sites would be occupied by new members of the community.

The original settlers in a town were likely to receive the most generous allocations of land, although in unusual cases a family allocation might be no more than it had held in England earlier, perhaps only twenty or thirty acres.[32] Many families, however, received as much as 500 acres by the time their towns had completed their several divisions of the common land.[33] Such families had plenty of land to divide among their children, who were then likely to stay in the town. After another generation or so, the farms would stand no more division. Newly formed families became candidates for emigration, and the extended family might become a scattered family.

[30]Wallace, "Colonial Settlement," 6.

[31]Joseph Wood, 48–49; Daniels, *Connecticut Town*, 124; William H. Wallace, "Compact Rural Settlement in Colonial New Hampshire" (manuscript), 1979; Garvan, 62.

[32]Allen, 32–33.

[33]Greven, 214–58; Kenneth A. Lockridge, *A New England Town: The First Hundred Years* (New York: W. W. Norton and Co., 1970), 153–59; idem, "Land, Population, and the Evolution of New England Society, 1630–1790," *Past and Present* 39 (1968): 62–80. Greven (224) found that thirty acres was as small as most Andover farmers would suffer farms to be divided.

The alternative was to stay in the familiar home with a skimpy holding to farm.

Woodstock, a town in northeastern Connecticut although originally in Massachusetts, illustrates one way of "hiving" a new community, and also epitomizes the transition from seventeenth- to eighteenth-century ways of laying out the land. Woodstock developed as an adjunct of the old Massachusetts town of Roxbury, which bought the land from a Connecticut land wholesaler in the 1680s as an outlet for its crowded population. The Roxbury residents divided voluntarily into "goers" and "stayers."[34]

The goers as a group were awarded the southern half of Woodstock (at first called New Roxbury) and were promised £100, to be paid by the stayers over the first few years, for building a meetinghouse and other public improvements. The first division of southern Woodstock gave about forty settlers home lots of ten to thirty acres laid out in strips along a few irregular roads at the present center of settlement in that township.[35] In this division at least, Woodstock resembled the seventeenth-century townships. Some of the later divisions, continuing to 1724, are described as being laid out in ranges,[36] and may have been more regular. Most of the hilly land is sparsely settled today, however, and the present road patterns give no suggestion of such ranges.

While the goers were settling in the southern portion, the northern half of Woodstock was reserved for the stayers, who were assigned lots in the first division of 1695 at the rate of ten acres for each shilling contributed toward the £100 promised the goers for public improvements. As no one settled in the northern half of Woodstock for fifteen years,[37] the surveyors were hardly rushed to get lots marked out for use. This lag in settlement may have provided time to plan the layout of fourteen north-south ranges, all of even width except for the tapering eastern range (fig. 3.5). The first division embraced only the southeastern part of northern Woodstock; completion of the survey awaited the second division in 1715 and third division in 1738. The proprietors had voted in 1713 to assign the rest of the northern half in proportion to holdings in the first division.[38] Most of northern Woodstock is very sparsely settled, but

[34]Clarence Winthrop Bowen, *The History of Woodstock, Connecticut* (Norwood, Mass.: Author, 1926), 18.

[35]Ibid., 14–15, 22–23.

[36]Ibid., 57, 62.

[37]Ibid., 42–43, 60.

[38]Ibid., 62.

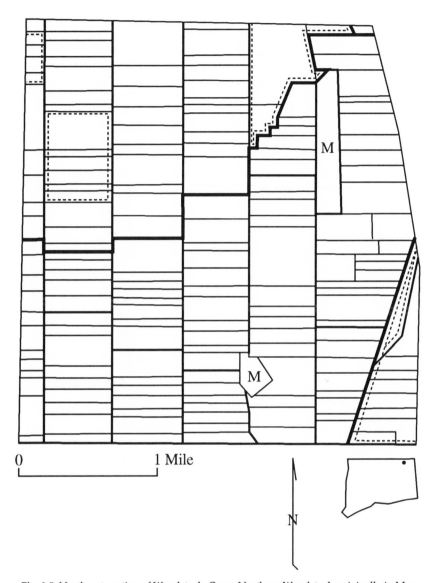

Fig. 3.5. Northeast portion of Woodstock, Conn. Northern Woodstock, originally in Massachusetts, had a plan of fourteen ladders or ranges, side by side. With ranges half a mile wide, every rod in the width of a lot would provide one acre. The first division of 1695 lies between the heavy black lines. The rest of the area is the second division of 1715, except for areas within dashed lines, which belong to the third division of 1738. M = meadow. From "A Plan of the North Half of the Township of Woodstock," eighteenth-century copy by G. C. Williams in Connecticut State Library Archives. Webster (southwest) and Putnam (northwest) quadrangles.

the topographic maps show roads running along seven segments of north-south lines spaced at intervals approximating the range lines. Several aspects of Northern Woodstock's settlement and layout can be recognized in the account of eighteenth-century changes below.

4

Tradition Recedes: Commercially Founded Towns

EIGHTEENTH-CENTURY New England towns departed more and more from the community settlement practice of early New England.[1] Real-estate development became more commercial and speculative. Towns or shares in towns were likely to be purchased, rather than simply granted. Towns were seldom founded by groups of people who expected to share their lives in them. Absentee ownership of land came to be tolerated. Even if original owners did settle in the towns, they were likely to sell their holdings and move again. A resident family's surplus acreage beyond the needs of farming was more likely to be sold and less likely to be held for division among its children. Owners might not be required to build on and cultivate their property in order to hold it.

An important external impetus late in the seventeenth century was at least partially responsible for these changes. Moves toward more direct rule by the crown had posed a threat to land titles conferred by towns.[2] The principal response of the New England colonies was a series of measures to place landownership in the hands of individuals rather than in corporate bodies such as towns and boards of proprietors, which were unrecognized in English law. Where town meetings had assumed control of the common land, the colonies restored control to the original proprietors and their successors.[3]

---

[1] Akagi, 204–5, 209–10; Bushman, 73–82.

[2] Martin, 262–66.

[3] Plymouth and Rhode Island restored the proprietors' right in 1682, Massachusetts in 1698, New Hampshire in 1718, and Connecticut in 1723 (Ray Allen Billington, "The Origin of the Land Speculator as a Frontier Type," *Agricultural History* 19 [1945]: 207). The separation of land control from the town meetings resulted in town meetings giving more attention than before to matters they could control. Through their newly won political powers, however, to tax, to appoint officials, to make laws, to select residents of the township, the nonproprietors were able to regain some of their influence on land policy (Martin, 266–93).

The new approach to town formation required modification of the traditional town layout. The new-style towns often had no house lots or successive divisions—only unitary farms with at most a few lots for meetinghouse, minister, church, and school. Farms of equal acreage were often laid out in a geometric grid with relatively little regard to terrain or soil quality. Fragmented farms or rights in future divisions would have been troublesome to handle in mass real-estate sales.[4] Complete division of the common land often was the first order of business rather than a process of adjustment over a generation or two.[5] Towns were sometimes laid out and sold in groups rather than being individual creations of the general courts and of their inhabitants.

Charles S. Grant's analysis of Kent, however, suggests that a speculative town origin, the consequent turnover of property, and the disparate origin of the settlers need not have prevented a town from developing as a community nor its institutions from being rather democratic.[6]

The Older Colonies

Massachusetts and Connecticut

Some of the variety of eighteenth-century land division in Massachusetts is illustrated by several townships in central Worcester County. Four of these towns were part of a speculative purchase made by settlers in the older town of Lancaster from five Nashaway Indians in 1686.[7] No effort was made to settle the tract until 1715, when the proprietors planned the town of Rutland for sixty-two families who would receive thirty-acre house lots. These house lots were grouped in traditional fashion with several separate rows of rectangular strips arranged around the ministry and school lots. By 1759 some settlers had filtered into Rutland's West Wing, which was set off first as a precinct, then as the town of Oakham. Like Princeton in the East Wing, Oakham had been subdivided in a grid of compact

[4]Wallace, "Colonial Settlement," 7.

[5]Charles S. Grant, *Democracy in the Connecticut Frontier Town of Kent* (New York: Columbia University Press, 1961), 14–15.

[6]Grant, 169–72.

[7]Material in this paragraph is based on Henry Burt Wright, *The Settlement and Story of Oakham, Massachusetts* (New Haven: H. B. Wright and E. D. Harvey, 1947), 13–25; and copies of two old undated maps in the Worcester County Engineer's Office: one of Barre, the other of Oakham, Princeton, and Rutland.

parallelograms, each of about 250 acres except for those truncated by the town limits (fig. 4.1). No town center was shown for either Oakham or Princeton. But Barre, a later town erected at least partly from the same purchase, focused on a small square green surrounded by about seventy rectangular-strip house lots averaging perhaps fifty acres and thirty-three outlots of 500 or more acres. Barre's house lots ran north-south, and the outlots were mostly compact parallelograms with sides parallel to those of the town.

At least two towns in central Worcester County, Leicester[8] (ca. 1715) and Holden[9] (ca. 1724), were laid out in an irregular manner more characteristic of the Southern colonies than of New England (fig. 4.2). The only conspicuous regularity on the plat of either town is that half the lots of Holden were rectangular. In the Southern system land choice was awarded in order of request on the basis of headrights or other entitlements determined by the colony. In New England, such pitching was more often under close control of the town, which determined entitlements and permitted those acquiring lots to make their choices in a sequence determined by drawing. Each recipient in turn might be given a day to select and lay out his lot.[10]

Holden was originally the northern part of the town of Worcester.[11] The land in North Worcester was awarded at the rate of sixty acres in the first division and 100 acres in the second division for each forty acres previously held in South Worcester (now Worcester). The lots of the first division, ranging from thirty to 125 acres, were mostly rectangular and strangely located near the hilly borders of the township, but not in such order as to suggest a planned survey. Second division lots ran up to 180 acres, still tending to be rectangular and near the township borders. Third and fourth division lots were less numerous. A few people obtained adjoining parcels from two, three, or even four divisions so as to get all or most of their holdings in a single parcel, which might amount to 500 acres in rare cases. Commons were quite irregular and seldom near town boundaries; they probably occupied leftover areas not chosen in the pitches. Today

---

[8]Jos. A. Denny, Map of the East Precinct or Settlers Part of Leicester as First Laid Out from 1714 to 1717 (1860), at Massachusetts Historical Society Library, Boston.

[9]Map from Worcester County Engineer's Office, recorded in Plan Book 24, plan 38, Worcester Registry of Deeds. William H. Wallace has identified several townships in New Hampshire that were mostly laid out in irregular lots; "Lines on the Granite Hills: Rectangular Land Survey in Colonial New Hampshire" (manuscript), 1981.

[10]Ford, 20; Egleston, 53.

[11]Samuel C. Damon, *The History of Holden, Massachusetts* (Worcester: Wallace and Ripley, 1841), 26–27.

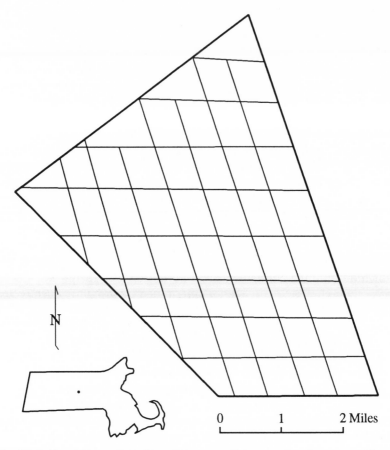

Fig. 4.1. Oakham, Mass., divided into 250-acre parallelograms for sale to nonresidents. After map in Worcester County Engineer's Office. Barre (south center) and North Brookfield (north center, northeast)) quadrangles.

the main axis of Holden's settlement runs northward from Worcester through the center of the township. The peripheral hilly parts of the township, where most of the first division lots fell, are wooded and unsettled.

In another eighteenth-century innovation, colony governments sometimes took the initiative in setting off new townships or groups of such townships.[12] Some of the townships they established were offered as bounties for military service. In 1697 Connecticut laid out Voluntown on its eastern border for 185 volunteers who had fought in

[12]Akagi, 191–202.

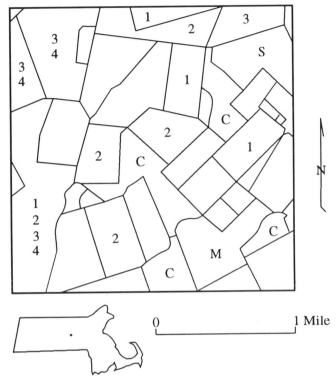

Fig. 4.2. Portion of Holden, Mass. Numbers indicate the division(s) on which lots were allocated. C = common; M = ministerial land; S = school land. First division tracts and one second division tract are rectangular. After map in Worcester County Engineer's Office. Worcester North (northwest) and Paxton (northeast) quadrangles.

King Philip's War.[13] Voluntown ended up being divided into 150 nearly equal-sized lots, the first town in Connecticut without common land for the meetinghouse, parsonage, and other purposes.[14]

Few of the volunteers, some of whom received only half a lot, actually settled in this rugged country.[15] Massachusetts followed suit a generation later with seven townships for veterans of King Philip's war. Mostly located in present New Hampshire and Maine, these townships were to be six-mile squares divided into 120 proprietorships.[16]

[13]Ibid., 192.
[14]Garvan, 65.
[15]Dorothy Deming, *The Settlement of the Connecticut Towns,* Connecticut Tercentenary Commission, Pamphlet no. 6 (New Haven: Yale University Press, 1933), 74.
[16]Akagi, 191.

In the 1730s Massachusetts established another dozen townships in north central Massachusetts and southern New Hampshire for veterans of King William's War.[17] Twenty-five "frontier" townships were also set aside in several groups in western Massachusetts and southwestern New Hampshire as defense outposts. Six-mile squares with sixty proprietors became the standard plan here.[18] Few of these townships even approximate squares in their present boundaries, however.

Connecticut and Massachusetts also laid out townships to sell.[19] Using land to produce income for the public treasury was a sharp departure from the earlier policy of getting land into settlers' hands solely to meet their needs and to develop the colony. Connecticut used its income for support of schools in the older towns.[20]

A historical accident kept open much of the rugged land of northwest Connecticut, for the land had been deeded by the colony to the old towns of Hartford and Windsor in 1687 to keep it out of the hands of the newly established Dominion of New England.[21] In the 1720s, long after the demise of the Dominion, the colony regained the western half of the area in exchange for leaving Hartford and Windsor in possession of the eastern half.

The Connecticut government used its half of the deeded land for the first townships to be put up for auction by a colony. The area was surveyed into seven townships, each to be divided into fifty-three shares (only twenty-five in Salisbury). Three shares in each township were set aside for public purposes, and the rest were sold at auctions held in several of the older county seats.[22] Most of the towns were quickly sold, some buyers taking more than one share. The buyers then met as proprietors of the new towns and put the survey and division of the respective towns in the hands of committees. Less than half the proprietors ever actually lived in their towns; the others sold their land to buyers who would settle there and thus validate the titles.[23]

---

[17]Ibid., 192–93. Volunteerstown (now Petersham), 1730, was also set aside for veterans (Joseph Wood, 99).

[18]Akagi, 195–96.

[19]Connecticut had ordered land sold to raise revenue as early as 1712, Massachusetts by 1727 (Billington, 210; Akagi, 181; Bushman, 75).

[20]Garvan, 73.

[21]Daniels, *Connecticut Town*, 28–31. The Dominion was a short-lived royal government over all the northeastern colonies.

[22]Grant, 14; Akagi, 198; Garvan, 68.

[23]Daniels, *Connecticut Town*, 30–31.

Maps of land division are available for Cornwall, Kent, and Norfolk among the seven auctioned townships.[24] Cornwall was divided in a series of eleven divisions, Kent probably in four, and Norfolk, which did not sell immediately, in three divisions; most proprietors received two lots in each of Norfolk's divisions. The parcels in these divisions were more often compact than elongated, often rectangular, and only locally in even rows or grids. These towns contained roughly 700 acres for each proprietor. Only the map for Kent shows a village plan, a row of narrow lots along both sides of a central street near the Housatonic River.

The Hartford-Windsor (eastern) portion of the northwestern lands was also divided into seven townships, which were allocated among the taxpayers of the two older towns in accordance with their individual estates. The people entitled to land in each township formed a company, which laid out the township in banks of north-south running ranges or ladders of half a mile or a mile width.[25]

The contrast in layout between the Connecticut colony towns and the Hartford and Windsor towns raises questions of why the difference and what the outcome. We may first identify some differences that might affect settlement incentives: (1) shares in the colony towns had been purchased by people who wanted to buy them, whereas the Hartford and Windsor shares were windfalls to all taxpayers, whether interested or not, in the older towns; (2) shares in the colony towns were equal except that a few people might have bought two or three each, whereas shares in the more eastern townships were unequal, and large holders held proportionately more of the land; (3) the colony imposed seating and planting requirements that were absent in the eastern towns.[26]

Consistent with the differences in incentives, the colony townships' series of land divisions probably shared the good land as equitably as possible, whereas the arbitrary division of the eastern townships into ladders of even width left the distribution of the better land to chance. The colony towns are reported as having been better provided with roads and with public land (for meetinghouse, minister, school).[27]

---

[24]George C. Harrison, compiler, Map of the Town of Cornwall, Original Surveys, 1896; Proprietor's Map of Norfolk, n.d.; Map of original land division in Kent; all foregoing in Connecticut State Library, Hartford.

[25]Garvan, 70–73. The statement about division patterns is based on data or suggestive evidence from all but one of the seven townships.

[26]Ibid., 74.

[27]Ibid., 71, 77.

The more remote colony townships actually grew faster than the eastern townships. In 1756, for example, the colony townships had 5,099 persons to 814 for the seven eastern townships,[28] although the eastern townships had been laid out first. The Hartford group actually lagged behind Windsor in development of the towns. Hartford had tended to lay out wider ranges, to divide each holder's land among all the ranges, and to neglect roads. The holders of lesser acreages in the Hartford towns consequently had small and inconveniently narrow parcels, hence little opportunity to sell except to adjoining larger holders.[29]

Massachusetts developed its own auction plan somewhat later than Connecticut, and sold nine six-mile townships in far western Massachusetts at a Boston tavern in 1762 at prices ranging from £1,350 to £3,200. One smaller tract was also sold. Unlike Connecticut's auctioning the individual shares of its townships, Massachusetts sold its townships whole to individuals or to small groups. Within a few years the towns had been sold at profits for the original purchasers.[30]

New Hampshire

Most of New Hampshire was still to be divided into towns when the eighteenth century opened. Although that colony shared in the changes that characterized New England as a whole, its town-founding agencies perpetuated in at least token degree the older practice of laying out central nuclei for most of the new towns. Few of New Hampshire's new townships were so large that they were subsequently divided; hence there was no question of developing additional town centers.

Five towns laid out by Massachusetts in southern New Hampshire shortly after 1725 were traditional in form. Among the townships Massachusetts established to secure its frontiers, these had good reason to concentrate residences in central villages.[31] The home lots of one and a half to ten acres in narrow strips along a single wide street, the intervale lots for hay and pasture, and the upland lots for cultivation also conformed with earlier town designs.

[28]Ibid., 76.
[29]Ibid., 71–72.
[30]Akagi, 199–200.
[31]Wallace, "Compact Rural Settlement," 2.

Another fourteen or fifteen townships were laid out similarly except that the home lots were larger, ranging from twenty to sixty acres.[32] Towns of this type were founded by Massachusetts in the southwestern part of New Hampshire and by New Hampshire in the southeast of the colony. These townships often maintained some central focus of settlement, but most of the farmers consolidated the fields they were actively using and chose to live on their farms.

Additional towns in central New Hampshire were cut from the 1629 grant to John Mason that included the present coast of New Hampshire and all the territory inland to a distance of sixty miles.[33] Mason did not live long after receiving this grant, and his heirs were either uninterested or unable to validate their claim until it was sold for £1,500 in 1746 to a group of influential New Hampshire capitalists, who became known as the Masonian Proprietors.[34] The proprietors judiciously issued quitclaim deeds for most of the settlements already established within their claim before they set about developing the rest of the land for profit.

Most of the land left in the proprietors' hands was granted in the form of forty-two towns. The shares in these Masonian towns were not subjected to quitrents. However, a share of each township (usually about 300 acres) was reserved for each of the fifteen proprietary shares. In addition three shares were saved for a school, the ministry, and the first minister; and two "law lots," a kind of title insurance, went to the proprietary lawyers charged with defending the titles.

The Masonian towns were normally surveyed before settlement. The most common survey pattern was a grid of rectangles or parallelograms 160 x 100 rods (100 acres) with parallel roads running between the ranges.[35] Some towns had more elongated lots: most of Salisbury, for example, was divided into four ranges of strips each a mile wide (320 rods), and each grantee received lots of 100, eighty, and sixty acres; in addition each holder received a strip of intervale land along the Merrimack River measuring about 3 x 50 rods. The little

[32]Ibid., 3.

[33]Wallace, "Colonial Land Survey, 'Centre Squares,' and Reality in New Hampshire: The Masonian Grants, 1748–1754" (manuscript), 1980, 1.

[34]*State Papers of New Hampshire*, ed. Albert Stillman Batchellor, *Town Charters* 28 (Concord: Edward N. Pearson, Public Printer, 1896): iii-v; William Henry Fry, *New Hampshire as a Royal Province*, Studies in History, Economics, and Public Law 19, no. 2 (New York: Columbia University, 1908), 303–4.

[35]This paragraph is based on Wallace, "Colonial Land Survey"; and *State Papers of New Hampshire* 28, including the town plats therein.

permanent common land provided in the townships was unsuitable for other uses. A lot of a few acres was platted, often at the geometrical center of the township, for the meetinghouse, and the lots for schools and the minister bordered it. Purchasers usually did their farming on only one of their lots, selling the others off as separate farms. If the meetinghouse lots were conveniently located, villages later grew around them, but more often the villages located elsewhere. The roads had similar fates. The three long roads separating the four ranges of Salisbury can be followed for eight or ten miles on the modern topographic map, even in rough terrain, but little trace of a regular road system can be discerned in many other townships.

The great arc that marked the northern and western limit of the Masonian grant also forms the boundary of several towns today. Other town boundaries have been shifted. At least two present townships and a number of gores were divided among the proprietors and disposed of by them individually.

The governor also was busy granting new townships in west central and northern New Hampshire—sixty-three new townships between 1760 and 1774.[36] Each township was granted to about sixty original proprietors, many of them speculators who acquired shares in a large number of towns. Additional shares in each town were reserved for the Society for the Propagation of the Gospel in Foreign Parts, for a glebe to support the Church of England, and for the first minister, not to mention two shares for Governor Benning Wentworth, for whom corner lots labeled "B. W." were often the only division of the townships shown on the published plats.[37] Quitrents were reserved for the royal government: an ear of corn per grantee, if demanded, for the first ten years, and a shilling per hundred acres afterward.

In a marked reversal from the earlier omission of house lots, the grants specified that an area as near the town center as practical should be developed in one-acre lots for the residents. The measure itself probably had little to do with effecting village settlement. Certainly villages were seldom precisely centered in the Wentworth towns. A plat of Lebanon of ca. 1800 shows an 8 x 8 checkerboard of small lots (labeled "acre lots," but actually scaling more than two acres).[38] The checkerboard is not near the present village of Lebanon, which is a mile or more away, very near the township center. In similar townships in Vermont, at least, the owner proprietors of

[36]Wallace, "Compact Rural Settlement"; *State Papers of New Hampshire* 24, 25.
[37]*State Papers of New Hampshire* 24–26.
[38]Wallace, "Compact Rural Settlement," map of Lebanon proprietors' lots.

many of these towns evidently made no serious effort to conform with the requirement of laying out the centrally located houselots.[39]

The Wentworth towns were approximately six miles square[40] and were platted much like the Masonian towns except that they exhibited somewhat greater variety and were planned to have the acre lots. The farmlands were usually surveyed into 100- or 200-acre lots, any intervale land being separately divided. Many towns straddling floodplains had their small intervale strips on either side of the stream in proximity to their owners' larger upland holdings. On major river plains, long narrow lots at right angles to the stream resembled the Connecticut River townships of Massachusetts and Connecticut of the previous century.[41]

The Frontiers

Vermont

The eagerness of Wentworth and his nephew and successor, John Wentworth, in granting towns found the Connecticut River no barrier, for they also granted 129 towns in what is now Vermont on the same conditions as those granted in New Hampshire.[42] The Wentworth grants, which helped make Vermont's layout of townships rather regular, although far in advance of settlement, were mostly in the south and along the eastern and western borders to the north. Bennington, Halifax, Marlboro, and Wilmington were planned on behalf of their grantees in sixty-four-square checkerboards with hexagonal reserves at the central intersections large enough to accommodate the acre lots.[43] In such towns Wentworth usually chose a lot bordering the hexagon for himself. Only in Bennington, of the four towns, does the present village location appear so central as to suggest that the plan might actually have been followed.

The Vermont grants began with Bennington, suitably named for the governor, in the southwest corner in 1749.[44] Little or no settlement

[39]P. Jeffrey Potash, *Vermont's Burned-Over District: Patterns of Community Development and Religious Activity, 1761–1850* (Brooklyn N.Y.: Carlson Publishing, 1991), 24–25.

[40]"Containing . . . Twenty Five Thousand Acres, which Tract is to contain something more than six miles square, and no more" (grant for Addison, now in Vermont, *State Papers of New Hampshire* 26: 4).

[41]Wallace, "Colonial Settlement," 16.

[42]*State Papers of New Hampshire* 26: viii and passim.

[43]Ibid., 34, 273, 561.

[44]Ibid., 630.

occurred, however, before 1760, when the Indian threat was reduced. As Wentworth's grants proliferated, Vermont was also claimed by New York, which began making its own military and speculative grants.[45] The results were often two conflicting grants for the same land, both in the name of the King of England. The New York grants were irregular in shape and location in contrast to the relatively orderly ranges of New Hampshire townships and their subdivisions.[46] In the contest for official English support, New York pointed to the higher quitrents available to the crown under its grants, while New Hampshire found supporters in the Society for the Propagation of the Gospel.[47] The ruling from London gave Vermont to New York, but most of the actual settlers there were land-hungry New Englanders under the New Hampshire grants faced with the threat of losing their land or buying it again at high New York prices.[48] Although New York did regrant some of the New Hampshire towns to their occupiers, most people of Vermont, whether settlers or speculators, found their interest tied to validating the New Hampshire titles. For them the American Revolution took the special twist of independence from New York, and the state of Vermont was the later result. Ethan Allen and his brothers and cousins, settlers and land speculators (through their Onion River Company) from Connecticut, have been particularly identified with this Vermont cause.[49]

Vermont was established by its legislature in 1778.[50] Soon it was selling any vacant land, regardless of New Hampshire or New York titles.[51] Resident holders under New York were required to repurchase their land, although at only about nine pence per acre. As early as 1780, Vermont granted more than sixty townships on the general Wentworth model without waiting for admission into the United States, which came in 1791. The revenue raised by selling the

[45]Donald W. Meinig, "Geography of Expansion," in *Geography of New York State*, ed. John H. Thompson (Syracuse: Syracuse University Press, 1966), 141.

[46]"Essays in the Social and Economic History of Vermont," *Collections of the Vermont Historical Society* 5 (1943): 92.

[47]Irving Mark, *Agrarian Conflicts in Colonial New York* (New York: Columbia University Press, 1940), 169.

[48]Ibid., 168, 170.

[49]Dixon R. Fox, *Yankees and Yorkers* (Port Washington, N.Y.: Ira J. Friedman, 1963; original edition, 1940), 168–71.

[50]Florence May Woodward, *The Town Proprietors in Vermont*, Studies in History, Economics, and Public Law no. 418 (New York: Columbia University Press, 1936), 110.

[51]Henry W. Tatter, *The Preferential Treatment of the Actual Settler in the Primary Distribution of the Vacant Land in the United States to 1841* (New York: Arno Press, 1979), 60–62.

townships saved the people of the state the payment of taxes.[52] Buyers in groups of about sixty-five proprietors were recruited by advertising all over New England and the middle states and in the continental army.[53] Unlike the New Hampshire town grants, the Vermont towns carried no quitrent.[54] No land was set aside for the governor, although it should be noted that Vermont Governor Thomas Chittenden did become a proprietor of at least forty-two townships.[55] Education was favored a little more than religion in awarding public shares in these towns. Hyde Park, for example, gave two shares to local public schools, one for a university, one for the support of a minister, and one to further the "social worship of God."[56] Vermont laws gave extensive powers to proprietors, most of whom sold their shares without ever visiting the state. But many proprietors still gained possession of most of one or more townships before the land finally passed into the hands of those who would actually settle there. A number of Vermont townships were taken up by pitches rather than more regular geometric division.[57]

Maine

Maine, with its marginal position and its vast lands of marginal quality, provided New England with a long-enduring frontier. The story of Maine land entails a complex of early grants and jurisdictions, and a prolonged and often sporadic division of those holdings into townships. Although many of those towns were in their turn divided in the manner of other New England towns, many remain undivided today.

A line running nearly east and west (about 44°40'N) limits the southern quarter of Maine as an area of irregular townships laid out and settled by about 1800. The area north of the line was laid out in townships that are mostly square or at least rectangular, largely in grids of six-mile squares. The southern half of the regular townships have boundaries oriented with the magnetic directions, about 11°

---

[52]Woodward, 112–13, 115–16. Three times as much was raised from the sale of confiscated property.

[53]Ibid., 114.

[54]Ibid., 126.

[55]Ibid., 130.

[56]Ibid., 127.

[57]Ford, 13.

west of north when the townships were created. The more northern townships are oriented with the true cardinal directions.

Important parts of Maine were covered by a number of early land grants. One of the most comprehensive of these was the royal grant to Ferdinando Gorges in 1639, finally sold by his heirs to the Massachusetts Bay colony in 1677.[58] Maine remained under the jurisdiction of Massachusetts until 1820. Before the Gorges grant, however, the Council for New England had made more than two dozen grants that together embraced the whole coast of Maine as far east as the Penobscot River and extended varying distances inland. Most of these grants received little attention and became dormant, but four were revived by the heirs or assigns in the eighteenth century with the formation of companies of proprietors that reestablished their claims in court.[59]

The Kennebeck Company holding originated in 1630 with a grant to leaders of the Plymouth colony extending some miles on each side of the Kennebec River. The grant was eventually turned over to all the freemen of Plymouth and later sold into private hands. It was confirmed and extended through Indian purchases. The original strategy of the grant was as a base for trade in furs and other commodities. When the grant was revived and the proprietors incorporated in 1749, they began promoting settlement. One hundred acres were offered each settler as underpinning for the efforts to recruit groups in Europe.[60] By the early 1760s, the company had settled at least eleven townships. The present town of Dresden derives from a settlement of Germans, who in fact were mostly Huguenots. More settlers came in with agreements regarding residence and clearing land, and the company had to deal with many squatters. Some grants or sales were as large as a few thousand acres, mostly made to individual members of the company.[61] The company finally auctioned off its last landholdings, divided its liquid assets of $48,000, and dissolved itself in 1822.[62] The Pejebscot Proprietors, Lincolnshire Company, and Pemaquid Proprietors were other holders of Maine claims who settled townships and promoted immigration in the 1700s.[63]

[58] Akagi, 230–33, 241–65; Gerald E. Morris, ed., *The Maine Bicentennial Atlas: An Historical Survey* (Portland: Maine Historical Society, 1976), plate 10.

[59] Akagi, 241–44.

[60] Gordon E. Kershaw, *The Kennebeck Proprietors, 1749–1775* (Portland: Maine Historical Society, 1975), 69–74.

[61] Ibid., 108.

[62] Ibid., 294–95.

[63] Akagi, 244–52.

Settlement by settlement, which actually meant town by town, Maine grew from its coast inland, with the greatest early concentration in the southwest. Settlement began with royal grants, proprietary grants, Indian deeds, and Massachusetts grants.[64] Land division patterns within these towns were varied, as we might expect from the variety of sponsors. A sample of late eighteenth-century Massachusetts grants shows cases of longlots (Farmington, fig. 4.3), grids of rectangles and parallelograms (Farmington, Freedom, Avon), and irregular rectangular division (Freedom), including townships with mixed patterns.

The regular townships of northern Maine were originally public lands that were systematically put on the market by Massachusetts after the Revolution to raise revenue. Townships east of the Penobscot received most attention at first. Alternate townships on the rivers were to be sold in 500-acre lots for at least six shillings per acre, others in 150-acre lots at the best obtainable price. Each non-riverine township was to be seeded by giving away 3,000 acres in 100-acre lots to actual settlers.[65] To speed up the slow sales, a lottery of fifty townships was ordered in 1786. Tickets were sold at sixty pounds each, and each holder would win a parcel that might be as small as 160 acres or as large as a township.[66] One township divided for the lottery contained forty-two lots of 160 acres and other lots of 320, 640, 1,280, 1,920, 2,560, and 3,840 acres in addition to four lots of 320 acres for support of schools and the ministry.[67] Only a few hundred tickets were actually sold and 165,000 acres awarded, but these were inconveniently scattered over the whole fifty-township area. Although Harvard College with nine tickets had purchased more than any other buyer, an individual received the largest prize of 5,440 acres.[68]

Between 1793 and 1818, Massachusetts granted a total of about thirty townships in Maine to thirty-seven colleges and academies.[69] Most of these grants were for half townships and several were for

---

[64]Morris, ed., plates 5 and 10.

[65]Frederick S. Allis, Jr., ed. "William Bingham's Maine Lands, 1790–1820," *Collections* (Colonial Society of Massachusetts) 36 (1954): 26.

[66]Ibid., 27–28.

[67]Township no. V of South Range North Division, Maine State Archives, book 26: 42.

[68]Allis, ed., 36: 28–29.

[69]Stanley Bearce Atwood, *The Length and Breadth of Maine*, Maine Studies no. 96 (Orono: University of Maine, 1973), 30; Moses Greenleaf, *Map Exhibiting the Principal Original Grants and Sales of Lands in the State of Maine* (Portland: Shirley and Hyde, 1829).

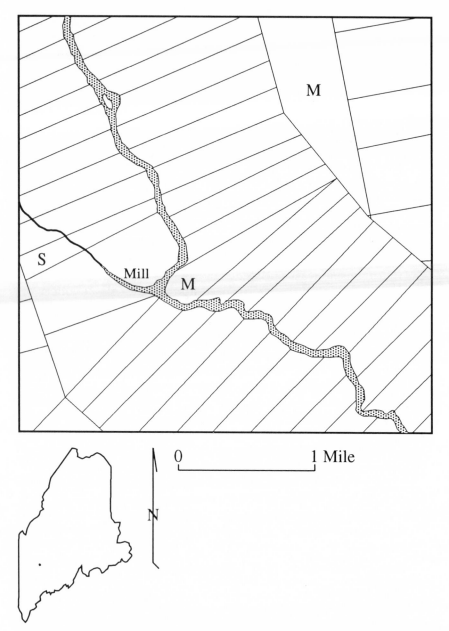

Fig. 4.3. Farmington, Me. Longlots along Sandy River; portions of more compact lots on each side of longlots are visible. M = ministerial land; S = school land. After map in Maine State Archives. Farmington (east) quadrangle.

full townships. Bowdoin College, in Maine, was the largest recipient with about seven townships, most near the center of the state. Eleven of the academic grants were in the two easternmost tiers of townships north and south of the town of Houlton. In addition to the colleges and academies, grants were made to aid the Massachusetts Agricultural Society and the Massachusetts Medical Society, the towns of Boston and Plymouth, "sufferers of Falmouth," improvements such as canals, bridges, and piers, and various soldiers and private parties, including one man (10,000 acres) for his "exploits in Tripoli."

Massachusetts also sold a few very large tracts amounting to as much as a million acres each. Two of these, with some adjoining lands, came under the control of William Bingham of Philadelphia in the early 1790s.[70] Bingham's Penobscot tract lay in a great square just inland of tidewater to the east of the Penobscot River, and came to include additional lands to the south and east. One of the tract's lesser problems involved the lands distributed earlier in the lottery. His Kennebec tract was a great square in the interior astride the Kennebec River. Bingham and his predecessors, associates, and European backers perceived the lands as generally favorable to farming and also as about to be engulfed in the great wave of settlement that the land hunger of the times would produce. They were wrong on both accounts. The lands have never favored farming and indeed have remained sparsely settled to the present day.

The first efforts were toward developing the Penobscot tract, partly because Bingham's European backers were willing to offer help for it alone. Alexander Baring, agent of the European banking concerns and soon to be Bingham's son-in-law, identified two avenues to profit, from his extensive observations of other American land speculations: resale to other speculators, or investment in improvements and attractions for early settlers in order to raise the land value for sale to later settlers. Bingham had not succeeded at the first, and, individual settlement proving very slow, Baring prepared a detailed plan for stimulating it.[71]

[70]Allis, ed.

[71]Ibid., 37: 919–34. Baring's strategies included: providing infrastructure in anticipation of needs (a wagon road into the heart of the country, laying out a principal town and port, smaller towns in main farming concentrations, regular packet connection with Boston, mills and stores, houses, land office, district surveyors); publicizing all progress (advertising in all principal New England papers, with considerable "puffing"); priming the pump (inducing settlers to come and scattering them through the tract, selling some farms around the town, selling larger tracts to small speculators who

So Bingham turned his effort toward the Kennebec tract.[72] In 1799 John Merrick, whom Bingham was considering employing as an agent, offered a plan for dividing each township into 200-acre lots a mile long and 100 rods wide, fronting on roads, one of which would connect with the older settlements. The 200-acre lots were thought more attractive than the standard 100-acre lots available elsewhere. Settlers could buy only 100 acres at first, but would receive options to buy the second hundred after paying for the first. A number of these lots would be held back for a higher selling price after the first were sold.

Bingham died in 1804 with little progress in the sale of either tract. Despite many financial squeezes, his heirs' resources were sufficient to hold onto the land, but its general sale and settlement lay nearly twenty years in the future. In the 1820s the demand for lumber (often satisfied earlier by piracy) opened a new market, especially on the Kennebec. The land was sold mostly by the township rather than by the small farms planned. The Bingham interests probably showed a profit on the original investment, but not enough to justify the long wait for it to materialize.[73]

The struggle between the great land speculators and the squatters had been especially bitter in Maine, where large tracts had been granted the wealthy from early in the seventeenth century and which was long treated by Massachusetts as its colony without all the corporate concern for its residents that was traditional in Massachusetts proper. Many settlers, who left their mark on Maine in such town names as Freedom, Unity, and Liberty, felt that they had liberated the land as soldiers and should not have to pay for it a second time. The land speculators considered that the settlers, by wanting to share in the increase in land values, were not playing their fitting roles.[74] The Betterment Act (ca. 1808) ended much of the altercation by recognizing the proprietors' claim to the wild value of

might have their own contacts with groups of immigrants); pleasing customers (encouragement and assistance, a good farm for every applicant, each sharing in meadows and waters, assistance to settlers, amicable settlements with squatters); establishing terms of sales (standardization on 160-acre farms except for twenty-five to fifty-acre farms around town, first-year price of $1 per acre, letting it be known that the second-year price would be $2, a few years to pay, no deed before substantial payments made); screening speculators (for respectability, for their interest in improvement, that none contemplate lumbering).

[72]Ibid., 983ff.

[73]Ibid., 1173–1255.

[74]Alan Taylor, *Liberty Men and Great Proprietors* (Chapel Hill: University of North Carolina Press for Institute of Early American History and Culture, 1990), 17–18, 51–57.

the land and the settlers' claim to the value of their improvements.[75] The wild value, however, tended to include the enhancement from increasing population density.

When Maine separated from Massachusetts in 1820, about half the state's area remained as public land. After Maine declined Massachusetts' offer of the area at little more than two cents an acre,[76] it was divided between Maine and Massachusetts, either in alternate ranges of townships or, to the northeast, in a checkerboard pattern of townships. The two states worked together in trying to sell and settle land, and policies changed frequently. Townships near the eastern border of Maine were designated as "settling lands," those to the west as timberlands. The policies protected squatters and offered 100–120 acres to settlers at modest prices that were sometimes to be paid off by working on the roads. Timberland was usually sold in tracts of 500 acres or more and sale was limited to only a few townships a year.

After Maine bought the Massachusetts lands in 1853, more than five million acres remained public. The eastern settling lands continued to be sold slowly, usually gravitating into the hands of large landholders. A thousand acres in each township had been set aside for support of education; sale of stumpage brought some revenue for that purpose. And Maine continued the grants to educational institutions begun by Massachusetts, a program that totaled nearly a million acres. Shortly after the Civil War, most of the remaining public lands, three-quarters of a million acres, were granted to a railroad running from Bangor eastward to the Canadian border. The remaining settling lands were declared unfit for that purpose and put up for sale.

Most of northern Maine went into the hands of large holders among whom the timber interests heavily predominated. Most of the townships there have never been organized, named, or divided. Their ownership has been split, however, creating outlandish fractions as in the case of a 31/52 part of an eighth interest. Even the public lots of 1,000 acres reserved in each town remained part of the undivided ownership pool until a recent program to mark them off. The principal owner of a town usually manages the timber, and all owners share proportionately in the expenses and income. The north-

[75]Ibid., 220–25.

[76]David C. Smith, "Maine and Its Public Domain: Land Disposal on the Northeastern Frontier," in *A History of Maine*, ed. Ronald Banks (Dubuque, Ia.: Kendall/Hunt Publishing Co., 1969), 192–98.

west quarter of Maine has few settlements except for logging camps; the people who work the timber live mainly around the edges of the area.[77]

Summary

Land distribution in colonial New England had two facets that were at least somewhat contradictory. On the one hand, land was the principal material tool of the region's church-centered communities—the basis of subsistence and a device for grouping the faithful in their pursuit of celestial goals. On the other hand, land was the chief form of personal wealth, providing affluence beyond the demands of subsistence. The ideas of land as a reward for special status or service and land as an avenue to speculative gain both resided in the first implantation of colonies on New England soil. Capitalistic activity steadily encroached on the cadastral interests of the theocratic community as the New England colonies matured.

The township was the basic unit of land granted by the colonies of New England, and became in turn the unit within which land was subdivided into private parcels. The township is still basic to the New England cadastral map, just as the town is basic to the social and political organization. New Englanders perceive an area and the locations within it in the frame of its townships. The town-to-town variation in landownership patterns often reflects the original land division. Many old boundaries of towns, which were mothers of that division, double as property lines along much of their length.

Most New England land was laid out in surveys before it was awarded to those who would possess it and use it. In the early towns these surveys often reflected careful assessment of both the terrain and of individual and community circumstances. The resulting organic land patterns were often replaced in later towns by geometric surveys that ignored both the terrain and the yet anonymous townsmen who would acquire the parcels. On New England's northern frontier land division frequently ended with laying out townships that have never been surveyed into lots, even though their ownership has been divided.

---

[77]Bret Wallach, "Logging in Maine's Empty Quarter," *Annals of the Association of American Geographers* 70 (1980): 544–46. David C. Smith, 193, identifies the public land in each township as 1,000 acres; Wallach's figure of 500 hectares is assumed to be an approximation.

Land assignments among early Puritans were aimed at meeting minimal needs of all families and more generous recognition of wealth and status in the community. Even with such unequal land division the order in which strips were placed in a field was usually determined by lot. Rarely did the principle of equality enter into land assignments as it did briefly in Plymouth and in two of the first towns of Rhode Island. Land, once granted, however, could be traded, at first only with town approval, but increasingly on a free market. The townships and their land became more and more objects of speculation, whether initially granted outright or sold. Ironically, the later townships that were given to people of influence or to soldiers or were sold to raise revenue were often divided in equal shares among their recipients.

The regularity of some late New England town layouts is often revealed in the landscape. To gain one measure of such regularity, topographic maps were examined for parallel roads that appear to be old range lines. Such evidence is scarce in Massachusetts, where it appeared in only two towns. In Connecticut, eighteen towns showed such indications, however. The number increased to twenty-seven in New Hampshire, and Vermont showed seventeen. There is more such regularity than reading topographic maps alone will show, however, for Wallace's more intensive search found evidence of old range lines in fifty-five townships in only a portion of New Hampshire.[78]

It is not only in regular surveys, however, that old lines persist on the New England land. Wallace found landscape evidence of original surveys in more than half the area of New Hampshire, the major exceptions being the mountainous north and smaller hill areas in the southern parts of the state.[79] Original surveys are etched in roads, as mentioned above. They are followed by fence lines in cleared areas and countless miles of old stone fences now lost in forests. They are revealed in the vegetation succession that follows on the heels of earlier land uses (fig. 4.4). Most directly of all, many original property lines persist as property lines and guide the activities of people on that land.

[78]Maps accompanying Wallace, "Lines on the Granite Hills."

[79]Maps accompanying William H. Wallace, "The Mark of the Past upon the Land: Colonial Land Survey and Territorial Organization as an Element in the Contemporary Landscape of New Hampshire" (manuscript), 1983.

0 N 1 Mile

Fig. 4.4. Epping, N.H., and adjoining townships. Range and lot lines revealed by roads, clearings, and vegetation boundaries. USGS, 1951. Epping (west center) and Mt. Pawtuckaway (east center) quadrangles.

Part III

The South Atlantic Region: Land Division by Individual Choice

THE SOUTH Atlantic colonies (fig. 5.1) were founded at different times, under different sponsorships, and with widely disparate goals. They included the first and last of all the English colonies planted in the present United States. The most significant unifying circumstances were proximity and climate. Their governments remained mostly independent of one another. The ultimate division of Carolina yielded two colonies that were sufficiently dissimilar to increase rather than decrease the variety among the colonies of the region.

Nevertheless, the South Atlantic colonies were clearly the hearth and core of the tradition of independent land surveys, which developed first in Virginia, then Maryland, Carolina, and Georgia. In spite of dissimilarities, specific even to their land plans, the colonies' land systems converged considerably as they faced common problems and the later colonies took cues from their predecessors.

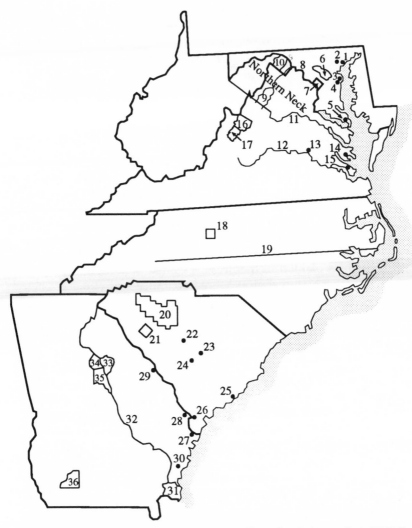

Fig. 5.1. South Atlantic locations: 1. Baltimore 2. Ellicott City 3. Annapolis 4. All Hallows Parish 5. St. Mary's City 6. Howard County 7. District of Columbia 8. Potomac R. 9. Shenandoah R. 10. Berkeley County 11. Rappahannock R. 12. James R. 13. Richmond 14. Ware Neck 15. Jamestown 16. Augusta County 17. Rockbridge County 18. Wachovia 19. Southern boundary of Granville proprietorship 20. Sumter National Forest 21. Hamilton's Great Tract 22. Saxe-Gotha 23. Amelia 24. Orangeburg 25. Charleston 26. Purrysburg 27. Savannah 28. Ebenezer 29. Augusta 30. Darien 31. Camden County 32. Western limit of headright grants 33. Greene County 34. Morgan County 35. Putnam County 36. Mitchell County.

5

Colonial Beginnings

IRREGULARITY of land division accompanied a system of warrants and independent layout that was closely linked at first with the granting of land on headrights. It moved on westward in Virginia and North Carolina, persisting through the settlement of what now are West Virginia and most of Kentucky and Tennessee.

Indiscriminate location came about as colonists asserted their individual choices in the absence of effective colonial management. The sponsors in England could not keep tabs on individual land decisions, and local leaders, like other settlers, were preoccupied with survival. Plans for controlled settlement, which were elaborate in the cases of Carolina and Georgia, were not sustained. Colonists in Virginia had been acquiring land for several years before the first authorized surveyor arrived in 1621. Sarah Hughes suggests that the practice of individual location and bounding of property became established during that initial period, then rushed ahead under the incitement of big tobacco profits.[1] Except for short periods, none of the Southern colonies surveyed lands in advance of settlement or held up the march of settlement for such surveys.

Although indiscriminate location originated in necessity and expediency, it became a tool of settlement highly valued by Southern pioneers. Such individual selection was one way of enabling farmers to find suitable sites in a region of varying land quality. Hughes considered individual selection a means of giving priority to "rapid economic development instead of planned and orderly growth."[2] Arbitrary land assignment did not work well in the colonial South. Failure of the 1664 colony at Cape Fear has been blamed on the Carolina proprietors' insistence on a preconceived compact settlement pattern in a region where the good land was scattered among

---

[1]Sarah Hughes, *Surveyors and Statesmen: Land Measuring in Colonial Virginia* (Richmond: Virginia Surveyors Foundation, and Virginia Association of Surveyors, 1979), 5.
[2]Ibid., 131.

swamps and pine barrens.[3] And in early Georgia so many settlers were assigned poor sites[4] that the colony trustees relented after a few years and permitted augmentation of unsuitable holdings with better land selected elsewhere.[5]

Prescriptions for good settlement practice that might be inferred from the previous paragraph do not hold up well in comparison with New England experience. There planned compact settlement survived very well in a land of varying quality, and, indeed, New England's compact settlement has been widely considered a forcing bed for rapid economic development *with* planned and orderly growth. Comparison of only the New England and Southern treatment of varied lands, however, will tell us little, for colonization in those two regions depended also on differences in objectives, social structure, and climate.

The land division of the Southern colonies was not all irregular. In one place or another the South tried most of the range of land division patterns found in all the Atlantic colonies. Thus the irregular land division had to compete at times with more formal plans proposed by colonial governments and their English sponsors or put into practice by local promoters and speculators.

The treatment of Southern land division will begin with the initial experience under the Virginia Company between 1607 and 1624, when many practices later used in Virginia and other colonies evolved. The varying origins and early land plans of the other Southern colonies will follow.

Land Distribution in Virginia, 1607–24

Business enterprise guided the founding of Virginia more than that of any other colony. Its inception and early management were in the hands of a joint stock company, which originally raised funds by the sale of stock, but later resorted to assessments, lotteries, and appeals

---

[3]Lawrence Lee, *The Lower Cape Fear in Colonial Days* (Chapel Hill: University of North Carolina Press, 1965), 45, 53.

[4]Phinizy Spalding, *Oglethorpe in America* (Chicago: University of Chicago Press, 1977), 73–74; Kenneth Coleman, *Colonial Georgia* (New York: Charles Scribner's Sons, 1976), 123–25.

[5]James Ross McCain, *Georgia as a Proprietary Province: The Execution of a Trust* (Boston: Richard C. Badger, 1917), 267; Allen D. Candler, comp., *The Colonial Records of the State of Georgia*, 26 vols. (Atlanta: Franklin Printing and Publishing Co., 1904–16), 2: 377.

to keep the colony alive. No doubt the investors, managers, and settlers were excited by their chance to expand England's domain, to build a new world, and to Christianize the heathen, but the project was to draw its nourishment from the coupled prospects of profit for its financial backers in England and of land for the settlers who were offering their labor and risking their lives in the new colony.

The anticipated forms of wealth did not materialize, and most of the basic industries tried in the colony were unsuccessful. Tobacco, the one product that did enhance the value of Virginia land, was at first discouraged by the company in England because it interfered with subsistence pursuits. The colony survived its early period of starvation, diseases, Indian wars, and shortage of women even though the company and most of the colonists did not. Virginia became a royal colony in 1624, the English government its sponsor until 1776.

The colonial tactics of the Virginia Company and of the crown were not very different. Each sought growth in number of settlers, development of more resources, and an economic surplus of benefit both to the colony and to the homeland. Lacking special religious, feudal, or charitable purposes, Virginia was the colony that most "seemed to conform to the English expectation of what a colony should be."[6]

Land was offered to both investors and settlers as the Virginia colony got under way in 1607. One early promise was 100 acres each for able-bodied men, their wives, and children old enough to work.[7] But delivery on the promise was deferred, for no land was planned to be distributed during the first years of the colony. Farming was to be carried out on the company's land, the produce to go into company stores for the common use of the colony.

Nova Britannia,[8] a prospectus of 1609, was more generous, quoting 500 acres as the amount the company hoped to distribute to the holder of each share costing £12 10s, or to each immigrant to the colony. The good land and poor land "in three or foure distinct differences" would be divided proportionally among all claimants. But this prospectus imposed another seven years of communal farming be-

[6]Charles M. Andrews, *Our Earliest Colonial Settlements* (New York: New York University Press, 1933), 27.

[7]Alexander Brown, *The Genesis of the United States,* 2 vols. (Boston: Houghton, Mifflin and Co., 1890), 1: 71.

[8]In Peter Force, comp., *Tracts and Other Papers Relating Principally to the Origin, Settlement, and Progress of the Colonies in North America,* 4 vols. (1836; reprinted New York: Peter Smith, 1947) 1, no. 6: 23–25.

fore the immigrant colonists, mostly transported to Virginia as indentured servants, would receive their land. Neither the promised quantity nor the systematic division by quality was to materialize.

Communal farming met with no more success in Virginia than it did a few years later in Plymouth, and, as a result, Governor Thomas Dale made the first tentative efforts at individual land assignment around 1613–14. He issued a three-acre parcel of "cleere Corne ground"[9] to each of eighty-one tenants, reportedly to every farmer in the colony except those in the Bermuda settlement, some thirty miles upriver from Jamestown, who worked under a special agreement. The tenants were freed of all obligations except one month's service to the colony and a payment of two and a half barrels of ears of corn each year. At the same time they were put on their own resources for raising food. This move toward free enterprise is credited with a great increase in the production of staples such as grains and beans.[10] These first land assignments were temporary and probably left no identifiable mark on Virginia property lines. About the same time, Dale promised twelve acres, a house, tools, livestock, and provisions to every man with a family who would come to Virginia at his own expense.[11] Families were to be self-sustaining after the first year, but it is probable that few were attracted by this offer.

By 1616, the colony began granting land in both small and large acreages—*farms* and *plantations* as they came to be called.[12] The time was ripe, for the seven-year period of communal land use prescribed in *Nova Britannia* was up, as were the terms of many indentured servants. Extant records of grants from 1616 and 1617 are very few. Share owners, however, had to put up another £12 10s in order to receive their dividends.[13]

[9]Ralph Hamor, *A True Discourse of the Present State of Virginia* (1615; reprinted, Richmond: Virginia State Library, 1957), 17.

[10]Ibid. Private holdings, however, were not so highly praised in all reports. The decline of the "Companies Garden" and salt works, which, with fifty-four men, had yielded a total of £300 in 1617, was blamed on the competition of individual holdings. Susan M. Kingsbury, ed., *Records of the Virginia Company*, 4 vols. (Washington: Government Printing Office, 1906–35), 1: 350–51; Wesley Frank Craven, *Dissolution of the Virginia Company* (1932; reprinted, Gloucester, Mass.: Peter Smith, 1964), 35–36.

[11]Marshall Harris, 181.

[12]Alexander Brown, *Genesis*, 2: 774–79. Even the small farmers originally were called planters. Farms and plantations in the present sense may be roughly distinguished by whether the labor was done by the family or by others. Farms seldom contained more than 300–500 acres, plantations seldom less.

[13]Ibid.; W. Stitt Robinson, Jr., *Mother Earth: Land Grants in Virginia, 1607–99* (Williamsburg: Virginia 350th Anniversary Celebration Corporation, 1957), no. 12: 16–17.

Land policies were set out in more explicit terms in 1618 in the company's instructions to Governor GeorgeYeardley as he took office, in a document that became known as the "greate Charter" because of its generous guarantees.[14] It contained the principle of the headright that was to guide Virginia land policy for the rest of the century.

The basic promise was a headright of fifty acres for each new colonist, the land to go to the person paying the passage, and 100 acres for the holder of each share of the company's stock. The "ancient planters," those who had endured and survived the hardships of the colony since a specified date in 1616, were granted 100 acres on completion of any service they owed. Most of the grants to shareholders and colonists were to be doubled on the declaration of a second division, provided that the original grants had been "peopled," but the second division was never declared. Privileged classes, generally stockholders and settlers who had paid their own passage, received their lands without quitrent; others were to pay each year a shilling per fifty acres after a short period of exemption. Headrights were contingent on the settlers' remaining in the colony for three years or, in recognition of the risks of this venture, dying in the effort. Artisans and tradesmen not interested in farms might be granted a house and four acres of land for the practice of their vocations at an annual rent of four pence.

The Great Charter also formalized two types of large holdings, one private and one public. Particular plantations[15] were large private grants put together by company shareholders from land dividends, importation rights, and additional grants of the company's common land. These enterprises were virtually independent colonies under the Virginia Company with their own sponsors, funds, and settlers, on their own for making gains or taking losses, and even possessing limited political independence.[16] Their existence evidenced

---

[14]In Kingsbury, ed., 3: 98–109.

[15]*Particular* to distinguish them from the whole colony, which was also referred to as a plantation. Particular plantations were also sometimes called *hundreds*, using an old English term of uncertain origin for minor political divisions. Some county subdivisions in Delaware are still called hundreds.

[16]Particular plantations were given representation in the Assembly along with the boroughs. The representatives of one plantation, Martin's Brandon, were not seated in the first Assembly, 1619, because its owner claimed not to be bound by the body's decisions. In return for his long services to Virginia, his grant had specified that "he was to enjoye his landes in as lardge and ample manner . . . as any Lord of any Manours in England." The only grant of true manorial prerogatives in Virginia, it was withdrawn a few years later; Alexander Brown, *Genesis*, 2: 943–44; Charles E. Hatch, Jr., *The First Sev-*

both shareholder dissatisfaction with the lack of return from the parent company's operation and the enticement of profits from tobacco cultivation. For several years these plantations absorbed most of the money and immigrant labor available for Virginia and received most of the land granted. A few had been established even before Yeardley's 1618 instructions. The company reported to the king in 1623 that forty-four patents for land had been granted within the previous four years to persons or groups who had each undertaken to transport at least a hundred men.[17] Many of these projected plantations never did come into being, as Virginia's entire non-Indian population did not reach 4,400 before 1630. By 1640 no vestige of the special status of the particular plantations remained. One of these plantations, Berkeley Hundred, and probably others as well, had planned to operate with tenants attached to the estate in feudal fashion, but keeping tenants beyond their indentures proved impractical.

The public holdings confirmed and created by the instructions of 1618 comprised several types of parcels: (1) 3,000 acres of "Governor's Land" adjoining Jamestown; (2) a 3,000-acre tract of company land in each of the four boroughs,[18] including Jamestown; (3) a 1,500-acre common for each borough or particular plantation; (4) 10,000 acres as the endowment of a college for educating the Indians; (5) 100 acres of glebe land for each borough or particular plantation. The first and third types of tracts were to help support the governor and local officials, with the intent of freeing the colonists from the burden of taxation. The company land, as well as some of the other public land, was to be worked by tenants brought to Virginia at company expense, half the profits going to the tenants.

We have only a vague idea of actual land patterns under the Virginia Company. Plats of surveys were not kept as permanent public records. The company ordered property maps in 1616 and apparently again in 1618,[19] but it is most unlikely that they were ever made. The required approval of land grants in England can hardly have been a meaningful procedure in the absence of such maps.

---

enteen Years, 1607–1624 (Williamsburg: Virginia 350th Anniversary Celebration Corporation, 1957), no. 6: 75–76.

[17] Kingsbury, ed., 2: 350.

[18] The designation of the four boroughs reflected a lingering perception of a township type of settlement with a village at the core. Particular plantations were probably similarly perceived. Virginia settlement actually showed little resemblance to such townships.

[19] Marshall Harris, 184; Alexander Brown, *Genesis,* 2: 779; Kingsbury, ed., 3: 108–9.

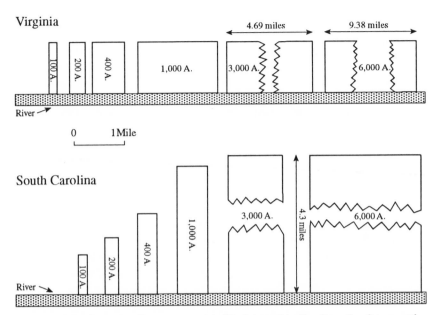

Fig. 5.2. Waterfront parcels as approved in Virginia and in Carolina. Carolina parcels conform with the requirement that depth be four times frontage.

The early planters and (untrained) surveyors developed a simple way of laying out their lands along the rivers that provided access to both large and small parcels. The valuable river frontage was limited to half a rod for each acre in a parcel. The simplest application of this formula would give farms a uniform depth of a mile running inland from the water. A grant of fifty acres would have twenty-five rods of river frontage, and a grant of 1,000 acres 500 rods (a little more than a mile and a half). The surveyor would measure a straight line along a river, ignoring the details of the stream's curves; then at each end of this baseline he would run a line a mile inland (fig. 5.2).[20] Thus the properties approximated rectangles or parallelograms with their inland boundaries paralleling the river at a mile distance. The origin of this pattern for dividing the land is unknown, neither the company nor the colonial Assembly having specified it.[21] The scheme was standard for laying out the land in

---

[20]Hughes, 40–44; T., "The Mode of Acquiring Land in Virginia in Early Times," *Virginia Historical Register* 2 (1849): 190–94 (attributed to Virginia lawyer and governor Littleton Waller Tazewell); J. Frederick Fausz, "Patterns of Settlement in the James River Basin, 1607–1642" (M.A. thesis, William and Mary College, 1971), 18.

[21]Hughes, 40–44.

Virginia until about 1642, when compass traverses and parcels bounded by more than four courses became common.[22]

In 1625 the Virginia governor presented the crown a list of the land titles current in the colony at the end of the company's administration the previous year.[23] The list cannot be regarded as complete, for it omits at least all the town lots. Many of the particular plantations mentioned in other sources are also missing. Of the 198 parcels listed in this inventory, 182 were smaller than 1,000 acres, averaging 161 acres. Ninety-five percent of the parcels under 1,000 acres contained even multiples of fifty acres, ranging from fifty to 750 acres. Twenty allotments were fifty acres each—one headright. Seventy-five were 100 acres, the standard grant for the ancient planter. However, more than half the grants identifiable as going to ancient planters included additional acreage for wives or other relatives, for shares held in the company, for importing servants, or for rights purchased from others.[24] The earliest known ancient planter patent went to William Fairefax and his wife in 1619, for 200 acres, twelve of which were in Jamestown and the rest a few miles away.

The sixteen tracts of 1,000 or more acres included seven of the public grants held by the governor, the boroughs, the company, and the Indian university. A 3,700-acre private tract of former governor Yeardley exemplified the practice of rewarding special service or influence. Few of the other tracts are identified by known names of particular plantations. Martin's Hundred, listed at 800,000 acres, and Southampton Hundred, at 100,000 acres, can have had such extent only on paper. They well may have been among the "enormous grants" that "lapsed because they could not be surveyed within the time limits imposed."[25] Berkeley Hundred was not listed; although it was crippled after the massacre of 1622, it was not sold until the 1630s.[26]

Settlement in Virginia at the end of the company's tenure was confined to the strip along the James River below the falls (site of Richmond) and a few localities on the Eastern Shore. The settlement along the hundred miles of river had only rare gaps of more than a

[22]Ibid., 45.

[23]Kingsbury, ed., 4: 551–59.

[24]Based on data from Nell Marian Nugent, *Cavaliers and Pioneers* (Richmond, Va.: Dietz Printing Co., 1934), xxviii–xxxiii, and passim.

[25]Hughes, 4.

[26]Wesley Frank Craven, *A History of the South,* vol. 1, *The Southern Colonies in the Seventeenth Century, 1607–1689* (Baton Rouge: Louisiana State University Press and Littlefield Fund for Southern History at the University of Texas, 1949), 161–62.

few miles.[27] The company's rules on spacing settlements spread out the population and gave each community room to grow.[28] Had all the forty-four particular plantations materialized at as little as 5,000 acres each, the entire length of the James below the falls might have been lined on both sides by holdings to a depth of nearly two miles.

The vague land distribution plans of the Virginia Company and their stumbling execution as the colony struggled for survival had finally crystallized in a firm policy in the Great Charter of 1618. The failure of the company in 1624, however, put land titles in doubt and removed the legal sanction for more grants, although the new royal governors continued to grant land on the old basis.[29] Step by step, however, the English government approved titles granted under the company, additional grants made under company obligations, lands already granted by the governors, and finally, after nearly ten years, the old headright formula for more grants. Thus was the basis laid for parceling out both small and large farms on through the seventeenth century.

The Virginia Company is to be credited with evolving the system of headrights, which was taken up by the other Southern colonies from their beginnings and which was also used at times in the middle colonies. Several additional Virginia land practices were also applied in later colonies: (1) free choice of location, (2) bonuses for settlement in the colony's first years, (3) land granted for investments and service, (4) temporary assignments of land for subsistence and gardens, (5) assignment of part of the farmers' acreage in a town, (6) rationing of river frontage, (7) requirement of seating and planting, (8) mixing of small and large grants, (9) requirement of quitrents, and (10) designation of the governor and council as agents for granting land.[30] Some of these practices antedated Virginia settlement, of course, but in that colony the English had their first opportunity to use them on previously undivided overseas land. It is not clear whether warrants authorizing survey were formalized during the Virginia Company's days. Virginia offered little precedent for the

[27]Hatch, 32–33.

[28]Particular plantations were to be placed ten miles from other particular plantations on the same side of the river and five miles from existing cities and boroughs. These were probably meant to be the distances between headquarters.

[29]Marshall Harris, 202–3.

[30]The last two are identified in Robert K. Ackerman, *South Carolina Colonial Land Policies* (Columbia: University of South Carolina Press for South Carolina Tricentennial Commission, 1977), 5.

manors and townships that would become important features of the land systems of some other colonies, although the short-lived particular plantations were conceived as having some elements of both.

Maryland, Carolina, and Georgia: Origins and Land Plans

Maryland

George Calvert's grant of Maryland in 1632 led to the first seigniorial colony in the present United States.[31] The generous terms of his charter, which gave the Calverts powers over Maryland land that the king himself did not enjoy in England, may have been "the achievement of a man who knew thoroughly the business of colonial grants and who had learned what forms were of most advantage to the grantee."[32] English seigniorial grants in the New World found their model in lordships established in Ireland where Calvert had received such a grant and gained his title of Lord Baltimore in 1625.[33] Calvert had held the office of secretary of state and had shown an active interest in American colonization as a member of the Virginia Company as early as 1609, of the provisional council for governing that colony during the transition to royal rule, and of the Council for New England. He had invested £25,000 in the colony of Avalon in southeastern Newfoundland in the 1620s, but had given the colony up as unsuitable for farm settlement after enduring the rigors and sickness of a winter there. On his way home he examined Virginia as a new outlet for his own colonization schemes, but his Catholicism as well as his threat to established interests there made him unwelcome.[34]

The motives attributed to Calvert by King Charles I in the Maryland charter—"a laudable and pious zeal for extending the Christian religion, and also the territories of our empire,"[35]—were likely subordinate to a more general excitement with opening up a new land to be governed under his own direction and landscaped to accord with his own ideal society. Land as enjoyed by the English country gentry

[31]Since Calvert died shortly before the grant was completed, it went to his son Cecilius.

[32]Barnes, 28.

[33]Ibid., 12–13, 22.

[34]John Thomas Scharf, *History of Maryland*, 2 vols. (Baltimore: John P. Piet, 1879), 1: 31–52.

[35]Ibid., 53–54. The same motives were also ascribed the proprietors of Carolina and Pennsylvania in later charters.

was central to Calvert's plans for Maryland,[36] and the colony's privy council was to include no one of rank lower than a lord of a manor.[37] Although a liberal provision of the charter served to guarantee all Englishmen access to property ownership in Maryland,[38] the proceeds from the rents, quitrents, and sale of real estate would flow to the Calverts. The concern with Christianity had a special facet in that Maryland was to offer a refuge for people of Calvert's faith, while practicing a tolerance toward other Christians that was not always reciprocated by the latter when they became the majority.[39]

Calvert's prospectus, "Conditions of Plantation," offered attractive "land rights" for immigration into the colony, but terms were even more generous for those adventurers who would be entitled to manors for importing servants. Few of the manor lords actually realized their prerogative of holding courts, but one set of court records, from St. Clement's Manor, has been preserved.[40] To accentuate the close tie between the manor lord and the land, a sixth of each manor had to be set aside as the lord's demesne,[41] an area that could not be rented out for longer than seven years. Manors in Maryland could be sold, however. A further feudal structure, division of counties into baronies, was proposed in Maryland, but was defeated in the colonial Assembly.

Carolina

The Carolina charters of 1663 and 1665 closely paralleled the earlier one for Maryland. Proprietors in both had palatine powers. But Carolina, instead of a single lord, had eight, representing a most imposing aggregation of titles, land, money, and influence, along with some colonial experience. These men saw the colony as a place to recreate their feudal privileges, almost in defiance of the recent En-

[36]Andrews, *Earliest Settlements*, 143–46.

[37]Ibid., 152.

[38]Matthew Page Andrews, *The Founding of Maryland* (Baltimore: Williams and Wilkins Co., 1933), 1. This provision may have been in recognition of the failure of common landholding in Jamestown and Plymouth.

[39]Maryland in its early days was a colony of Catholic gentry and Protestant servants (Mitchell, "Seventeenth Century Chesapeake," 411).

[40]John Johnson, *Old Maryland Manors*, Johns Hopkins University Studies in Historical and Political Science, ser. 1, no. 7 (Baltimore: Johns Hopkins, 1883), 12, 23–28.

[41]Demesne land is reported actually to have been set aside on only the first three manors. Newton D. Mereness, *Maryland as a Proprietary Province* (1901; reprinted, Cos Cob, Conn.: John E. Edwards, 1968), 53.

glish Revolution. Probably because of the need for written agreements to coordinate policy and action among so many leaders, more elaborate land plans were prepared for Carolina than for any of its predecessors. The proprietors knew that "ye whole foundation of ye government is setled upon a right and equall distribution of Land, and the orderly taking of it up is of great moment to ye welfare of ye Province."[42]

Three phases of the Carolina proprietors' planning should be distinguished: (1) the liberal "Declarations and Proposealls" of the years before 1669 when the greater interest lay in what is now North Carolina; (2) the *Fundamental Constitutions* of 1669 (with later revisions), which replaced the liberal policy with an elaborate feudal structure; and (3) instructions of 1671 and 1672 from the proprietors implementing the Fundamental Constitutions without, however, ignoring the earlier policies.

The proposals of 1663 provided 20,000 acres in each settlement for the proprietors, and headrights for the colonists.[43] The land for the colonists was to be laid out in lots of 2,200 to 22,000 acres in what was evidently planned as a presettlement survey. An eleventh of each lot would be reserved for the proprietors before the colonists received their headrights.[44] A special inducement was offered immigrants from the West Indian island of Barbados, many of whom had taken an early interest in the Carolina venture: 500 acres of land for every 1,000 pounds of sugar contributed toward early Carolina exploration and settlement.[45]

The feudal trappings of the Fundamental Constitutions[46] are attributed to Lord Ashley Cooper, who soon became the most active of the proprietors. Under that plan the eldest of the lords proprietors

[42]Various instructions from the Lords Proprietors to the Governor and Council of Carolina in 1671, 1672, 1682, compiled in W. J. Rivers, *A Sketch of the History of South Carolina to the Close of the Proprietary Government* (Charleston: McCarter and Co., 1856), 355.

[43]Rivers, 335–37.

[44]William L. Sanders, ed., *The Colonial Records of North Carolina*, 10 vols. (Raleigh, N.C.: State Printer, 1886; reprinted, New York: AMS Press, 1968), 1: 90–91.

[45]Ackerman, 13.

[46]Printed in *Old South Leaflets* (Boston: Directors of the Old South Work, n.d.), no. 172, 393–416; also in Sanders, ed., 1: 187–205. Ironically, the feudal document was written by the famous philosopher, John Locke, whose ideas of natural rights, social contracts, property, and revolution later got him in trouble in England and are often considered as ideological sources for American democracy. The preamble of the Fundamental Constitutions states its goal to "avoid a numerous democracy." Locke wrote the document as secretary to the proprietors.

was to hold the highest office of palatine, while the other seven were to be the heads of the major branches of the government. Each county was to have its own nobility—a landgrave, two caciques, and the lords of any manors that might be created. The government structure assumed control by the nobility, and a landownership requirement of 500 acres was stipulated for any freeholder who might be elected to the parliament or serve in other stated capacities. At the bottom of this neofeudal order was a class of *leetmen,* who would voluntarily become attached to estates of nobility, and whose descendants would remain leetmen.

The formality and symmetry of this anachronistic hierarchy were to be embodied in the layout of the land (fig. 5.3), as specified in the implementing rules that followed the Fundamental Constitutions. Each county of 750 square miles was to be divided into forty squares of 12,000 acres each (about four and one-third miles on a side), "by lines running East and West, North and South," beginning at the river mouth and "soe following the course of it into the country."[47] Eight of the squares would be seigniories with the administrative status of manors, one for each of the proprietors. Another eight would be baronies, four for the landgrave, two each for the caciques. These baronies,[48] like the status of their owners, were to be hereditary. They were also indivisible and, after 1700, inalienable. A third of each barony was to be demesne. The other twenty-four squares in each county were designated as colonies that were to be settled by smallholders or manor lords, with each six colonies forming a precinct. Baronies and colonies were to be mixed together on each side of any river to assure that the colonies received proportionate shares of the most accessible land. Any square containing an Indian village, along with the adjoining square, was to be "left untaken up and unplanted on for the use of the Indians."[49]

Leetmen and leetwomen were to receive ten-acre life tenancies on the occasion of their marriage at a rent of no more than an eighth of the yearly produce.[50]

Settlement in townships, although not mentioned in the Fundamental Constitutions, was an important part of the colonial plan de-

[47]Rivers, 356–67.

[48]The term *barony* will be used generically for the class of both seigniories and baronies.

[49]Rivers, 358.

[50]Article 26 of the Fundamental Constitutions.

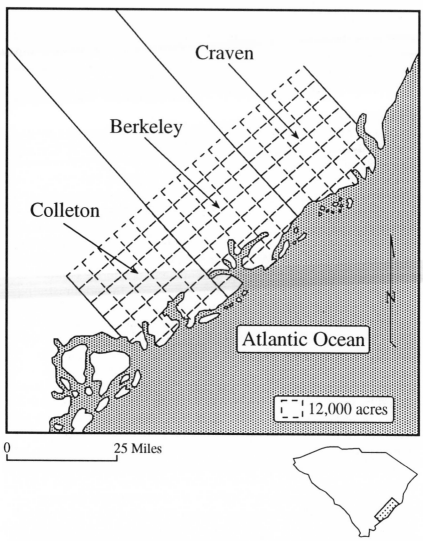

Fig. 5.3. Early South Carolina counties as conceived by proprietors (except that boundaries do not follow cardinal directions). Such regularity never developed. The proprietors ordered a map of the colony as laid out under their directions, but it too never materialized. From map of WPA Historical Records Survey distributed by South Carolina Department of Archives and History.

tailed in the 1671 and 1672 instructions.[51] Lord Ashley showed considerable knowledge of New England's compact settlements, which he believed had built more substantial colonies than Virginia's dispersed pattern.[52] All the settlers in a Carolina colony were "to set their houses together in one place," fronting on "large, convenient, and regular streets."[53] A 200-acre common was to be located near the village, initially to be used for planting provisions. Each settler was to get a "home Lot" near town (apparently in addition to his house lot), containing not more than a twentieth of his total right, as well as an "out Lot." The lots were to be laid off in a systematic manner and distributed by chance.[54]

With Carolina's land scheme, the art of planning a colony had made great advances on paper, but the art of making the colony conform to the plan remained little developed. The layout of land and houses in Carolina never took on much resemblance to the proprietors' abstract plan. The colonial Assembly never ratified the Fundamental Constitutions, which faded into disuse as the proprietors lost control.

Sir Robert Montgomery's plan of 1717 for the Margravate of Azilia must be mentioned as another example of a geometric layout matching a feudal hierarchy, with its intricate checkerboard of estates for the gentry fringed by neat but irregularly shaped parcels for the cultivators.[55] Azilia was to be a part of South Carolina located in what is now Georgia, but in fact no settlement was ever made. James Edward Oglethorpe's benevolent plan for the later colony of Georgia, however, projected its own expression of controlled equalitarian order in the land geometry. Unlike the preceding plans, Georgia's was engraved on the land during the earliest days of the colony (fig. 8.5).

Georgia

The philanthropic purpose of providing a new start for the deserving poor led to many unique policies in Georgia, chartered in 1732

[51]Rivers, 365; Craven, *Southern Colonies,* 342.

[52]Ackerman, 28.

[53]Rivers, 366–67, 371.

[54]Ibid., 371.

[55]Ford, 23, 45; Sir Robert Montgomery and Colonel John Barnwell, *The Most Delightful Golden Isles* (1717; reprinted, Atlanta, Ga.: Cherokee Publishing Co., 1969), frontispiece.

and settled the next year.[56] The trustees of the trust that governed Georgia from England were to receive neither salary, profit, nor land in reward for their services. Slavery was prohibited; in fact all Negroes were excluded. Even rum was officially prohibited for some years. Charity colonists, who settled at the expense of the trust (which got some of its funds from the British Parliament), would each receive "so much land in Quantity as would support such Planter, and his Family; and Fifty Acres were judged sufficient, and not too much."[57] Township settlement was an integral part of the colony plan.

To insure that Georgia land should remain in these smallholdings and not be parceled into still smaller ones, the trustees decreed that it was to be held in tail male; that is, it could be passed on only to male heirs.[58] Any other form of transfer—sale, lease, trade, or inheritance by female heirs—required specific permission of the trustees. The discrimination against women was a device to prevent engrossment of property in cases of a series of marriages. The tail male restriction actually made titles uncertain and thus inhibited the opportunities (including borrowing on mortgages, profiting on sales, and providing for survivors) that made socage tenure so popular elsewhere. The trustees' controls also made squatting unattractive, virtually eliminating the practice.

The special conditions prescribed for Georgia's land and labor were not destined to last long. In practice, the trustees usually approved requests for the sale of land and for widows to assume the property of their deceased husbands. Economic pressures from other colonies were readily transmitted into Georgia. By 1750 the trustees had relented on the issues of both land tenure and slavery.[59] The colonial South apparently could not endure four-fifths slave and one-fifth free.

[56]Other purposes specified in the charter were development of trade, navigation, and wealth and serving as a barrier for the defense of South Carolina (McCain, 17).

[57]*An Account Shewing the Progress of Georgia in America,* written ca. 1740 by order of the trustees, in Candler, comp., 3: 373. In addition to charity colonists deemed worthy of sponsorship, Georgia was open to farmers who would come at their own expense and receive headrights, and also those who would bring servants and receive up to 500 acres in headrights.

[58]McCain, 227–28, 267; Coleman, 122; Paul S. Taylor, *Georgia Plan: 1732–1752* (Berkeley: Institute of Business and Economic Research, University of California, 1972), epigraph.

[59]Harold E. Davis, *The Fledgling Province: Social and Cultural Life in Colonial Georgia, 1733–1776* (Chapel Hill: University of North Carolina Press, 1976), 12, 13.

6

Control and Disposition of Land

Control of Land

CORPORATE ownership of Southern colonies proved short-lived, less than twenty years in the cases of both Virginia and Georgia. The Carolina proprietorship was replaced by royal government with the final separation of the two Carolinas only in 1730 after more than sixty years. The Calverts maintained their control of Maryland, with two interruptions, until the Revolution.

Within two of the colonies appeared great proprietorships that were subordinate to the royal governments in matters other than land. Virginia's Northern Neck (fig. 5.1), probably vaguely understood at first as the narrow tidewater peninsula between the Potomac and Rappahannock Rivers, was granted by Charles II in 1649, during the dark days of his exile, to seven loyal supporters.[1] Virginia was then one of the few British domains still loyal to the king, but when it surrendered to Parliament in 1652, the grant seemed a paper of scant value. The grant was renewed, however, after the monarchy was restored in 1660, to the consternation of Virginians, whose land titles and other rights suddenly seemed less secure.[2] With further renewals of the grant the Neck grew into "neck and body also"[3] by extension to the "first springs" of the bordering rivers, widening as it reached inland. Ownership was concentrated by sale, marriage, and inheritance, finally devolving on Lord Thomas Fairfax in 1719. Fairfax's domain was extended further with the final settlement of disputed boundaries along the northern (although

[1]One of the most straightforward accounts of the Northern Neck to 1745 is that in Douglas Southall Freeman, *George Washington*, 7 vols. (New York: Charles Scribner's Sons, 1948), 1: appendix I-1, 447–513.

[2]The insecurity was greatest when the rest of Virginia, too, was turned over to one of the Northern Neck proprietors, Lord Culpeper, and another lord in 1673, but the crown repurchased Virginia in 1684.

[3]Statement of a London observer ca. 1737, quoted in Fairfax Harrison, "The Northern Neck Maps of 1737–1747," *William and Mary Quarterly*, ser. 2, 4 (1924): 7.

shorter) branch of the Potomac, and along the southern branch of the Rappahannock (the Rapidan), to include well over five million acres—twenty-two counties of present Virginia and West Virginia, and parts of four other counties. The proprietors had almost unrestricted rights of ownership.

The other such grand proprietorship went to the heir of the one Carolina lord proprietor who had refused to sell his interest to the crown. For several years Lord Granville retained an undivided eighth interest in the lands of both Carolinas and Georgia. Finally, in 1744, his interest was set off as a separate sixty-mile wide strip constituting approximately the northern half of North Carolina.

Thus the land of the original Southern colonies came under control of five colony governments and two private proprietorships, a total of seven different organizations. Virginia had begun as a trading company, Georgia as a charitable venture. Maryland and Carolina began under proprietors who saw land as the base for their aristocracies. Fairfax and Granville viewed their land primarily as sources of income. All the colonies, however, found that the land was their chief source of wealth, whether that wealth flowed to the proprietors, to the crown, or to support the public or private interests of the colonies. The palatinate of Maryland was described as "originally nothing but a great land market";[4] and the lords of the palatinate of Carolina tried to launch their colony with little effort other than opening a land office.[5] The meaning and management of the colonies' lands showed much less divergence than the intents of their founders and interests of their officials might have led us to expect.

Disposing of Land

The procedures by which undivided land was converted into parcels of private property are discussed below, in the following order: headrights (including distribution by townships and homestead plans), sale, military grants, squatting, wholesale grants for promoting settlement, large feudal grants, and grants to Indians. Grants for special service or influence will be mentioned only through occasional examples.

[4]John Kilty, *The Land-Holder's Assistant and Land-Office Guide* (Baltimore: G. Dobbin and Murphy, 1809), 299.

[5]Craven, *Southern Colonies*, 324ff. The original hope was to attract most of the settlers from other colonies.

The headright was designed as an incentive for peopling the colonies and a way of keeping the amount of private land in line with the number of people and their ability to use it.[6] It proved effective as an immigration incentive, but fraudulent claims and limited adjustments for deaths led to grants in excess of the labor supply. Had the seating and planting and quitrent laws been enforced, most of the surplus land would have reverted to the granting authority. Leasing, sale and purchase, and hiring of labor, however, all helped to unite land with those who would use it.

The fifty acres per person established early as the headright in Virginia continued there without basic change as long as headrights were honored. Other colonies showed more variation in the size of their headrights, which ranged from six to 150 acres[7] (summarized in table 6.1). Headrights were often greater in the earliest years of a colony's settlement or, in the case of Carolina, in counties the proprietors were anxious to develop. They were often greater for free settlers than for servants, for men than for women, for adults than for children, for servants entering the colony than for those gaining freedom.

Maryland's initial headright was 100 acres, but an adventurer who brought in five men in the first years was awarded 2,000 acres. The basic headright fluctuated until the governor cut it down to fifty acres in 1651, warning, "The people will be too remotely situated from one another and the whole Province perhaps in a short time taken up by a few people."[8] Fifty acres in Georgia was the headright for an individual as well as the allotment for a whole family of charity settlers (who had their passage paid and were not indentured). The trustees did not want much surplus acreage to end up in the hands of people who had been unsuccessful in managing their affairs previously.[9] Those who got all their land in cultivation, however, were soon permitted another fifty acres.[10] But the maximum holding of 500 acres was initially offered to anyone who brought in six servants.

[6]Headrights were normally granted following entry into the colony, but occasionally in advance; e.g., see Robert Bruce Harley, "The Land System in Colonial Maryland" (Ph.D. diss., University of Iowa, 1948), 28–30.

[7]Marshall Harris, 228; Rivers, 337.

[8]Harry Wright Newman, *The Flowering of the Maryland Palatinate* (Washington: Author, 1961), 64–67.

[9]E. Merton Coulter, *A Short History of Georgia* (Chapel Hill: University of North Carolina Press, 1933), 52.

[10]McCain, 230, 267.

TABLE 6.1. Representative headrights granted in southern colonies, in acres

	Man	Wife	Child	Man-servant	Maid-servant	Freed servant
Virginia						
Resident by 1616	100	100	—	100	100	100
Resident after 1616	50	50	50	50	50	__a
Maryland						
1633	100	100	50	100	100	—
1648	40	40	40	40	40	40
Carolina						
Albemarle Co.						
1665	80	80	80	80	80	80
1667	40	40	20	40	20	20
1670	60	60	—	50	—	50
Craven Co.						
First year	150	—	75	150	75	75
1667	60	—	60	60	60	30
1670	100	—	50	50	50	—
Both Carolinas						
1700s[b]	50–100	50	50	50	50	50
Georgia						
Trustees, 1730s	50[c]	—	—	—	—	20
Royal gov't., 1750s	100	50	50	50	50	50

Sources: Primarily Marshall Harris, 199–236; also: Craven, *Southern Colonies,* 325; Ackerman, 106; Merrens, *Colonial North Carolina,* 25.

[a]Often none; sometimes fifty acres.

[b]Both Carolinas.

[c]Per family of charity colonists; adventurers bringing in six servants were entitled to 500 acres for a short time.

Headrights did not evolve apace in all the colonies. Maryland abolished them in 1683, half a century before Georgia was founded. When Virginia and North Carolina proceeded to change their ways similarly, headrights remained the most common way of granting land only in the southernmost colonies, South Carolina and Georgia.

Headright provisions for indentured servants and slaves varied. Generally the person paying the servant's fare received the land. Most of the colonies eventually provided an equal headright for the servant himself after his indenture was up. In Maryland before 1646, however, the servant's master was expected to provide the land.[11]

[11]Robinson, 37; Newman, *Flowering of the Maryland Palatinate,* 65–66. The land for freed servants in Maryland was known as "freedom rights."

Except for the promise to ancient planters, Virginia is considered to have made the least provision for the freed servant, who usually would receive land from his master only in the infrequent case that the indenture called for it.[12] Although freed servants were entitled to land under both English instructions and a Virginia law of 1705, they seldom actually received it.[13] Many servants were unable to pay the fees and surveying costs. The headright was originally not intended for importation of slaves; it was often so used, however, legally or illegally, depending on the colony.

Land distribution by headrights was difficult to control, loosely administered, and subject to fraud by duplication of claims and other devices. Ship captains sometimes claimed the land for importing passengers whose headrights were also claimed by those who had paid the fares.[14] Captains and sailors might claim rights for transporting members of ships' crews, then appoint agents in Virginia to manage their lands.[15] A person might enter a colony more than once, claiming a headright for each entry. The headright for a slave might be exercised by the person importing him, the planter who bought him, and possibly a middleman who arranged the deal. A South Carolina settler increased his family entitlement by "borrowing" two neighbor children.[16] Fictitious names were sometimes submitted; one applicant is said to have listed as indentured servants the names "of some of the principal gentlemen of the English county of Kent."[17] Another man multiplied his estate by adding a "0" to his acreage rights—20,000 acres for importing forty colonists.[18]

Distribution of land by townships may be mentioned here, for township land in the South was usually metered out on the headrights formulas. The most significant period of township founding in the South came in the 1730s with South Carolina's scheme for open-

[12]Newman, *Flowering of the Maryland Palatinate*, 65–66.

[13]Manning C. Voorhis, "Crown versus Council in Virginia Land Policy," *William and Mary Quarterly*, ser. 3, 3 (1946): 501–2; William Walker Hening, ed., *Statutes at Large: Being a Collection of All the Laws of Virginia*, 13 vols. (New York: editor, 1823), 3: 304. The law, however, provided that the servant might waive his right. Another obstacle to acquiring land by servants and others of limited means was the minimum surveying fee set in 1666 to equal that charged for 1,000 acres (Hughes, 68–69).

[14]Henry Hartwell, James Blair, and Edward Chilton, *The Present State of Virginia, and the College* (1727; new ed., Williamsburg: Colonial Williamsburg, 1940), 16–17.

[15]Robinson, 41.

[16]Ackerman, 106.

[17]Voorhis, "Crown versus Council," 503.

[18]Voorhis, "Land Grant Policy," 30; Richmond Croom Beatty, *William Byrd of Westover* (Boston: Houghton, Mifflin Co., 1932), 68–69.

ing up its interior and with Georgia's brief initial phase of colonization.

Beginning about 1700, the English government promoted a homestead plan for Virginia settlement. The homestead idea differed from headrights in that land was to be available on the basis of family size (including laborers) without the requirement of immigration. Such a practice might have disrupted the stratification of Virginia society, but had only limited adoption, as will be explained.

Direct sale and purchase is a second major method by which land passed into individual hands. The distribution of land to shareholders of the Virginia Company was one way of selling land; and when the first land dividend required the payment of additional money, the transactions remained peculiar types of sales. The Carolina proprietors began selling land as early as the 1680s.[19] In the ensuing decade, they established prices of twenty pounds per 1,000 acres for land near the settlements, and ten pounds per 1,000 acres for land near the "mountains."[20] The Carolina quitrent on purchased lands was typically lower than the rate common on headright grants;[21] some purchased land carried a nominal quitrent of only a peppercorn. In effect the purchase money went to buy up part of the value of the quitrent.

The sharpest break with the headrights occurred in Maryland in 1683 when Lord Baltimore put all the remaining unalienated land on a sale basis.[22] Headrights, with all their irregularities, although profitable for speculators, had returned the proprietor a softer currency than the tobacco he now proposed to accept—100 pounds for fifty acres or half that price near borders disputed with Penn. The land price, called "caution money," rose to five pounds sterling per 100 acres by 1738.[23] Virginia's headrights suffered from the same abuses as Maryland's, but its transition to sales was more gradual. Virginia had had a secondary market in land since the first grants of private land. Headrights and warrants also were bought and sold, and sale was the way in which Northern Neck land passed into private hands. By late in the seventeenth century, labor was available

[19]Ackerman, 27.

[20]Ibid., 38.

[21]Ibid.; Beverley W. Bond, Jr., 118–19.

[22]*Archives of Maryland,* 72 vols. (Baltimore: Maryland Historical Society, 1883–1972), 5: 390–91.

[23]Clarence P. Gould, *The Land System in Maryland, 1720–1765,* Johns Hopkins University Studies in Historical and Political Science, ser. 31, no. 1 (Baltimore: Johns Hopkins, 1913), 9–10.

without the expense of importing servants,[24] while land, partly because of the headright frauds, was on the market at a low price.[25] While people were thus reluctant to import servants, clerks in the secretary's office began accepting a few shillings per fifty acres in lieu of headrights.[26] The "treasury right" was set at five shillings per fifty acres by Governor Francis Nicholson in 1699 and reaffirmed by an act of the Assembly in 1705.[27] After 1717 county surveyors were authorized to receive money for land, thus saving buyers a trip to Williamsburg to pay for it.[28] The headright in Virginia was largely displaced by sales after 1715, although it continued to be legal throughout the colonial period.

The two private proprietorships of Virginia and North Carolina also sold their land, having little raison d'être other than such sale and subsequent collection of quitrents. In the Northern Neck sales began in 1670 when a relative of one of the proprietors opened a land office on the tidewater peninsula itself.[29] For a time immigrants

[24]Philip Alexander Bruce, *Economic History of Virginia in the Seventeenth Century*, 2 vols. (New York: Macmillan and Co., 1896), 1: 524.

[25]I do not know whether there is a contradiction in the reports that both labor and land were plentiful. Headrights were reported on the market at "a piece of eight" (Robert Beverley, *The History and Present State of Virginia* [1705; reprinted, Chapel Hill: University of North Carolina Press for Institute of Early American History and Culture, 1947], 274), approximately the five shillings that became the government price for fifty acres (Hartwell, Blair, and Chilton, 16). Five shillings is estimated to have been one or two days' wages; Robert E. and B. Katherine Brown, *Virginia, 1705–1796: Democracy or Aristocracy?* (East Lansing: Michigan State University Press, 1964), 11. The plentifulness of land was blamed for such varied eighteenth-century shortages as towns, labor, artisans, manufacturing, ships' crews, and soldiers; Brown and Brown, 7–10; Anthony Langston, "Anthony Langston on Towns, and Corporations; and on the Manufacture of Iron," *William and Mary Historical Quarterly*, ser. 2, 1(1921): 100–106.

[26]Hartwell, Blair, and Chilton, 17–18. A contemporary reported the change as occurring in 1699 when "several persons having Rights to Land in Pamunkey neck, and on the Southside of Blackwater swamp, who could not well procure legal Rights for patenting thereof, and the Treasury of the Country for support of the Government being very Low, a method was established of selling those Rights at a certain rate for money to be paid to the Auditor and Receiver of the Revenues for the use of the Crown." William Robertson, "An Account of the Manner of Taking up and Patenting of Land in Her Majesty's Colony and Dominion of Virginia with Reasons Humbly Offered for Continuance Thereof," *William and Mary Quarterly*, ser. 2, 3 (1923): 137–42.

[27]Faye Bartlett Reeder, "The Evolution of the Virginia Land Grant System in the Eighteenth Century" (Ph.D. diss., Ohio State University, 1937), 17; Voorhis, "Crown versus Council," 504; Hening, ed., 3: 305.

[28]Hughes, 107.

[29]Freeman, 1: 458; Beth Mitchell, *Beginning at a White Oak . . . : Patents and Northern Neck Grants of Fairfax County, Virginia* (Fairfax: Fairfax County, 1977), 4.

coming into Virginia and buying land in the Northern Neck were entitled also to Virginia headrights, which they could sell on the market. Virginians long distrusted Northern Neck titles and were reluctant to pay quitrents to the proprietors rather than to the colony (if they paid them at all). Competition kept Northern Neck land prices and quitrents in line with those in Virginia—five shillings to purchase and a shilling quitrent for fifty acres.[30] Seating and planting were not required in the Northern Neck, but large holdings were still discouraged by doubling the price on land in excess of 500 acres in any purchase.

The Granville lands in North Carolina embraced the more populous northern half of the colony. Land prices and quitrents there were in line with those in the southern part of the colony, and sales were normally limited to 640 acres.[31] Granville's agents, however, were known for their maladministration, charging settlers extortionate rents and fees, selling lands already sold, and remitting little of their collections to the proprietor. Granville's land office was closed during many of the troubled late colonial years, and his land was finally confiscated by the state of North Carolina in 1782.[32]

Land was granted for military purposes both for the location and support of soldiers and in reward to soldiers for past service.[33] Grants of the first type began in Virginia as early as 1630 for soldiers who would live on frontiers where the Indians were considered a threat.[34] A commander could be granted several hundred acres on condition of maintaining a number of men in the locality for three years. Such tracts were later shared among the men who agreed to settle. Maryland made a similar offer in 1661.[35] In Carolina and Georgia, for some time, the military settlement was integral with agricultural settlement. The Carolina proposals of 1663 specified the arms and ammunition for each servant for whom land was granted, and enjoined the colony government to maintain an armed man for each fifty acres granted.[36] The compact settlement planned for Georgia

[30]Fairfax Harrison, *Virginia Land Grants* (Richmond: Old Dominion Press, 1925), 128–29.

[31]A. Roger Ekirch, *"Poor Carolina": Politics and Society in Colonial North Carolina, 1729–1776* (Chapel Hill: University of North Carolina Press, 1981), 128–29.

[32]R. D. W. Connor, *History of North Carolina*, vol. 1, *The Colonial and Revolutionary Period, 1584–1783* (Chicago: Lewis Publishing Co., 1919), 222–27.

[33]Ford, 103–5.

[34]Marshall Harris, 259–61.

[35]Ibid., 262.

[36]Rivers, 337.

was also conceived in terms of military readiness, with a settler-soldier for every fifty acres.[37]

Professional soldiers in early Georgia were given five acres each with a promise of an additional twenty acres after seven years of service.[38] The record, however, shows a number of fifty-acre grants to disbanded soldiers of General James Oglethorpe's regiment after the 1749 war with the Spanish.[39] These grants apparently began the practice of giving land to veterans in the South. The scale of bounties greatly increased in 1754 when Governor Robert Dinwiddie of Virginia set aside 200,000 acres on the Ohio River for men who would enlist in the campaign against the French and settle on their land afterward.[40] In 1763 George III declared a general bounty for disbanded soldiers ranging from fifty acres for a private to a hundred times as much for a field officer.[41]

Squatting played its unrecorded and unmeasured role in the Southern colonies, as can be inferred from laws passed for the apparent purpose of dealing with it. Virginia's Great Charter of 1618 required that settlers whose land claims had not been authorized should pay the company a quarter of the profits until the land was legally granted.[42] In 1639 the governor was authorized to make grants to people who had "set down upon" certain unplanted or abandoned lands.[43] In 1663, the Maryland Assembly, recognizing that some people were ignorant of the laws of England, provided that a person in peaceful possession of land for five years could hold it against the claims of any legally competent person.[44] South Carolina passed a similar law with a seven-year limit in 1712.[45] But the South Carolina Council had been even more explicit forty years before when it ordered that persons in possession of unsurveyed lands should acquire warrants and have surveys made within three months.[46] Squatting

[37]Spalding, 73–74; Marshall Harris, 262.

[38]McCain, 268.

[39]Pat Bryant, *Entry of Claims for Georgia Landholders, 1733–1755* (Atlanta: State Printing Office, 1975), 150–53. Coleman, 52–53, mentions 150-acre bounties for disbanded soldiers; Bryant lists very few 150-acre grants, none identified as going to disbanded soldiers.

[40]Hening, ed., 7: 662, 666.

[41]Ackerman, 112.

[42]Kingsbury, ed., 3: 105.

[43]"Abstract of Instructions to Sir Francis Wyatt, January 1638/9," *Virginia Magazine of History and Biography* 11 (1903–4): 54–57.

[44]*Archives of Maryland* 1: 501–2.

[45]Ackerman, 40.

[46]Ibid., 33.

meshed readily enough with indiscriminate location—choosing the land in the field. It was especially advantageous when the settlers' migration routes to the land they would occupy did not go near the land offices in the colonial capitals (e.g., Pennsylvanians moving by the Great Valley to Piedmont locations in the South).

Large tracts were granted in a number of ways. We can distinguish between (1) those intended to remain large estates for the glory and financial benefit of their owners and (2) those intended to be subdivided into smaller holdings for resale to farmers. Some tracts, of course, were granted with no concern as to how they might be used.

The clearest examples of the first type of large estate were the baronies and manors of Carolina and Maryland. These feudal fiefdoms were expected in many cases to be family seats. Many estates granted as manors, and others without such status, but nonetheless called manors, were operated by subdivision into leased farms.

Virginia was the principal colony to dispose of its western lands wholesale, that is, in large tracts intended for redistribution into small farms. Land was offered to enterprising pioneers in quantities ranging from 10,000 to more than 100,000 acres on condition that a family be settled for each 1,000 acres. The entrepreneurs had a chance to profit from sales to settlers as well as from gaining most of the land for themselves. Land companies also received grants as large as 800,000 acres that were not tied directly to colonization. Most of these grants were unspecified as to exact location; they were merely licenses to survey and sell so much land in a general area rather than grants of ownership.

Occasionally we find the anomaly of colonial grants of land to Indians. In 1658 the Virginia Assembly extended the fifty-acre headright to Indians as a measure of the land to be reserved for each tribe.[47] Although fifty acres often proved adequate for English farmers, it was not likely to be so for Indians who lived by a combination of farming and hunting. Calverton, one of Lord Baltimore's manors in Charles County, Maryland, was laid out as a home for six tribes of Indians, but their nomadic way of life just did not fit with the plan of fifty-acre feudal leases for the tribesmen and 200-acre leases for their werowances (chiefs).[48]

[47]Robinson, 6. A later (1714) agreement with Indians in Virginia provided a minimum of 100 acres per person for reservations. Leonidas Dodson, *Alexander Spotswood* (Philadelphia: University of Pennsylvania Press, 1932), 76.

[48]Newman, *Flowering of the Maryland Palatinate*, 112–13. The tenure of the leases was *copyhold* (Matthew Page Andrews, 179: Chandler, 289), under which the tenant was bound by the customs of the manor (Marshall Harris, 31).

Seating and Planting

All the Southern colonial governments required that land distributed by them be settled and put to use. Although seating and planting were conditions of Virginia grants from a very early date, they were not defined by law until 1666.[49] Seating was then specified as building a house and keeping livestock on the land, and planting as clearing, tending, and planting an acre of ground. Either seating or planting within three years was then sufficient to hold the land. Later it was required that the house be built of wood and at least 12 x 12 feet in size.[50] By 1713 a patentee was required to plant three acres for every fifty acres certified by the surveyor as cultivable, or to clear and drain three acres of swamp or marsh; three neat cattle or six sheep or goats were to be kept for every fifty acres of barren land. The minimum house size was increased to 16 x 20 feet. Quarrying or mining became an alternative form of development.[51] In 1720 improvements costing ten pounds per fifty acres were accepted as planting.[52] Seating was required in Northern Neck grants until 1687, but not after that time.[53]

The other Southern colonies also evolved policies for seating and planting. The Maryland Assembly as early as 1639 took action against manor holders who had not settled their land as their grants specified, declaring such properties open to long-term leases to others.[54] In 1663 the assembly recognized that Baltimore County, where the land was largely taken up but little settled, was defenseless, and decreed that such unsettled lands be seated by grantees or become open to anyone who would seat them with three able hands within two months.[55] In Carolina, baronies were to be peopled with thirty persons within seven years or their lords subject to fines; and no lord could claim his second barony until he had 100 people on his first.[56] In the 1690s the proprietors encouraged the governor to reclaim land

---

[49]Marshall Harris, 204; Hening, ed., 2: 244.

[50]Hening, ed., 3: 312–13.

[51]Ibid., 4: 39.

[52]Ibid., 81. One man soon made a claim of eighty pounds in such improvements, citing wear and tear and personal risk on a journey to look at his land, and adding lobbying expenses for his effort to acquire the land, when the only tangible improvements on the property were blaze marks on boundary trees (Voorhis, "Crown Versus Council," 511).

[53]Robinson, 72.

[54]*Archives of Maryland* 1: 63.

[55]Ibid., 499–500.

[56]Rivers, 352, 357–58.

if no clearing was done within three years.[57] A North Carolina grantee, according to a law in effect in 1722, could "save" his grant by building a house and planting, fencing, and tending an acre of land.[58] North Carolina had so much unplanted land in 1736 that the crown directed every owner to enclose and clear three acres in every 100 and to pasture at least five cattle on every 500 acres within three years.[59] Georgia, with its focus on small farms, also emphasized planting, with five acres in every fifty to be cultivated and 100 mulberry trees to be planted on every ten acres cleared, all within ten years. The royal government later required five acres in every 100 to be cleared and cultivated *each year,* until it was realized that the policy would lead to both deforestation and potential forfeit of all land after twenty years.[60]

[57]Ackerman, 38.
[58]Sanders, ed., 2: 457.
[59]Ibid., 4: 185.
[60]Marshall Harris, 235–36.

7

Seventeenth-Century Land Division

THE FIRST settlements in all the Southern colonies were necessarily in the coastal lowlands where the ships from Europe could unload passengers and supplies. The premium land continued to be the tidewater shores of bays and rivers with access for personal movement and marketing. Competition for real estate focused as much on the water frontage as on the soil quality of land itself. Such an evaluation of site was bound to affect the shapes of land parcels and to be reflected in public regulations.

The Virginia formula for water frontage, requiring a mile depth inland from the shore, has already been examined. A Maryland provision in the 1641 Conditions of Plantation limited shore frontage to fifty poles (rods) to each fifty acres, requiring only a half-mile depth for waterfront lots.[1] But a generation later, when frontage must have been scarcer, the allowance was down to fifteen poles for each fifty acres, requiring a mile and two-thirds of depth.[2] The example of parallel strips ending at the jagged edge of an estuary on the southern reaches of Maryland's Eastern Shore (fig. 7.1) may be as close to conformance with Baltimore's order as the surveys actually ran.

Carolina's approach to allocating frontage was somewhat different: the depth of the lot must be a multiple of the river frontage (four, five, or six times in different regulations),[3] and thus adjacent longlots of differing width might reach inland different distances (fig. 5.2). But, for grants larger than about 2,000 acres, the original Carolina instructions resembled the customs in Virginia and Maryland in requiring only a certain minimum depth. That lot depth in Carolina, however, was much greater, 346 chains (about four and a

---

[1]Ralph H. Donnelly, "The Colonial Land Patent System in Maryland," *Surveying and Mapping* 40 (1980): 52.
[2]*Archives of Maryland* 5: 95; Kilty, 63.
[3]Rivers, 367, 400, 401; Ackerman, 30, 109.

117

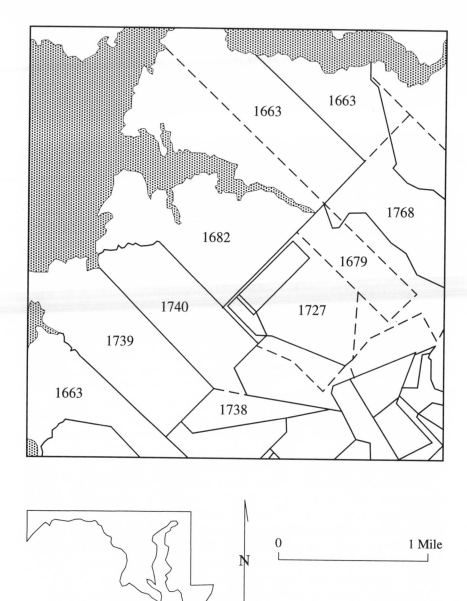

Fig. 7.1. Part of Somerset County, Md. Solid lines represent the original survey. Dashed lines are resurvey lines. Later dates may well be second grants of property abandoned earlier. Simplified from map by Harry L. Benson, northwestern part, Brinkley's election district no. 3, in Hall of Records, Department of General Services, State of Maryland. Marion quadrangle (east center).

third miles), a figure calculated to permit a 12,000-acre barony or colony to be square.[4]

The Carolina proprietors were also concerned about the shapes of parcels not bordering rivers.[5] Properties farther inland than 346 chains, that is, beyond the influence of the river frontage rules, were to be square. New properties not actually bordering earlier properties were to come no closer to the earlier properties than twelve chains if near a navigable river, otherwise twenty chains. The intent was to avoid narrow slivers of unclaimed land that would be awkward to include in new parcels.

Division in Farm-Size Parcels

The oldest Southern tract for which a land grant map is available is the St. Mary's Townlands set aside as the capital of Maryland. The first settlers who landed here in 1634 were instructed to build their houses close together to form a town.[6] Their leader soon reported having "seated ourselves, w[th]in one halfe mile of the river, w[th]in a pallizado of one hundred twentie yarde square, w[th] fower flankes." The map of the area in the early 1640s (fig. 7.2) shows a dozen holdings ranging from about twenty to 250 acres, hardly suggesting a town. Indeed the colonists had already scattered by 1637, and three decades passed before the capital developed into a settlement concentrated enough to resemble even a small town. Although various of the lots contained the original fort, the governor's house, the provincial secretary's house and office, a Catholic chapel, and a Jesuit establishment, St. Mary's in the 1640s was still a rural farm settlement. The lots of this early community were simple in outline and mostly compact in shape, although one did have a length four times its width. Most lots bordered the estuaries of the St. Mary's River and St. Inigoe's Creek. Surprisingly, about half the

---

[4]Rivers, 401. One early proposal for Carolina specified banks of riverfront lots one chain wide and 100 chains long for planters and servants alike. These were apparently the ten-acre planting lots to support the early settlers and, at the same time, a way of concentrating militiamen for defense. Such lots probably never materialized (Sanders, ed., 1: 505).

[5]Rivers, 401-2.

[6]The account of early St. Mary's depends on Lois Green Carr, "The Metropolis of Maryland: A Comment on Town Development along the Tobacco Coast," *Maryland Historical Magazine* 69 (1974): 124-29.

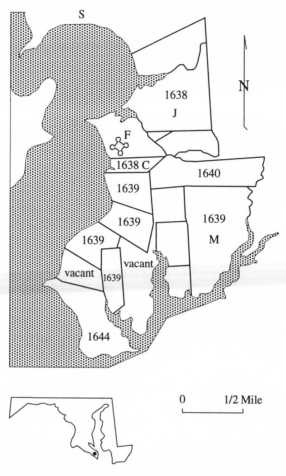

Fig. 7.2. The St. Mary's City original land division included both public and private holdings. C = property on which the chapel was located. F = Governor's Field, including the 1634 fort, a 1636 mill, and the governor's house. J = St. John's. M = St. Mary's Freehold. Governor's Field became the core of the community when it began to grow in the 1660s and a square mile was incorporated. From Lois Green Carr, "The Metropolis of Maryland," *Maryland Historical Magazine* 69 (1974): 124-45. St. Mary's City quadrangle (east center).

bounds surveyed followed mutually perpendicular directions close to the cardinal magnetic directions at the time.[7]

[7]The north-south boundaries are about 5° west of north. *The Report of the Superintendent of the Coast and Geodetic Survey,* 1895, 54th Congress, 1st Session, Senate Document no. 25 (Washington: Government Printing Office, 1896), estimates 9° west for the

A tentative land grant map of St. Mary's County for the seventeenth century,[8] at the end of which much of the land was still vacant, gives a more typical view of rural property. Most holdings are simple in shape; a large portion are bounded by only four or five courses. Many are rectangles, mostly drawn square with the compass directions. The holdings with water frontage—on the Potomac and Patuxent Rivers and on Chesapeake Bay—mostly date from the 1660s or earlier. The interior parcels mostly date from later decades. The manors held a disproportionate share of the water frontage, often having frontage exceeding their inland depth.

The earliest Virginia area for which a satisfactory land grant map is available is Ware Neck (fig. 7.3a), between two small rivers that empty into a protected bay on the peninsula between the York and Rappahannock Rivers.[9] The original Ware Neck properties all had broad frontage on the water, not difficult to arrange on that site, but showed no evidence of adherence to a uniform mile depth, and none of the rectangularity or compass orientation of St. Mary's.

The first grant on Ware Neck (marked A), to Thomas Curtis in 1642, gave access to both the Ware and North Rivers. Curtis's headquarters and his early clearings were near the Ware River, whereas his channel to the North River was designated Back River. Three more grants followed within three years, all on the Ware River upstream from Curtis. An Indian massacre interrupted settlement for a few years before the lower part of Ware Neck was taken up. The Curtis property was originally surveyed at 400 acres. An early resurvey determined its area to be 730 acres, and the owner probably had to buy or produce headrights for the 330 acres of "surplus lands." Modern measurements show the property to have contained about 1,000 acres. Early Virginia surveyors have been styled "more generous than accurate."[10] It was the grantee who paid the surveyor's fee and who was likely to be on hand to demand what he wanted.

Baltimore magnetic declination in 1640 (p. 219), but calculates it from an extrapolating formula at 5° west (p. 308). The St. Mary's declination varied from about 40' east of Baltimore in 1945 to 20' east in 1975.

[8]Map and accompanying data from working files of the St. Mary's City Commission, Annapolis, compiled for the Commission by Russell Menard. Some holdings are located, but not bounded. In many places groups of several adjoining properties are shown with boundaries.

[9]The map and historical material below are taken from Ludwell Montague, "Landholdings in Ware Neck, 1642–1860," *Virginia Magazine of History and Biography* 60 (1952): 64–88.

[10]Ulrich Bonnell Phillips, *Life and Labor in the Old South* (Boston: Little, Brown and Co., 1930), 32.

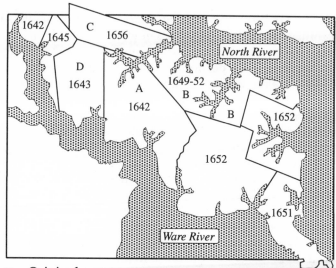

a. Original grants

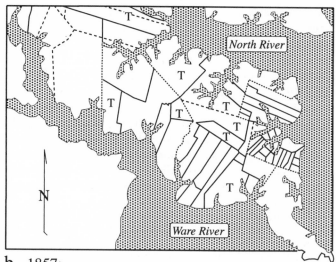

b. 1857:

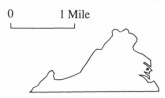

	Original property line still property line
- - -	Original property line no longer property line
—	Property line not bounding original grant

0   1 Mile

The most thorough analysis of tidewater land division has been done by Carville Earle for All Hallows Parish several miles south of Annapolis, Maryland, settled in the latter half of the 1600s.[11] His map was put together by plotting the parcels in the order of their survey, literally following the original property descriptions as they gave dimensions, directions, and bounding of one property against another (fig. 7.4). This technique emphasizes two aspects of land division that usually do not appear on land grant maps. First it shows the large number of overlaps and smaller number of gaps in the property net that the original surveyors left for later owners and surveyors to untangle or fill in.[12] Second, what appears as a long, jagged ungranted area running northeast-southwest is really an artifact of the disparity between the recorded acreage and dimensions and those actually laid out on the land. The apparent vacancy is merely the accumulation of errors from frequent understatement of sizes. The properties in reality took up nearly all the space.

As in most of the Chesapeake, the shoreline sites sought by All Hallows settlers lay along the intricate edge between necks of land and stream estuaries filled by the geologic drowning of the terrain. Surveyors often approximated the irregular shores as straight lines for simplicity of description.[13] Properties frequently included entire necks of land, never straddling estuaries and seldom straddling creeks.[14] By 1669, most of the estuarine shores had been taken up, and new settlers were forced inland.[15]

Another tidewater land grant map covering Fairfax County, Virginia (fig. 7.5), near the Fall Line between the Potomac River and its tributary, Occoquan Creek,[16] is notable for the range of property sizes it reveals. The colony of Virginia granted land here before the

[11]Carville Earle, *The Evolution of a Tidewater Settlement System: All Hallows Parish, Maryland, 1650–1783* (Chicago: University of Chicago Department of Geography Research Paper no. 170, 1975).

[12]Methods for resolving disputes included resurveys, resort to courts of arbitration, and reliance on knowledgeable neighbors (ibid., 191).

[13]Ibid., 183.

[14]Ibid., 23–24.

[15]Ibid., 21.

[16]"Patents and Northern Neck Grants," map accompanying Beth Mitchell, *Beginning at a White Oak. . .*; Fairfax Harrison, *Landmarks of Old Prince William* (Berryville. Va.: Chesapeake Book Co., 1964), 41–42.

Fig. 7.3 *(facing page)*. Ware Neck, Va. a. Original grants. b. Holdings in 1857. T = properties held by members of the Taliaferro family. Maps adapted from Montague, "Landholdings in Ware Neck," by permission of Virginia Historical Society. Ware Neck quadrangle.

0   1 Mile

N

Fig. 7.4. Part of All Hallows Parish, Md.: original property lines. The checkered area, not shown as part of the grants, is a measure of the land surveyed in excess of the amount actually reported by surveyors. From Carville Earle, *Tidewater Settlement System*. South River quadrangle (center).

return of Charles II in 1660, but was forced later to recognize the Northern Neck claim. The Virginia grants, probably representing speculation by downriver planters using purchased headrights, were seldom smaller than 500 acres and took up much of the accessible tidewater frontage. One of the larger grants, 5,000 acres for 100 headrights, to Nicholas Spencer and John Washington, was not patented under Virginia until after it had also become the Northern Neck's first grant. The claimants were taking no chances in their quest of the land.[17] Washington's half of the tract passed by way

[17]Harrison, *Landmarks*, 49–50.

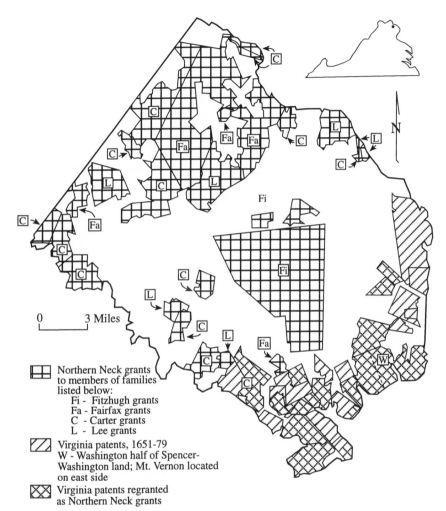

Northern Neck grants
to members of families
listed below:
Fi - Fitzhugh grants
Fa - Fairfax grants
C - Carter grants
L - Lee grants

Virginia patents, 1651-79
W - Washington half of Spencer-
Washington land; Mt. Vernon located
on east side

Virginia patents regranted
as Northern Neck grants

Fig. 7.5. Fairfax County, Va., selected land grants. The Virginia patents, which came first, took up the more accessible water frontage. Several were regranted by the Northern Neck Proprietors to the original owners or to new owners. Fitzhugh, Fairfax, Lee, and Carter were Northern Neck agents who, with their relatives, received much land. Spencer and Brent were also Northern Neck agents whose claims were mostly in the area of Virginia patents. From map, "Patents and Northern Neck Grants." in Mitchell, *Beginning at a White Oak. . . .*

of five other members of his family to his great grandson, George Washington, as the site of Mount Vernon (fig. 9.1).

As the ungranted land in the county diminished in quantity, the fraction of small grants steadily increased. The median of the

ninety-five Virginia grants was 2,000 acres, whereas the median of
the 448 Northern Neck grants up to 1780 was little more than 300
acres. Measured by total acreage in larger parcels, however, the disparity is much less: more than half the area in Virginia grants was
in parcels of 2,000 acres or more, while the comparable measure for
Northern Neck grants was parcels larger than 1,500 acres. Most of
the Virginia parcels were recorded in multiples of 100 acres, and
more than a third in multiples of 1,000 acres, in contrast with only
unusual round numbers for Northern Neck's sales of land.

The early foci of settlement in Carolina were Albemarle Sound,
the Cape Fear River, and the Charleston area. The Albemarle settlements began as part of Virginia and depended so closely on that
colony that the Carolina proprietors were forced to make the "Great
Deed of Grant" in 1668, accepting Virginia land policies there, especially regarding quitrents and free choice of land.[18] The Cape Fear
settlement, without benefit of the deed, had failed the year before,
and a second attempt there did not come for another half century.

The studies of H. A. M. Smith along the Cooper and Ashley
Rivers on and above the site of Charleston are our best guide to early
tidewater land division in South Carolina.[19] Charleston, of course,
occupied the tip of the peninsula above Oyster Point where the two
rivers flow together. Although Smith's maps show properties after
they had developed into plantations, he traces them to the original

[18]Lee, 52.

[19]H. A. M. Smith, "Charleston and Charleston Neck," *South Carolina Historical and
Genealogical Magazine* 19 (1918): 3–76; "The Ashley River: Its Seats and Settlements,"
ibid., 20 (1919): 1–51, 75–122; "The Upper Ashley and the Mutations of Families," ibid.,
151–98; "The Baronies of South Carolina, XVI: Quenby and the Eastern Branch of the
Cooper River," ibid., 18 (1917): 3–36.

The records of warrants reveal the range of South Carolina land arrangements (A. S.
Salley, Jr., ed., *Warrants for Lands in South Carolina, 1672–1711* [1910–15; revised with an
introduction by Nicholas Olsberg, Columbia: University of South Carolina Press for
South Carolina Department of Archives and History, 1973]): "twelve thousand acres
for a Collony in a square"; "One hundred and seaventy acres . . . being the proporcon
allowed him for two serv^{ts}"; "five hundred acres of land being the proporcon allowed
to him . . . for his disbursements on the discovery of this Province"; "one hundred acres
of land . . . arriveing a Servt. in the first ffleet"; "Tenn acres of land for his present
planting near Charles Town"; "one hundred acres of land being the proporcon allowed
him by the lords prop^{rs} concessions arriveing in February 1670/1: deducting therefrom
his Towne and Tenn acre lot if any." Each grant contained these conditions: "in such
place as you shall be directed by him soe as the same be not within the compass of any
lands heretofore layd out for any other person . . . and if the same happen upon any
navigable River . . . you are to allow only the fifth part of the depth thereof by the wa-
terside."

grants in most cases. Most of the properties on the maps are elongated, with their narrow sides along the rivers, but length-width ratios vary from one to ten or twelve without any regularity (fig. 7.6). The first three parcels above the site originally assigned Charleston (running about four-fifths of a mile above Oyster Point) crossed the neck to front on both rivers. Then for a few miles the properties fronting the two rivers met in the middle of the neck, which often still had less than a mile of firm land between the marshes bordering the water on each side. The original warrants were for only a few headrights, but many of them called for more acreage than the narrow peninsula provided.

Six miles above Oyster Point the peninsula abruptly widens, permitting the strips to become much longer. The plantations, limited to a few hundred acres downstream, ranged from several hundred to several thousand acres upstream. Inland properties were often compact in shape. Many of the plantations shown on the maps were formed by aggregating several of the smaller grants. Sometimes the smaller grants had been made to different people. In other cases they were grants to the same owner for successive imports of servants. Aggregation was more common than subdivision up to the Civil War, but both processes as well as many exchanges of property occurred.

Taken together, the above examples of seventeenth-century land division show few common characteristics beyond their irregularity and a preference for waterfront sites that themselves contribute to the irregularity. Elongation of parcels as a way to control the appropriation of water frontage appears most clearly along the Cooper and Ashley Rivers, but even there without regularity. Some elongation occurs also in available Maryland examples, especially rows of strips along both sides of the Anacostia River in present District of Columbia.[20] The Virginia cases, however, show very little evidence of elongation; a Virginia plantation with a mile of depth back from a river would more likely stretch along the river than perpendicular to it. The preference for necks of land and avoidance of straddling estuaries noted in All Hallows Parish is another way of adapting parcels to shore features, most readily realized when necks are about the size of the parcels to be laid out. The use of necks is evident in most of the Maryland maps and in Fairfax County, Virginia, but one property in Somerset County, Maryland, and several on Ware

---

[20]Louise Joyner Hienton, *Prince Georges Heritage: Sidelights on the Early History of Prince Georges County from 1696–1800* (Baltimore: Garamond Pridemark Press, 1972), land grant map.

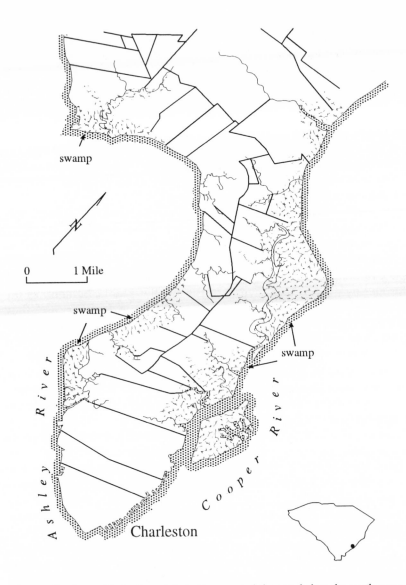

swamp

swamp

swamp

Ashley River

Cooper River

Charleston

Fig. 7.6. Charleston Neck. The original city occupied the area below the southernmost line on the peninsula. From H. A. M. Smith, "Charleston and Charleston Neck." Charleston quadrangle.

Neck not only straddled estuaries, but embraced whole systems of estuaries and their tributaries.

Other contrasts emerge when land grant systems are compared. Rectangularity, for example, is most conspicuous on the St. Mary's

City plat and was noted in other Maryland examples. It is rare on parcels fronting the Ashley and Cooper Rivers, but more common inland. Rectangularity, however, does not seem to be a feature of the Virginia examples. The largest land parcels appear in the two Virginia cases, whereas the smallest appear in All Hallows Parish and, in a few cases, along the Ashley and Cooper Rivers.

Understatement of property sizes is shown explicitly in both the large parcels of Ware Neck and the small parcels of All Hallows Parish. Confusion from overlapping titles is clearly shown on the maps of All Hallows Parish and Somerset County, both in Maryland. These defects of surveying cannot have been absent in the other cases: recently prepared land grant maps have probably been drawn to eliminate the early ambiguities.

Persistence and Change of Land Parcels

We return here to the examples of Ware Neck and All Hallows Parish for the light they throw on persistence and change of property ownership and property lines.

Ware Neck illustrates an evolution of property succession by sale and purchase, consolidation and subdivision, marriage and inheritance, and expropriation. Thomas Curtis, who had come to Virginia as an indentured servant, added property B (fig. 7.3a) to his original grant (A) of 1642, and his son patented parcel C. Robert Bristow, who came to Virginia in 1660, married a daughter of Thomas Curtis, acquiring as a result two of the Curtises' parcels, first C and later A, and he independently acquired D, which had been abandoned by its first owner. About 1677 he returned to England, and eventually placed his property under the management of Thomas Booth, who, like Bristow, became both planter and merchant. Booth and his descendants continued to manage the Bristow property and gradually acquired most of the rest of the Neck on their own. For some of the Booths, at least, Ware Neck lands were more an ambiance for gracious living than a means to financial gain. The Booths' dominance of the Neck was in decay by the time of the Revolution, and the Bristow interests were expropriated shortly after it. Virginia also, after disestablishment of the Church of England, took over a parish glebe (most of C) that had been purchased from the Bristows. By the time of the Civil War several branches of a new family, the Taliaferros, held much of the Neck (fig. 7.3b); their first acquisitions had been by marriage, one of them to a Booth descendant.

Fig. 7.7. Ware Neck. Northeast portion of figure 7.3. The North River cuts across the northeast corner. The diagram relates to information visible in the photograph: lines may be original property boundaries. A represents areas of subdivision lines on figure 7.3b not visible here, and B represents the area of subdivision lines that are visible. USGS, 1963.

Fig. 7.8. Houses and woods near the center of Ware Neck.

Although boundaries changed as property was traded, none of the Ware Neck holdings was really fragmented until 1804, when a parcel that had been purchased from one of the Booths was divided among four heirs by approximately parallel boundaries forming strips with frontage along the Ware River. About 1840 two other estates were divided among five and fifteen heirs respectively. Only then, after nearly 200 years of settlement, did a few inland properties without water frontage appear.

Subdivision has continued to characterize land change in Ware Neck. Small plots were sold to former slaves in 1870. Division of land among heirs has been the major process of fragmentation. The tax map current in 1977 showed some 300 parcels ranging from about a tenth of an acre to a little more than a hundred acres (fig. 7.7). Some of the most recent subdivision has probably been commercial, but "almost all landholdings are now essentially residential, be they modest cottages with their small gardens or the old plantation houses in their spacious settings."[21] Most of the houses are near the water where the early clearing and settlement occurred; others are near the main road, which makes a loop in the interior (fig. 7.8). Oc-

[21]Montague, 88.

casional cultivated clearings in the interior interrupt woods that have succeeded earlier farming.

Half the length of the original seventeenth-century property lines of Ware Neck were still property lines in 1857, and later boundaries from both the seventeenth and nineteenth centuries are discernible on the present tax map. The directions of property lines from the earliest subdivisions have often been paralleled in more recent subdivisions. Ware Neck's present settlement density is typical of the popular extremities of Virginia peninsulas reaching into Chesapeake Bay. The interiors of peninsulas are heavily wooded and sparsely settled, and settlement along the rivers thins out westward away from Chesapeake Bay.

In All Hallows Parish, Maryland, also, the property maps record a relatively stable cadastral stage for the flux of its colonial history, this in spite of rapid changes in population, settlement, roads, the tobacco economy, and the condition of the land.[22] Stability does not imply absence of ownership changes or of subdivision, but rather a persistence of property sizes and boundaries in spite of the uncertainties of the original surveys. Between 1730 and 1774, the majority of original parcels were sold not more than once each. About a sixth of the parcels were involved in five or more sales; these frequently traded parcels were concentrated near towns, roads, and the head of navigation.[23] The same busy areas had the most subdivision and the most legal actions to clarify boundaries.[24] Between 1675 and 1783, the number of landholdings nearly doubled, and the median size of landholdings dropped from 300 to 204 acres. During the same period, population grew faster than the number of landholdings, tenancy increased, and the nonlandholding households increased markedly to 50 percent of the total.[25] It appears that colonial-period subdivision of properties went on somewhat faster in All Hallows Parish than in Ware Neck, where the land was probably less intensively populated and used.

[22]Earle, 182.

[23]Ibid., 197–98.

[24]Ibid., 190, 200–201.

[25]In Maryland as a whole, more than half the free whites were members of land-owning families as late as 1755. Elizabeth Hartsook and Gust Skordas, *Land Office and Prerogative Court Records of Early Maryland* (Annapolis: Hall of Records Commission, State of Maryland, 1946), 13.

Manors and Baronies

Great estates for the nobility were features of the plans for only Maryland and Carolina among the Southern colonies. Most of those granted in Carolina were actually in South Carolina. Few of the estates developed into the lordly fiefs they were intended to be.

The manors in Maryland were both private and proprietary. Private manors were granted between 1633 and 1684 to people who brought settlers into the colony and, more commonly in the latter part of the period, as gifts to relatives, friends, officials, and others who had performed services for the colony.[26] Although the law did not provide for new private manors after 1683, large tracts continued to be granted, and some of them were still called manors. Proprietary manors were those retained by the Calverts themselves, withheld from the land available for headrights and sale. The Calverts' interest in holding these manors seems to have been mostly the anticipation of profits from increasing land values.[27]

The map of manors in Maryland (fig. 7.9) shows how they were distributed and how much of the colony's area they actually took up. Manors were heavily concentrated in the southern counties between the Potomac and Chesapeake Bay where the first settlement of Maryland took place. A number occupied tidewater locations on the Eastern Shore.

Although manors in America were sometimes looked on as opportunities for younger sons of aristocratic English families,[28] few, if any, of the private manors of Maryland became seats of long family dynasties. Some were sold almost immediately, others after twenty or thirty years, and still others were divided on inheritance or regranted after reversion to the proprietor. Kent Fort Manor, on Kent Island in Chesapeake Bay, for example, was granted Giles Brent in 1640 in return for his services in the extended dispute with William Claiborne, who claimed the island as a part of Virginia. Claiborne's sporadic control of the island ended only in 1658. The successive owners were mostly absentee, and the island had passed out of the Brents' hands by 1700. In 1709 the southern half of the 2,000 acres was sold off. After more sales, a resident of Annapolis reassembled

---

[26]Donnell MacClure Owings, "Private Manors: An Edited List," *Maryland Historical Magazine* 33 (1938): 309.

[27]Gregory A. Stiverson, *Poverty in a Land of Plenty* (Baltimore: Johns Hopkins University Press, 1977), 1.

[28]Newman, *Flowering of the Maryland Palatinate*, 102.

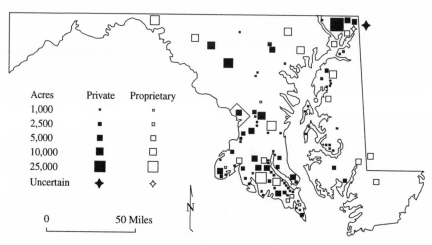

Fig. 7.9. Manors of colonial Maryland. The symbols showing manor size are on the same areal scale as the map itself. A few locations are no closer than in the proper county. The manors mapped are not complete, but include those from (1) a list of private manors from Owings, "Private Manors," (2) a list of proprietary manors from Stiverson, *Poverty in a Land of Plenty*, (3) a list in Harry Wright Newman, *Seigniory in Early Maryland* (Washington: Descendants of the Lords of the Maryland Manors, 1949), and (4) a few eighteenth-century estates popularly called manors, but not technically so established.

the separate parts of the manor. Several additional families owned the manor before a new division in the 1780s. The northern half was sold off as three farms in the mid-1800s. Division of the southern half into five farms began after 1861. One of these farms, containing 170 acres, is still known as Kent Fort Manor.[29]

One of the later manors was granted to Augustine Herman for his services in making a map of Maryland and Virginia, one of the best seventeenth-century maps of American territory. Bohemia Manor, and Augustine Manor across the line in present Delaware, were entailed by Herman on the male line, which they followed for at least two generations.[30]

---

[29]Erich Isaac, "Kent Island: Part I—The Period of Settlement; Part II—Settlement and Land Holding under the Proprietary; Part III—Kent Fort Manor," *Maryland Historical Magazine* 52 (1957): 93–119, 210–232.

[30]Owings, 332–34. Herman's lands eventually sheltered two unpopular causes. He sold one tract comprising four necks of land in 1684 to a group of Labadists, members of a European utopian group, who held forth there for a few decades (Bartlett B. James, *The Labadist Colony in Maryland*, Johns Hopkins University Studies in Historical and Political Science, ser. 17, no. 6 [Baltimore: Johns Hopkins, 1899]). For some time, after about 1744, Bohemia Manor was the site of a Jesuit school for instructing young Catholics, an

More than twenty large private grants were made after 1684, predominantly in central and northern Maryland west of Chesapeake Bay. The Charles Carroll family was one that came into great holdings through such grants and trades. The first Charles Carroll came to Maryland late in the 1600s as attorney general and later served as Lord Baltimore's agent.[31] Among the Carrolls' purchases were all or part of at least three earlier manors.[32] New estates such as Doughoregan and Carrollton were direct grants to the Carrolls. Doughoregan, first granted in 1711, long remained their country seat. It is still identified as Doughoregan Manor on a 1977 Howard County tax map, with about 2,500 of its 13,500 acres still held by descendants named Carroll.[33] Large private grants continued to be made or confirmed even after the Revolution; large tracts named Potomac Manor and Yough Manor in westernmost Maryland are not included on figure 7.9 because their grant dates (to the same man) are 1800 and 1804.

The Calverts retained possibly thirty of the Maryland manors for themselves. Two proprietary manors of 600 acres each had been planned for every county in 1665.[34] Figure 7.9 shows the twenty-three proprietary manors known to have been in existence in 1767.

The Calvert manors were variously treated. Parts of most of these proprietary manors were sold within a score of years of their formation. The greater part of their land, however, remained vacant until the demand for rented land showed a marked increase in the eighteenth century.[35] An earlier deterrent to renting had been a consideration fee of four pounds to be paid by the tenant on assuming the

---

illegal institution under the Protestant government of that day (Ellen Hart Smith, *Charles Carroll of Carrolton* [Cambridge: Harvard University Press, 1942], 29).

The Jesuits themselves held five of the private manors in early Maryland, and still had one as recently as 1977 (John Johnson, *Old Maryland Manors*, Johns Hopkins University Studies in Historical and Political Science, ser. 1, no. 7 [Baltimore: Johns Hopkins, 1883]: 20; Joseph Agonito, "St. Inigoes Manor: A Nineteenth Century Jesuit Plantation," *Maryland Historical Magazine* 72 [1977]: 83). Baltimore had denied the Jesuits the prerogative they claimed of receiving land directly from Indians (Mereness, 436). The mortmain provision (dealing with ecclesiastical holdings) in early Maryland forbade large holdings by religious bodies without specific approval of the proprietor. The proprietor's power in this regard descended to the State Assembly (Marshall Harris, 216).

[31]Mereness, 63; Ellen Hart Smith, 9.

[32]Owings, 307, 312–13, 319.

[33]Also Mary H. Cadwalader, "Charles Carroll of Carrollton: A Signer's Story," *Smithsonian* 6, no. 9 (1975): 70.

[34]Mereness, 53. In 1754 the Maryland governor reported to the proprietor that he could not find large enough parcels in the settled areas for all the manors the proprietor wanted (*Archives of Maryland* 6: 52–53).

[35]Stiverson, 1–3.

lease. The fee was dropped in favor of *developmental leases* under which improvements such as planting orchards and building houses were required. The cash part of the rent remained low, usually ten shillings per hundred acres.[36] Tenant holdings, averaging more than 100 acres, seem to have been laid out in irregular parcels, suggesting that many tenants were allowed to choose the land they would use.[37] Large private holdings were similarly divided into leaseholds.[38]

Leasing of the manors was not well managed by the proprietors' agents and stewards, and the return from them was low.[39] For this reason, or perhaps a shortage of cash, or some prescience of trouble to come, the last Lord Baltimore, in 1766, against the advice of his Maryland governor, ordered that his manor lands be sold. Less than half of the 120,000 acres offered was sold within the next five years. A few tenants were able to buy their land. Most had long leases, often for three lives, so that only a minority were forced to leave.[40]

The proprietary manors, along with a great deal of private land, were confiscated during the Revolution. Maryland moved rapidly to sell the land to raise money for the war. This gave tenants a new chance to buy their land, but many were displaced.[41] Maryland manors and any special status they had enjoyed came to an end.

In Carolina only five or six seigniories, a dozen baronies, and a very small number of manors can be identified as ever having been definitely located (fig. 7.10). Even a few of those surveyed were probably never occupied. These estates were hardly the compass-oriented squares of the proprietors' model. Of thirteen large estates mapped by Smith,[42] three were nearly square in shape and one close

[36]Ibid., 9–13.

[37]Ibid., 16–17.

[38]Craven, *Southern Colonies*, suggests that tenancy was the next step up for the freed servant and that these tenants of absentee landlords operated with considerable independence. Although entitled to fifty-acre freedom rights, most servants could not afford the survey and patent fees immediately (Lois Green Carr, personal communication, March 25, 1981).

[39]Mereness, 53, says many manors diminished in size through the agents' failures to keep track of boundaries.

[40]Stiverson, 17–27, 104–11.

[41]Ibid., 111–36.

[42]"The Baronies of South Carolina," series of articles in the *South Carolina Historical and Genealogical Magazine*: "I: Ashley," 11 (1910): 75–91; "II: Fairlawn," 11: 193–202; "III: Cypress," 12 (1911): 5–13; "IV: Wadboo," 12: 43–54; "V: Seewee," 12: 109–17; "VI: Winyah" and "VII: Wiskinboo," 13 (1912): 3–20; "VIII: Boone's," 13: 71–83; "IX: Oketee or Devil's Elbow," 13: 119–75; "X Hobcaw," 14 (1913): 61–80; "XI Raphoe," "XII: Tomotley," and "XIII: Malling," 15 (1914): 3–17; "XIV: Ashepoo," 15: 63–72; "XV: Land-

to a rhombus. Two or three had sides close to the cardinal directions, but without appearing to lie exactly along the magnetic directions. Ten, however, derived their orientations from bordering rivers. Only one estate lacked river frontage entirely. The following paragraphs present examples of the fates of these supposedly entailed and indivisible fiefdoms.

The first of the 12,000-acre estates was a seigniory taken up by Lord Ashley Cooper on the Ashley River about twelve miles above Charleston. Cooper had written that he wanted help in choosing "a place of the greatest pleasantness and advantage for health and profit which must be where there is high ground neare a navigable River and if it be above the tydes flowing 'tis the better." He intended "to stock it and lay out a good deale of money in making a Plantation for myselfe." His title to the land was finally buttressed by a separately negotiated purchase from the Indians.

Even Ashley Cooper could be disappointed with his acquisition on one of the rivers bearing his name; he soon complained that earlier claimants had taken up the most convenient places, and considered moving his estate to Edisto Island, but finally accepted the original location. Cooper never actually visited Carolina. His heirs sold the property in 1717 to a merchant, who soon sold off two 3,000-acre parcels. The merchant's descendants continued in possession of most of the retained half of the property until the last one died in 1875. Several parts of Ashley Barony were important plantations until the Civil War (fig. 7.11).

Fairlawn was early granted as a seigniory to Sir John Colleton, eldest son of an original proprietor, and it became the Colleton family seat. Cypress, Wadboo, and Devil's Elbow were baronies of other members of the Colleton family, some of whom, alone among the original proprietary families, actually did make their homes in Carolina. The proprietary permission to divide Cypress in 1704 was already evidence of decay of the landed aristocracy scheme.[43] The other three Colleton estates survived until after 1750. Wadboo, however, was the only seigniory or barony in Carolina to survive essentially intact and in possession of the original family until the Revolution. Because the heirs were then residing in England, however, Wadboo was confiscated, divided into a grid of twenty-eight

grave Ketelby's," 15: 149–65; "XVI: Quenby and the Eastern Branch of Cooper River," 18 (1917): 3–36.

[43] Ackerman, 40–41.

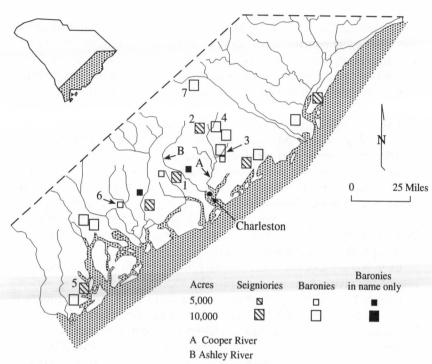

Fig. 7.10. Baronies of colonial South Carolina. The areal scale of the symbols is the same as the scale of the map. 1. Ashley 2. Fairlawn 3. Cypress 4. Wadboo 5. Devil's Elbow 6. Ashepoo 7. Raphoe. Compiled primarily from the maps and articles of Henry A. M. Smith, "The Baronies of South Carolina," *South Carolina Magazine of History and Biography* (1910–17).

nearly square rectangles, and sold (mostly in groups of two to five rectangles) for a total of £26,000. Although the barony was removed from the list of condemned estates the next year, it was too late to put the pieces together again; inflation and embezzlement ate up most of the monetary compensation due the British heir.

Ashepoo and Raphoe Baronies were both holdings of landgraves. Ashepoo, consisting of only half the standard 12,000 acres, was granted to Edmund Bellinger in 1702 and broken up by his descendants before 1750, with at least one portion continuing in the hands of Bellingers until after 1860. Raphoe was farther from the coast than any other barony. Never properly patented, it was sold by the owner's agent in the 1720s. It was probably never occupied, and seems to have lain abandoned until its land was taken up by new claims about 1747.

0 _____ 1 Mile

N

Fig. 7.11. Part of Ashley Seigniory, S.C., including most of the largest parcel into which it was divided, reported to have had 200 slaves in the early 1790s. Forestry and hunting clubs are two of the much less intensive land uses now present in the vicinity. Phosphate was mined at one time. The Ashley River is at the upper right. USGS, 1971. Stallsville quadrangle (southeast).

The Carolina baronies usually had select locations on rivers and estuaries. Subdivided, most of them lent the glitter of their names and hopes to plantations that flourished between 1700 and the Civil War.

Manors and baronies did not prove to be viable in most of the colonies. They could not retain free labor in the face of abundant land for family farms. The introduction of slave labor depended on a rule of force rather than the give and take of customary feudal tenures. Manors and baronies not transformed into plantations were broken up or abandoned and regranted.

8

Eighteenth-Century Land Division

THIS CHAPTER deals with eighteenth-century land development in new parts of the Coastal Plain, the Piedmont, and the Virginia mountains. By way of introduction I will discuss certain land reforms attempted in Virginia and South Carolina during the first half of the eighteenth century. The land division of particular areas will then be discussed in this order: (1) areas of small to moderate land parcels of the Piedmont; (2) land operations of western Virginia: large tracts and their subdivision; (3) township settlements and other group settlements resembling townships.

Land Controversies and Reforms

The distribution of land was a topic of continual controversy in most of the colonies. Two efforts at reform are presented here, more to illuminate the perennial issues than to mark them as milestones that really changed practices.

Alexander Spotswood, governor of Virginia from 1712 to 1722, applied his energies toward carrying out the numerous royal instructions to enforce the laws on land acquisition, on seating and planting, and on quitrents. Applicants for more than 400 acres were required to provide evidence to the governor and council that they could put so much land to use before a survey would be allowed.[1] Forfeiture was threatened if quitrents were not paid or seating and planting did not occur within the time limit. Patenting of land was required soon after the survey in order to get the land on the rent rolls and to discourage abandonment after collection of the valued pitch, tar, and pitch-rich "lightwood." Owners were to buy or give up any land in excess of the acreage granted. Grantees were expected to take up poor land along

[1]Michael L. Nicholls, "Origins of the Virginia Southside, 1703–1753: A Social and Economic Study" (Ph.D. diss., College of William and Mary, 1972), 77–78; Dodson, 135–36; Voorhis, "Crown versus Council," 507.

with the good, so that the poor land would not be left unclaimed; gerrymandering of boundaries to include only good land was discouraged by the requirement that each parcel be at least a third as broad as long (barring hindrance by streams or earlier boundaries).[2]

Spotswood's efforts were largely thwarted by the Virginia Council, which was composed of landholding interests.[3] After several years of contention, he gave up and joined the land grab himself. His holdings, eventually amounting to 85,000 Piedmont acres along the Rappahannock and Rapidan Rivers, were acquired through a series of grants to accomplices who then turned the land over to him.[4] His tracts were variously rented to a group of German colonists, used for iron and naval stores, and rented out as small tenant farms.[5]

Spotswood and his defenders claimed that his land operations advanced the settlement of the Piedmont. The Virginia Assembly in 1720 had created two huge new Piedmont counties, Spotsylvania north of the James, and Brunswick to the south.[6] For seven years beginning in 1721, the land would be granted for surveying and filing fees only, and exempted from quitrents and other levies for ten years—the so-called homestead scheme. The Board of Trade in England tried, with scant success, to limit land so obtained to 1,000 acres.[7] The activities of Spotswood and other large speculators there encouraged smallholders also to move into Spotsylvania, which developed rapidly. Brunswick, without the speculators and with few tracts of more than 1,000 acres, lagged far behind.

In South Carolina the administration of Governor Robert Johnson, 1730–35, focused many of the land distribution questions with which that colony had to deal. The Carolinas had just been placed under royal government after a period of uncertainty following the overthrow of the proprietors in South Carolina and the crown's purchase of the land rights of seven of the eight proprietors. The land offices in both Carolinas had been closed, but a number of baronial patents for still unlocated land granted by the proprietors served as a reservoir from which new parcels were sold, however doubtful the legality.[8]

[2]Dodson, 135.

[3]Voorhis, "Crown versus Council."

[4]Voorhis, "Land Grant Policy," 142; Dodson, 278–80.

[5]Dodson, 293–300.

[6]Hening, ed., 4: 77.

[7]Dodson, 244–48, 279–93.

[8]Richard P. Sherman, *Robert Johnson: Proprietary and Royal Governor of South Carolina* (Columbia: University of South Carolina Press, 1966), 138. Somewhat parallel in North

Under Governor Johnson, the South Carolina Assembly passed a liberal land law known as the Quit Rent Act, which was considered by many as the "Magna Carta of Carolina" for its securing of land titles.[9] Under this act, nearly all grants and patents from the proprietors were recognized along with claims to any other land that had been held in peaceful possession for seven years.[10] When quitrents could not be ascertained, they were set at a shilling a hundred acres, the most common rate under the proprietors, but only a quarter of the new rate being established.[11] Arrears of quitrents were remitted. All land had to be registered, to the end that future quitrents could be collected.

Johnson, as claimant to 19,000 acres of land inherited from his father, was among the many holders, large and small, who stood to benefit from validation of the proprietary patents.[12] James St. John, South Carolina's surveyor general, led the opposition in the colony to the Quit Rent Act and sought to have it declared void in London. His stated position was that the proprietary patents were not legal and that their approval would deprive the crown of quitrent collections. His true interest showed, however, when he approved new surveys of some of the lands in the proprietary patents for a group with which he was in league, and which proceeded to offer the land for sale.[13] The Quit Rent Act was never voided,[14] and the patents remained with their holders.

The case of Johnson, like that of Spotswood, illustrates the constant tension between governments trying to effect orderly land development and individual colonists taking liberties to make the land policies serve their own purposes. Many colonial officials were among those taking the greatest liberties.

Carolina were a number of "blank patents" signed by the last proprietary governor without date, location, amount paid, patentee, or acreage. Intended perhaps only as signed forms available for legal transactions, some of them got into circulation and were used to claim about half a million acres of land at quitrents of only a shilling or half a shilling per hundred acres. These "wild cards" in the hands of their holders could be predated to gain priority over claims staked out years earlier. Lee, 105–6; Hugh Talmadge Lefler and Albert Ray Newsome, *North Carolina* (Chapel Hill: University of North Carolina Press, 1954), 143–44; Beverley Bond, 294.

[9]Ackerman, 73.

[10]Ibid., 69.

[11]Beverley Bond, 318–19.

[12]Ackerman, 67.

[13]Ibid., 77–78; Sherman, 163–65.

[14]M. Eugene Sirmans, *Colonial South Carolina: A Political History, 1663–1763* (Chapel Hill: University of North Carolina Press, 1966), 180.

Settlement of New Lands

Settlement of the South proceeded from the coast into the interior differently in different colonies. By 1700 the Virginia Coastal Plain was well settled except for the Southside (south of the James), the Piedmont had hardly been touched, and the first publicized expedition across the Blue Ridge, by Governor Spotswood and his "Knights of the Golden Horseshoe," was still sixteen years ahead. The total land per person in the settled areas was about forty acres, most of it already taken up. Settlement on the Western Shore of Maryland had moved onto the Piedmont in the north where the Coastal Plain was narrow, while the interior of the Eastern Shore still had only limited settlement. The Carolinas had only limited coastal settlement by 1700. Movement onto the Piedmont of the Carolinas began only after royal government was established in 1729, and followed favored river corridors, especially those of the Peedee and Santee systems, before the Coastal Plain had filled up.[15]

Indiscriminate Location on the Piedmont

Land grant maps are available for only two areas that might be expected to be typical of eighteenth-century land division on the Piedmont. The two, from Maryland and South Carolina, stand in such contrast as to raise doubts about how representative they may be. They are probably closer to the opposite ends of the spectrum of property patterns than to the middle. At least their contrast provokes some questions that need to be studied. The Maryland Piedmont map covers Howard County, west of Baltimore. The South Carolina map covers parts of seven counties in the northwestern part of the state now in the Sumter National Forest.

The Howard County map[16] exhibits the greatest irregularity of property shapes encountered in this entire study, parts of it more befitting the scheme of a jigsaw puzzle than of surveying or landownership. The outlandish shapes occur in most parts of the county, but dominate in the northwestern areas of somewhat greater relief,

---

[15]Herman Friis, "A Series of Population Maps of the Colonies and the United States, 1625–1790," *Geographical Review* 30 (1940): 463–70.

[16]Caleb Dorsey, "The Original Land Grants of Howard County, Maryland," *Maryland Historical Magazine* 64 (1969): 287–94; and map of same title on file in Maryland Hall of Records, Annapolis.

where most of the grants came after 1750 (fig. 8.1). An area south of Ellicott City in the eastern part of the county had large compact parcels (ca. 1,000 acres) dating as early as the 1680s. The most conspicuous cadastral features of the central part of the county are the 7,000-acre parallelogram of Doughoregan Manor and other grants to Charles Carroll in the early 1700s.

Characteristic land parcels of Howard County are bounded by a large number of short courses, totaling more than a hundred in extreme cases. Edges of parcels often zigzag, with many reentrants. Some of these polygons are compact in shape, but others are formed of tentacles reaching out in three or more directions, or make great S-shapes winding around other properties. Some of the strange shapes must be late claims that were missed or rejected in earlier surveys. But when the boundary between two parcels changes direction ten, twenty, or thirty times, some additional explanation is needed, for the most conspicuous zigzag boundaries do not follow streams. Boundaries along the Patuxent and Patapsco Rivers are often shown as straight lines, sometimes crossing these rivers into adjoining counties. Creeks are usually ignored as boundaries. The rough terrain explains some of the irregularity: upland parcels sometimes wound around the edges of stream lowlands, jogging upstream around tributary valleys, or downstream possibly to capture springs. However, the boundaries simply do not fit the topography very closely. Jagged boundaries are found on relatively smooth land, and straight boundaries, such as the six-mile sides of Doughoregan, proceed indiscriminately across ravines and ridges.

The 1977 tax map of Howard County shows, at first glance, little resemblance to the land grant map. Old parcels have been consolidated and divided. New residential lots of one to ten acres abound near the main roads. But close examination shows that many of the less rational bends in the modern boundaries duplicate lines of the original grants.

The land patterns of the South Carolina Piedmont, on the other hand, were as simple as the practice of indiscriminate location would be likely to produce (fig. 8.2).[17] Parcels were relatively compact in shape, had relatively few sides, and nearly all fell in the range between fifty and 1,000 acres in size. The most unusual feature of the land parcels here is a scattering of square parcels exhibiting

[17]Statement based primarily on *Land Grant Maps* (Union, S.C.: Union County Historical Foundation, 1976). These published maps are believed to have been prepared in the acquisition of land by Sumter National Forest.

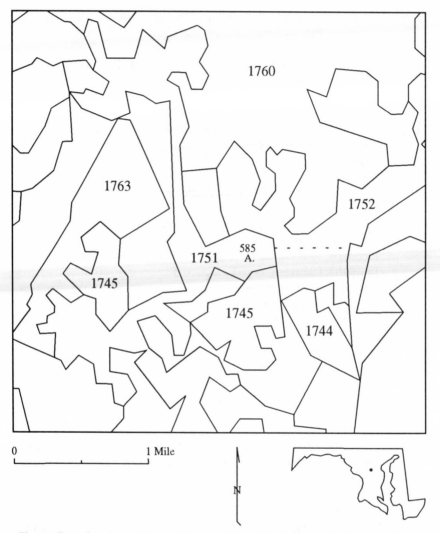

Fig. 8.1. Part of northwest Howard County, Md.: original land grants. The patent dates given do not necessarily reflect the survey dates. "Henry and Peter," the parcel indicated by the 1751 date, is bounded by more than eighty courses. From Caleb Dorsey, "Original Land Grants of Howard County," copyright 1968, by permission. Woodbine (east central) and Sykesville (west central) quadrangles.

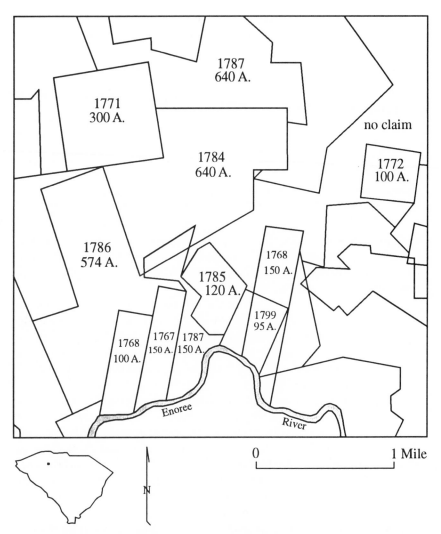

Fig. 8.2. Land grants in Sumter National Forest, Spartanburg and Union Counties, S.C. The earlier grants were longlots on the Enoree River or squares. From *Land Grant Maps,* Union County Historical Foundation. Philson Cross Roads quadrangle (northwest).

TABLE 8.1. Area of Sumter National Forest: Distribution of land grants in time

Period	Sample of all parcels (%)	Sample of square parcels (%)	Sample of riverfront parcels (%)
1749–61	5.9	4.6	29.0
1762–69	11.3	35.4	10.1
1770–79*	28.3	46.4	34.8
1780–94*	39.1	13.1	17.4
1795–1822	13.9	0.4	8.7
1836–57	1.5	—	—
Totals	100.0	99.9	100.0

Sources: Data from *Land Grant Maps* and its separately bound "Index."
*Most of the grants date in the intervals 1772–75 just before the Revolution, and 1784–86, just after.

the full range of property sizes, totaling nearly a tenth of all the parcels. The squares do not show compass orientation. Occasionally two squares share a common boundary, and in one or two places several squares form a limited grid.[18]

The Broad River and most of the course of the Enoree River, as navigable streams, were used as property boundaries. Most commonly the riverfront grants were compact in shape. A few riparian parcels had their long sides along the river, although more were laid out with their short ends abutting the river in accordance with official policy.

The plats on the rivers and the square plats tended to come early in the land appropriation sequence (table 8.1). Sites on the rivers, of course, were traditionally preferred by early settlers. The first settlers away from the rivers were expected to lay out their land in squares, but later settlers had to run their boundaries around the earlier parcels, making squares less likely. The early preference for river sites, however, was not to stand the test of time. Piedmont residence today is concentrated on the divides.

The terrain offers no explanation for the differences in land division patterns of the Maryland and Carolina Piedmont areas just described, for both areas are rolling upland with local relief on the order of 200 feet and occasionally steep valley sides. In both areas today the settlement and roads are mostly on the divides and woods are more frequent in the valleys. Roads cutting across valleys or run-

[18]Squares similarly occurred near Bishopville, S.C., on the upper Coastal Plain (map by J. F. Stuckey, MC3–10 in South Carolina Archives). Headrights grants in Georgia showed a comparable use of squares.

ning along valley floors are more frequent in the Maryland than the South Carolina example, where we find patchy clearings among extensive woods; in Maryland it is the woods that occur in patches.

The origins of people settling these Carolina and Maryland areas are also of little help in explaining the differences. Most of the Piedmont settlers in South Carolina had previously been neither residents of that colony nor immigrants entering through the port of Charleston, but were rather Pennsylvanians and Piedmont Virginians, many of them Scotch-Irish.[19] Many of the Howard County settlers were descendants of Puritans who had staked out mostly quadrangular lots in the lowland near Annapolis.[20] In neither case do we find specific similarities of land patterns in the areas of origin and of later settlement.

The differences in the South Carolina and Maryland surveys do not seem explainable by differences in terrain, colony policies, or cultural baggage of the settlers. This leaves as a possibility differences in the way in which surveying techniques evolved in the two localities. The square parcels we find on the South Carolina Piedmont seem extensions of that colony's earlier emphasis on squares, a tradition more likely pressed by the colony government and surveyors than by the settlers.[21] The contorted Maryland boundaries, on the other hand, find no precedent in that colony, or, so far as I know, in any other. Maryland instructions of 1712, in fact, called for parcels as regular and square as possible.[22] The irregular boundaries may somehow represent the reaction of a later generation of surveyors, armed with new instruments, to the irregular terrain. Demonstration of such an explanation would require deeper inquiry into the surveyor's art in eighteenth-century Maryland.

One anomaly of Piedmont land distribution in Georgia remains to be mentioned, in the area originally comprising Wilkes County, west of the Savannah River and north of Augusta.[23] More than a million

---

[19]Robert L. Meriwether, *The Expansion of South Carolina, 1729–1765* (Kingsport, Tenn.: Southern Publishers, 1940), 161–62, 261.

[20]Dorsey, 289.

[21]Linda Marie Pett-Conklin, "Cadastral Surveying in Colonial South Carolina: A Historical Geography" (Ph.D. diss., Louisiana State University, 1986), reports that a majority of parcels in a sample of eighteenth-century frontier surveys were squares or rectangles (p. 110). This surprising rectangularity may be partially explained by the fact that most of the sample comprised townships.

[22]Harley, 82.

[23]This discussion of the ceded lands is based on Alex M. Hitz, "The Earliest Settlements in Wilkes County," *Georgia Historical Quarterly* 40 (1956): 260–80.

and a half acres were ceded to Georgia in 1773 by the Creek and Cherokee Indians in return for cancelation of their considerable debts to Georgia traders, at the same time ending the hostility between the two tribes over possession of the land. The traders were to be paid by the colony from the proceeds of selling the Indians' land. An elaborate scale of land prices was worked out: a shilling to five shillings an acre depending on quality, with surcharges for good mill sites or river frontage near the fork of the Broad and Savannah Rivers, where the town of Dartmouth was laid out. The tract was to be used to attract new settlers to Georgia: no buyer was to be a resident of Georgia, and sales were limited to 100 acres. Possibly a quarter of the land was sold before the Revolution disrupted the plan. But payments were slow, many buyers left the area, more than half the warrants issued were for more than 100 acres, and the aggrieved traders received none of the proceeds. This departure from Georgia's policy of giving land to all qualified settlers was based on the need to repay the merchants and on the evaluation that the ceded lands were of better quality than other lands available in the colony.

Opening Virginia's West

The areas in which the various authorities in Virginia granted land were not always clearly separated. Tidewater lands of the Northern Neck were partly granted by Virginia before the proprietary was definitely established.[24] Several of Virginia's grants to pioneer promoters lay on Shenandoah Valley land also ultimately adjudged to belong to the Northern Neck. Wholesale grants and promises of unlocated acres entailed potential conflict among the different companies, promoters, and grantees.

Virginia's Northern Neck, as a privately held domain, was not subject to the efforts of the crown to spread landownership among as many settlers as possible. The great tract is widely considered to have been a channel by which large tidewater landholders extended their individual holdings and their collective dominion west into the Appalachian mountains.[25] Not least among these tidewater

---

[24]Land grant maps of Westmoreland County appear in David W. Eaton, *Historical Atlas of Westmoreland County, Virginia* (Richmond: Dietz Press, 1942). From these maps it is not always possible to distinguish colony grants from Northern Neck grants.

[25]James Blaine Gouger, III, "Agricultural Change in the Northern Neck of Virginia, 1700–1860" (Ph.D. diss., University of Florida, 1976), ix, 13, 15; Robert D. Mitchell, *Commercialism and Frontier: Perspectives on the Early Shenandoah Valley* (Charlottesville: Uni-

landholders were the Northern Neck proprietors' agents, who have been characterized as "their own best customers."[26] Fairfax County illustrates the agents' activity (fig. 7.5). Although Nicholas Spencer obtained his part of the Spencer-Washington property and William Fitzhugh his 20,000-acre tract of Ravensworth before they were agents, Fitzhugh's purchase was confirmed in 1694 by a new grant from his coagent, George Brent, who in turn received grants from Fitzhugh.[27] Robert Carter, agent from 1702 to 1712 and from 1722 to 1732, made fourteen grants to his son Robert Carter, Jr., beginning in 1707 when the son was three years old. "King" Carter was the largest Virginia property owner of his day except for the proprietor himself; his 30,000 acres in Fairfax embraced about a tenth of that county. The four agents who succeeded Carter were Lord Fairfax's relatives, all of them also land operators.

Carter extended his appropriations of large tracts westward across the Piedmont, and eventually gained strategic gaps in the Blue Ridge and 58,000 acres in the Shenandoah drainage.[28] By the time other Virginia lowlanders had made their own purchases, most of the Northern Neck Piedmont was blocked off by what Harrison described as "The Barrier of the Manors." Many of the manors were rented out on long-term leases for three lives,[29] but large parts remained unsettled and uncultivated wilderness, quitrents in arrears, and inaccessible to settlers.[30] Some tracts were being held as estates for the younger sons of tidewater owners.

When Fairfax moved to Virginia in 1735, becoming "probably the first owner of the Northern Neck ever to set foot there,"[31] he was shocked to find so much of the land tied up in these so-called manors. His response was to grant no more manors to others, but to stake out six for himself. His manor of Leeds, more than 100,000 acres, straddled the Blue Ridge, and reached into the Shenandoah Valley near Front Royal.[32] The much smaller manors of Greenway Court, where

versity of Virginia Press, 1977), 31; and "Content and Context: Tidewater Characteristics in the Early Shenandoah Valley," *Maryland Historian* 5 (1974): 79–92.

[26]Harrison, *Virginia Land Grants*, 88–90.

[27]Beth Mitchell, 168–69; Richard Beale Davis, ed., *William Fitzhugh and His Chesapeake World* (Chapel Hill: University of North Carolina Press for Virginia Historical Society, 1963), 44–45.

[28]Harrison, *Landmarks*, 239–45.

[29]Ibid., 247.

[30]Robert D. Mitchell, *Commercialism and Frontier*, 31.

[31]Freeman, 1: 502.

[32]Harrison, *Landmarks*, 246; Josiah Dickinson, *The Fairfax Proprietary* (Front Royal, Va.: Warren Press, 1959), caption to map.

Fairfax lived for thirty years, and Gooney Run lay nearby in the valley. On these manors lived more than 600 tenant families. Fairfax offered ninety-nine-year leases to squatters he found settled there, and charged new settlers ten shillings per 100 acres in rent.[33] The boundaries between parcels shifted frequently as tenants took and relinquished leases.[34] The final outcome after the Revolution and Fairfax's death in 1781 was the assumption by Virginia of the Northern Neck's unappropriated lands, which proved to be limited in area, and the sale of the manors by Fairfax's heirs to a syndicate in which John Marshall and the ubiquitous Robert Morris were involved.[35]

Virginia had embarked on a program of large grants to individual promoters beginning about 1730. Most of these grants required that the promoter settle a family within two years for each 1,000 acres in the grant. In this manner the Virginia Council passed to the promoters the problems of settling remote lands that were threatened by French forces to the west.

Most of these promotional grants were in the Appalachian Valley portion of western Virginia. Two prominent grants on colony land of the upper Shenandoah were the "Manor of Beverley," 118,000 acres granted to William Beverley in Augusta County,[36] and 92,000 acres granted Benjamin Borden adjoining Beverley's tract on the south in Rockbridge County.[37] At the southern end of the valley, beyond the Shenandoah drainage, 120,000 acres were granted a group headed by James Patton, who had recruited Irish settlers for Beverley.[38] Seaward of the valley, William Byrd II had received 105,000 acres along the Dan River for his direction of the survey of the Virginia–North Carolina boundary (he also bought 20,000 acres in North Carolina from that colony's participants in the survey).[39]

Virginia grants on Northern Neck land of the lower Shenandoah Valley included 40,000 acres to John and Isaac Van Meter, who sold their land to Jost Hite; 100,000 acres to Alexander Ross and Morgan

[33]Reeder, 79.

[34]Dickinson, caption to map.

[35]Marshall Harris, 91; William Couper, *History of the Shenandoah Valley*, 3 vols. (New York: Lewis Historical Publishing Co., 1952), 1: 421–29.

[36]Mitchell, *Commercialism and Frontier*, 31; Couper 1: 266–67.

[37]Mitchell, *Commercialism and Frontier*, 31.

[38]Reeder, 81; Thomas Perkins Abernethy, *Western Lands and the American Revolution* (New York: A. Appleton Century, 1937), 4–5.

[39]Richard L. Morton, *Colonial Virginia*, 2 vols. (Chapel Hill: University of North Carolina Press, 1960), 2: 568.

Bryan;[40] and, apparently, additional land to Benjamin Borden.[41] The people to whom these promoters sold land came largely from Pennsylvania and other middle colonies, as did some of the promoters themselves. The promoters' sales put land directly in the hands of pioneer farmers, in contrast with many Northern Neck sales to tidewater planters. As with some land sold by the colony, the small farmers were often paying the higher unit price.[42] Most of the lower Shenandoah land sold by promoters was surveyed in 1734 and 1735, as incoming settlers picked out the land they wanted.

Lord Fairfax's arrival brought the dispute over land titles into the open, and initiated the long process of settling the bounds of the Northern Neck. Meanwhile Fairfax offered to confirm the promoters' sales provided (1) the usual fees be paid for titles, (2) Fairfax receive the quitrents, and (3) the lands be surveyed in accordance with existing laws, or be resurveyed to conform. Fairfax's terms were accepted by all promoters in the Northern Neck except Hite.[43]

One view of land division in the Shenandoah Valley is offered by land grant maps for the vicinity of Martinsburg in the eastern panhandle of present-day West Virginia (figs. 8.3, 8.4).[44] Of the early patents sold by the promoters, nearly half had generous frontage on Opequon Creek, the largest stream in the area. After Fairfax's claim was confirmed, settlers moved onto the rest of the broad valley floor, virtually filling it by 1774. Parcels usually had only four or five sides, stayed well within the length:width limit of 3:1, and often had one or more right angles. Early in the 1750s the first settlements reached North Mountain, the first prominent ridge of the Folded Appalachians, but the ridge itself was avoided until the 1790s,

---

[40]Voorhis, "Land Grant Policy," 162.

[41]Stuart E. Brown, Jr., *Virginia Baron: The Story of Thomas Sixth Lord Fairfax* (Berryville, Va.: Chesapeake Book Co., 1965), 72.

[42]Ibid., 73–77. The promoters, selling land at three pounds per 100 acres, six times the cost of land sold directly by either the colony or the Northern Neck, had to give the settlers easy terms of payment.

[43]Fairfax's case against Hite hinged heavily on charges of illegal surveys: (1) properties more than three times as long as broad, especially stringy parcels along streams, (2) excess acreages, (3) Hite's failure to settle the specified number of families. The first suit went in Fairfax's favor, but Hite's titles were finally established on appeal in 1786 after both principals and most of the settlers were dead.

[44]Land grant maps for Jefferson, Berkeley, and Morgan Counties result from the work of two historically minded surveyors in Martinsburg. Francis Silver assembled copies of the grants in the Berkeley County Surveyor's office, and Galtjo Geertsema put together the maps. The discussion is based on the land grants of two USGS quadrangles, Martinsburg and Tablers Station, 1:24,000, W. Va.

0 _____ 1 Mile

N

Fig. 8.3. Northern Neck grants in Great Valley, Berkeley County, W.Va. The long north-south lines near the center are boundaries of older (and larger) Virginia grants. Parcels here were relatively simple in shape. Late grants are elongated along an Appalachian ridge cutting across the northwest corner. The heavy lines represent early boundaries that are visible in the aerial photograph of figure 8.4. From land grant map of USGS Tablers Station quadrangle (south central) by Galtjo Geertsema.

Fig. 8.4. Same area as in figure 8.3. USGS, 1971.

when adjoining owners began to claim it, perhaps to secure its timber. Long narrow parcels along the mountain then cut a conspicuous swath abutted by the more compact holdings of the valley.

Late in the 1740s, the grants of western land began going to land companies. In 1748 the Ohio Company, dominated by prominent landholders of the Northern Neck tidewater, received a grant in the Pittsburgh area (then claimed by Virginia) on orders of the English crown.[45] The original 200,000 acres would be extended to 500,000 acres as soon as two hundred families were settled. The Ohio Company's affairs dragged on until 1821, but wars, legal technicalities, and the critical failure of official support in both Virginia and England

[45] Abernethy, *Western Lands,* 5–8.

meant that the company never gained a significant portion of its promised land.[46] Then another group that had bases in Albemarle County and the upper Shenandoah Valley, known as the Loyal Company, received a Virginia grant of 800,000 acres to the south, along the North Carolina border and reaching across the Blue Ridge into Kentucky.[47] The closely allied Greenbrier Company was then formed to market an earlier grant of 100,000 acres on the Greenbrier River between the other two grants.[48] There was plenty of land for all three, but there was no certainty that their claims would not conflict. The claims of James Patton and of the Loyal Company were sure to overlap; and the Virginia governor's promise in 1754 of 200,000 acres to soldiers who would fight the French in the interior greatly increased the chance that there would be further conflict.[49]

Although the Loyal Company, unburdened with requirements as to number of settlers, was originally given only four years in which to survey and pay for its land, its claims were pursued for more than a century. Land sales began in 1753 at three pounds per 100 acres plus certain fees and a charge of £3 2s. 6d. per survey. The war with the French and the reservation of Indian land interfered with sales, but the claim was revived indirectly by an order of the governor and council in 1773.[50] Most of the company's sales were to squatters.[51] Indeed, for a time it was able to select land simply because squatters were there, and to force them to pay the company price when the settlers had actually qualified for land at the lower preemption price.[52] The company sold about 200,000 acres to a thousand set-

---

[46]Ibid., 38, 90, 135, 224; Kenneth P. Bailey, *The Ohio Company of Virginia and the Westward Movement, 1748–1792* (Glendale, Calif.: Arthur H. Clarke Co., 1939), 31, 259–63; Alfred P. James, *The Ohio Company: Its Inner History* (Pittsburgh: University of Pittsburgh Press, 1959), 159–63, 170, 175–76, 179. The company tried to offset its failures in Pennsylvania with 1775 surveys in the heart of the Kentucky Bluegrass, but its surveyors were never properly deputized.

[47]Anne M. O'Hara, "The Loyal Land Company of Virginia" (M.A. thesis, Columbia University, ca. 1954), 1.

[48]Otis K. Rice, *The Allegheny Frontier: West Virginia Beginnings, 1730–1830* (Lexington: University of Kentucky Press, 1970), 30, 34–35.

[49]Abernethy, *Western Lands*, 70. The soldiers' claims, many of which were acquired by George Washington, were surveyed between the Great and Little Kanawha Rivers in 1769, avoiding the claims of the Loyal and Greenbrier Companies. Several other land companies, most based in the middle colonies, also claimed territory south of the Ohio River, but the land they expected failed to be granted.

[50]Abernethy, *Western Lands*, 90.

[51]O'Hara, 8–9.

[52]Abernethy, *Western Lands*, 90, 256.

tlers,[53] but payments dragged out long after the state of Virginia had taken over all remaining ungranted land. In 1818, the heirs of the original grantees incorporated, as "Successors of the Loyal Company," to pursue payment. The last lawsuit was settled in 1872.[54]

Few comparably large grants were made in other colonies. "Hamilton's Great Survey" of 1751, at 200,000 acres the largest speculative tract in colonial South Carolina, comprised four adjoining parcels, all square, except that two had sides on the Saluda River, largely in what is now Greenwood County in the western Piedmont.[55] Henry McCulloh, a London merchant,[56] and his associates acquired more than a million acres in North Carolina, by far the largest speculative acreage in that colony[57] (save, of course, the Granville District marked off a few years later). McCulloh was soon involved in an unambiguous conflict of interest when he secured appointment as royal commissioner for controlling revenues and grants of land in both Carolinas.[58] One of McCulloh's grants was in the Cape Fear area[59] for settling poor Protestant families to produce flax and hemp, but most of his lands were on the Piedmont, where the emphasis was on naval stores, potash, and furs. Most of his sales were in small tracts, originally planned to be 100 acres each. He and his agents were reported "Hawking it about . . . thrò all the back parts of the Province and . . . even to Boston."[60] Sizable parts of his grant were eventually returned both to the crown and to Lord Granville. In Maryland in the eighteenth century, speculators had become active in the western Piedmont and Great Valley, but mostly through acquiring warrants to numbers of small parcels rather than through large grants. They sometimes held enough warrants to block surveys for settlers until their own land had been picked out.[61]

[53]O'Hara, 14, 39; Abernethy, *Western Lands*, 90, 220.

[54]Daphne S. Gentry, *Virginia Land Office Inventory* (Richmond: Virginia State Library, 1976), xviii.

[55]Meriwether, 116, 125–26.

[56]John Cannon, "Henry McCulloch and Henry McCulloh," *William and Mary Quarterly*, ser. 3, 15 (1958): 71–73.

[57]Harry Roy Merrens, *Colonial North Carolina in the Eighteenth Century* (Chapel Hill: University of North Carolina Press, 1964), 26.

[58]Ackerman, 102–5; Sanders, ed., 4: 1083–86.

[59]Lee, 183.

[60]Sanders, ed., 4: 1083–86.

[61]Harley, 139; Carl Bridenbaugh, *Myths and Realities: Societies of the Colonial South* (Baton Rouge: Louisiana State University Press, 1952), 138–39. One of these speculators expressed the view that the lands beyond the mountains would be more quickly settled by giving land to pioneers free of quitrents than by large private grants; Charles Carroll,

Township Settlements

It was hardly coincidental that township settlement was revived simultaneously with the first settlement of Georgia and the first thrust of settlement under the royal government in South Carolina. The impetus for a new colony beyond the Savannah River had come largely from South Carolina. Twenty thousand acres was adopted as a standard township size in both colonies.

Georgia was the only Southern colony that began with a settlement laid out on a preconceived plan. Savannah, its first community, enjoyed a conventional tidewater site, but individual farms were largely assigned in the surveyed grid rather than lined up along the water in the fashion of earlier colonies. The settlement combined the paternalistic assumptions of compact settlement and the uniform fifty-acre farm. The unusual geometric plan of the city of Savannah has been the subject of much comment, speculation, and admiration.

Initially Savannah comprised six geometrically identical wards, each containing forty building lots 60 x 90 feet (about an eighth of an acre) and some land for public buildings centering on an open square. The arrangement was replicated as the city plat was extended. Outside the city were lands for a public garden or nursery, for private gardens and farms, and commons for grazing. The outlying lands were in grids oriented with the grid of the city (fig. 8.5).

Adjoining the city were the blocks of garden plots, probably four and seven-eighths acres each, as halves of squares divided diagonally. Next came the individual farm plots of forty-five acres, bringing each person's total to fifty. Blocks of garden and farmlands were matched with the wards and tithings of the city. Blocks of a dozen farms, arranged in a 3 x 4 pattern, included two public farms in the center of each block, resembling the public squares of the city surrounded by private lots in each tithing.[62] The orderly clustering of farms would aid in the mustering of their yeomen-militiamen in an emergency. The city squares may have been intended as assembly places for troops as well as refuges for residents of surrounding villages in need of protection.[63] The map shows also a fourth order of land division in the form of nearly square tracts of about 600 acres ly-

"Extracts from Account and Letter Books of Dr. Charles Carroll, of Annapolis," *Maryland Historical Magazine* 26 (1931): 55–56.

[62]Farris W. Cadle, *Georgia Land Surveying History and Law* (Athens: University of Georgia Press, 1991), 12.

[63]Orville Park, "The History of Georgia in the Eighteenth Century," *Report of the Thirty-Eighth Annual Session of the Georgia Bar Association* (1921), 156.

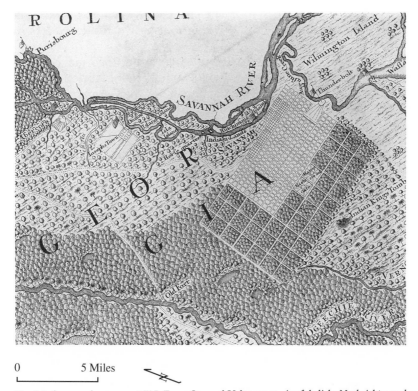

0   5 Miles

Fig. 8.5. Savannah area, ca. 1735. From Samuel Urlsperger, *Ausfuhrliche Nachricht von den Salzburgischen Emigranten*, 1740. Photograph provided by Library of Congress.

ing beyond the farms. A few of the squares were set aside as farm villages, notably Highgate, settled by French Swiss, and Hampstead, settled by German Swiss. Each was radially divided around a central circle into twelve farms.[64] The land patterns shown for other villages such as Thunderbolt, Joseph's Town, and Abercorn are very likely only schematic, although there was more radial division. No land had been granted at Joseph's Town at the time of the map, nor did the later 500-acre grants of record along the river there conform with the map.[65] Georgia settlers who came at their own expense and

[64]Charles C. Jones, Jr., *The Dead Towns of Georgia* (Savannah: Savannah Morning News Steam Printing House, 1878), 248; sketch maps provided by Shelby Myrick, Jr., Savannah, from Book B, Chatham County Surveyor's Office. Radially divided villages showed up earlier in the farm areas around Philadelphia, among French settlers in the St. Lawrence Valley, and on Long Island (Reps, 165, 195).

[65]Federal Writers' Project, Savannah Unit, "Mulberry Grove in Colonial Times," *Georgia Historical Quarterly* 23 (1939): 238–40.

were entitled to more than fifty acres had some freedom in choosing sites beyond the town lands, and might also own residence lots in town.[66]

Savannah was the principal model for other Georgia colonial towns.[67] Oglethorpe followed its block-and-square fabric in laying out Ebenezer, up the river from Savannah, for the German Salzburgers, and Darien, near the mouth of the Altamaha, for a group of Scottish Highlanders. Brunswick and Hardwick, later laid out by the royal government, continued the general plan, as, in lesser degree, did the later Puritan settlement of Sunbury and the Quaker settlement of Wrightsborough.

The clustering of outlots as an integral part of town settlement was continued in several of these cases. Frederica, a port south of Darien, and Augusta, a fall-line frontier center on the Savannah River, were early settlements that did not share the Savannah town pattern. The block of farmland in Ebenezer was divided into longlots,[68] and Frederica had mostly rectangular farm lots with one square cut into a dozen parallel longlots about the same size as the more compact rectangles.[69]

The original survey of gardens and farms around Savannah persisted as a frame for some of the later expansion of the city to the south and southeast. Some of the main roads of the suburban grid carry the orientation of the garden and farmlands (and of the city grid) more than four miles from the riverfront into the 600-acre squares, and one road follows one of the diagonal boundaries between garden plots.[70] A Chatham County real-estate map of 1875 showed many of the forty-five-acre farm plots still intact as well as several of the 600-acre squares in the first two rows beyond.[71]

Hampstead was shown divided radially into its twelve sectors (although it and Highgate had proven poor farmland and had lost most of their Swiss settlers by 1740). By 1906, subdivision had obliterated most of the original survey of Highgate and Hampstead, but

---

[66]Federal Writers' Project, "Plantation Development in Chatham County," *Georgia Historical Quarterly* 22 (1938): 310.

[67]Joan Niles Sears, *The First One Hundred Years of Town Planning in Georgia* (Atlanta: Cherokee Publishing Co., 1979), 34–52; Reps, 192, 195, 198.

[68]Charles W. Wilson, "The Salzburger Long-Lots of Colonial Georgia," mimeographed report on file in office of Georgia Surveyor-General, Atlanta.

[69]Reps, 194–95.

[70]Ibid., 187.

[71]By Charles Platen, on file in Georgia Surveyor-General Department.

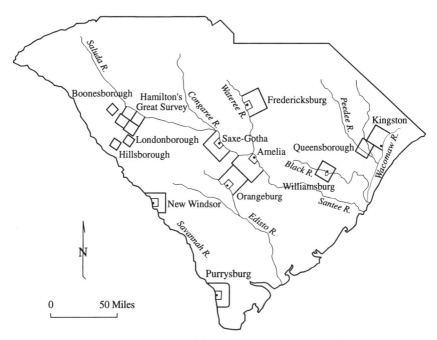

Fig. 8.6. Carolina townships of the 1730s and 1760s. The three townships of the later period are in the northwest near Hamilton's survey, which was not a township plan. The rest of the townships are from the earlier period. From William DeBrahm, "Map of South Carolina and a Part of Georgia," 1757 (copy in Georgia Surveyor-General Department); and maps in Meriwether, *The Expansion of South Carolina.*

the latter, containing a racetrack and crossed by three roads, was still identified.[72] Most of Hampstead was absorbed into the Hunter Air Force Base after 1930.[73]

South Carolina's township program, which was backed by the resources of an older colony, was a specific plan for expanding settlement beyond the limited area near Charleston where most South Carolinians were living in 1730 (fig. 8.6).[74] Governor Robert Johnson's revival of the proprietors' earlier preference for townships envisioned a group of eleven such settlements on major rivers in an irregular ring about eighty miles from Charleston. Some of the sites were

[72]Chatham County real-estate map by T. M. Chapman, on file in Georgia Surveyor-General Department.

[73]Communication from Ben P. Axson, Savannah, October 1, 1979.

[74]The best treatment of the township project is in Meriwether. See also Sherman, 107–17; Ackerman, 65–66.

to be at the inner edge of the Coastal Plain, others near the coast (two of the latter in what soon became Georgia). The townships were to be peopled by European Protestants, who might be recruited in groups.

In addition to opening up the interior, the townships were intended to increase the security of the colony by forming a band of communities around the coastal core and by increasing the ratio of the white to the black population. Custom duties on slave imports would provide the European settlers with provisions and tools as well as land. No other English colony executed so comprehensive a settlement plan or provided a subsidy to settlers comparable with the £60,000 that South Carolina put into the township plan over three decades.

The South Carolina townships were planned as compact rectangles of 20,000 acres bordering on the rivers. Each township was to focus on a town located centrally on the river, where each settler family would receive a house lot. Three hundred acres near the town would be reserved as a common. A band of land six miles wide and running around the three sides of the township not bordered by the river was reserved for expansion. Each township would become a parish, which could send two representatives to the Assembly when it had a hundred householders.

Purrysburg, the first of the townships settled, was developed under the leadership of Jean Pierre Purry, a Swiss who had already dealt with the proprietors on an earlier unfulfilled colonization plan. He picked a bluff site on the northeast side of the lower Savannah River where he was to bring 600 colonists on headright grants and receive 48,000 acres for himself. Several hundred Swiss and other Europeans were settled in the area, but only half that number were probably ever in the area at any one time. Much of the land, which the government insisted be distributed to colonists by lot, proved unsuitable for farming. A major but unsuccessful experiment with silk culture gave way to general farming. Several large grants, up to 2,000 acres, opened the way for plantations, which were worked first by servants, then by slaves. The colonists dispersed, and the town planned at its core never materialized. The proximity of Savannah, which was founded across the river almost simultaneously, thwarted Purrysburg's urban ambitions.[75] Purrysburg appears on the modern topographic map as a road junction with two cemeter-

[75]The best account is that of Henry A. M. Smith, "Purrysburgh," *South Carolina Historical and Genealogical Magazine* 10 (1909): 187–219.

ies.[76] Along the rural roads in the vicinity is a scattering of houses, many recently built, and a band of land that has been cleared of its forests.

As might be expected for a township initiated by a government plan and promoted by an entrepreneur, Purrysburg was surveyed in regular grids.[77] The square and rhomboidal blocks of the town were bisected along both axes into four lots each.[78] A glebe was laid out next to the town and common lands farther out. Surrounding the 800-acre townstead was a regular grid of more than 300 fifty-acre lots, each four times as long as wide, ready to be assigned headright by headright. Grants totaling about 40,000 acres were made to some 250 individuals. Purry himself received grants of nearly 20,000 acres, and his son made additional claims after Purry's death.[79]

Another township for which we have a land grant map is Amelia (fig. 8.7), on the southwest bank of the Congaree-Santee River thirty miles below Columbia, near the center of South Carolina and along the old Cherokee path connecting the upcountry with Charleston. Land in Amelia was taken up slowly. By 1740, about thirty-five surveys included 12,000 acres, many in the hands of nonresidents. Grants increased after 1749, the greatest part "evenly divided between German and English names."[80]

Although Amelia does not appear to have been laid out before settlement like Purrysburg, the land grant map (fig. 8.7) shows a surprising rectangularity. Many properties are squares and rectangles. At least three-quarters of the holdings have boundaries that run northeast-southwest and northwest-southeast. The surveys of the 1730s show this orientation in scattered parts of Amelia, and the pattern continues in later parcels surveyed on into the nineteenth century. The survey rectangularity is hardly evidence of strong central guidance in Amelia's growth, but it suggests that head surveyors or other authorities managed some control over the boundary orientation in the prolonged laying out of this township.

Amelia, like most of the other townships, soon lost any community coherence or tradition and developed a plantation economy.[81] The directional stamp the survey left on the land, however, can still be seen in field boundaries and roads (fig. 8.8).

[76]*Hardeeville*, USGS quadrangle, 1:24,000, South Carolina, Ga., 1962, photorev. 1979.
[77]Map of Purrysburg, n.d., MC5-14, in South Carolina Archives map collection.
[78]Map in Smith, "Purrysburgh," 187.
[79]Meriwether, 34.
[80]Ibid., 44–46, 51.
[81]Ibid.

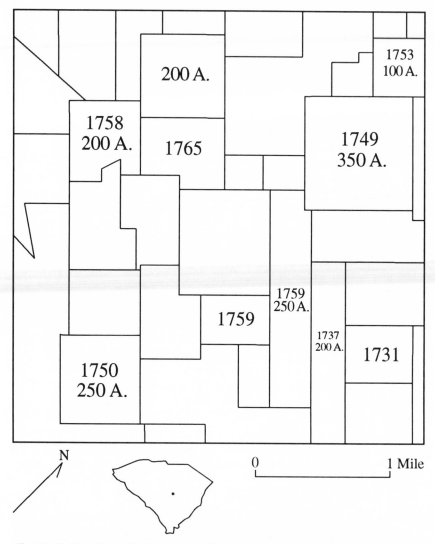

Fig. 8.7. Portion of Amelia Township, Calhoun County, S.C., from "A Map of Amelia Township: An Approximate Register of Original Grants, 1704-1785," compiled by Susan Smythe Bennett, n.d., on file in South Carolina State Archives. Ft. Motte quadrangle (northwest of center).

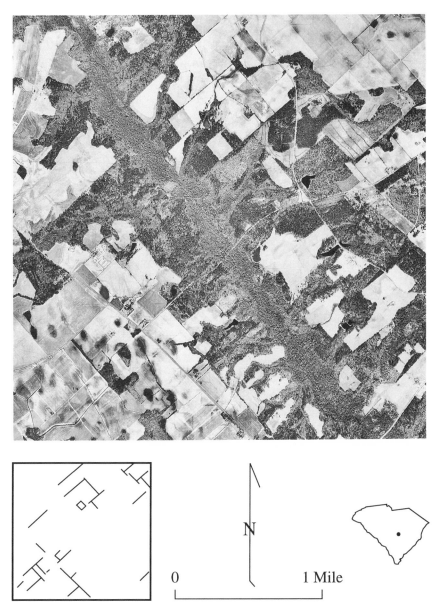

Fig. 8.8. Portion of Calhoun County, S.C., showing the imprint of the eighteenth-century survey of Amelia Township (main lines about 45° to cardinal directions). USDA, 1973. Ft. Motte and Cameron quadrangles (east).

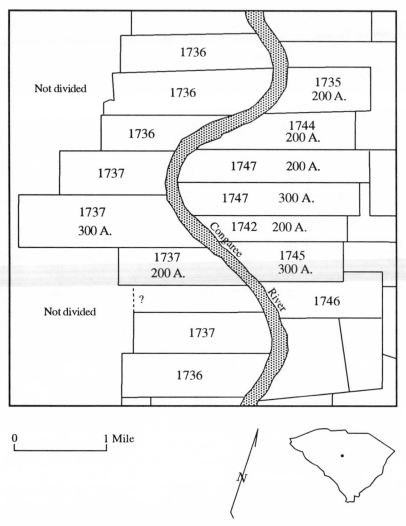

Fig. 8.9. Portion of Saxe-Gothe Township, Lexington County, S.C. The east side of the Congaree was not within the township, but offered a wider lowland (Meriwether, 54). Properties at a distance from the river were often square and astride streams. From Meriwether. Southwest Columbia (southeast) and Fort Jackson South quadrangles (southwest).

The land grants of Saxe-Gotha township, a few miles up the Congaree River from Amelia and near the Piedmont, have also been mapped (fig. 8.9). The floodplain strips approximating the practice of laying out the depth to equal four times the frontage[82] present one of the most consistent arrays of riverfront longlots I have found in the South Atlantic colonies. Saxe-Gotha was settled by English, Swiss, and German farmers, but this river lowland is now mostly forested and bears virtually no population today. A few present-day property lines and vegetation boundaries may line up with the old strips.

The land parcels of the South Carolina townships were typically consolidated into plantations, and their central towns usually failed to develop. An exception on both counts was Orangeburg, where the land remained in the hands of its German Swiss farmers, and the town did become the county seat.[83] Nonetheless the townships played an important role in bringing in immigrants who opened up the interior for settlement.

In the 1760s, while South Carolina was planting a few more townships on the Piedmont under a new settlement law, Georgia announced its own plan to encourage group settlement of Protestant families. Queensborough, a Scotch-Irish community near the present town of Louisville southwest of Augusta, and Wrightsborough, a Quaker town northwest of Augusta, were settled under the Georgia program.[84] Both towns were exposed to Indian attacks in their early days, and both suffered divided loyalties in the Revolution with some consequent land confiscation. Queensborough hardly survived the Revolution. Wrightsborough lost its last Quaker by 1803, and faded completely by 1840. Although land grant maps have not been published for these townships of the 1760s, both the Georgia townships contained platted village centers, and it is likely that the rural surveys had some of the regularity found in other townships.

A greater cadastral anomaly in the colonial South was a settlement of Huguenots, who, at the beginning of the eighteenth century, brought French longlots to the bastion of English settlement on the James River. Seven or eight hundred Huguenots sailed for Virginia in 1700 and 1701 under an arrangement with English and Virginia authorities to settle in Norfolk County near the Virginia-Carolina

[82]Ibid., 20.

[83]Ibid., 51.

[84]E. R. R. Green, "Queensborough Township: Scotch-Irish Emigration and the Expansion of Georgia, 1763–1776," *William and Mary Quarterly*, ser. 3, 17 (1960): 183–99; Alex M. Hitz, "The Wrightsborough Quaker Town and Township in Georgia," *Bulletin of Friends Historical Association* 46 (1957): 10–22.

border.[85] The designated area proved to be unattractive, for it was low and wet (it was located in or near the Dismal Swamp) and possibly beyond the limits of Virginia. William Byrd, one of the colony's most important landholders, promoted in its place a new site on the Piedmont along the south side of the James River some miles above the falls and the future site of Richmond. The Manakin Indians had only recently given up the area, and Byrd undoubtedly calculated that settlement there would enhance the value of some of his adjoining land.

The French, at least two or three hundred of whom settled in the area, received two contiguous tracts of 5,000 acres each, extending a total of ten miles along the river. The combined tract was bounded on the south by the "French Line," which lay roughly parallel to and, for much of its length, about a mile and a half from the river.[86] More than half the eighty-four lots surveyed for French settlers ran with parallel or nearly parallel sides from the James River to the French Line. About twenty-five additional lots with their narrow sides on the river were cut off from the French Line by interior lots or by butting against other longlots. Eleven lots had no frontage on the river.

The French originally planned that the lots to be assigned families should all be 133 acres, regardless of the family's size.[87] In actuality the lots ranged from twelve to 444 acres.[88] Only eleven were surveyed as 133 acres, and four others within ten acres of that figure. More than half the Huguenot settlers received less than 133 acres, and many considered their acreage inadequate. A dozen of the settlers patented more than one lot; one held a total of 1,298 acres in five lots.[89]

The longlots running from the river crossed its floodplain and climbed a slope onto the Piedmont upland 100 or 200 feet above. The lowland was subject to floods, and there appears to have been no effort to locate homes near the river in the style of longlot settlement in Louisiana or Quebec. Rather the original plan for settlement in one

---

[85]James L. Bugg, Jr., "The French Huguenot Frontier Settlement of Manakin Town," *Virginia Magazine of History and Biography* 61 (1953): 359–94.

[86]From maps accompanying Priscilla Harriss Cabell, *Turff and Twigg,* vol. 1, *The French Lands* (Richmond, Va.: Author, 1988).

[87]Bugg, 377. It may be significant that forty arpents, the standard depth of French longlots in Louisiana and in much of Quebec, is about a mile and a half, and that 133 acres is nearly the area of a 4 x 40-arpent strip.

[88]Cabell, 26–30.

[89]Ibid., 14.

or two villages suggested a township type of community. The principal village, Manakin Town, was laid out around a central square near the French Line. The French farmers, however, soon left the village to live on their own farms. The settlement succeeded agriculturally, and population grew after the uncertain early years. The French culture and economy were absorbed into Virginia ways, and gradually the concentration of French stock too disappeared through intermarriage and exchange of land with English Virginians.[90]

Several reminders of the early Huguenots do survive in the area today. A small Episcopal church is the direct descendant of the original parish church established at Manakin Town. Founded under the Anglican aegis in the absence of any other church organization in Virginia, the parish had French rectors during the colonial years. Most of the rural property in the western part of the tract is still in long strips from the river at least most of the way to the French Line (fig. 8.10). These include attractive residential estates with modern houses overlooking the James Valley (fig. 8.11). Subdivision by subdivision, however, the suburbs of Richmond are moving westward onto the French tract. One of these subdivisions, a real-estate firm, and several stores are using "Huguenot" in their names. Had the plan for village residence and an entirely French community been realized, the tract might well have functioned as a township within Virginia's county organization.

Another Southern community originally planned in the nature of a township, although larger and more complex, was Wachovia,

---

[90]One of the French farmers discovered a coal outcrop while hunting along a creek in the early years of the colony. William Byrd acquired this coal land in a 1704 patent for a parcel of land "laid out for the French refugees but not by any of them seated" with a headright for bringing seven persons into the colony. The parcel, bounded by two straight lines and the meanderings of a stream, did not conform with the French pattern. It may have been the site of the coal mine operated by William Byrd II several years later. Henrico County Patent Book 9: 612; William Byrd, *The Secret Diary of William Byrd of Westover, 1709–1712*, ed. Louis B. Wright and Marion Tinling (Richmond, Va.: Dietz Press, 1941), 61, 70, 351.

An intriguing footnote to the Anglicization of the French colony occurs in the land dealings of the brothers John, Benjamin, James, and William Harris, descendants of a 1611 Virginia settler. John Harris acquired two of the French parcels in 1730 and at least nine more in the period 1739–49. Benjamin obtained four in 1737 and 1738, five more in the 1740s, and the last of four more in 1768. James's fourteen were acquired between 1743 and 1771, and six of William's eight in 1745–7. Many of the parcels were passed on to their sons and grandsons, some of whom acquired new parcels even after 1800. At one time or another the Harris family held all or part of forty-one of the original French grants (see fig. 8.10) in addition to other property outside the French tract (Cabell, passim).

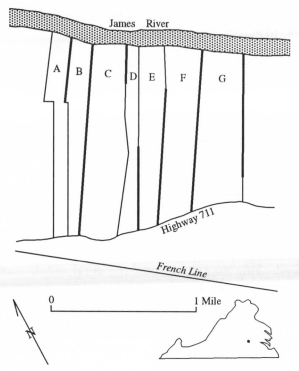

Fig. 8.10. Powhatan County, Va., tax lots in a portion of the French tract north of the highway, ca. 1940s. Most of the elongated lots do not now extend south of the highway to the French Line. The northern part of A was originally two lots; the disposal of the southern part of one of them probably explains the offset in the western boundary. C embraced four of the original lots, and E, F, and G comprised two each. All seven of the lots belonged to the Harris family at one time or another. The heavier lines present boundaries that are visible on the airphoto mosaic (Midlothian quadrangle orthophotoquad, 1974) as vegetation boundaries, roads, or fence rows (by decreasing order of frequency).

planted by Pennsylvania Moravians on the North Carolina Piedmont. The period of settlement in Wachovia was longer than that of most townships because a high price was set on lots in order to recover the cost of the tract.

Under an agreement with Lord Granville, a band of Moravians in 1752 crossed North Carolina seeking a square tract of 100,000 acres that would be bisected by a river, on which they planned to place their town at the center of the square.[91] Unable to find a single tract

[91]Notes on the Moravian expedition are given in the diary of Bishop August Gottlieb Spangenberg, published in Adelaide L. Fries et al., eds., *Records of the Moravians in*

Fig. 8.11. View north toward the James River from the southern edge of former Huguenot properties, 1977. Row crops and elongation of the field parallel the old longlots. The plat on the real-estate sign at the left probably embraces three or four of the original lots (507 acres).

of available land in the Granville proprietorship that would meet all their desires, they first chose several separate parcels, some west of the Blue Ridge, but found it difficult to mark off the rich lowlands from the uplands with the compass-oriented lines ordered by Granville.

On their return eastward, however, they managed to locate their requisite acreage on three adjoining parcels that together shaped a compact although not exactly square tract containing at least its share of good land.

The £500 purchase price (plus nearly as much for deeds and surveys) was raised by selling about half the land to a company of twenty-six European investors, each of whom would receive a 2,000-acre rectangle.[92] The bounds of the whole tract and of the investors'

North Carolina, 11 vols., Publications of the North Carolina Historical Commission (Raleigh: Edwards and Broughton Printing Co., 1922–69), 1: 30–36.

[92]Ibid., 66–69.

rectangles within it were all square with the cardinal directions.[93] Subdivision of both the investors' land and of the "Unity" land, however, was on a piecemeal basis of individual sales without restrictions on acreage.[94]

The Moravians had planned long, narrow lots as a strategy for assuring each owner water, wood, meadow, and probably a representative portion of good land and poor land. Actual knowledge of the land, however, indicated that lots "more nearly square" would accomplish the same ends.[95] Two villages and the town of Salem were assigned surrounding land for outlots distinguished from the other rural holdings.[96] The Moravian territory was marked off as a separate parish by the colony.[97]

The foregoing cases of townships and other group settlements in the South exhibit a variety of relatively regular land division patterns. Such regularity is to be expected in compact communities organized by leaders who were often on the spot. The communities have long since been absorbed into the general structure of the population and civil divisions common to their regions, but their land patterns often survive as conspicuous anomalies in the surrounding fabric of irregularity.

[93]Ibid., maps, opp. 310, 364; 2: opp. 616; 3: opp. 1342. The colony of North Carolina had established a policy as early as 1715 that land grants should be laid out as rectangles oriented with the compass (Ford, 16, 26). Examination of a number of aerial photographs of Piedmont areas shows only a little evidence of the cardinal directions in the present landscape.

[94]Fries et al., eds., 2: 598.

[95]Ibid., 540–41. Merrens (211, n. 23), suggests that high stream densities on the Piedmont obviated the need for shaping properties to share water access.

[96]Fries et al., eds., 1: 433; Bridenbaugh, *Myths and Realities*, 151.

[97]Adelaide L. Fries and J. Edwin Hendricks, eds., Stuart Thurman Wright, comp., *Forsyth: The History of a County on the March* (1949; rev. ed., Chapel Hill: University of North Carolina Press, 1976), 16–17.

9

Farms and Plantations in the Colonial South

Property Sizes

THIS SECTION will use statistics on sizes of land parcels to compare different areas and periods as a summary of the foregoing discussion. Parcel size distribution data and comments on the sources and uses of the data are given in Appendix C.

Most of the grants in the colonial South were in multiples of fifty acres,[1] and the median size of grants in most localities fell between 100 and 400 acres. The median size for all data in the colonial South was about 200 acres. It was unusual for more than 10 percent of any population of grants to be larger than 1,000 acres. In short, the preponderance of grants were in the sizes to be expected for family farms. Even many larger than average farms, such as those of 400 or 500 acres, represented simply the grantee's hope to provide family farms for his children or grandchildren out of the abundance of American land.[2] Some larger grants were also issued expressly for subdivision into family farms.

As a very general rule, frontier land grants in a given locality were larger than grants made after the land was partly taken up. In Frederick County, Maryland, for example, the average size of grants before 1700 was 750 acres; the figure dropped in each succeeding

---

[1] A notable exception occurred in Carolina, where 640 acres was specified in 1709 as the maximum grant to be issued by the governor (Sanders, ed., 1: 346). A spate of such grants began in South Carolina late in 1709 and continued at least during the two ensuing years (Salley, 652–72), but they were not used in South Carolina long. They appeared in North Carolina about the same time (Sanders, ed., 1: 346) or earlier (Ford, 44), and continued to play an important role there and in what is now Tennessee.

[2] Langston.

decade through the 1740s, when it was only 150 acres.[3] An increase to 285 acres for the next quarter century may be explained by settlement on new frontiers in the mountains in the western part of the county.

The earliest records of property sizes show variety among the colonies. We have seen that most holdings in Virginia in 1625 were small farms in spite of some larger grants of particular plantations. In Maryland's first years, most of the warrants issued authorized the survey of a thousand acres or a multiple of that size.[4] By 1642, sixteen private manors had been surveyed, but not more than ten of the forty-one landowners of that year actually held as much as 1,000 acres.[5] Just over half of those landowners held 125 acres or less. Even so, Maryland's landownership reflected the aristocratic dominance planned there by Baltimore in a degree not found in other Southern colonies at similar stages. The early land warrants in South Carolina showed much less evidence of that colony's seigniorial plan. The median South Carolina grant in 1672 ran 150 acres, with only 6 percent as large as 1,000 acres. North Carolina's early grants in the Albemarle area followed Virginia patterns of small farms. Georgia's peculiar philanthropic land policies resulted in a unique bimodal distribution of property sizes with most of the grants either fifty acres for charity settlers or 500 acres for colonists with servants.

In Virginia the average patent size increased during the seventeenth century from about 400 acres in the 1630s to a peak of 890 acres between 1666 and 1679; the average between 1650 and 1700 was 674 acres.[6] Headrights were evidently being aggregated by importing numbers of servants, by purchase, or by frauds. By 1704, however, the rent rolls of Virginia counties gave an average holding not much above 400 acres with a median of only 200.[7] Large plantations had not been very successful in Virginia during the seventeenth century; the larger tracts had often been broken up into smaller farms as the 1704 rent rolls indicate.[8] During the ensuing century, however, the large plantation with slave labor used land more profitably.[9]

[3]Harley, 258.

[4]"First Land Grants in Maryland: A Note on All the Warrants for the Granting of Land in Maryland," *Maryland Historical Magazine* 3 (1908): 158–69.

[5]Russell R. Menard, "Economy and Society in Early Maryland" (Ph.D. diss., University of Iowa, 1965), 68, 83.

[6]Bruce, 1: 527–32.

[7]Thomas J. Wertenbaker, *The Planters of Colonial Virginia* (Princeton: Princeton University Press, 1922), 183–247.

[8]Ibid., 44–59

[9]Ibid., 155–56.

Favored property sizes in Maryland seem to have paralleled those in Virginia. Following the original manor grants, immigration of servants and small farmers soon transformed the colony into a land of smallholders.[10] From studies of grants and sales between 1663 and 1700, V. J. Wykoff discerned a tendency for properties of more than 450 acres to break up and parcels under fifty acres to be consolidated.[11] Between 1690 and 1699 three-fourths of properties sold and two-thirds of those granted were between fifty and 249 acres. In All Hallows Parish the median holding declined from 300 acres in 1675, to 176 in 1707, then rose to 204 in 1783.[12]

Eighteenth-century land acquisitions on the Virginia Piedmont reflected the newly generous practices following Spotswood's reform attempts. The most common patent, and possibly the median, was for the 400 acres that did not require special approval. The average in the Southside (south of the James) between 1703 and 1753 was probably between 500 and 600 acres. More than 40 percent of the new land patented was in parcels smaller than 405 acres, and more than 60 percent in parcels smaller than 1,001 acres.[13] Very large grants were concentrated to the north of the James. In all, the Piedmont grants probably were not very different from the earlier grants of the tidewater. Contrary to popular belief, however, the tidewater counties in the mid–1700s probably had a greater portion of land in smallholdings (as under 200 acres) than the Piedmont and Great Valley counties.[14]

Comparison between Virginia and Northern Neck grant sizes is difficult, for the data are spotty. Available lists of parcel acreages, however, do not support the frequent statements of monopoly of the Northern Neck by large estates.[15] The distribution of Northern Neck

---

[10]Menard, 241.

[11]V. J. Wykoff, "The Sizes of Plantations in Seventeenth-Century Maryland," *Maryland Historical Magazine* 32 (1937): 331–39.

[12]Earle, 204–5.

[13]Nicholls, 80–82.

[14]Brown and Brown, 12–15. The data Brown and Brown present in support of the statement come from both Northern Neck and colony grant areas. Bridenbaugh, *Myths and Realities*, 139, reports 300 to 400 acres as the land taken up by the average settler in the Great Valley.

[15]The acreage data come from Virginia State Archives' indexes to land patents of several counties both in the colony proper and the Northern Neck; colony rent rolls of 1704; documents in the Henry E. Huntington Library listing lands granted by Northern Neck agents in 1690–92 and 1713–14 as well as lists of landholdings in Frederick County in 1744 and Prince William County in 1762; land grant records in Berkeley County, W. Va.; land grant lists in Fairfax County.

grant sizes was comparable with that of Virginia grants. Large grants, which occurred on both Northern Neck and colony lands, may have differed more in intent than in size or number. Many colony grants went to speculators ready to sell parcels to farmers, sometimes on the explicit condition of their doing so. The Neck grants were more often retained as "manors," either farmed out on leases or left vacant because their wealthy owners held them for heirs, while farmers preferred to settle where they could own land.[16]

Large grants played a lesser role in the Carolinas and Georgia during the last decades of the colonial period. Both Carolinas had a spate of large grants during the 1730s as they worked out the old proprietary patents.[17] In South Carolina these brought the average grant up to 627 acres during the years 1733–39.[18] During the period 1735–39, the average in the townships was 361 acres,[19] a figure compounded of more modest grants to the immigrants and grants to tidewater planters that often ran 500 acres and occasionally 1,000.[20] In the Piedmont generally, however, the role of planters played a smaller part than it had earlier on the lowlands.[21] A sampling of all South Carolina grants in the years 1745–70 gave a lower average of 232 acres,[22] a figure consonant with the median of about 150 acres in the vicinity of today's Sumter National Forest.

North Carolina was especially noted as a land of small farms, although the 640-acre grant was common in Granville's northern District. In the colony lands to the south, most grants were smaller, 640 acres being the legal maximum.[23] A sample of North Carolina grants made between 1768 and 1773 in what is now South Carolina[24] shows parcels running only slightly larger than the contemporary South Carolina grants and may be indicative of North Carolina grants generally.

Parcels granted in Georgia under royal rule between 1755 and 1775, with median values of 200 to 250 acres, were appreciably larger than

[16]Harrison, *Landmarks,* 247–49.

[17]In Carolina proprietary orders to issue warrants were called patents, a term used elsewhere for the final stage of acquiring land from the crown.

[18]Ackerman, 98.

[19]Ibid.

[20]Meriwether, 50–51, 81, 86–87, 109.

[21]Ibid., 257–61.

[22]Ackerman, 114.

[23]Bridenbaugh, *Myths and Realities,* 139.

[24]Brent Holcomb, *North Carolina Land Grants in South Carolina,* vol. 1, *Tryon County, 1768–1773* (Clinton, S.C.: Author, 1975).

grants in South Carolina at the same time or in Georgia earlier under the trustees. Headrights in both colonies were 100 acres for the family head and fifty acres for others after 1755. By this time much of South Carolina settlement was on the Piedmont, and the farmers coming there were less likely to have servants.

Over the whole period, large grants were probably dealt out more frequently in Virginia than in the other colonies. In given areas, grants tended to be smaller as open land became scarcer. Small farms were favored in interior areas settled by migrants from Pennsylvania in the eighteenth century. Plantations, most frequent in the tidewater area, were often aggregated from smaller holdings.

Plantations

The cadastral background of the traditional Southern plantation[25] has not been the subject of a broad investigation, although the cadastral histories of many individual plantations have been worked out. Plantation estates can have been (1) created in original land grants, (2) split off by subdivision of still larger tracts such as baronies or particular plantations, or (3) aggregated by purchase of smaller tracts. Plantations that had long lives were likely to have undergone occasional changes in their land bases, making their cadastral histories complex. The practice of *entailing*[26] estates was common in the colonies, and served to hold many plantations together. The rigidity of entail was modified in some colonies, and entails were abolished after the Revolution.

The cadastral histories of three plantations are presented here as examples. Berkeley Hundred and Mt. Vernon in Virginia began as large holdings and went through periods of growth and decline. The third estate, Whitehall in Georgia, really had no core of plantation size and quality, but was put together from somewhat smaller holdings.

Berkeley Hundred was a well-known plantation on the James River that had its origin as a particular plantation of 8,000 acres in 1619. Its original staff of some ninety workers was depleted by the high death rate prevalent in Virginia, especially the massacre of

---

[25]The traditional plantation is defined here as a large farm producing commercial crops with slave labor.

[26]The legal status of an estate requiring that it remain intact and normally be inherited by male primogeniture.

1622, and the expiration of the servants' terms.[27] By 1636 the estate had been sold to a group of London merchants. It was again sold in 1691 to Benjamin Harrison, a merchant and planter in the process of increasing his holdings.[28] Harrison's six successive descendants of the same name were to live on the estate until the early 1840s. The first three of these Benjamin Harrisons built up their holdings of land. The third left the "six plantations that comprise Berkeley" to his eldest son, dividing eight separate plantations among four other sons in 1744. The family holdings shrank under the last four holders of Berkeley until the estate was taken over for debts. The youngest son of the fourth Benjamin Harrison, although inheriting a parcel within the original Berkeley Hundred bounds, took up an army career in the West, was elected President of the United States in a campaign that featured the rustic log cabin, and returned to the manor house where he was actually born to write his inaugural address. The headquarters of Berkeley Hundred, along with a portion of its land, survives today as a public exhibition of plantation days in Virginia as well as a working farm with access by road, by Harrison's Landing on the river, and by a landing strip for airplanes.[29]

Mt. Vernon, famous as George Washington's home, had its cadastral roots in the 5,000-acre grant to Nicholas Spencer and John Washington (figs. 7.5 and 9.1). In 1690, the holding was divided, the Washingtons receiving the eastern half. In 1738–39, the Spencers sold 256 acres[30] of their holding to the Washingtons, and in 1739 sold 2,153 acres in five parcels to other parties.[31] George Washington came to occupy the estate, by then known as Mt. Vernon, after the 1752 probating of the will of his half-brother Lawrence, made his home there, and entered on a calculated campaign of purchases of nearby property between 1757 and 1779 that increased the estate to more than 8,000 acres, including all the Spencers' original portion. In its heyday, Mt. Vernon comprised five separate operating farms and a large extent of forest.[32] But the plantation seems to have absorbed

[27]Craven, *The Southern Colonies*, 261–62.

[28]Material on Berkeley Hundred, unless otherwise indicated, is taken from Clifford Dowdey, *The Great Plantation* (New York: Rinehart and Co., 1957).

[29]*Westover*, Va., topographic map, 1:24,000, USGS, revised 1974.

[30]Two hundred acres of this purchase went to a relative not connected with the estate, were sold outside the family, and were purchased by George Washington in 1769.

[31]These land exchanges are identified in Mitchell, *Beginning with a White Oak*.

[32]The story of the estate is told in Paul Wilstach, *Mount Vernon* (Garden City, N.Y.: Doubleday, Page, and Co., 1916).

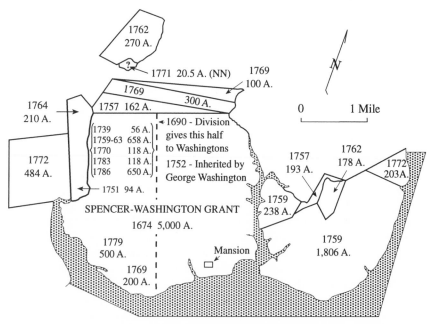

Fig. 9.1. The growth of Mt. Vernon. From map and text of Beth Mitchell, *Beginning at a White Oak* . . . ; and Freeman, *George Washington* 6: appendix VI-1. The two sources are not entirely complete or mutually consistent. The map represents what seemed the most likely matching of date and acres purchased with the parcel. The five bracketed purchases in the former Spencer Property are not individually locatable with the data available. A. = acres.

profits from other ventures rather than generating its own. Between the Revolution and Washington's death in 1799, he sold off much of his extensive real-estate holdings elsewhere, some of it dating from his days as a surveyor in the West, to support the lavish living style that had become customary at Mt. Vernon. The core with about 1,200 acres remained in the hands of Washingtons until 1858, when the house and central area were purchased as a public memorial.

Berkeley Hundred and Mt. Vernon exemplify the classical plantation sites in the coastal lowlands of Virginia, Maryland, and South Carolina. In Virginia, the plantation tradition was carried onto the Piedmont, especially in the Northern Neck, but not much in the southwest, for the movement of Pennsylvania frontiersmen onto the Piedmont in southwestern Virginia and the Carolinas made those areas into a mosaic of predominantly small farms. In North Carolina, plantations were common only in the Cape Fear area. In Georgia, large holdings had originally been forbidden. Most of the prime wet sites along the lower Savannah River were taken up quickly. The rice plantations that formed there after 1750 had to be assembled from smaller holdings.[33]

Whitehall Plantation, several miles upriver from Savannah, illustrates a contorted relation between original land divisions and their integration into a long-lived estate.[34] Only an aggressive entrepreneur could have seized the opportunities for putting this plantation together.

At least five immigrants with small farms and three with 500-acre farms settled in the 1730s near the meeting of the Savannah River with Pipemaker Creek, the future site of Whitehall. These early claims were often uncertain. Two of the farmers, unable to get their land surveyed because of a shortage of surveyors in early Georgia, gave up and moved to South Carolina rather than risk making improvements they might lose with the land. A third found that his farm was on a larger and earlier grant. One of the 500-acre tracts, claimed by both a settler and another resident of the colony, was not cleared before their respective heirs had sold the tract to new parties. A squatter on another 500-acre tract later established his claim by some years of adverse possession. A 100-acre parcel remained for many years as a reserve of the Georgia trustees.

Tracts changed hands through inheritance, sale, abandonment, default on payments, and marriage. One man came into control of 1,100 acres and had the whole confirmed by a new royal grant in 1758. After that holding was divided among his heirs, an adjoining owner added part of the tract to his own land held since the 1730s. With twenty-three slaves the new owner cultivated rice on the river lowlands, but began to sell off land before the Revolution. An additional slave-worked plantation had evolved across a channel in the river on Argyle Island (now east of the mainstream between two earlier courses).

Building Whitehall, a more impressive plantation, took more than another generation (fig. 9.2). This was done in the early nineteenth century by Thomas Gibbons, lawyer and statesman, who in 1769 inherited his father's 1759 grant of 1,000 acres of pine land three miles inland from the river properties mentioned above. Gib-

---

[33]A series of articles by the Federal Writers' Project, Savannah Unit, in *Georgia Historical Quarterly*, 22–27 (1938–43), deals with development of plantations in the Savannah area.

[34]Federal Writers' Project, Savannah Unit, "Whitehall Plantation," *Georgia Historical Quarterly* 25 (1941): 343–63; 26 (1942): 40–64, 128–55.

bons's property was one of several that had been confiscated by Georgia during the Revolution, but he managed to have it returned. By 1820, he had put together a thriving plantation uniting the pine and river land, including some of Argyle Island—perhaps ten parcels formerly belonging to more than forty different parties during the preceding eighty-five years. After Gibbons's death in 1826, his son added a few hundred more acres to bring the total near 4,000, as the plantation reached its most profitable days. As with many other plantations, the capital needed to create Whitehall was not generated by farming. Like one of its predecessors, however, it was built from an earlier family holding. Although Gibbons's original holding was taken over by the Savannah airport and Argyle Island by a National Wildlife Refuge in the 1930s, a surviving private estate continued to be identified as Whitehall past the middle of the twentieth century.

Summary: Southern Colonial Land Distribution

The Southern colonies' land distribution policies were flexible and liberal in several ways. Much of the land was distributed on the basis of headrights without charges other than fees to cover immediate costs, or by sale at relatively low prices. Land was distributed in a great range of parcel sizes from small family farms to estates of thousands of acres. Grantees normally chose their own parcels and designated the boundaries thereof. The colonists' freedom to choose led to a relatively rapid advance of pioneers into the interior frontiers in the eighteenth century. Although the liberal policies were often manipulated by insiders for their own benefit, land was still widely distributed among the population.

Headrights and sales particularly facilitated grants of widely varying size. Even the rigidly prescribed military bounties created holdings that ranged widely in acreage. Land parcels of acreage suitable for family farms predominated in actual numbers, but larger holdings occupied a significant part of the total land area in many parts of the region. Slave-worked plantations became the most characteristic large holdings in the eighteenth century. The so-called manors, whether or not they were manors in the feudal sense, operated as plantations, were divided into tenant farms, or were simply held for speculation. Large speculative tracts granted explicitly for subdivision into farms were most numerous in the western part of Virginia.

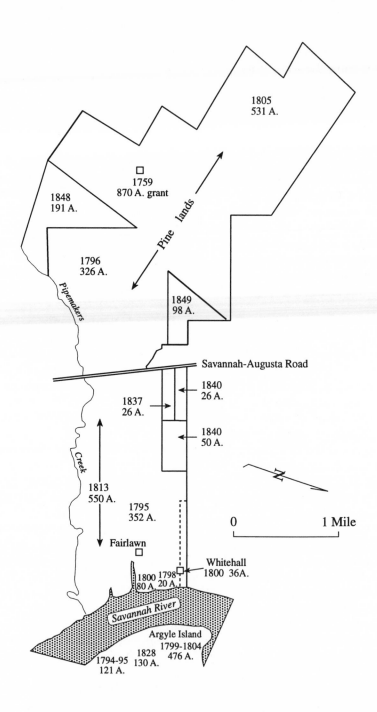

1805
531 A.

1759
870 A. grant

1848
191 A.

Pine lands

1796
326 A.

Pipemakers

1849
98 A.

Savannah-Augusta Road

1840
26 A.

1837
26 A.

1840
50 A.

Creek

1813
550 A.

1795
352 A.

N

0   1 Mile

Fairlawn

Whitehall
1800 36A.

1800   1798
80 A.   20 A.

Savannah River

Argyle Island
1799-1804
476 A.

1794-95   1828
121 A.   130 A.

Free choice of land led to irregular shapes of parcels over most of the area of the Southern colonies. Such irregular division often occurred even when owners of larger tracts sold their smaller parcels to their tenants. In mostly undeterminable ways, the surveyors must have influenced the geometry of many of the parcels they laid out. The rectangularity of survey in Amelia Township of South Carolina and the contorted shapes of parcels in Howard County, Maryland represent polar extremes of the surveyors' choices and skills. The most regular surveys in Southern colonies developed in townships or other group settlements and, here and there, from colonial rules regarding river frontage.

Cessions of Indian land, free choice of location, and promotional land grants all encouraged westward movement, while cheap land encouraged the migration of Pennsylvanians along the Great Valley to the Southern interior.[35] In 1780, Maryland, Virginia, and the Carolinas together contained more than half the settled territory and the most inland settlements of the thirteen states.[36]

[35]Bridenbaugh, *Myths and Realities*, 122.

[36]Settled area as measured by appearance on the maps of Herman Friis at a scale of 1:12,500,000. Settlement was more dense in the middle and northern states. The total amounts of land granted are not easily compared.

Fig. 9.2 (*facing page*). The Growth of Whitehall plantation from the original 1759 grant of pineland, actually only 870 of the 1,000 acres of the entitlement. The pineland was of some use for feeding Gibbons's sawmill, but his son and grandson eventually connected it to more valuable rice land near the river and on Argyle Island . Whitehall absorbed at least two waterfront longlots, but did not have such an origin itself. The open squares identify residence centers. From Federal Writers' Project, "Whitehall Plantation."

10

The National Period

New Land Policies

THE SUCCESS of the Revolution gave the colonies—which were now states—control of their public land, free from the policies of an overseas government. The new federal government had no jurisdiction over the unassigned lands that remained as parts of the original states or over the lands that would become Kentucky, Vermont, Tennessee, Maine, and, later, West Virginia.[1]

The land policies of the original states, retaining much colonial practice, changed in three main directions: (1) further reliance on selling land rather than headrights; (2) preemption practices favoring settlers who were already in possession of land; and (3) land bounties for Revolutionary soldiers.

Land was a source of revenue the states were not inclined to forego. Headrights, which had been available until 1774 in all the Southern colonies but Maryland, were terminated in all the other original states except for Georgia. The prices put on the sale of land were not high, however. Virginia's initial price of forty pounds in inflated currency per 100 acres was probably not very different from the colonial price of ten shillings plus quitrents.[2] Virginia land was offered for sale in whatever quantities the purchaser wished, a policy without basic change until 1950. Six hundred forty acres was the limit for purchasers in South Carolina, where the price was ten dollars per 100 acres.[3] In North Carolina a family head could buy 640 acres plus 100 acres for his wife and each child at two and a half pounds per

---

[1] One portion of western Kentucky and Tennessee became federal land, as will be explained later.

[2] Abernethy, *Western Lands,* 225.

[3] *Land Grant Maps,* foreword.

185

100 acres; additional land was twice as much.[4] Georgia's new headright, no longer linked to immigration, was 200 acres to any family head who had previously received no headright grant.[5] Additional land, up to 800 more acres, but not exceeding fifty acres per family member, could be purchased at a graduated rate of a shilling for the first hundred acres up to four and a half shillings for the eighth 100 acres. Soon the entire family allowance was free for all who had not previously used their headrights.[6]

Virginia's preemption law of 1779 confirmed earlier promises of 400 acres each for bona fide settlers—with outright grants for those who had settled on the "western waters"[7] before 1778, and rights to purchase the land for those who had come later.[8] The first group received a further *preemption*[9] to buy an additional 1,000 acres of adjoining property. Maryland's legislature gave preemption rights to 323 families settled on lots surveyed as land bounties for soldiers.[10] North Carolina's preemption gave purchase rights of up to 640 acres to first settlers. In Georgia, preemption rights were extended to settlers who had been invited to migrate into the state by a proclamation of 1778 and had "sat down on pieces or parcels of vacant land."[11] All these particular preemption acts, however, were retrospective; they did not guarantee land in the future on the basis of occupation only.

Military bounties for service in the Revolution were offered by all the Southern states. The acreages offered were sensitive to the land at each state's disposal (table 10.1). North Carolina was the most generous with the ordinary soldier. Georgia, of the states with abundant land, was least generous with the officers. Maryland surveyed more than 4,000 military lots of fifty acres in its westernmost counties, much of it in grids of square and compact rectangular parcels to be allocated by lottery.[12] The other four states followed the cus-

[4]Lefler and Newsome, 291.

[5]Candler, comp., 19, pt. 2: 201–2.

[6]Ibid., 434–35.

[7]Land draining to the Mississippi River.

[8]Hening, ed., 10: 38–40; the new preemption laws helped implement colonial statutes of 1752 and 1754 designed to encourage settlement on the waters of the Mississippi system.

[9]Prior right, on the basis of settlement, to buy.

[10]Kilty, 343.

[11]Candler, comp., 19, pt. 2: 209–10.

[12]Marshall Harris, 264; *Map of Military Lots, Tracts, Escheats, &c.* in *Garrett County, Md. and Allegany County, Md.,* and similar map for Garrett County only, both on file in Maryland Hall of Records.

TABLE 10.1. Bounties for service in the Revolution: Acres offered, by rank and state

	Virginia	Maryland	N. Carolina	S. Carolina	Georgia
Private	100–300*	50	640	100	230–287.5
Captain	4,000	200	3,840	300	575–690
Brigadier-General	10,000	200?	12,000	850	1,955

Sources: Hening, ed., 10: 331, 375; Kilty, 343; Marshall Harris, 264; Connor, History of North Carolina, 1: 500; Land Grant Maps, foreword; Candler, comp., 19, pt. 2: 202; Hitz, "Georgia Bounty Land Grants," 339.
*Depending on enlisting and serving for duration of conflict.

tomary practice of letting the warrantees choose their own lands, but usually within specific reserves set aside for the bounties.

Virginia reserved the most land for bounties, for it not only had many soldiers and had promised them good land, but also had charter claims to vast western areas. First it set aside all the land between the Green and Tennessee Rivers from the Allegheny Mountains to the Ohio River except for a tract already granted.[13] For fear that this would not be enough, Virginia later reserved the tract in Ohio between the Little Miami and Scioto Rivers.

North Carolina reserved the major part of what is now middle Tennessee for its veterans, with a provision that soldiers could make their claims elsewhere if the reservation did not contain enough land fit for cultivation.[14] South Carolina's military reservation was very small, the area between the Tugaloo ("Togolo") and Keowee Rivers, approximately Oconee County, the westernmost in the state today.[15]

Georgia's soldiers and sailors could claim any land open to settlers, except that, in Franklin and Washington Counties, they would be limited to a special military reserve.[16] The most unusual feature of Georgia's bounty was its extension to civilians who had been loyal to the American cause, liberally defined to include any citizens who "cannot be convicted of plundering or distressing the country" during a period of about ten months from the passage of the law until the withdrawal of British troops from Georgia.[17] Twice as many civilians as fighting men made bounty claims in Georgia. Thus Georgia had two distinct ways of distributing free land to civilians.

[13]Hening, ed., 10: 159.
[14]Sanders, ed., 24: 483; 25: 4–6.
[15]Marshall Harris, 266.
[16]Act of March 2, 1784.
[17]Alex M. Hitz, "Georgia Bounty Land Grants," Georgia Historical Quarterly 38 (1954): 341; civilians qualifying were entitled to 250 acres.

Kentucky and Tennessee

Disorder and confusion marked the distribution of land in the western parts of Virginia and North Carolina that became Kentucky and Tennessee. General conditions contributing to such disorder included the remoteness from centers where policies were formulated and administered, the unsettled post-Revolutionary times themselves, and the later land fever that led pioneers in person, and speculators through "locators"[18] or simply on paper, far beyond the frontiers of continuous settlement. More specifically: squatting was common and sometimes covered by later grants of preemption; entries occurred on Indian lands years ahead of their actual cession; unlocated acreages promised to soldiers and speculators intensified an atmosphere of doubt and urgency; rustic speculators known as *outlyers* marked off and built on land, intending to sell it quickly and move on; the acceptance of actual surveys sometimes hinged on later rulings on whether the surveyors had proper credentials. Meanwhile interested parties, both with and without official positions, vied for legislation favorable to their schemes.

The grand strategy of westward expansion hinged on the changing "Indian Line," marking the western limit of English and later American, legal settlement, and on the claims of the great land companies. The minor strategy, equally important, depended on actual settlement and surveys of individual properties. The Indian boundary had been fixed along the divide limiting the Atlantic drainage by the British proclamation of 1763. Then at Fort Stanwix, five years later, the Six Nations (who scarcely controlled the area) ceded the lands south of the Ohio River. Shortly after that the Cherokees ceded lands in West Virginia and Kentucky as far west as the Kentucky River.

Among the pre-Revolutionary land companies, the Ohio, Loyal, and Greenbrier, all of Virginia origin, have already been identified. Competing interests in the middle colonies and in England sought land south of the Ohio River and west to the Kentucky River under the names of the Indiana Company and the Grand Ohio or Walpole Company, and its prospective colony, Vandalia. The Transylvania

---

[18]Neal O. Hammon, "Land Acquisition on the Kentucky Frontier," *Register of the Kentucky Historical Society* 78 (1980): 297–321. These advance men would pick out good property in return for as much as half the land acquired. For examples see Abernethy, *Western Lands,* 263; Abernethy, *From Frontier to Plantation in Tennessee* (University: University of Alabama Press, 1967) (originally published 1932), 53.

Company, with its base in North Carolina, claimed Kentucky west of the Kentucky River and some of Tennessee. The Indiana, Vandalia, and Transylvania schemes collapsed through their failure to obtain land grants (except for consolation grants by Virginia and North Carolina to the Transylvania interests).

Kentucky

In distributing its Kentucky land, Virginia recognized military bounties from both the French and Indian and Revolutionary Wars, preemption rights of early settlers, and sales by the Virginia colonial and state governments as well as those by land companies. Priority went to surveys previous to the land law of May 1779: first, surveys on military warrants properly filed before 1779, next, land of bona fide settlers (those who had made improvements and grown a crop of corn) before 1778, then land of outlyers who had made improvements, and finally other settlers during 1778 and early 1779. Later claims were given preference according to date of entry.[19]

Land surveys in Kentucky, made by several different parties, began in the summer of 1773 and continued during the following two summers.[20] Only deputies of the Fincastle County (Virginia) surveyor were properly accredited for this work. Claims based on the work of unauthorized surveyors representing speculative interests were mostly not recognized, but some surveys even in what was legally Indian country west of the Kentucky River were accepted. Pioneer settlers depended on preemption to establish their rights. The sites most sought during those early years were at the Falls of the Ohio River near Louisville and on both sides of the Kentucky River in the Bluegrass. Although Kentucky was temporarily abandoned by all settlers by the fall of 1774 because of Indian hostility, some of the surveys endured, particularly at the Falls and in the Bluegrass east of the Kentucky River.

Surveyors marking off a number of parcels under a single command could readily lay out grids, especially where the terrain was even and the woodland open.[21] Much of greater Louisville's street grid

---

[19]Hammon, 309–12.

[20]Ibid., passim.

[21]Hammon, "The Fincastle Surveyors in the Bluegrass, 1774," *Register of the Kentucky Historical Society* 70 (1972): 285; "The Fincastle Surveyors at the Falls of the Ohio," *Filson Club Historical Quarterly* 47 (1973): 20–21.

today is oriented with boundaries of the 1774 survey.[22] Three or four original grid lines bounding rectangular properties are still preserved in long, straight rural roads of the Lexington area.[23] The parcels in these 1774 surveys were mostly 1,000, 2,000, or 3,000 acres, laid out for men who had bought military warrants.[24] West of the Kentucky River, the pioneer James Harrod and his followers were laying out parcels of 400 and 1,000 acres in accordance with older settlement and preemption rights.[25]

A large portion of Kentucky, perhaps most of the good land, was distributed under policies established in Virginia before Kentucky became a state in 1792.[26] Although Jillson in *The Kentucky Land Grants*[27] identifies only 9,500 Virginia grants, their acreages ran large. Some of the speculative tracts counted several tens of thousands of acres, and the financier Robert Morris and his Philadelphia associates held rights to more than a million acres, mostly purchased from Virginia.[28] Many of an additional 9,000 grants, classified as "Old Kentucky Grants," were also based on Virginia warrants and surveys.

Much of the confusion in these early land claims stemmed from the fact that the claims or *entries*[29] were not necessarily fixed in their original locations. The office issuing warrants for surveys had no way of knowing what claims might overlap.[30] The warrants issued for surveys in some areas authorized more acreage than the areas contained. If an entry was vague about describing the location, the settler might be able to use it for a different parcel. A claimant losing his land to an older entry might then move to a location already covered by a later entry and assert priority there (illegally,

---

[22]Hammon, "Surveyors at the Falls," 25.

[23]Hammon, "Surveyors in the Bluegrass," 280–85.

[24]Ibid., 294; Abernethy, *Western Lands*, 103.

[25]Abernethy, *Western Lands*, 105. Harrod's town had thirty-one half-acre lots with ten-acre outlots for the settlers' subsistence. Cabins built by Harrod's men to secure nearby springs were assigned by lottery, and property lines were drawn midway between adjacent cabins. Hammon, "Land Acquisition," 301; Hammon, "Captain Harrod's Company, 1774: A Reappraisal," *Kentucky Historical Register* 72 (1974): 225.

[26]Abernethy, *Western Lands*, 305–6.

[27]Willard Rouse Jillson, *The Kentucky Land Grants* (Louisville, Ky.: Standard Printing Co., 1925); the different groups of grants are identified on pp. 3–12.

[28]Abernethy, *Western Lands*, 228, 263.

[29]In Kentucky, as in Tennessee, land claims often began with a crude survey called an entry, which was filed with an entry-taker, who then issued a warrant for an official survey (Abernethy, *From Frontier to Plantation*, 50).

[30]Hammon, "Land Acquisition," 312–16.

of course); however, such a claimant could legitimately use his entry to gain vacant land elsewhere.

Many disputes, naturally, went to the courts for settlement. Some courts handed down novel rulings on the shapes of claims.[31] One of these specified that when an entry identified only an improvement, such as a house, the parcel should form a square oriented with the cardinal points and having the improvement at the center. But by 1800, court rulings were accepting more of the older casualness and flexibility of indiscriminate location.

The 200,000 acres given by Virginia to Richard Henderson's Transylvania Company were laid out along the Ohio River just below the mouth of the Green in 1778, and comprise most of Henderson County, Kentucky, today.[32] Nearly twenty years passed before those holding shares in the partnership found it advantageous to divide the tract. The town of Henderson was laid out with 264 one-acre lots, wide streets, and an ample municipal park. The adjoining thirty-two ten-acre outlots covered scarcely more area. The rest of the tract was surveyed into farming lands of 400 to 2,250 acres, which were chosen by lot among the partners. The town lots were ordered sold or were donated to squatters who had settled nearby a few years before. The town lots and outlots were to be seated or planted in accordance with time-honored customs.

Beginning in 1797, Kentucky opened its remaining land on terms attractive to small farmers. More than 40,000 claims were made under these later laws, but the parcels were much smaller than before. The first law promised what were called "headright claims"[33] of 100–200 acres in the former military reserve south of Green River to any person over twenty-one with a family. A broader law of 1815 offered any vacant land, except that west of the Tennessee River, to anyone in Kentucky except aliens at twenty dollars per 100 acres. Then in 1835, Kentucky turned over all the remaining vacant land east of the Tennessee River to its counties, which subsequently issued nearly 70,000 grants.

Although the land west of the Tennessee was ceded by the Chickasaw Indians and became federal property in 1818, it was actually surveyed by the state of Kentucky into six-mile-square townships.

---

[31]Ibid., 317, 320.

[32]William Stewart Lester, *The Transylvania Colony* (Spencer, Ind.: Samuel R. Guard and Co., 1935), 275–81.

[33]"Headright," as a term in common rather than historical use, may never have been connected with immigration.

These were distributed almost entirely in quarter sections,[34] except for a few earlier grants.

The only other significant group of Kentucky land grants was made in Tennessee, beginning in 1825, in a strip six to ten miles wide between the state boundary and the parallel of 36°30' north where the boundary was supposed to have been run.

A great deal of rectangularity in Kentucky property lines, far surpassing that of any South Atlantic colony, somehow emerged from the confusion of overlapping surveys and claims.[35] The rectangularity was part of the more regular patterns shared with other frontier lands. The concurrent failure to control the staking out of claims, however, made Kentucky a paradise for lawyers.[36]

Tennessee

Lasting settlement in Tennessee began in 1769 with the colony on the Watauga River in the northeast. The settlement was made without the authorization of any colonial government, and its land was obtained by private Indian purchases six years later.[37] Settlement in the Nashville area on the Cumberland River was organized under the Transylvania Company following a land purchase in 1779. North Carolina, however, no more willing than Virginia to confirm Henderson's deals with the Indians, finally granted him only 200,000 acres in Carter's Valley among Appalachian ridges far to the east of Nashville.[38]

Other North Carolina land speculators soon found rich opportunities in Tennessee. They bought up the generous military bounties as well as confiscated Tory lands, although much of the latter eventually reverted to the original owners. They accumulated nearly three million acres through the 1783 "Land Grab Act" that offered land at

[34]Darrell Haug Davis, *The Geography of the Jackson Purchase* (Frankfort: Kentucky Geological Survey, 1923), 2–3.

[35]In addition to material already cited, sample land grant maps can be found in Joan E. Brookes-Smith, comp., *Master Index: Virginia Surveys and Grants, 1774–1791* (Frankfort: Kentucky Historical Society, 1976); and James Franklin Sutherland, *Some Original Land Grant Surveys along Green River in Lincoln and Casey Counties (1781–1836)* (Casey County, Ky.: Casey County Bicentennial Committee, 1975).

[36]Thomas D. Clark, *Kentucky: Land of Contrast* (New York: Harper and Row, 1968), 31.

[37]Robert E. Corlew, *Tennessee: A Short History* (Knoxville: University of Tennessee Press, 1981), 50; Abernethy, *From Frontier to Plantation*, 24.

[38]Abernethy, *From Frontier to Plantation*, 49–50.

ten pounds in depreciated currency per 100 acres. Entries under the law had to be filed at the land office at Hillsborough, North Carolina, 500 miles east of most of the good land. When the land office closed after seven months, few ordinary settlers had had time to mark out their distant land and file their claims at Hillsborough.[39] The speculators' agents, however, had not been held back by the encumbrances of subsistence farming. Another manifestation of land dealing was the new state of Franklin in eastern Tennessee and southwest Virginia. The interests of at least two groups of speculators and of many settlers frustrated in their efforts to get adequate farms were tangled in its brief history.[40]

The Nashville settlements were included in the fifty-mile strip across the northern part of middle Tennessee set aside for military claims. Few of the original settlers there had been able to afford the 640-acre preemptions of their farms, but a law of 1784 gave them free title to such vacant lands as they could still locate.[41]

North Carolina's western lands were finally ceded to Congress in 1790 with provisions that existing North Carolina land claims would be honored and that North Carolina would continue to issue grants to meet the seemingly endless claims of its soldiers.[42] Tennessee, admitted to statehood in 1796, opposed both North Carolina's continuing issuing of land titles and Congress's claim to the remaining public lands. Agreement, finally reached in 1806, gave to Congress the unclaimed lands west of the Tennessee River (still in Chickasaw hands) with an adjoining block on the southeast, and to Tennessee the administration of land titles and ownership of ungranted land outside the congressional land, but North Carolina soldiers were still guaranteed their bounties in cultivable land.[43] This last provision ultimately took eight million acres more than were in the military reserve, leaving Tennessee with little discretion in granting its own lands. The state was able to give squatters in certain areas preemption rights to 200 acres.[44] A sample of Tennessee grants from ensuing decades showed a median acreage of only fifty, with an average of about 140.[45]

[39]Ibid., 58.

[40]Ibid., 89–98.

[41]Harriette Simpson Arnow, *Seedtime on the Cumberland* (New York: Macmillan Co., 1960), 311–12, 328–35.

[42]Abernethy, *From Frontier to Plantation*, 112–13.

[43]Ibid., 184–87.

[44]Corlew, 157.

[45]Random sample from alphabetical file of grants in Tennessee State Archive.

When the congressional lands west of the Tennessee River were finally opened after the 1820 Chickasaw cession, they were surveyed into five-mile-square townships, and a new land rush ensued. Those whose land had been located by entries and surveys in the 1780s and squatters who could show warrants held their land without disturbance.[46] Then in poured agents choosing the best remaining land for holders of military warrants, mostly public officials and other prominent persons. The one Revolutionary soldier actually claiming land for himself so late was accorded the special privilege of having it surveyed with as many corners and offsets as he chose. Nearly half the congressional lands remained. In the absence of any marketing arrangement, these less desirable lands attracted large numbers of squatters. Only in 1841 were the squatters, championed in Congress by David Crockett, finally granted preemption rights.[47]

Tennessee ultimately gained control of the remaining Cherokee tracts of its southeastern areas, some 3,000 square miles. These were surveyed into townships and sections and sold at a progressively declining price as the favored lands were taken up.[48] Preemption rights in these last areas were limited to 160 acres.[49]

Kentucky and Tennessee had little opportunity to develop their own land distribution policies, bound as long as they were to control by their parent states. The general offering of land for sale was an old practice, but the allocation of so much land to veterans was new. Both practices lent themselves to formation of great speculative tracts, often by the officials who made and administered the laws. Squatting and preemptions played larger roles than before. The 400-acre claim introduced on the Virginia Piedmont before 1720 was extended as a preemption into Kentucky, more than the private soldier might claim on his military service. North Carolina's 640-acre claim became an important unit in Tennessee, alike for purchases, preemptions, and military bounties.

Rectangular surveys were made in the last Indian cessions in both Kentucky and Tennessee. Individual choice of land continued until the land was entirely taken up, whether or not it had been surveyed in advance. The declining price schedule in Tennessee's late land sales was a final adjustment to the "first come . . . " principle.

---

[46] Abernethy, *From Frontier To Plantation*, 257–58.

[47] Ibid., 260.

[48] Ibid., 257–58; Corlew, 157–58; *American State Papers: Class 8, Public Lands,* 8 vols. (Washington: Gales and Seaton, 1832–61), 5: 514–16.

[49] Abernethy, *From Frontier to Plantation*, 252–55.

Land Distribution under the State of Georgia

Georgia, like Virginia and North Carolina, had extensive wilderness lands west of its populated areas at the time that it became a state. Even after the separation in 1802 of what later became Alabama and Mississippi, the state of Georgia still had most of its cadastral history to write in its own fashion. By 1800, the Indian boundary lay along the Oconee River, leaving the western two-thirds of the state in Indian hands. East of the Oconee River headright laws remained in force until 1909 except in three counties where they had been declared inoperative during the latter half of the nineteenth century.[50] The reasons stated for suspending headrights there were that little, if any, land remained ungranted, and that records were missing and boundaries and names forgotten. Evidently land disputes were difficult enough to resolve without allowing new and merely adventurous claims to cloud property titles long accepted by custom.

Unusual changes in one Piedmont headrights survey are shown on figure 10.1. The land grant map (fig. 10.1A) is probably typical of its time in its exhibit of overlaps, gores (unclaimed slivers of property between grants), and rectangularity. The gores and overlaps of the original survey are small and simple in shape compared with some occurring elsewhere on the Georgia Piedmont.[51] The rectangularity represents an effort to conform with instructions that parcels, when possible, "be square or oblong, the length not to exceed double the width."[52] The recent cadastral map of the same area (fig. 10.1B), however, shows striking and unexpected changes: The fragmented parcels now bear little relation to the property lines of the 1786 survey, and the rectangularity has disappeared. The unusual sweep of a string of property lines across the southern part of the map marks the course of parallel highway and railroad, and raises a question as to which of the other changes may also be ascribed to the railroad. The virtual disappearance of the original property lines suggests some unusual wholesale consolidation, abandonment, or resurvey. One might imagine a latifundium of at least 6,000–7,000 acres compounded of all the parcels in the area of the map, then the building

---

[50]Laws of August 13, 1909; December 14, 1858; December 14, 1859; and February 26, 1877.

[51]Sam B. Hilliard, "Headright Grants and Surveying in Northeastern Georgia," *Geographical Review* 72 (1982): 423–24, 426.

[52]Gerald L. Holder, "The Eighteenth Century Landscape in Northeast Georgia," *Pioneer America* 13, no. 1 (March 1981): 41.

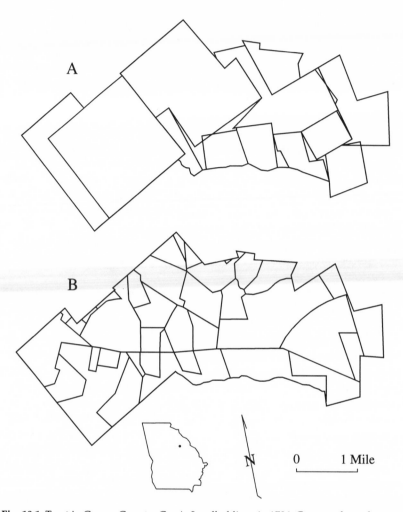

Fig. 10.1. Tract in Greene County, Ga. A. Landholdings in 1786. Gores and overlaps are evident, as are efforts to conform with the rule that surveys enclose squares. B. Same area, 1968. The transportation line (rail and highway) following the stream divide across the map is the most conspicuous feature of the new land division. From Holder, "Eighteenth Century Landscape." Union Point quadrangle (northeast).

of the Georgia Railroad about 1835,[53] stimulating resubdivision of the area. Or could the railroad itself, one of the earliest in the United States, have bought up a two-mile swath for its right-of-way and subsequent development?

[53] Arthur F. Raper, *Tenants of the Almighty* (New York: Macmillan Co., 1943), 33–35.

Another anomaly of the 1968 property lines is the presence of the curved boundary, in the eastern part of the tract, suggesting the arc of a circle. The only explanation of it that occurs to me may seem far-fetched, but is more likely in Georgia than it would be anywhere else. The center of the circular arc falls nearly two miles away near the hamlet (about six houses and two commercial buildings today) of Robinson on the railway. One wonders if the rail line puffed up Robinson ambitions to be a railhead or junction point and led the city fathers to incorporate and draw a circular boundary like the first incorporated towns at present in either direction on the rail line. Admittedly two miles or nearly so exceeds the ambitions of most towns with such corporation lines. If Robinson indeed had such a town boundary, it could have been a logical locus for a property line of somebody's parcel.

The meting out of land by headrights in the early 1790s could not keep pace with the great land grabs for parts of Georgia's tempting western territory stretching to the Mississippi River. In the massive Yazoo frauds of 1795, four private land companies bribed many Georgia legislators with shares of stock in order to purchase millions of acres for unduly small sums. When the nature of the transactions emerged, the land was taken back by the legislature, the records publicly burned, and a few innocent purchasers of lots compensated.[54]

Whereas the Yazoo frauds dealt with real land located far beyond the western frontier, the Pine Barrens frauds between 1789 and 1796 involved imaginary lands in the Georgia frontier counties themselves. The Georgia Surveyor-General's Office has on file several thousand plats, usually of 1,000 acres each, representing tracts sold mostly to Northern investors, tracts their inheritors have never been able to locate.

An illustrative file contains seventy plats, each labeled "1,000 acres pine land," in Washington County, east central Georgia, all purportedly surveyed for Richard Dawson by a single crew in four days during January of 1793. Each tract is in the shape of a square a mile and a quarter (100 chains) on a side. The seventy plats, numbered in boustrophedon sequence,[55] can be assembled in a compact grid, in which the streams form a coherent drainage system labeled

---

[54]Kenneth Coleman, "Political Development in a Frontier State," in *A History of Georgia*, ed. Kenneth Coleman (Athens: University of Georgia Press, 1977), 96–97, 101; S. G. McLendon, *History of the Public Domain of Georgia* (Atlanta: Foote and Davies Co., 1924), 104–6. The U.S. Supreme Court eventually ruled that Georgia could not revoke the sale, and Congress compensated the purchasers.

[55]Consecutive rows alternating in direction, in the manner in which an ox plows.

with the names of three tributaries of the Ogeechee and Ohoopee Rivers. Since three drainages meet at only one point, we should be able to locate the area on topographic maps. But much of the land on the Dawson plats drains southwestward, whereas the topographic maps show drainage to the south and southeast. Thus the survey does not seem to fit the land. An agent commissioned in 1900 to locate 20,000 acres of Pine Barrens lands for other owners failed to find them, and complained, "I could locate the same if I had the names of the streams that run through it or ... only two or three larger streams."[56] The sample survey cited did name the streams; their networks, however, did not conform with reality.

The grants of this exuberant period totaled more than three times the land area of the existing counties of Georgia, and in some counties more than ten times the county area.[57] Pennsylvania land speculator Robert Morris held nearly 500,000 acres in pineland claims, one contribution, perhaps, to his later bankruptcy.[58] Although the fraudulent grants all originated in the counties, they required the governor's signature in the face of the legal grant limit of 1,000 acres per person. Today the Surveyor General's Office in Atlanta contains an accessory of these frauds in the form of four old plat books with 1,000-acre squares printed on the pages. The "surveyor" needed only to fill in streams, bearings, witness trees, dates, and other such data. Some forms even had the surveyor's name printed on them.

The paper representing ownership of these bogus lands, most of it in the hands and vaults of people far from Georgia, developed histories of its own. Secondary transactions sufficient to develop long chains of title were recorded in Georgia courthouses.[59] An agent representing Philadelphia interests came to Georgia in the late 1830s to dispossess squatters allegedly occupying the owners' lands.[60] Some Georgia counties have 1882 quitclaim records from a bankruptcy trustee still settling Robert Morris's affairs.[61] But Georgia counties could claim the land for nonpayment of taxes, thus nullifying any obligation to produce the land,[62] and any identifiable squatters on that land were amply protected by adverse possession rights.[63]

[56]Quoted in McLendon, 176.
[57]Coleman, 106–7.
[58]McLendon, 166–67.
[59]Cadle, 106.
[60]Ibid., 104–5.
[61]Ibid., 103.
[62]Ibid., 98.
[63]Ibid., 106.

For land west of the Oconee, Georgia developed a new distribution system that departed radically from practices in any of the colonies. Presurveyed land lots were distributed by lottery to citizens residing in Georgia and registering for chances in the drawing. A lottery, prompted perhaps by the earlier land frauds, promised to be beyond the reach of bribes, speculation, or bogus surveys.

Several lotteries were held between 1804 and 1832 as successive new tracts became available for settlement.[64] Lottery lands were divided into square land districts (except that districts in the first lottery were rectangular), which in turn were divided into square lots for distribution to individual winners. The first districts and lots, near the center of Georgia, were oriented with the main rivers; later districts conformed with the cardinal directions. Land lots were most commonly 202.5 acres (forty-five chains on a side). The largest lots of 490 acres (seventy chains) were in poor areas of the mountains or Coastal Plain. The smallest lots of forty acres (twenty chains) were in the northwest part of the state where gold discoveries were anticipated. Other lots were 160 acres (forty chains) and 250 acres (fifty chains). These Georgia land lot surveys also reached south into a strip of land that was finally awarded to Florida.[65]

The Georgia lotteries were not entirely free of fraud. Ineligible winners were sometimes identified by informers who were rewarded by the state with half the land or its value. A commissioner of the lottery was convicted in 1832 of rigging the results to give five of his friends sites variously favored with mills, ferries, a courthouse, and a stream confluence.[66]

Land lot surveys were not as well monumented as the federal land survey, and discovery of the original boundaries is sometimes impossible today. There were cases in which surveyors had probably not actually been over the land and in which some winners could not even locate their property.

Land lots came easy and were not, on the whole, highly treasured. Relatively few winners actually settled on their lots, many of which were indeed poor in quality. Lots might be far from their winners' homes. If they were too distant to visit, the winners could examine the survey reports for evidence of what they had won. Many winners sold their lots, and some sold their chances even before the drawings.

---

[64]*Hall's Original County Map of Georgia* (Atlanta: Hall Bros., 1898).

[65]Burke G. Vanderhill and Frank A. Unger, "The Georgia-Florida Land Boundary," *West Georgia College Studies in the Social Sciences* 18 (1979): 59–73.

[66]*Journal of the Senate of the State of Georgia* (November and December) 1832.

If grant fees were not paid, lots reverted to the state. One recent sampling of 1805 lottery lots in southeastern Georgia showed no significant relation between physical qualities of the land and reversions. Strangely, however, reversions ran as high as 80 percent for people who lived within fifty miles of their lots, compared with considerably lower rates for those who lived farther away.[67] But another study in central Georgia showed a clear recognition of land quality in the lotteries of 1805 and 1807. Reversions were more than a third in the inner Coastal Plain (primarily lots on the sandy Tifton Upland), and less than 1 percent on the adjoining part of the Piedmont.[68]

The fates of land lots drawn in Morgan County on the Piedmont about 1806 measure the continuing cadastral change. In northeastern Morgan County less than a fifth of the lottery winners ever took up residence on their lots,[69] and by 1830 only three of 204 original families still held their full lots undivided. Through the 1820s most transfers of land were in whole lots of 202.5 acres. The earliest land exchanges tended to produce even larger holdings; after 1810, holdings decreased in size, but were increasing again after 1830. Such change, of course, never stops. In 1910 farms in this county averaged less than half the size of the original lots, but today they are nearly twice the original lot size,[70] and much of the county is in very large timber holdings. In the early 1970s only five or six properties in the county coincided exactly with original land lots, and some of those had once been part of a single larger holding.[71]

The lines of the land lot grid are still conspicuous on property maps of Georgia's lottery lands. On the relatively smooth parts of the Coastal Plain, field and clearing boundaries frequently run along or parallel to the land lot lines (fig. 10.2). On the rougher land of the Piedmont, field boundaries and roads more often reflect the terrain

[67]C. Frederick Payne, "A Geographic Analysis of Responses to the 1805 Lottery Lands in Wayne County, Georgia," 1970, manuscript on file in Georgia Surveyor-General Department.

[68]Paul Starrett, "Appraisal: The Creek Nation—Lands in Southern Georgia and Southeastern Alabama," before the Indian Claims Commission, Docket no. 21, n.d., on file in Georgia Surveyor-General Department.

[69]Steven Engerrand, "The Evolution of Landholding Patterns on the Georgia Piedmont, 1805–1830," *Southeastern Geographer* 15 (1975): 73–80.

[70]U.S. Agricultural Censuses. Rural property in Carroll, another Piedmont County, still averages little more than a third the size of the original land lots. John Fraser Hart, "Land Use Change in a Piedmont County," *Annals of the Association of American Geographers* 70 (1980): 498–500.

[71]Property map of Morgan County (Atlanta, Ga.: Land Data Corporation, 1973).

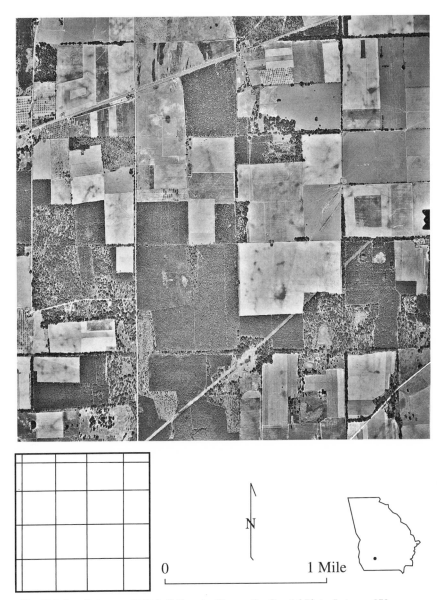

Fig. 10.2. Landlot area of Mitchell County, Ga., on the Coastal Plain. Lots are 250 acres, drawn in 1820. Land is mostly in cultivation. Local roads and fields conform with land lot boundary directions. Land lot squares are plainly visible (specified as 5/8 mi. on a side). USGS, 1968. Branchville quadrangle (center).

(fig. 10.3). Here aerial photographs give an impression of irregularity, for field boundaries are more conspicuous than property lines. The farmers seem not to recognize their acres as having a rectangular frame.

More surprisingly, perhaps because of shortcomings in the original surveys, land lots are often ignored in modern property descriptions. A sample of descriptions in Morgan County deeds showed that some relied on the original survey, whereas others ignored it. In Putnam County, a lawyer explained that only the electric utility company, which has extensive holdings, regularly has its land described in terms of the land lot system. Most deeds now identify property by the previous owner and the bounding neighbors. New property lines often follow roads.

The boundaries of some of Georgia's civil divisions do reflect the land systems. In the whole headrights section of Georgia east of the Oconee, there are probably not more than ten miles of county boundary that are square with the cardinal directions. However, original counties[72] laid out with the surveying of the lottery land districts had much of their bounds coincident with the land district and land lot lines. Perhaps half the boundaries of the present counties in the land lot area are square with the cardinal directions. The boundaries of the present smaller counties usually do not coincide with land district lines, but probably run along land lot lines. Some of the southern Georgia county lines that follow land lots feature strange small offsets, often less than a mile in extent, detouring around individual properties, for, during the middle half of the nineteenth century, Georgia made it very easy for border landholders to pick their county.[73] Their choices variously gained them a more accessible county seat, qualification for a county office, consolidation of property in a single county, lower taxes, or maintenance of personal contacts.

Georgia militia districts, which are county subdivisions, show boundaries similar to those of the counties—skew and often curving lines in the headrights area, and a major proportion of lines along cardinal directions in the land lot area. Census county divisions, established for the federal census, however, ignore the land survey in their quest for stable and recognizable boundaries. Depending on such

[72]Original counties signify the first counties laid out in any part of the state. Smaller counties were later split off from the original counties.

[73]Burke G. Vanderhill and Frank J. Unger, "Georgia's Crenelated County Boundaries," West Georgia College Studies in the Social Sciences 16 (1977): 59–72.

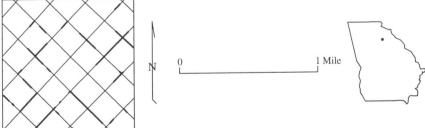

Fig. 10.3. Land lot area of Morgan County, Ga., on the Piedmont. Lots are 202.5 acres, oblique to cardinal directions, drawn in 1806. Roads and field boundaries reflect terrain more than land lot boundaries. USGS, 1971. Rutledge North quadrangle (center).

features as streams, roads, and railroads, they show abhorrence of any straight line (very short sections excepted) in both headrights and land lot areas.[74] Highways in Georgia show no respect for cardinal directions, but many minor roads of southwest Georgia do run along land lot lines.

The grids of the early nineteenth-century Georgia land lot surveys were projected on far grander scale than the original grids of small eighteenth-century holdings laid out around Savannah. Both systems were designed to put the land in the hands of the ordinary farmer: in the Savannah area a paternally guided system with hand-picked clients, in the landlots a blatant expression of wide-open expansionist democracy. Assignment of land by lottery was hardly less arbitrary or more random than the original assignments at Savannah. The fee simple tenure of the lottery lands led to an open market in land, contrasting with the tail male tenure of the Georgia trustees. The open market permitted a continuing cadastral adjustment that might or might not accord with the democratic assumptions of the system.

The Georgia land lotteries represented the most significant departure in the original Southern states from the free choice of land so long practiced and so strongly advocated. Georgia was the only Southern state to distribute much land free of cost (beyond surveying and filing fees) to people other than veterans. The survey and the lotteries provided for quick disposal of new lands as they were ceded by the Indians, and reduced the ambiguities and disputes that invariably accompanied indiscriminate location.

Summary: Land Distribution by the States

Following independence the Southern states mostly continued the division of land by indiscriminate location. Squatting and entering claims by marking them off in the field became more frequent ways of initiating land acquisition. Bounty rights for soldiers, Georgia's new headrights for all citizens, and Virginia's grants to settlers who were in the west before 1778 were the counterparts of the free land granted immigrants under colonial headrights. Except for Georgia, however, the general policy of the states was to sell their land.

---

[74]John L. Andriot, *Township Atlas of the United States* (McLean, Va.: Andriot Associates, 1979), 156–65.

The generous land policies ostensibly designed to make Western lands available to settlers also made it easy for speculators to aggregate huge acreages. The entrepreneurs then played the role of middlemen in actually distributing land to settlers. The great rush to distribute and settle the Western lands resulted also in confusion regarding property boundaries and titles.

Except for Maryland's military lands, the Southern states surveyed land in grids only after that pattern had been adopted by Congress in 1785. Beginning in 1804, Georgia applied its land lot surveys to new lands as fast as they were released by the Indians. Township surveys in Kentucky and Tennessee began only with the Chickasaw Cession of 1818. By then little unsettled land remained in those two states, which had theretofore been unable to exercise much discretion over their land division. Georgia, however, where early growth had been late and slow, had both the space and time for some of the most extensive regular surveys outside the federal system.

Officials involved in distributing land may have been more supportive of the transition from individual surveys to grids than were the pioneer recipients. Resistance to the transition, however, does not seem to have run very deep. As suitable tracts became available, they were surveyed into grids even when partly encumbered already by squatters and other claimants.

Part IV

The Middle Atlantic Region

THE MIDDLE Atlantic region (fig. 11.1) for our purpose comprises the present states of New York, Pennsylvania, New Jersey, and Delaware. The first European settlements in the area were established by the Dutch along the Hudson River, on the islands near its mouth, and on Delaware Bay. For a time during the mid-seventeenth century, Sweden was the controlling power on the west bank of the lower Delaware in what are now Delaware and Pennsylvania. In 1655 the Dutch took command of New Sweden, again uniting all the tidewater settlements of the Middle Atlantic region under a single European nation. Nine years later the region came under English control when New Amsterdam was captured by a fleet under the Duke of York. The areas east of the Delaware River were assigned to the duke as proprietor, and he extended his control over the settlements on the west bank of the Delaware also in the absence of any explicit disposition of them.

The unity of the Middle Atlantic colonies under the duke was short-lived. Even before the surrender of the Dutch, he had granted New Jersey to his friends, Lord John Berkeley and Sir George Carteret. In 1681, Pennsylvania was granted by King Charles II to William Penn, and the Duke of York turned Delaware over to Penn the following year. When the duke succeeded to the throne as James II in 1685, his remaining holding of New York became a royal colony. When New Jersey also became a royal colony in 1702, its land remained in the hands of the proprietors who had succeeded Berkeley and Carteret.

The dominant land division patterns of colonial Pennsylvania and Delaware were similar to those of the South. New Jersey's were

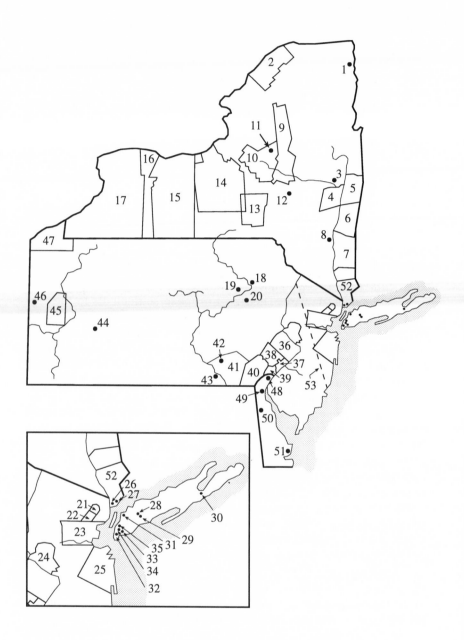

more diverse and resembled the South's somewhat less. New York's original land division was dominated by large tracts, resembling neither the patterns to the South nor those of New England to the east. A wedge between the contrasting land systems on either side, it was no transition area, but shared its peculiar cadastral history only fragmentarily with other colonies.

Pennsylvania and New York were never meaningfully linked in the shifting colonial administrations. Their common border lay remote from the tidewater settlements, and remains a rugged and sparsely populated border zone separating the subcultures spread from the cores in southeastern Pennsylvania on the one hand and southeastern New England and the lower Hudson on the other. (Curiously, Connecticut interests asserted serious territorial claims on both sides of this boundary, actually establishing permanent settlement in northeastern Pennsylvania, but were unable to hold them against more powerful neighbors with later grants from the crown.)

Fig. 11.1 (facing page). Middle Atlantic locations: 1. Plattsburgh 2. St. Lawrence Ten Towns 3. Schenectady 4. Albany County 5. Rensselaer County 6. Columbia County 7. Dutchess County 8. Kingston 9. Herkimer County 10. Oneida County 11. Steuben Township 12. Cooperstown 13. Chenango Township 14. Military Tract 15. Phelps and Gorham Purchase 16. Morris Reserve 17. Holland Company Tract 18. Muncy Township 19. Kingston Township 20. Dennison Township 21. Aquackanonk Patent 22. Newark tract 23. Elizabethtown 24. Hunterdon County 25. Navesink Patent 26. Yonkers 27. Pelham 28. Garden City 29. Hempstead 30. Southampton 31. Flushing 32. Gravesend 33. Flatlands 34. New Utrecht 35. Breuckelen 36. Bucks County 37. Philadelphia County 38. Montgomery County 39. Delaware County 40. Chester County 41. Lancaster County 42. Rapho Township 43. Springetsbury Township 44. Cherryhill Township 45. Butler County 46. Neshannock Township 47. Erie County 48. Wilmington 49. New Castle 50. Middletown 51. Lewes 52. Westchester County. 53. Final dividing lines between East Jersey and West Jersey (surveyed 1743).

11

New York:
The Dutch Period, 1624–64

A LAND grant map of New York appeared in an atlas of 1895, showing nearly all the state as divided between 1629 and 1800 into some 500 to 600 parcels (fig. 11.2).[1] Perhaps half the parcels shown were areas of between 1,000 and 3,000 acres. The other half were mostly much larger and took up most of the area. No other colony had so pervasive a pattern of large grants that a small-scale map could present its land division history meaningfully. The New York map does ignore some limited areas of small parcels.

The large grant was a thread that bound New York's cadastral history through successive governments under the Netherlands, England, the Confederation, and the United States. For most of the first century the grants were feudal in spirit, intended to support a landed gentry.[2] Subsequently land grants gradually became more speculative, sought as a way to profit through later division and sale. Finally, after the Revolution, most of western and northern New York was granted in tracts of a million or more acres to individuals and companies that entered the land division process as jobbers. Although these tracts were even larger than in colonial days, it was clear that their division would respond to the demand of ever more numerous migrants for family-size, family-owned farms.

---

[1]Joseph R. Bien, *Atlas of the State of New York* (New York: J. Bien and Co., 1895), map 3. The map is reproduced with minor changes in Ruth L. Higgins, *Expansion in New York* (Columbus: Ohio State University Studies, Graduate School Series, Contributions in History and Political Science, no. 14, 1931), map 1 in end pocket; and in Robert Rayback, ed., *Richards Atlas of New York State* (Phoenix, N.Y.: Frank E. Richards, 1957–59), 36. Two earlier maps with some of the same material for eastern New York were Claude J. Sauthier, *A Chorographical Map of the Province of New York in America* (London: 1779); and Simeon DeWitt, *Map of the Head Waters of the Rivers Susquehanna and Delaware Embracing the Early Patents on the South Side of the Mohawk River* (1790). Both were reprinted in Christopher Morgan, ed., *The Documentary History of the State of New York*, 4 vols. (Albany: State Printer, 1849–51), 1: 420, 774.

[2]Rayback, 35, 65.

211

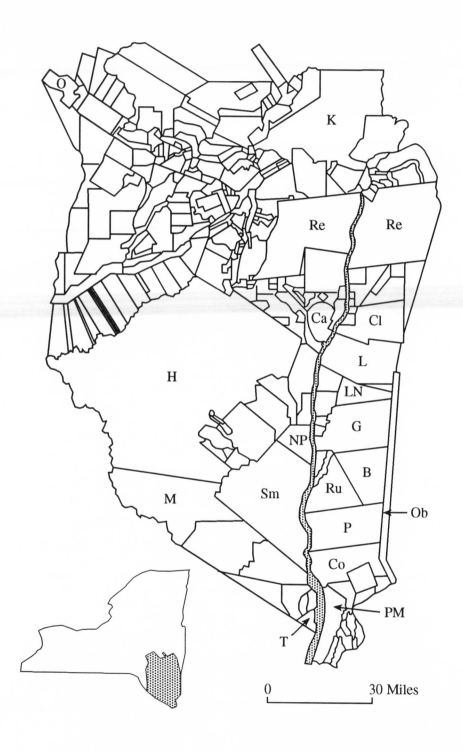

0   30 Miles

Although we separate colonial New York into Dutch and English periods, each period was influenced by participants and traditions of both nations. English legal interpretation too gave final form to some earlier Dutch grants. The brief Dutch repossession of New Netherland in 1673–74 seems to have been cadastrally unimportant.

New York's origin as the colony of New Netherland fell under the management of the Dutch West India Company, an organization concerned primarily with trade rather than colonization. The company enjoyed monopoly control over the land, but not actual ownership of it; granting land to settlers came as an afterthought, to increase local supplies and to strengthen the military potential of the colony. Under its monopoly, the company found little reason to grant land to small farmers in tenures as free as those then enjoyed in the Netherlands. The special "Freedoms and Exemptions" in a charter of 1629 and a somewhat more liberal charter of 1640 provided, however, for a variety of land grants.[3]

The 1629 charter created the neofeudal status of *patroon* for any stockholder of the company who would plant a colony of fifty persons more than fifteen years of age within four years after announcing his intention. The patroon would receive a grant of land extending as much as sixteen miles along a river (eight miles if along both banks) and running an undefined distance inland from the river. A patroonship was equivalent to a large manor in the English colonies. The patroon could hold courts, appoint officers, and enjoy exclusive rights of hunting, fishing, and milling. His land was a "perpetual fief of inheritance" subject to renewal on inheritance by "doing homage" to the company and paying twenty guilders. With the company's agreement, the patroonship could be willed to other than natural heirs. Once a patroon identified the location he claimed, he would "have the preference over all others of the absolute property of such lands." An estate could be enlarged if an increase in the number of colonists justified it.

[3]Higgins, 3; S. G. Nissenson, *The Patroon's Domain* (New York: Columbia University Press, 1937), 22–24. The 1629 document was published in J. Franklin Jameson, ed., *Narratives of New Netherland, 1609–1664* (New York: Charles Scribner's Sons, 1909), 90–91, under the title "Privileges and Exemptions."

Fig. 11.2 *(facing page).* Southeastern New York land grants: B = Beekman, Ca = Catskill, Cl = Claverack, Co = Cortlandt, G = Great Nine Partners, H = Hardenbergh, K = Kayaderosseras, L = Livingston, LN = Little Nine Partners, M = Minisink, NP = New Paltz, O = Oriskany, Ob = Oblong, P = Philipse's Highland Patent, PM = Philipsborough, Re = Rensselaerswyck, Ru = Rumbout, Sm = numerous small tracts, T = Tappan. Redrawn from *Richards Atlas of New York State,* 36, copyright 1957-59, by permission.

The original charter also provided for farmer settlers coming either at their own expense or under the sponsorship of others. The grants for such farmers were like headrights, providing, however, only so much land as they could improve. Farmland was, or soon came to be, granted in free and common socage, subject to tithes (a tenth of the crops and of the increase of livestock) after several years of initial exemption.[4]

A new charter in 1640 reduced the maximum size of a patroonship to a quarter of the earlier limit, still a very large grant. The charter also created the status of "master" or "colonist," providing 100 morgen (200 acres) for settling five adults in the colony. And it required that municipal charters be conferred when these settlements grew into villages or towns.[5] Thus New Netherland developed manor, village or township, and individual farm settlements, to equate them with the variety of settlements in the English colonies. Between fifteen and twenty patroonships were claimed in all New Netherland, not more than eleven of which were in present New York State.[6] Between fifteen and twenty townships or villages were granted municipal privileges. Of the smaller Dutch grants there were perhaps 350 farms in present New York State and nearly 200 city lots in New Amsterdam.[7]

Patroonships

Some accounts of New Netherland give the impression that the Hudson River was lined with patroonships from its mouth all the way north to the vicinity of Albany. Actually the concentration of patroonship claims extended only about thirty miles, from the mouth of the Hudson to the southern parts of the present counties of Rockland and Westchester. Only three claims can be identified farther up the river. Three of the patroonships in present New York State were never settled. Three others were destroyed by Indians;

---

[4]Michael Kammen, *Colonial New York* (New York: Charles Scribner's Sons, 1975), 34.

[5]Irving Elting, *Dutch Village Communities on the Hudson River,* Johns Hopkins University Studies in Historical and Political Science, ser. 4, no. 1 (Baltimore: Johns Hopkins, 1886), 18; Clarence White Rife, "Land Tenure in New Netherland," *Essays in Colonial History Presented to Charles McLean Andrews by His Students* (New Haven: Yale University Press, 1931), 47–48.

[6]Nissenson, 27–30, 243–44; Higgins, 4–7.

[7]Jessica Kross, *The Evolution of an American Town: Newtown, New York, 1642–1775* (Philadelphia: Temple University Press, 1983), 13.

one of these later developed into a village, and one was repurchased by the company. Two more patroonships were annulled or turned back to the company after settlement had begun.[8] The only patroonships extant when the English took New Netherland were Rensselaerswyck, originally including the present site of Albany, and Colendonck, including the site of Yonkers. Colendonck had few settlers, and was subsequently divided into two English grants.[9] Thus, Rensselaerswyck, which operated for two centuries, was the only patroonship grant of any great duration and, indeed the only one that ever operated as a great estate with a significant number of tenants.

Rensselaerswyck, granted to Kiliaen van Rensselaer in 1629, was one of the five patroonships authorized immediately on adoption of the Freedoms and Exemptions. It quickly became the principal settlement and economic force of interior New Netherland. Extending on both sides of the Hudson, it was vaguely defined to reach as far inland as the "situation of the occupants would permit."[10] The first patroon estimated his domain at 330,000 acres, but several purchases subsequently extended and consolidated it. In 1685 the English governor issued a new grant confirming the van Rensselaers in what they claimed: twenty-three miles along the Hudson and twenty-four miles inland on each side (most of present Albany and Rensselaer Counties). The later English grant of Claverack to the south added ten more miles of frontage on the east side of the river to bring the holding to a million acres.

The English grant did not perpetuate Rensselaerswyck's status as a manor, placing it only in Kentish free socage "as of our manor of East Greenwich," with a quitrent fixed at fifty bushels of good winter wheat delivered at New York each March 25. As early as 1652 the settlement of Beverwyck (earlier Ft. Orange, later Albany) had been given separate municipal jurisdiction, as had also the east-bank village of Greenbush. Freed of the patroon's restraints, the people of these two communities could more readily pursue their own commercial interest, retaining, however, the right to collect firewood and timber in Rensselaerswyck.

The loss of manorial status, the loss of Albany and Greenbush, and the sale of a few small parcels did little to inhibit the van Rensse-

---

[8]Nissenson, 247.

[9]Thomas F. O'Donnell, Introduction to Adriaen Van Der Donk, *A Description of the New Netherlands,* trans. Jeremiah Johnson (Syracuse, N.Y.: Syracuse University Press, 1968), xxvii, xxxviii.

[10]Nissenson, 22. The following material on Rensselaerswyck is drawn largely from Nissenson, passim.

laers' lordly dominion over their vast estate. The first patroon, who never actually visited New Netherland, saw the estate as a means of effecting the cooperation of capital and labor "so the rich may stay at home and send their money thither and the poor may go and perform their work with the money of the rich."

Tenants and workers were recruited to settle the estate. The first farmers took land on the basis of share leases, the patroon providing animals, tools, and even helpers in return for half the crop and half the increase of animals. The patroon was also entitled to buy the tenant's share of animals as a way of stocking additional farms. Tenants objected when an additional eleventh of the crop was levied as a tithe for church support. The share leases soon evolved into more conventional leases for a fixed rent, usually payable in wheat. In addition the tenant paid a fixed tithe and a surrent such as "two fowls" to the domain's manager. The tenants' farms were scattered along the river, their boundaries often indefinite. In this casual selection of land, the landlord tried to discourage a tendency of the tenants to cultivate only the good land and ignore the poor land.

In the early years, the fur trade was the profitable business of the manor, not only for the patroon, but also for many of the tenants, to whom it had at first been forbidden. The traders centered their activities in Greenbush, which had developed around the minister's house as adjoining land had been leased for mills and for house and garden sites. As the fur trade faded, farming replaced it as the long-term economic basis of the manor.

Ownership of Rensselaerswyck was complicated by two conditions. First was an agreement among four of the original patroons to pool their holdings and share the profits. Although Rensselaerswyck was the only one of the four estates that ever actually operated, the interests of the other patroons had to be considered until the van Rensselaers finally bought them up. The second condition was the division of ownership on inheritance. The death of the first patroon left ownership divided nine ways among his children. By 1674 the shares of some heirs were as little as a fortieth of the whole. The estate itself, however, remained undivided and under the unified management of the family member holding the title of patroon, which passed by male primogeniture. Various arrangements among the van Rensselaers resulted in reconcentrating the ownership. First the members of the family in Europe gave up their shares to those in New York. Finally a new patent in 1704 put most of the holding back in the hands of the patroon, as the Claverack portion was conveyed to his brother.

Near the end of the seventeenth century the van Rensselaers fashioned a new type of tenancy described as a *perpetual lease,* a form believed to have been customary in parts of the Netherlands. The tenant gained an inheritable interest in the land and improvements, but still had to pay rent to the landlord. The rent would be low for the first five or ten years while the lessee was building a house and clearing the land. When the farm was in full operation, the rent was raised, typically to about a tenth of the crop. The lease could not be sold without permission of, or at least notice, to the landlord. Since giving up his lease meant sacrificing his stake in the farm, the leaseholder was not really free to bargain for better terms. The system of perpetual rents continued for a century and a half, when it became a cause of protest in the nineteenth-century antirent agitation.

Grants of Farms and Townships

Although most of the land granted by the Dutch was in the Hudson River patroonships, grants of farms and townships accounted for the immediate settlement of a greater number of people. Most of the separate farms granted in Dutch New York were within the present limits of New York City and in Westchester and Rockland Counties. Township grants were mostly on Long Island. The Kingston area, farther up the Hudson, was a locus of both farm and township grants.

Manhattan Island was originally reserved for the Dutch West India Company, which at an early date laid out a dozen *bouweries* (farms) assigned to company officers or head farmers. The farms were worked by company-paid labor, and the assignee received a tenth of the cattle and produce.[11] Other farms were granted as private property, and at least part of the company farms remained in the hands of erstwhile Dutch officers after the English took over. Part of Peter Stuyvesant's land still belonged to his descendants well over a century later. As the southern end of Manhattan became divided into streets, blocks, and nearly 200 city lots,[12] the farms of a variety of shapes and sizes, but mostly smaller than 100 acres, were excluded from the area south of the wall (present Wall Street) limiting the city on the north. Additional farms were located nearby, on Long Island to the east, and up the Hudson River to the north.

[11]I. N. Phelps Stokes, *The Iconography of Manhattan Island,* 6 vols. (New York: Arno Press, 1967) (originally published 1915), 6: 65–71, 141–43.
[12]Stokes, 2: plate 87.

Township and farm village settlement in New Netherland was initiated under English rather than Dutch impetus. This came about from the proximity of southern New England to Long Island and the 1635 granting of Long Island by the Council for New England to the Earl of Stirling.[13] With England and the Netherlands both claiming Long Island, the Dutch kept control of its western third near New Amsterdam, but lacked strength to challenge English activity in the eastern two-thirds. This division was formalized by a treaty in 1650.

Two townships, Southampton, settled by colonists from Lynn, Massachusetts, and Southold, by colonists from New Haven, were founded near the eastern end of Long Island about 1640 on grants from Stirling's agent.[14] These townships represented the first implantation of New England settlement and land division patterns beyond the area conventionally recognized as New England. Additional English townships in eastern Long Island soon followed.

Although Dutch authorities had forced out the Southampton settlers when they had earlier tried to land in western Long Island, New England towns were very soon accepted in Dutch territory. In 1644 and 1645 Hempstead in present Nassau County, Gravesend in Brooklyn, and Flushing in Queens were all settled under Dutch charters. Later New England communities included Newtown (Middleburgh) and Jamaica in Queens and Pelham in Westchester County on the mainland.[15] As in New England, these towns had the prerogatives of local government and of distributing their own land.[16] Conditions usually placed on the towns by the Dutch were, first, settling 100 families within five years and second, after ten years, payment of a tenth of all return from soil and pasture. This tithe was a novelty to New Englanders, but it is doubtful that much of it was ever collected.[17] The land of most of these towns was distributed in divisions of longlots in keeping with New England custom.[18]

---

[13]Isabel MacBeath Calder, "The Earl of Stirling and the Colonization of Long Island," Essays in Colonial History Presented to Charles McLean Andrews by His Students (New Haven: Yale University Press, 1931), 74–95.

[14]Calder, 81–85.

[15]Donald Meinig, "The Colonial Period, 1609–1775," in Geography of New York State, ed. John H. Thompson (Syracuse: Syracuse University Press, 1966), 126.

[16]Rife, 54–55.

[17]Ibid., 63–64.

[18]Bernice Marshall, Colonial Hempstead (Port Washington, N.Y.: Ira J. Friedman, 1962), 138–41; James Truslow Adams, History of the Town of Southampton (Port Washington, N.Y.: Ira J. Friedman, 1962), 12, 120, 150–51. The Southold USGS topographic map (1:24,000, 1956) shows a pattern of elongated fields around the village of Southold, which may derive from the original division.

The township of Hempstead was founded on a large Indian and Dutch grant that extended the full width of Long Island. Over the years adjoining townships less generously endowed were awarded parts of Hempstead's grant. Each of Hempstead's several divisions of its land was allocated on a different formula, as determined by the townsmen at the time.[19] Other parcels were awarded to individuals or sold by the town. The cleavage of the township into Hempstead and North Hempstead grew out of divided loyalties in the American Revolution.[20] A sizable part of Hempstead's huge common land (which remained because of colonial disagreements about how to divide it) was sold for the founding of Garden City as late as 1869. Gravesend in contrast was founded on a much smaller grant a year after Hempstead. Its central village was laid out in a square that was cut into quadrants by two main roads. Each quadrant had a common in its center surrounded by house lots. The farm plots of the householders extended out radially from the village. The four quadrants of the original village are still outlined by Brooklyn streets, but the radial farms have been obliterated by the modern city's grid of regular blocks.[21]

Dutch villages in New Netherland were incorporated only after some of these New England villages had appeared. Since farm villages were as well known in Dutch tradition as they were in English, the division of Dutch village lands into house lots and gardens, arable plots, common pastures, and woodland[22] was probably taken over from Dutch tradition more than from contact with local New England villages. Villages of Dutch settlers, however, were never given the independence they saw and envied in the New England settlements.[23] Although the village leaders might be permitted to plan the layout of the land, the grants were made only by the colony government, with acreage often assigned in proportion to individual payments toward the land purchase and patent. In several cases incorporation came only after settlement had occurred family by family and sometimes only at the instigation of colonial authorities.

A variety of other early villages also developed into communities well known today. The present Borough of Brooklyn incorporated the

[19]Marshall, 20–21, 138–41.
[20]Ibid., 271.
[21]H. Arthur Bankoff, "The Gravesend Project: Archaeology in Brooklyn," in *Brooklyn, U.S.A.: The Fourth Largest City in America,* ed. Rita Seiden Miller (New York: Brooklyn College Press, 1976), 61–62.
[22]Elting, 24, 27, 32.
[23]Rife, 57; Kammen, 40.

English village of Gravesend (1644), the French village of Bushwick (1660), and the four Dutch villages of Breuckelen (1646), New Utrecht (1661), Amersfort (Flatlands), and Midwout (Flatbush); the last two had been founded as one village in 1654 and separated in 1661. New Harlem at the northern end of Manhattan was established by the New Netherland government in 1656 after individual settlement efforts there had failed.[24] Its land was opened up in a series of divisions, the first comprising house lots and the next several comprising longlots, most of which fronted on the shores or creeks. The original settlers represented several European nations, French, Dutch, Walloons and Danes, Swedes, and Germans in decreasing order of numbers. The land divisions were not completed until long after the English had taken New York. The old divisions have been obliterated by the modern street grid except that the main road originally separating the lots of the east side from those of the west side is traced today by parts of St. Nicholas Avenue and Broadway, running oblique to the principal street grid. The only Dutch village between Manhattan and Rensselaerswyck was Esopus, a small-farm community near Kingston, given village status near the end of the Dutch period. Schenectady, northwest of Albany, got its start as a community settlement for farmers dissatisfied with the constraints of tenant farming in Rensselaerswyck.[25]

Summary

The period of Dutch administration left its impressions on the land of New York as it did on the culture. These marks included one great patroonship, many farms, a score of villages with their division often in longlots, and the urban division of southern Manhattan. The roads and property boundaries of the smaller Dutch farms survive here and there today in the fabric of the metropolis that has spread over much of the original farm area. The patroonship system had far more carryover into the English period than might have been expected from its lone embodiment in Rensselaerswyck.

[24]James Riker, *Revised History of Harlem* (New York: New Harlem Publishing Co., 1904), 167ff. and map following 832.
[25]Higgins, 12–17.

12

New York's English and American Periods: Lordly Estates and Land Developers' Tracts

ALTHOUGH the Duke of York was awarded more power over his domain than any other English proprietor (he was the king's brother and lord high admiral over the fleet that took New York from the Dutch), he gave relatively little attention to the society emerging in his colony.[1] Of the thirteen English colonies, New York showed the least evidence of a guiding philosophy that might have led to a coherent scheme for land distribution. New Netherland was the only part of the original United States already developed into a going colony before English acquisition. The English entry there was effected by a fleet of mere warships rather than a settlement fleet replete with committed colonists attracted by the plans for their new community.

The Dutch trading company's land policies, including the patroons' estates and tithes on farm production, did not offer the best models for the new British regime. While other British colonies were offering small farms on attractive terms, New York made them relatively expensive and scarce. The granting of large estates proved to be a more convenient model for the English governors, who hoped to gain some influential allies while encouraging settlement at the same time.[2]

The large tracts, however, actually discouraged settlers, who could not acquire their own land as readily as they could in other colonies. The estate owners who fancied the status of landed gentry proposed to keep their land whether or not they succeeded in recruiting tenants. Those who viewed their land as speculation tended to

[1]Kammen, 76.
[2]Sung Bok Kim, *Landlord and Tenant in Colonial New York* (Chapel Hill: University of North Carolina Press for Institute of Early American History and Culture, 1978), 18–43.

hold it for higher prices at a later time. The frequent vagueness of estate boundaries (many grants did not even specify acreages)[3] also cast a cloud over bordering land where potential settlers feared that clear titles could not be obtained. Thus the distribution of land proceeded much faster than its settlement, contrasting with a more even pace of the two in most other colonies.

The damping effect of land policy on immigration into New York is emphasized by the fact that the five colonies that had more people than New York during the period 1750–70 included the small colonies of Massachusetts, Connecticut, and Maryland as well as Pennsylvania, which was not founded until eighteen years after the English conquest of New York. Some of the population growth that New York did gain was absorbed on new farms as a limited number of estates were broken up. By around 1750 New York was developing both urban and rural proletariats, even while far more land than was needed to provide them with farms lay unused on large holdings.[4]

The English Period, 1664–1776

Granting Aristocratic Estates

The colonial governors of New York did not share equally in their propensity to grant large estates. Before 1685 land grants were relatively few and were largely regrants of earlier Dutch holdings, made to assure the cooperation of their owners. The first two governors after 1685 gave out estates so generously that their successor, for reasons that were partly personal and partly in the interest of the colony, sought, with limited success, to annul some of the large grants to make the land available to more settlers.[5] The next governor resumed the large grants, but in 1708 the English government ordered a grant limit of 2,000 acres per person, which was lowered in 1753 to 1,000 acres.[6] Large grants could still be issued to partnerships of several persons, as will be discussed below. The total amount of land granted between 1708 and 1732 was insignificant, but a final surge of

---

[3] Alice Maplesden Keys, *Cadwallader Colden* (New York: AMS Press, 1967), 96.
[4] Kammen, 279.
[5] Rayback, 35; Kim, 75–86.
[6] Armand Shelby La Potin, *The Minisink Patent* (New York: Arno Press, 1979), 48–49. The 1708 regulation also set quitrents on new grants at two and a half shillings per 100 acres, less than a day's labor at the time, but a considerable increase over the quitrents assessed on older grants, which, on many large estates, were mere tokens.

large grants saw the alienation of another four million acres before the Revolution.[7]

The sizes of many manor holdings in New York dwarfed the plantations of the South, being more comparable with the great speculative tracts in Virginia that were held only for sale and profit. The special legal jurisdictions of these manors were merged into the regular counties during the first two decades of the eighteenth century.[8] Owners of nonmanor estates, like owners of manors, often divided their land into parcels farmed by tenants and enjoyed comparable prestige and power. At least three of the manors were represented in the New York Assembly, their seats virtually the property of their lords, and other great landowners were influential enough in their counties to gain regular election to the Assembly.[9] The leading manor families, who were closely intermarried, dominated politics and trade in New York for a long time.[10] Privilege was rooted in the land.

Estate by estate, the choice lands fronting the Hudson River passed into private hands. By 1710 nearly all the land east of the river and south of Rensselaerswyck was in as few as ten great holdings. Livingston Manor began as two discontinuous grants, but they were soon expanded sixtyfold into a single estate of 160,000 acres by virtue of a vague patent and an all-encompassing survey.[11] Frederick Philipse and Stephanus van Cortlandt also received manors that incorporated earlier purchases of land; their two manors took up the greater part of Westchester County, including all its frontage on the Hudson. Adolph Philipse obtained a large grant that is now Putnam County. Other large grants went to the Beekmans and Rumbouts, and several smaller tracts on the river went to members of the Schuyler family. In 1697 Morrisania, a tract of nearly 2,000 acres comprising the southwestern corner of the present Borough of the Bronx, was given manor status nearly a generation after Lewis Morris had bought it from an earlier owner.[12] The estates on the west bank of the

[7]Rayback, 35.
[8]Kim, 87, 93ff.
[9]Keys, 96.
[10]Prominent landed families linked by marriage included Beekman, Livingston, Philipse, Schuyler, van Cortlandt, and van Rensselaer. Most were also linked by mercantile interests.
[11]Lawrence H. Leder, *Robert Livingston (1654–1728) and the Politics of Colonial New York* (Chapel Hill: University of North Carolina Press for Institute of Early American History and Culture, 1961), 32–35.
[12]Rayback, 35; Kim, 3–43.

Hudson were more mixed in size. Even those that were as large as the estates on the east side bore less prestige.

As the last tracts of the Hudson River corridor below Albany were taken up, large new group grants by Governor Edward Cornbury (1702–8) pushed out the frontiers between granted and ungranted land. The Minisink Patent of more than 200,000 acres and the Hardenbergh Patent of more than 1,500,000 acres reached west to the Delaware River, and the Kayaderosseras tract of 400,000 acres took up a large area north of Albany. The relatively small Oriskany Patent of 1705 reached more than fifty miles beyond the frontier of its day and thirty to fifty years ahead of other grants in its vicinity. More than 30,000 acres, it had a quitrent of only ten shillings and no clause requiring prompt settlement. It was probably selected as a strategic portage site between the Mohawk River and Lake Ontario, which indeed it later became.[13] Here Fort Stanwix was located in 1758 and the city of Rome platted in 1786.

Later governors shared personally in the final orgy of grants that began in 1732. Governor William Cosby (1732–36) required that a third of each grant be deeded to him, a feature of land division the maps do not show. Some governors after Cosby took their share in cash, often at seven pounds per thousand acres. When that rate did not seem enough, the same charge might be levied on each partner in a large tract for the full acreage. The cost of such grants held down their sizes: 10,000 to 30,000 acres was typical in the continued expansion to the north and west (see northwest quarter of fig. 11.2). Sir William Johnson, who lived among the Indians, held their confidence, and represented the New York government in dealing with them, was the most successful frontiersman in the colony when it came to gaining land. Some of the most important tracts among his half million acres were in the southern Adirondacks. He was also rumored to have had a hand in the Totten and Crossfield purchase of the 1770s, the last of the giant colonial tracts, which stretched north into the central Adirondacks.[14]

In addition to the large tracts granted to individuals or families, several estates were granted to groups of partners. Pooling several interests could greatly reduce the per capita and per acre load of surveying and filing fees.

Thus many grants were officially for acreages equal to 2,000 or 1,000 times the number of partners, but actual acreages might be much

[13]Higgins, 58–60.
[14]Rayback, 35.

larger. Sometimes most of the partners were merely "dummies" who deeded their shares to the principals as soon as the patents were obtained. Thus the group grant was sometimes a direct way of getting around the acreage limitation.

The group grant also had disadvantages that may not have been foreseen by the grantees. Since the shares of the grantees were undivided, no one of them could use part of the grant without his improvements becoming the common property of all, nor could he sell any specific parcel to any other person. Division of the holding required agreement of all holders, and, at times, even a court order. Some of these speculative grants lay dormant for many years, while shares might have been sold or passed to heirs, often having been divided in the process, and the heirs themselves likely became more scattered in residence. Getting agreement for division among all the partners could be difficult and expensive. Dividing the holding could subject the current owners to all the costs the original partners had sought to avoid in the first place.

Reports on three partnership purchases illustrate varied fates. The Tappan Patent was a rather small group grant intended as farmland for its purchasers, but not planned as a New England-style township.[15] The purchasers were residents of Bouwery Village on Manhattan Island and of New Jersey, some of them with maturing children who would need more land. In 1682 spokesmen for the sixteen shareholders negotiated with the Tappan Indians for the purchase of 5,000 acres west of the Hudson and believed to lie in New Jersey. In 1686, after the New York–New Jersey boundary had been surveyed through the tract, the New York governor granted the shareholders a patent for about 8,000 acres, designated as the township of Orange with a quitrent of sixteen bushels of wheat. Soon the Tappan purchasers established three clusters of settlement without any formal assignment of land either to individual farmers or to subgroups.

The first formal division of the Tappan lands occurred in 1704 when the settlers, purchasers, and their heirs released the land they had been using in exchange for about 250 acres each, including lots of about 100 acres in a range along the east side of Hackensack Creek and about twelve acres of meadow. The expenses of division

---

[15]George H. Budke, "The History of the Tappan Patent," *Rockland Record* 2 (1931–32): 35–50; Peter O. Wacker, *Land and People: A Cultural Geography of Preindustrial New Jersey: Origins and Settlement Patterns* (New Brunswick, N.J.: Rutgers University Press, 1975), 244–45.

were raised by selling a lot or two. The second division in 1721 parceled out the remainder of the patent at probably seven or eight hundred acres a share, including land in New Jersey. The lots seem to have been irregular, as they were adapted to fit existing fences and land uses that had already encroached on the common land. The courses bounding the parcels were described in relation to the thirty-two points of the mariner's compass, as in "east-north-east, six degrees north."

The Little Nine Partners tract, a speculative grant east of the Hudson, was more systematically divided than the Tappan Patent. Along with the Great Nine Partners tract, it was laid out in the early 1700s in northern Dutchess County (fig. 11.2) in a vicinity mostly taken up by large individual grants. The Little Nine Partners tract filled a wedge-shaped area between the Great Nine Partners tract and Livingston Manor, and was separated from the Hudson by several miles. The tract is reported originally to have contained 18,000 acres, or 2,000 acres per partner, but it scales three times as much on the maps that represent it.[16] It remained undivided for nearly forty years, with settlement only by squatters.[17] In 1743–44 it was divided into sixty-three lots, seven for each proprietary interest (fig. 12.1A), but remained largely unsettled until 1755, when the area was organized in townships.[18] Problems with the surveys led to boundary disputes that were not settled until the 1790s when resurveys were made.[19] The tract stands as an example of geometrically simple division among the heirs of the original proprietors. The further subdivision of one lot is shown in figure 12.1B. This second division was less regular, but maintained approximate rectangularity. Several roads, field boundaries, and a township boundary in the area today preserve the directions of these old subdivision boundaries.[20]

A recent analysis of the Minisink Patent, although it does not deal with the geometry of the subdivision, illuminates several aspects of land dealings in colonial New York.[21] This speculative grant of 1704, with its eastern edge twenty miles west of the Hudson, reached westward another forty miles, bordering on New Jersey and

[16]Rayback, 35; and see figures 11.2 and 12.1.
[17]Isaac Huntting, *History of the Little Nine Partners of North East Precinct and Pine Plains* (Amenia, N.Y.: C. Walsh and Co., 1897), 38.
[18]Ibid.
[19]Ibid., 34–36.
[20]Pine Plains USGS topographic map (1:24,000, 1960).
[21]La Potin.

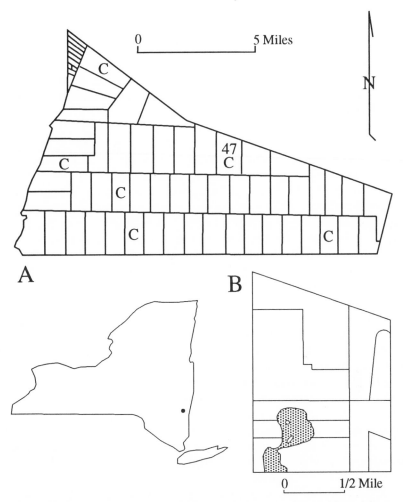

Fig. 12.1. Little Nine Partners Tract. A. Division of the tract, 1743–44. Most of the partners or their heirs each received six of the fifty-four main lots, approximately 1,000 acres each lot. Probably each also received one of the small lots at the northwest. C = lots received by George Clarke, Governor of New York, 1736-43. B. Division of lot no. 47, 1797. Both plats from 1809 copies of earlier maps in New York State Archives, Office of Cultural Education, Department of Education.

Pennsylvania. Its size, not specified in the patent, appears to be about 230,000 acres in figure 11.2. The eastern point of Minisink, known as the Angle, in the choicer area east of the Appalachian ridges, was divided into fifty-one lots for distribution to the proprietors in 1711. The rest of the patent lay beyond the frontier for many years. The twenty-three original grantees, nearly all residents of New York City, included a high proportion of merchants, men who had held public office at some time, and owners of lands elsewhere. But only four of these grantees ever lived in the area of the patent. The sixty-seven people who subsequently acquired shares in Minisink—by purchase, later patent, or inheritance—show up as a less influential group, relatively fewer of them merchants, lawyers, officeholders, or residents of New York City. A larger fraction, however, owned other land, evidencing continued speculation. The later owners were less successful in holding onto the tract than the more influential original buyers had been in obtaining it.

Although the Minisink grant appeared duly legal when it was made, New York officials were able to force a radical reduction on its shareholders more than half a century later. The flaws of the grant lay in its lack of a clear definition of the boundaries, both in the purchase from the Indians and in the patent itself, and in its omission of a statement of total acreage granted. The tract was defined to include certain natural landforms identified by names that were not uniformly accepted. It was stated to bound an earlier patent, also of uncertain limits, which had been annulled. The Minisink owners may not have intentionally claimed more land than intended in the grant, but with these uncertain boundaries, they could not disprove the government's accusation that they had done so.

The New York government's ostensible motives for pursuing the Minisink case were to increase quitrents to the level set in 1708, to effect settlement of vacant lands, and to respond to competing claims, including those of Indians and farmers already settled on the land. The genuine efforts of some shareholders to sell property for settlement had run afoul of the legal difficulties of dividing the land, the danger of Indian attacks, and the uncertain locations of the tract boundary and of the New Jersey border. Rather than face a threatened suit in a court where they were sure to lose, the Minisink owners in 1765 gave up the contested portion of the Angle, accepted resurveys with all the attendant costs, and one by one surrendered their patents for new issues with the higher quitrent.

Of the three partnership patents discussed, the Tappan Patent was the earliest and smallest and the only one designed for farming by the partners or their descendants. Virtually a communal project, its land was divided as fast as it was needed for farming and largely in accordance with the original intent. Little Nine Partners and Minisink were larger and speculative projects, the purposes of which remained unfulfilled for about half a century. The former was the smaller and lay closer to the settled areas. Most of Minisink lay beyond the frontier. Although its owners sponsored some settlement earlier than had the Little Nine Partners, its frontier location led to doubts about its boundaries and to conflicting settlements, which led to the renegotiation of the grant on terms less favorable to its owners.

Smaller Grants

Like the Dutch, the English also distributed some land in smaller parcels. A very early offering of headrights found few takers.[22] In the Kingston–New Paltz area the land of several villages or townships was divided among numerous farmers, essentially on a headright basis. The settlers here were mostly Dutch, and Dutch land customs prevailed. New Paltz had originated as a Huguenot settlement in 1677, but the Dutch gradually replaced the Huguenots. On Long Island in the same year the English approved an addition called New Lots to the Dutch village of Flatbush (Brooklyn).[23] The patent covered 1,426 acres, but the tract was actually three times as large. One part of New Lots was divided into parallel strips of about thirty acres, about 232 feet wide and over a mile long, and another into smaller strips of meadow. New Lots Avenue today follows the southern margin of the original farm strips. The streets north of New Lots Avenue run very close to the direction of the strips they replaced, whereas those to the south are oriented perpendicular to the avenue.

The modern land grant maps (fig. 11.2) show several hundred square miles in northern Orange and southern Ulster Counties as having been devoted to "numerous small tracts." The Sauthier map of 1779 shows this area to have contained many tracts averaging about 2,000 acres, small parcels by New York standards. This area had been opened up by the disallowance of a huge earlier tract, and most of the smaller holdings were granted after 1708 during the twenty-four-year lull in larger grants.

A unique plan in New York's land history was Governor Cosby's 1754 offer of 100,000 acres in grants of 200 acres each to the first 500 Protestant families to come to settle in New York. Land was set aside in the Saratoga area, but eighty-three families of Scots Highlanders arriving a few years later were informed that the land had

---

[22]Kim, 18–19.

[23]Alter F. Landesman, *A History of New Lots, Brooklyn* (Port Washington, N.Y.: Kennikat Press, 1977), 11–13.

already been taken up (apparently by the governor himself).[24] After another thirty years about a hundred of the still landless Scots were granted 47,000 acres that were incorporated in Argyll Township between the Hudson River and Lake George.[25]

Another source of small grants lay in the military bounties from the French and Indian War, accounting for the alienation of 200,000 acres in the vicinity of Lakes George and Champlain. The land grant map[26] shows in this area many rectangular tracts elongated east-west and about 2,000 acres in size, the amount of land promised staff officers; the fifty-acre parcels allotted for privates would not be represented on this small-scale map.

The high fees charged for obtaining land have already been mentioned as one discouragement to small farmers. A 200-acre parcel in the early eighteenth century might cost the grantee as much as nine pounds in fees, a sum equal to the annual cash income from the farm.[27] The fees provided the principal income of those colony officials who dealt with the various stages of the patent process. Also, an individual farmer seeking land usually lacked the resources to make the necessary bargain with the Indians. The uncertainty of titles and boundaries, particularly in the vicinity of large tracts, was another discouragement. For a time, still another obstacle was the contradiction between the requirement of clearing three acres in every fifty within three years and the prohibitions on burning woodland and cutting pines that might be suitable for ships' spars.[28] The largest number of small farms during the English period came from purchase of parcels cut from larger private tracts.

Cadwallader Colden and New York Land

No one person was more involved with the land system of New York during the eighteenth century than Cadwallader Colden, who, in the period 1720–75 held the offices of surveyor general and of lieutenant governor.[29] Colden was a Scot of broad knowledge, who was

---

[24]Cadwallader Colden, "Letters on Smith's History of New York," *Collections* (New York Historical Society) 1 (1868): 226–35.

[25]Higgins, 88–90.

[26]See chapter 11, n. 1.

[27]La Potin, 59.

[28]"Letters and Papers of Cadwallader Colden," *Collections* (New York Historical Society) 50 (1917): 135–37.

[29]This account of Colden's career depends primarily on Keys, passim.

practicing medicine in Philadelphia when the New York governor invited him to accept a job in New York that would soon include the surveyor generalship. Between 1720 and 1760 he was the colonial official principally concerned with surveying and distributing land. In the latter year he became acting governor, a position which, as lieutenant governor, he was to fill on four separate occasions before English control of the colony finally collapsed in 1775 when Colden was eighty-seven. Thus Colden managed the distribution of New York land at two different levels of authority.

A man of strong conscience and personal integrity, Colden saw his duty in loyalty to the crown and in the enforcement of laws as they were written. Colonial New York was a place to strain the strongest of consciences, given the combination of the land-grabbing schemes of high officials and influential citizens with the frequent absence in the British colonial system of funds to pay those officials' salaries. Colden, as surveyor general, seems to have felt sometimes that he had no choice but to assist the powerful with their land acquisitions. As both surveyor general and governor, he kept for his own stipend some of the fees collected from buyers of land. Although Colden did not become one of New York's biggest landowners, he did manage to acquire holdings that would have been impressive nearly anywhere else.

Colden's 1732 report on New York lands summarized the views he developed as he became familiar with the history and state of the colony's land.[30] He explained how great estates had arisen through grants that either stated bounds vaguely without specifying acreage or specified a modest acreage but defined bounds that actually included much more. He questioned also the legality of many of the Indian purchases on which the estates were based. These great tracts, he found, were often little cultivated, deprived the crown of quitrents, and drove legitimate settlers to other colonies where they could find suitable land for their own. Colden believed the simplest solution to the problem would be reassessment of quitrents at a uniform rate of two and a half shillings a hundred acres. The higher quitrent, although still moderate for productive land, would greatly benefit the colonial treasury and would force dilatory estate owners to develop their holdings or give them up.

In his efforts to enforce the laws, Colden regarded the revision and division of Minisink with the higher quitrent as one of his sig-

---

[30]Cadwallader Colden, "The State of the Lands in the Province of New York," in *Documentary History of the State of New York*, ed. Morgan, 1: 382–87.

nal successes. As part of his long crusade against the great manors, he gave considerable support to the antirent forces in the disturbances of 1766.[31] In another matter of law and land, he was aggressive, but largely unsuccessful, in his efforts to bring Vermont under the control of New York in accordance with the official boundary decision of 1764.

New York Land in the American Period, Following 1776

Well over half of New York lay ungranted at the close of the Revolution. Soldiers and other potential settlers were demanding farms, and, by 1800, all of western New York except a few reservations had been purchased from the Six Nations of the Iroquois. To the north, in the region of the Adirondacks, little of the land, unattractive as it was, had been claimed even by Indians, but it too was made available quickly.

One large military tract and several huge private purchases took up most of the total area of New York's west and north. The state and the private wholesalers usually divided the western land into townships for purposes of survey and sales and occasionally for group settlement. While the federal government was developing the rectangular survey for its trans-Appalachian land, many of New York's new tracts were being similarly laid out.

Most veterans were unable to claim bounty lands until several years after they had been promised, although some tried to settle illegally in Indian territories. A 1781 law permitted groups of soldiers to acquire tracts of 30,000 acres by pooling their military warrants; the town of Plattsburgh was named for the leader of such a group who secured part of an old royal grant confiscated as Tory property.[32] New York's Old Military Tract, laid out as a strip of twelve large townships between the Totten and Crossfield Purchase and the Canadian border, was perceived as wilderness and attracted no settlers.[33] The much larger (New) Military Tract on attractive land just west of the center of the state became available in 1789. It was laid out in twenty-eight townships with their famous classical names (Aurelius, Camillus, Cato . . .). Each 60,000-acre township contained land enough for 100 square lots of 600 acres each for the ordinary

[31]Kim, 350–65.
[32]Higgins, 139.
[33]Ibid.

soldier (officers, depending on rank, could get up to ten times as much). If the soldier had already taken 100 acres elsewhere from the United States, New York retained the "State's Hundred" in the southeast corner of the square. And the "Survey Fifty," also in a corner, would be taken and sold if the forty-eight shillings to cover survey costs were not paid. A major portion of the soldiers sold their rights in the tract, with the result that most of it was ultimately marketed by speculators. In each township 400 acres were set aside for support of the Gospel and two 200-acre parcels for schools.[34]

Smaller tracts were allocated in a number of ways. Many townships were sold or granted to individuals. The St. Lawrence Ten Towns were laid out by the State Land Office, perhaps with defense as the underlying purpose.[35] After reserving in each township square miles for support of the Gospel and schools and for encouraging literature,[36] the townships were sold at auction, and the land then retailed to individual farmers. Road and field patterns in the tract still reflect the original orientation to the St. Lawrence River. A township in Chenango County was reserved for "Vermont Sufferers," who had lost their New York claims in Vermont.[37] A tract of 130,000 acres in far northeastern New York was set aside for refugees from Canada and Nova Scotia, but of the many who drew lots, few actually settled there.[38] Baron von Steuben, for his Revolutionary aid, was granted 16,000 acres in an Oneida County township named for him. Steuben's selection of land missed the portage site near Ft. Stanwix for which he had aimed, making his holding much less attractive to the tenants he sought. However, by 1791, he had more than 3,000 acres under perpetual lease and was offering for sale ninety-six lots averaging about 100 acres.[39] By his death three years later he had not gained much profit.

One of the most active land promoters of the period was Judge William Cooper, who founded Cooperstown (about 1790) on Otsego Lake at the edge of a 25,000-acre tract he had obtained in lieu of repayment of a loan to that acquisitive frontiersman George Croghan,

---

[34]Jeannette B. Sherwood, "The Military Tract," *Proceedings of the New York State Historical Association* 24 (1926): 169–79.

[35]Charles H. Leete, "The St. Lawrence Ten Towns," *Quarterly Journal of the New York State Historical Association* 10 (1929): 318–27.

[36]Higgins, 142, 145.

[37]Ibid., 109.

[38]Ibid., 139.

[39]David Maldwyn Ellis, *Landlords and Farmers in the Hudson-Mohawk Region, 1790–1850* (Ithaca, N.Y.: Cornell University Press, 1946), 50–51.

its original owner. Cooper's land dealings actually ranged far and wide, embracing not only tracts bought and sold on his own account, but also similar dealings with partners and sales as agent for other landholders.[40] He was involved in the sale of ten tracts in Otsego County in addition to the one he obtained from Croghan.[41] His records deal with land in nine other counties, several adjoining Otsego and others reaching to New York's northernmost border. His hand was recorded in at least seven townships of the Military Tract.[42]

Cooper's tracts, like most New York tracts after the Revolution, were subdivided before sale and settlement. This practice, which may reflect the influx of New England farmers, had obvious advantages for any land speculators. Cooper offered terms he thought would be attractive to impecunious farmers. He sold his land on time rather than rent it like colonial estate holders, and offered immediate title rather than withhold it like some other subdividers. The farms he sold were mostly in lots of 100 acres that would not load the farmer with much more land and debt than needed. His policies of not reserving the good land for himself and of selling all land in a tract at the same price won the confidence of farmers and favored the growth of well-settled communities. He did hope to gain also from the poor land that would remain unsold until the demand for timber would make it valuable.[43] Cooper's land brought prices of one to five dollars an acre. His records show 7 percent interest on mortgage loans and 5 percent commissions on sales. Near the end of his life he claimed to "have already settled more acres than any man in America. There are forty thousand souls now holding directly or indirectly under me." Butterfield credited him with converting "upwards of 750,000 acres from forests into farms."[44]

New York's six million acres west of Seneca Lake, except for a mile-wide strip along the Niagara River, came under the property

[40]Cooper's papers at the Stevens-German Library, Hartwick College, Oneonta, New York, include a land book with many maps of tracts as subdivided, and two land ledgers with records of lot sales and payment receipts.

[41]Otsego County's civil township boundaries often follow the boundaries of early subdivisions.

[42]It seems doubtful that he actually owned at one time the 750,000 acres mentioned by Ellis, 55, on the basis of a statement by his son, James Fenimore Cooper.

[43]William Cooper, *A Guide in the Wilderness, or the History of the First Settlements in the Western Counties of New York with Useful Instructions to Future Settlers* (Dublin: Gilbert and Hedges, 1810; reprinted, Rochester, N.Y.: George P. Humphrey, 1897).

[44]L. H. Butterfield, "Judge William Cooper (1754–1809): A Sketch of His Character and Accomplishment," *New York History* 30 (1949): 386.

ownership of Massachusetts, in satisfaction of its claim to western land. First the Phelps and Gorham partnership and then Robert Morris tried their hands at jobbing the area, only to find that they could not sell the land fast enough to make their purchase payments.[45]

This entire area was first purchased by Oliver Phelps and Nathaniel Gorham, who cleared the eastern part of it by an additional purchase from the Seneca Indians, surveyed it into seven ranges of ten to twelve townships, and opened a land office in the territory.[46] Most of their sales were by townships or half townships,[47] and some settlement resulted, but most of this huge purchase was still undivided in 1790 when Phelps and Gorham sold the eastern portion and reconveyed the larger western portion to Massachusetts. Robert Morris then purchased both parts of the tract, the western part from Massachusetts through his agent. These New York lands represented the most promising part of all Morris's investments, but the many millions of acres he acquired in all the states outside New England, as well as in Kentucky, Tennessee, Ohio, and the District of Columbia, overextended his credit, and he was soon bankrupt.[48]

Most of Morris's New York land was sold to English and Dutch interests, who, in their return to New York, proved better able to carry them pending settlement than had the Americans.[49] The million acres Morris kept as reserve between the two tracts he sold was used to pay off some of his debts through the sale and mortgaging of properties ranging between 15,000 and 175,000 acres.

Morris's eastern tract, which included more than a million acres of still undivided land, was obtained by an English company headed by Sir William Pulteney. Pulteney's agent, Charles Williamson, proceeded with plans to develop the land, laying out roads, improving streams, building stores, mills, and hotels, equipping the principal town of Bath with a theater and race track, and advancing needed equipment to settlers.[50] By 1800 all of these improvements had cost more than a million dollars, nine times the gross receipts to that

[45]Barbara Ann Chernow, *Robert Morris, Land Speculator, 1790–1801* (New York: Arno Press, 1978), 35–88.
[46]Ibid., 115–18.
[47]Paul D. Evans, "The Pulteney Purchase," *Proceedings of the New York State Historical Association* 20 (1922), 85.
[48]Chernow, 171–72.
[49]Evans, 83–85; Chernow, 65–75.
[50]Evans, 85–90.

date. The holding was divided in 1800, Pulteney himself getting most of the unsold land, which continued to be taken up over the ensuing decades.

The western part of Morris's holdings, more than three million acres, was sold in four tracts to Dutch interests that formed the Holland Land Company. Morris was obligated to survey part of the purchase into lots of 450 to 500 acres, but appears not to have done so.[51] Joseph Ellicott, surveyor and local agent for the company for more than twenty years, proceeded with dividing the holding into townships six miles square.

After few buyers appeared for the fairly large tracts first offered, the decision was made to sell land to small farmers in a fashion similar to William Cooper's successful sales farther east.[52] Little settlement occurred before 1800. Ellicott's improvements were significant, but they were not on the scale of Williamson's.[53] The Holland Company gave 100,000 acres to New York in appreciation of the completion of the Erie Canal in 1825.[54] Thus the Dutch returned to open New York's far west, as they had its southeast much earlier, but with considerable differences in managers, settlers, and their relationships.

Northern New York had several large tracts, but most of the land, more than three million acres, including most of the St. Lawrence Ten Towns, went to Alexander Macomb and his associates. His 1792 purchase of 1,920,000 acres, the largest grant made by the state of New York to an individual, cost eight pence an acre contingent on settling a family for every square mile within seven years. Macomb had to sell most of his property in several large tracts, which were usually subdivided wholesale at least once more before they were ready for sale in farms.[55]

[51]Chernow, 67, 79.

[52]William Chazanof, *Joseph Ellicott and the Holland Land Company* (Syracuse: Syracuse University Press, 1970), 25–28, 39–42.

[53]Williamson hoped to sell relatively large parcels of 320 acres at higher prices of three to five dollars an acre to "genteel" farmers whom he recruited from Pennsylvania, Maryland, and Virginia rather than from New England. Paradoxically, he sold land on easier terms than Ellicott, leading his company into financial straits. William Wyckoff, *The Developer's Frontier: The Making of the Western New York Landscape* (New Haven: Yale University Press, 1988), 46, 69; Evans, 94, 100–103.

[54]Higgins, 132–37.

[55]Ibid., 141–44.

Agrarian Rebellions in New York

The Hudson Valley, in both the eighteenth and nineteenth centuries, was shaken by forceful agrarian rebellions for which the early patterns of land division and tenure bear partial responsibility. The original division of land, to be sure, cannot by itself account for the social conditions that later develop on that land. The slave-worked plantations of the South did not all develop on property originating in large grants, nor did small farms persist in Pennsylvania solely because of their early dominance. Each type of holding depended on tradition and external conditions that made it economically and socially viable.

In New York, to some extent, the large estates proved suitable seedbeds for propagating the feudal ambitions of their original owners. Many estate owners fancied their roles as great landlords over tenants far beneath them in status. The conflicts understandably emerged when these feudal estates were juxtaposed with more egalitarian settlements in their environs. Although the tenants' rents were often set at a reasonable level, there were sometimes annoying additional burdens such as fees as high as a third of the price of the farm on sale of the tenants' interests.[56] Interestingly, for our study of land division, the disturbances on the estates were accompanied by challenges to the landlords' titles to their property.[57]

In the eighteenth-century disturbances, which occurred on estates east of the Hudson, the egalitarian challenges came from New England just beyond New York's eastern boundary. Massachusetts and Connecticut claimed the eastern portions of some of the New York manors and granted freehold farms there not only to settlers from their own territories, but also to squatters already on the estates, and even to some manor tenants, who, naturally, preferred freeholds to the leases they had held. Wappinger and Stockbridge Indians, who had originally held much of the land along the Hudson, contended that they still owned some of the eastern parts of the manors, and they proceeded to sell and lease this property on their own. While the New England colonies and the Indians were opposing New York's jurisdiction, Cadwallader Colden and other officials were encourag-

[56]Kammen, 301–2.

[57]The materials on the eighteenth-century agrarian disturbances draw principally on Patricia U. Bonomi, *A Fractious People: Politics and Society in Colonial New York* (New York: Columbia University Press, 1971), 180–224; Kim, 381–415; Mark, 13–84, 131–63. The material on nineteenth-century disturbances depends principally on Ellis, 1–65, 225–312.

ing certain competing New York land interests who claimed parts of these manors on the grounds that the manors had not been properly granted by the Colony of New York in the first place.

Philip Livingston of Livingston Manor had foreseen the threat from Massachusetts, and sought to protect his eastern boundary by obtaining a Massachusetts title to the adjoining Massachusetts township in partnership with two influential Massachusetts residents. A deadlock developed, however, for the New Yorker wanted to lease the land to New York Dutch and German farmers, whereas one Massachusetts partner's plan to sell the land to Yankees would have defeated Livingston's purpose. Livingston died in 1749 shortly after relinquishing the township in question, and his manor along with the ensuing years of troubles passed on to his son, Robert.

Although tenants and landlords maneuvered for position on several manors, the violence during 1751–57 was confined to the Livingston and Claverack manors on the New York–Massachusetts border. Typical incidents of the disturbance included forcible dispossession of tenants, destruction of their belongings, houses, and crops, arrests of claimants and law officers, and, rarely, beating and killing. Peace was restored when the English Board of Trade settled the New York–Massachusetts border in New York's favor, although, for a number of years, the squatters in one part of Claverack continued to recognize Massachusetts's jurisdiction rather than that of New York and the manor proprietor.

The rebellion of 1766 began in Philipse and Cortlandt Manors opposite the Connecticut border, and spread north to include Livingston and Claverack again. These land disturbances were reinforced by concurrent protests against the Stamp Act and the agitation of the Connecticut "levelers," who sought repudiation of all their debts. Among the many actions of the rebellion itself, tenants on both sides were forcibly evicted, and an extended gun battle between the Dutchess County sheriff's party and a band of farmers left four dead and a number wounded. In the end the protesting farmers were controlled by armed forces, and most were defeated in courts made up of landowners and their allies. The owner of Claverack won a court case on his title, but without getting rid of his troublesome squatters. He finally gave up some of his land, not to the squatters, but to the colony, and the squatter issue remained unsettled into the Revolution.

In summary, a variety of conditions led to the disturbances of the 1750s and 1760s. Mark, in his account, emphasizes the inability of the tenants on the estates, who wanted to be landowners, to change conditions they disliked. Bonomi emphasizes the role of the freehold tenures customary across the border in New England in engendering discontent, which had manifested itself only in the eastern parts of estates bordering Massachusetts or separated from Connecticut only by the narrow and contended Oblong Patent. Kim argues that rent conditions were oppressive on only one of the estates, and assigns the principal impetus for the disturbances to Massachusetts agitators and squatters seeking for themselves a share of the land. Other conditions that must be repeated were the presence of Indians asserting their ancestral rights and the vulnerability of the manors to reexamination of their titles. Farther north, in Vermont, the contest between New York and New England land tenures was joined while there was still a wide unsettled frontier zone. Even had there been no Revolution, the New York manor system could have made little headway there.

The energy of New York's farm causes soon went into the Revolution, which resulted in some important changes. Feudalism was abolished, at least officially. Landowners were permitted to buy up their quitrents, which, in any case, fell into disuse. Some of the manors were confiscated as Tory property and divided up among yeoman farmers. The abolition of entail and primogeniture allowed other manors to be divided. Independent farmers held most of Westchester County by 1790. In 1848 land under lease was estimated at 1,800,000 acres, a significant figure, but only a small part of what was originally granted in great estates.

Much of the land continuing under lease after the Revolution lay in surviving portions of the colonial estates, some of their owners among famous patriots of the war. Many of these estates lay in the counties along the Hudson, but leases were also important in a scattering of counties to the west. Rensselaerswyck, now surveyed into 120-acre farms with more than 3,000 tenants, contained a fifth of the leased acreage in 1848. Its perpetual leases or "incomplete sales" required as rent ten to fourteen bushels of wheat, four fat hens, and a day's work with a team of oxen and horses. Livingston Manor had most of its farms let for "two lives" (during the survival of either of two persons named in the lease), and others for "three lives." The Livingston rent was fourteen bushels of wheat per hundred acres, later changed to eighteen dollars, in addition to certain other obligations. Some landlords reserved the right to buy the tenants' grain and fruit. On many estates the tenant had to pay the taxes. But the most controversial provision on most of the estates had become the quarter sale, under which the landlord claimed a quarter (or some other fraction) of the value when the property changed hands by sale or inheritance.

By the mid–1840s cash rents for typical farms ran about thirty dollars, equaling perhaps a tenth of the gross production and a third of the cash income. These were not promptly collected by all the landlords, and back rents, like the earlier quitrents, were sometimes allowed to accumulate, evidence of some leniency with the tenants.

Whether or not rents and working conditions were oppressive, tenant farmers frequently felt a discontent that was likely directed against their landlords. The underlying problems might range from their struggles in trying to cultivate worn-out soils to their envy of freeholding neighbors. A great portion of the nineteenth-century immigrants into New York were New Englanders, who, as tenants, were most likely to be dissatisfied. The discontent among leaseholders had not died out following the riots of the eighteenth century. In the 1790s Livingston and Claverack were again the scenes of disturbances as farmers united to protect their fellows from rent collection and eviction. Nearly half a century later the next major outbreak began on Rensselaerswyck, which had previously escaped trouble.

When Stephen van Rensselaer died in 1839, the back rents on his estate had accumulated to the ominous level of $400,000. To make the matter critical, van Rensselaer's personal debts also amounted to $400,000, and immediate payment of the back rents was demanded by his heirs. Most of the tenants were not ready, or even able, to comply with this demand. In their defense, tenants questioned the landlord's title to the land. The van Rensselaer interests reminded all that the tenants had originally been settled on the land rent-free for several years. When compromise failed, the farmers resolved to stop paying rents entirely. As the situation deteriorated, the farmers, alerted by the blowing of horns, gathered in noisy bands dressed in outlandish Indian costumes. They turned away process servers and, on one occasion, a strong sheriff's posse. Some of their enemies were tarred and feathered, and a few were shot. As the Rensselaerswyck farmers' organization proved effective, their movement spread to other estates operated on leases. Basically it was fueled by the farmers' claim to the American promise of independence.

From a local contest of force and law, the issues moved into the state political arena. A new state constitution in 1846 forbade new leases longer than twelve years. Court decisions held farmers with perpetual leases to be freeholders and therefore not subject to quarter sales. The device of the "incomplete sale" would work no longer. The landlords realized that the old regime could not last and began selling their land and residual rent rights both to tenants and to others (fig. 12.2). Antirent unrest flared up occasionally as late as the 1870s, but the tenant farmers were fast becoming landowners.

Tenancy and rent were contentious issues on New York estates for well over a century. Although land distribution was an issue in most of the colonies, there was no parallel to New York's extended land-lord-tenant disturbances. Other colonies began their existence with plans for aristocrats' estates, but only New York persisted in granting so much of its land in large holdings. New York had to contend, as other middle and Southern colonies did not, with the possessive attitudes of New England farmers toward land. Even without New England at its door, however, New York's tenanted manors could not have survived indefinitely in a democratic United States.

Subdivision of New York Estates and Tracts

The subdivision of the great estates and tracts in New York was often more geometrically regular than the original division itself. The best summary of information on subdivision of the large holdings is an atlas published in 1829, which shows the main survey lines in most of the counties, presumably those counties with the more regular subdivision.[58] These survey lines, with their wide spacing, represent the first gross division of the tract, and not the bounds of individual farms into which the land was eventually divided.

Generally the oldest counties show the least evidence of regularity in this subdivision. East of the Hudson and south of Rensselaer County, no indication of subdivision appears (the atlas was published before the antirent movement, while several original estates were intact). Some lot patterns do appear in northern Rensselaer County and western Albany County. Common patterns in eastern New York are rectangular grids, variously oriented, grids of parallelograms, and ranges of strips, usually along water frontage. The farther west one looks, the more likely are division lines to conform with the cardinal directions.

The Military Tract and the lands to the west of it were mostly surveyed into square townships and sections, but not so uniformly as in the federal survey. The grid of 600-acre sections in the Military Tract often was discontinuous across township boundaries, and some of the lake frontage was in longlots.

[58]*Atlas of the State of New York* (1829; rev. ed., Ithaca, N.Y.: N. C. Burr, 1841).

0 ———————————— 1 Mile

Fig. 12.2. A portion of Rensselaerswyck, near the old headquarters. There is little evidence of any plan in dividing the estate. Tenant farmers probably took over the land they had been farming. USGS, 1952. East Greenbush, N.Y., quadrangle.

Much of the variety of surveys in western New York is illustrated in Allegany and Monroe Counties. Portions of the former lay in the three major tracts, the Holland Purchase, the Morris Reserve, and the Pulteney Purchase. The two western ranges of townships, in the Holland Purchase, were mostly divided into 8 x 8 grids of 360-acre lots, but two townships were cut into arrangements of rectangular strips. The next two ranges to the east were in the Morris Reserve, where some townships were in 360-acre sections, one in 640-acre sections, and others in a mixture of various-sized rectangles. The easternmost range, in the Pulteney Purchase, also showed a variety of rectangular division, with none of its townships fitting in a single pattern. The townships in Monroe County south of Rochester were rhomboidal rather than square and were divided into parallelograms.

Longlots occasionally fitted into the rectangular grids of the townships or, fronting on streams, interrupted the compass orientation of the grids. Joseph Ellicott was particularly ready to insert longlots in surveys when he saw advantages in it.[59]

Summary: New York Land Division

Although New York was eventually divided into small farms as in most parts of the United States, most of its land was originally laid out in large tracts, with less concern for the yeoman farmer than occurred elsewhere in the colonies or early states. The tracts granted by the Dutch and English governments in the seventeenth century were often feudal in nature and intended for rental in smaller parcels. The more speculative tracts granted in the eighteenth century were more likely to be divided in freeholds, although slowly. Many of these eighteenth-century colonial grants went to groups of individuals on a formula of 1,000 or 2,000 acres per grantee; the laws of the colony often made partition of these tracts among their individual owners difficult. Most of the land granted by the states of New York and Massachusetts was in a few huge tracts that were openly speculative. By this time there was a great demand for land by potential settlers and little doubt that the tracts would end up in the hands of farmers.

Thus, very little of New York was ever patented directly in small farms. Townships that would be divided among smallholders were

[59]Wyckoff, 51, 138–40.

introduced during the Dutch period by New Englanders, and were granted occasionally thereafter by Dutch, English, and New York State administrations. Most of the townships granted by New York State went to veterans or other needy groups. The large Military Tract was laid out in 600-acre lots, which were rather large for family farms, but even most of these were engrossed by speculators before being sold again in smaller parcels.

Many large tracts were held for one or more generations before their final division into small farms. Breakdown of large tracts into family farms often occurred in stages, with holdings of intermediate size between the original tracts or estates and the later farms. Some of the land in the tracts of western New York, for example, was sold in townships or half townships before it was divided into sections or smaller farm parcels. By 1850 New York farms averaged only 112 acres, a figure that decreased to 97 acres in 1890 and had risen again to 218 acres in 1982.[60]

The justification for large grants in New York, beginning with the patroonships, was usually the implementation of settlement. The patroonships were offered as an incentive for their masters to import and settle colonists. The English manors, likewise, were designed, or at least rationalized, to place the responsibility for settling the land in the hands of people better able to effect population growth than the impoverished government. In practice the colonial estates did not prove effective instruments of settlement. After the Revolution the states of New York and Massachusetts again farmed out the settlement process. Massachusetts' direct interest extended only to immediate sale of its land, and the first buyers of the great tracts proved to have resources little better than that state's. The demand for farmland proved inadequate, however, to fill up New York's great space in a short time.

The renter disturbances on New York manors lack close parallels in other American areas. Tenancy on the manors of Lord Fairfax in Virginia, Lord Baltimore in Maryland, or the Penns in Pennsylvania lacked both the characteristics and circumstances that led to disturbances in New York. Slaves on Southern plantations were given little chance to revolt.

---

[60]Figures from U.S. Censuses. The tenancy rate was about 20 percent in 1890 and less than 6 percent in 1982.

13

Land Division in New Jersey, and on the West Bank of the Delaware River up to 1682

Lands under the Dutch and Swedes

THE DUTCH activity in New Jersey and Delaware grew as an extension from the Dutch West India Company's primary base in New Amsterdam. Five patroonships were claimed in New Jersey and Delaware, three along the Hudson in northeastern New Jersey and one on each side of Delaware Bay. As we have seen, none of the five achieved any lasting settlement.

Delaware, however, was resettled beginning in 1638 under the auspices of the New Sweden Company, which, although chartered by Sweden, was in its first years supported at least as much by Dutch as by Swedish capitalists and settlers. As New Sweden became more a Swedish enterprise, the settlement of Swedes and the Finns who accompanied them reached between the present locations of Wilmington and Philadelphia. Reconquest of New Sweden by the Dutch in 1655 was followed by a mixed immigration of Dutch and other Europeans and settlement downstream from the capital at Amstel (Newcastle). In 1656 control of Delaware south of the Christina River was turned over to the City of Amsterdam, while the Dutch West India Company kept northern Delaware and the settlements of southeastern Pennsylvania. Amsterdam interests, primarily in trade, still gave more attention to settlement than had the West India Company. Shortly before the English conquest, the city of Amsterdam took over government of all colonies on the west bank of the Delaware.

The Swedes and Finns seem to have settled on scattered farms with little concern for exact boundaries until Dutch laws regarding fences and taxes made more precise property demarcation impor-

245

tant.[1] Records of Swedish grants are not available, probably because few, if any, deeds were issued.[2] The Dutch Governor Peter Stuyvesant's order that settlement be in groups of sixteen to twenty persons or families so as to form villages[3] suggests that the Swedes themselves were not inclined to such grouping. The Dutch tax of twelve stivers per morgen was designed to discourage holding of excessive acreage. Deeds were finally issued during the Duke of York's regime, and the map of landownership in early Pennsylvania (fig. 14.1) shows several irregular parcels near the Delaware River that are considered to have originated with the earlier Swedish settlers. Following the Dutch conquest a few Swedish farmers moved into southwest New Jersey, probably as squatters.[4]

The Dutch were more systematic than the Swedes in laying out farmlands, characteristically arranging holdings in parallel longlots, each including waterfront, meadow, and high ground.[5] When the present site of Lewes in southern Delaware was reoccupied by the Dutch in 1659,[6] a series of eight longlots of varying width was laid out to front on Lewes Creek, which paralleled the coast behind the beach.[7] The streets of the old core of Lewes still maintain the directions of the old longlot boundaries. A reconstruction of the former plan of Appoquinimink, between the present inland communities of Odessa and Middletown, shows a dozen longlots taking up more than three miles of frontage along a creek.[8] This late Dutch settlement is said to have been planned as a new capital. One modern farm still has boundaries that coincide with the old longlot; other lot boundaries survive in field lines, and a long driveway runs in the same direction.

In New Jersey at the end of the Dutch period, the township of Bergen was the only node of permanent settlement.[9] Property claims had been made there as early as 1629 when it was granted as the

---

[1]John A. Munroe, Colonial Delaware (Millwood, N.Y.: KTO Press, 1978), 44–45.

[2]Israel Acrelius, A History of New Sweden (1874; reprinted, New York: Arno Press, 1972), 106.

[3]Amandus Johnson, The Swedish Settlements on the Delaware, 2 vols. (Philadelphia: University of Pennsylvania, 1911), 2: 657.

[4]Wacker, 169–70, 246.

[5]Delaware Department of State, Division of Historical and Cultural Affairs, Historic Preservation Section, Delaware State Historic Preservation Plan, ca. 1977, 11.

[6]Munroe, 48. Lewes had been the site of one of the original abortive patroonships.

[7]Delaware Historic Preservation Plan, maps between 4 and 5.

[8]Louise B. Heite, "Appoquinimink: A Delaware Frontier Village," manuscript, Delaware Historic Preservation Section, 1972.

[9]Wacker, 239–43.

patroonship of Pavonia. After Pavonia's abandonment, settlement was begun again in the 1650s, but acquired a clear focus only with the platting of Bergen village in 1660. Some of the earliest properties were relatively large (a few hundred acres), compact but irregular in shape, and fronting on the Hudson River.[10] Bergen village was laid out around a central square, which survives in the present Jersey City. Most of the landholdings around the village were longlots, ranging from a few acres up to fifty or more acres. Where there were rivers or creeks, the longlots bordered on the water, but more often they were arranged along relatively straight paths or roads. The outlying part of Bergen Township was divided under the English in 1668 and 1764, extending the preference for longlots already established.[11] Longlots persisted in the expansion of Dutch people into northeastern New Jersey during the English proprietary period, especially in the Aquackanonk Tract of 1679, where they had the same dimensions (10 x 100 chains) specified by the English in West Jersey about the same time.[12]

New Jersey under the English

Administration and Policies

New Jersey's succession of governments and proprietors under English rule provided little continuity of land policy and practice in either space or time. The first policies and land grants were made by Richard Nicolls, who commanded the squadron that took over New Netherland and who became the duke's deputy governor over the conquered land. The validity of his grants was clouded, however, by the fact that, unknown to him, the duke had granted New Jersey to his friends Berkeley and Carteret more than two months before the conquest.

The regime of Berkeley and Carteret lasted less than two decades. By 1674 New Jersey had been divided, and Berkeley had sold his West Jersey share. By 1682 George Carteret had died, and East Jersey had been sold also. The ownership of both halves of New Jersey soon passed into the hands of separate bodies of proprietors, comprising

---

[10]D. Stanton Hammond, map of *Bergen Town and Township, November 1660– September 22, 1668, Hudson County, New Jersey,* Genealogical Society of New Jersey, Collections, map ser. no. 1, 1957.

[11]Wacker, 242.

[12]Ibid., 242, 244.

100 shares in West Jersey and twenty-four shares in East Jersey.[13] Some individual proprietors soon held more than one share, as many as twenty in one West Jersey case, while "fractioners" might hold only part of a divided share.

A large part of the original proprietors of both parts of New Jersey were Quakers, English in West Jersey and Scottish in East Jersey, and William Penn played a leading role in both groups. When Penn then was awarded Pennsylvania by the king and soon Delaware by the Duke of York, it might have appeared that the development of all these colonies would advance under a single plan. Penn's interests, however, had shifted to the west side of the Delaware River. Pennsylvania-Delaware and the two Jerseys separately then went their own uncertain ways with only incidental similarities.

Although the proprietors' ownership of the land itself was not generally questioned, their claim to govern the colonies was constantly in dispute. Even when New Jersey was made a royal colony under a single government in 1702, the land in each of the two divisions remained in the hands of its proprietors. Authority among the proprietors was frequently in question, however, sometimes between proprietors in Britain and those in New Jersey, at other times between major shareholders or groups of proprietors and the commissions they designated to administer their land.

The plans for land division in New Jersey drew on practices common in other colonies. Nicolls favored townships on the New England model, and the East Jersey proprietors were still insisting on townships with compactly settled cores as late as 1685.[14] Two of the early towns of West Jersey, Burlington and Salem, were the cores of townships, among two dozen officially recognized there in 1702.[15]

The early land plans set forth in the Concessions and Agreements of 1665 closely paralleled the contemporary plans for Carolina, where Berkeley and Carteret were also proprietors.[16] Land was to be laid off into lots of 2,100 to 21,000 acres, each to be divided into seven parts, one of which the proprietors would retain.[17] Such parcels seem large for fitting into townships, but smaller parcels were offered on a headright basis in all the proprietary plans. Headrights ran as

[13]John E. Pomfret, *The New Jersey Proprietors and Their Lands, 1664–1776,* New Jersey Historical Series, vol. 9 (Princeton: D. Van Nostrand Co., 1964), 23, 36–37.

[14]Wacker, 246–48, 251, 304, 325; Pomfret, *Proprietors,* 47.

[15]Pomfret, *Proprietors,* 75.

[16]Pomfret, *The Province of East New Jersey* (Princeton: Princeton University Press, 1962), 28.

[17]Ibid., 31.

much as 150 acres for first settlers and decreased to as little as twenty-five acres in later plans.[18] New Jersey headright plans aimed mostly at importing servants, who, on redemption, would receive land in addition to what their masters had received for bringing them in.

West Jersey policies of 1681–82 limited stream frontage to forty or fifty rods per 100 acres, thus requiring property depths to be a mile and a quarter or a mile, respectively.[19] East Jersey apparently had longlot policies too, for they were laid out along the Raritan River and across the valley between the First and Second Watchung Mountains before 1686.[20] None of the foregoing plans, however, was followed in the division of any major portion of New Jersey.

More than half the land in New Jersey was distributed through the East New Jersey Board of Proprietors, the Council of Proprietors of West New Jersey, and the West New Jersey Society, the last a stock company that bought or received as dividends more than a fifth of the West Jersey shares and proceeded independently to claim, survey, and sell land. The Board and the Council granted a great part of their proprietary lands in dividends to individual proprietors. These dividends were typically in parcels of 500 acres or more, and the further disposal of the land was up to the individual proprietor owners. The Society sold land through its own agents.[21]

Thus the distribution of proprietary land to individual owner-users was carried out separately by a large number of proprietors. This fact implies the absence of consistent policies and procedures as well as the impossibility of general statements about the results until some review of the more than 100,000 surveys can be made. For the present, the patterns of New Jersey land division can be presented only in terms of those examples that are available.

Patterns of Land Division

New England–style townships were the first English settlements to be planted in New Jersey. We have seen that the Dutch settlement

---

[18]Wacker, 253–54, 285, 304.

[19]Ibid., 242, 292; Pomfret, *Proprietors*, 65.

[20]Wacker, 316–19.

[21]An early plan of the West Jersey owners to divide their land into "Tenths" fronting on the Delaware (the southern five were actually delimited) may have interesting implications for varying patterns of division. Lacking the data to test such meaning, the matter will not be further considered.

of Bergen already resembled such a community and that the early authorities in New Jersey were favorable to township settlement. More important for the persistence of township character, several of these new communities were actually populated by New Englanders.

Very quickly after the conquest, Governor Nicolls responded to petitioners from Long Island townships by making two large grants. The Elizabethtown tract of about 400,000 acres between the Raritan and Passaic Rivers went to a group with a predominantly Connecticut background.[22] The southern part of Elizabethtown was sold in 1666 to Massachusetts settlers for the founding of Woodbridge, and one of the Woodbridge founders in turn granted part of his holding to four New Hampshire men for the town of Piscataway. Nucleated settlement was required or clearly expected for these villages, and quitrents were specified after a period of exemption. The other grant, Navesink, included much of Monmouth County, south of Staten Island and Lower Bay. The villages of Middletown and Shrewsbury quickly grew there; their early settlers from Rhode Island, Massachusetts, and Long Island were largely Quakers. In addition to the two large grants, the founding of Newark by more conventional Puritans from New Haven Colony[23] and the incorporation of Bergen[24] completed a group of seven townships that included much of the population of New Jersey under Berkeley and Carteret.

These towns followed the New England custom of distributing their land in a series of divisions. The townships proper were reported as containing typically about 10,000 acres, with an additional 20,000 to 40,000 acres in "outplantations." The deeded land in the outplantations was sometimes widely dispersed. The town lots in these New Jersey settlements were sometimes more compact in shape than typical New England longlots, and divisions made in the eighteenth century were likely to be laid out in uniform rectangles. As in New England, landowners often consolidated their farms, and village centers decayed as the farmers dispersed to reside on their holdings.

It must be added here that the New England cadastral traditions and the legal questions over the Nicolls grants precipitated conflict

[22]Pomfret, *Proprietors*, 9–13. Elizabethtown had scarcely been settled before Philip Carteret, the proprietors' governor, arrived, bought a share in it, and proceeded to live there and to take an active and sometimes autocratic part in its affairs. His purchase seemed to compromise the proprietors' position that Nicolls's grant of Elizabethtown was not legal (Wacker, 125, 248–49, 270–71).

[23]Pomfret, *Proprietors*, 13–14.

[24]Wacker, 240.

between the townspeople and the proprietors. Some township land-holders secured proprietary grants that confirmed their claims. Most, however, claimed validity for the Nicolls patents or for direct purchases from Indians, refusing in either case to pay the quitrents, which had been explicit in the Nicolls patents. Decades into the eighteenth century both Elizabethtown and Newark were still sub-dividing new tracts of thousands of acres originally claimed on their early Indian purchases. Mobs of township claimants harassed and evicted settlers holding parts of these tracts under conflicting pro-prietary titles;[25] the rioters freed their own people from jail, and Essex County juries refused to convict those accused of rioting. The Newark lands were brought under the proprietors' policies by an agreement consummated in 1771, but negotiations of 1760–62 between Elizabethtown and the proprietors were unsuccessful and no general agreement was ever reached there.

In the distribution and settlement of proprietary lands, West Jersey was probably more successful than East Jersey. The East Jersey Board of Proprietors granted seven dividends of land to shareholders between 1692 and 1744, totaling 23,500 acres per share.[26] The West Jersey Council, by 1756, had distributed 26,250 acres per share in five dividends.[27] With four times as many shares outstanding, West Jersey was evidently distributing much more land.

One reason for West Jersey's more rapid growth lay in the greater interest of its proprietors, more than a quarter of whom actually came there to live, whereas only one original East Jersey proprietor took up permanent residence in the colony.[28] In West Jersey the Quaker design for settlement was preserved for several years, but in East Jersey not a single Quaker settlement was established under the increasingly Scottish proprietors, who fostered business speculation with a Scottish landlord type of settlement.[29]

The special nature of the early settlement under the East Jersey proprietors was drawn from the lowland of northeast Scotland where virtually all the land was owned by landlords and worked by tenants and laborers without significant rights.[30] The Scots among

[25]Ibid., 350–62; Pomfret, *Proprietors*, 108–16.

[26]Wacker, 319–20.

[27]Ibid., 340.

[28]Pomfret, *East New Jersey*, 229. A number of the original proprietors' heirs and other successors did, however, eventually settle in New Jersey.

[29]Ned C. Landsman, *Scotland and Its First American Colony, 1683–1765* (Princeton: Princeton University Press, 1985), 108–20.

[30]Ibid., 17–35.

the proprietors proposed to locate their land dividends in one contiguous tract, people them with tenants and servants, and discourage smallholdings by forbidding both the sale of freeholds and the division of proprieties into fractions that would be entitled to less than 500 acres. They did, however, plan to grant land under quitrents (not a part of native Scottish tradition) to servants at the end of their terms and to tenants after fourteen years. Permitting quitrents to be bought up, as under the English proprietors, was not part of their plan. A concentration of proprietary estates worked by tenants and servants provided support for an influential elite through central New Jersey in the eighteenth century.[31]

Nevertheless, the evidence indicates that, even in East Jersey most of the land distributed by the proprietors from their dividends went into small farms. Parcels of land received by shareholders themselves were often smaller than the dividend sizes seem to imply, because dividends were often not made in single parcels.

Farms in West Jersey, typically between 100 and 200 acres, were smaller and probably more intensively used than farms granted in East Jersey. The West Jersey policy of granting small farms was sometimes defeated, however, by the acquisition of adjoining tracts from two or more proprietors. Even the free-dealing West Jersey Society's grants between 1695 and 1700, however, showed medians of only about 300 acres in the Cape May area and considerably less near the Delaware Falls.[32]

West Jersey proprietors had freedom in assigning quitrents on their own sales. Since they were all competing to sell land, quitrents were seldom assigned. In East Jersey, by contrast, quitrents were regularly stipulated, with a discouraging effect on settlement. Many of the smaller East Jersey farms derived from headrights, which, by 1702, had totaled some 19,000 acres; some of this headright land, however, was assigned by servants to their masters.

Small to medium farms continued to predominate in New Jersey. A sample of those advertised for sale between 1700 and 1730 had a median of a little over 300 acres. By 1780, however, the median was down to 180 acres, presumably the result of subdivision among a growing population.[33]

A substantial portion of New Jersey land parcels was surveyed on warrants in accordance with the wishes of the purchaser—following

[31]Ibid., 124–29.
[32]Wacker, 322, 300–301, 302.
[33]Ibid., 399.

the practice of indiscriminate location. Laws limiting parcels to four boundary courses had moderate success and helped prevent the marked irregularity found in some of the other colonies. Relatively regular surveys such as longlots in townships and along rivers and rectangular surveys in some of the New England townships have already been mentioned. The surveys in Hunterdon County during the first two decades of the eighteenth century emphasized longlots fronting on the Delaware River.[34]

Other land grant maps also illustrate the preference for streams in location of the first settlements in new areas. A group of Anglo-Irish Quakers pooled their rights to acquire a block of land on the Delaware River opposite Philadelphia in 1700.[35] Here they scattered their houses before finding that common landownership was inconvenient. Nonetheless they were able to divide the land into moderately compact parcels, most of which were bordered by streams and no more than three straight courses and contained the houses already occupied by the owners. Some mid-eighteenth-century maps of the first land grants in interior highland areas also illustrate the preference for streamside sites.[36]

Except for the New England town grants and proprietary dividends, both of which were usually subdivided into small parcels, relatively little New Jersey land was granted in large tracts. Early in the Berkeley-Carteret regime some large grants went to planters from the West Indian island of Barbados.[37] Barbadian land acquisitions in New Jersey, as in South Carolina, were likely a reflection of the scarcity of land in the Lesser Antilles. New Barbados, between the Hackensack and Passaic Rivers, contained some tracts as large as 15,000 acres, and received the first slaves brought into New Jersey. Two West Jersey proprietors tried to establish manors, but manors could not survive where land in smallholdings was so readily available.[38] The West Jersey Society managed to obtain several large tracts for speculation, including more than 90,000 acres in the Cape May area, surveyed in 1699, and a similar amount in the Great Tract of Hunterdon County surveyed in 1711. It was apparently in the latter that the society's agents let purchasers pick out 10,000 acres in select small parcels here and there, to the detriment of the remainder

[34]Ibid., 341.
[35]Ibid., 296–98.
[36]Ibid., 373, 375.
[37]Ibid., 271–72; Pomfret, *Proprietors*, 16–17.
[38]Wacker, 302; Pomfret, *Proprietors*, 65.

of the area.[39] The company that bought the remainder of the Great Tract in 1752 sold four tracts of about 10,000 acres each, but another 150 parcels in small farms averaging 200 acres.

Hunterdon in West Jersey is the only county of the state for which a land grant map is available.[40] The Hunterdon map shows a number of long straight lines bounding several parcels on each side. These long lines are clearly sides of earlier and larger tracts, probably including the Great Tract and its 10,000-acre subdivisions, which were in their turn divided into farms as they were sold off. Rectangularity, in which adjoining parcels have their boundaries running in the same directions, is the pattern in several parts of Hunterdon County, most commonly in the vicinity of the long lines mentioned. A sizable minority of all parcels on the Hunterdon County map are rectangles, and a great part of all parcels are four-sided.

Summary

The land division patterns of New Jersey are not yet known well enough to compare them meaningfully with those in other states. The Dutch made the first settlements in New Jersey, and, later, as their numbers increased, continued longlot division in the northeast of the colony. The New Englanders added several of their townships, but probably made more impression on New Jersey cadastral matters through contentious assertion of what they saw as their property rights than from their characteristic ways of parceling out the land. Most of the proprietary land of New Jersey went into small farms laid out one at a time without a general plan. The manner of dividing land among many proprietors, each of whom would further dispose of his tracts, was a unique feature of New Jersey colonial land distribution.

More surprising, and unique to New Jersey, was the survival of the state's proprietary establishments after the Revolution. The West Jersey Society sold its shares to a single real-estate dealer in 1814, and finally distributed its treasury in 1876.[41] The East New Jersey Board of Proprietors and the Council of Proprietors of West New Jersey, however, are still in existence. Although they have no invento-

[39]Ibid., 302, 343–44.

[40]D. Stanton Hammond, map of *Hunterdon County Tracts, 1688–1785*, Genealogical Society of New Jersey, map ser. no. 4, 1968.

[41]Pomfret, *Proprietors*, 119.

ries of unalienated land, occasional patches do turn up as results of surveying oversights or errors or coastal accretion. The West Jersey Council surveyed 20,000 acres of land between 1900 and 1922, but reported less than a dozen surveys in the next forty years.[42] Each body still maintains its own original land grant records; in New Jersey alone are such records not in public archives. The proprietors' quitrents, never assiduously collected, quickly disappeared through disuse rather than legal abolition. The town of Bergen, however, did pay $1,500 in 1809 to buy up its fifteen pounds quitrent.

Delaware under the Duke of York

Between the 1664 English conquest of New Netherland and the 1682 cession of Delaware to William Penn, Delaware was under the control of the Duke of York. Little of Delaware had been granted under the Netherlands and Sweden, and the new grants in the duke's name were also limited in number. The Duke's policy was based on fifty-acre headrights,[43] but his grants were fairly large. A sample of fifty grants, mostly between 1670 and 1680, ranged from eighty acres to 2,531 acres with a median of 400 acres.[44] The largest tract was actually granted to five owners. Consistent with the grant sizes, rent rolls of 1689 show that more than half the landowners in Kent and Sussex Counties owned 500 acres or more, whereas properties were probably smaller in more populous New Castle County, as they were in adjoining Chester and Philadelphia Counties in Pennsylvania.[45]

---

[42]Ibid., 118.

[43]Munroe, 74.

[44]Sample from original land titles in *Duke of York Record, 1646–1679* (Wilmington: Sunday Star Print by order of General Assembly of Delaware, 1903).

[45]Munroe, 94.

14
Pennsylvania and Delaware: The Penn Proprietorship

WILLIAM Penn saw the founding of Pennsylvania as a "holy experiment" for which the new land offered "room" that might not be found in England.[1] Pennsylvania abounded in land, but Penn soon found that his promises of grants in his principal city created a kind of presettlement urban congestion that exceeded the space in even the expansive plat of Philadelphia.[2]

The resources and planning of Penn and of the people he recruited to organize the initial colonization got the Pennsylvania settlement off to an unparalleled beginning. Eighteen ships had brought in about 2,000 people in the ten months preceding Penn's arrival in October 1682, and sixty more ships brought in a larger number in 1683.[3] One result of his preparation is the land pattern in the original counties of southeast Pennsylvania, which is more orderly than that found in any comparable area in any other colony.

Penn and the other Quakers developing Pennsylvania did not find their business interests incompatible with the "holy" nature of the venture. Many of the people who helped finance the colony by their advance purchases of land were Quakers who had been quite successful in their businesses in England. Penn himself distributed and managed the land of Pennsylvania with a view to personal profit, which, however, he failed to realize.

The land plan began with a 500,000-acre purchase from the Indians to be divided into fifty blocks of 10,000 acres each.[4] The land was

[1]Edwin B. Bronner, *William Penn's "Holy Experiment": The Founding of Pennsylvania, 1681–1701* (New York: Temple University Publications, 1962), 6.

[2]Reps, 163, 165.

[3]Bronner, 31–32; Joseph J. Kelley, Jr., *Pennsylvania: The Colonial Years, 1681–1776* (Garden City, N.Y.: Doubleday & Co., 1980), 33; Philip S. Klein and Ari Hoogenboom, *A History of Pennsylvania* (University Park: Pennsylvania State University Press, 1980), 25.

[4]Pomfret, "The First Purchasers of Pennsylvania," *Pennsylvania Magazine of History and Biography* 80 (1956), 146–48.

to sell at 100 pounds for 5,000 acres, one pound for fifty acres, with a quitrent of a shilling per 100 acres, which could be covered in perpetuity on payment of eighteen shillings.[5] Those buying large tracts were promised 2 percent of their acreage in Philadelphia, 100 acres for a purchase of 5,000 acres, ten acres for a purchase of 500. Alternatively, those who settled in rural communities could set aside 2 percent of the land for a village. Penn offered to lease land to settlers at a penny an acre, and he offered a headright of fifty acres for importing a servant as well as fifty acres for the servant at the end of his term. The quitrent was increased on the headright—two shillings for the servant, four for the master.[6] Even the servant would pay in quitrents more than the equivalent cost (sale price plus quitrents) of fifty acres for first purchasers. The 10,000 acres in each 100,000 to be reserved for Penn's own use provided land for many proprietary manors.[7]

Penn's precolonization sales in tracts of 125 to 10,000 acres were almost entirely within the community of Friends in the British Isles. By May 1682 sales exceeded the planned 500,000 acres, and by 1700 the total reached 800,000. In addition 165,000 acres in tracts of more than 10,000 acres were sold to half a dozen large speculators, all but one after Penn's return to England in 1684. More than half of the 700 purchasers of Pennsylvania land before 1700 actually settled in the colony, although those settlers included only a dozen who bought as much as 5,000 acres.[8]

Early Land Division as Shown on the Holme Map of Pennsylvania

By the time Penn returned to England, he was already pushing the surveyor general, Thomas Holme, for a map of the settled part of the colony.[9] The map, which materialized in 1687 (fig. 14.1), made Pennsylvania the only North American colony that provided its sponsors with a comprehensive map of its land grants. The difficulties under which Holme prepared the map explain a number of omis-

---

[5]Prices of Pennsylvania land went up. Between 1732 and 1765, 100 acres sold for £15 10s with a quitrent of half a penny sterling per acre.

[6]Bronner, 61.

[7]William H. Kain, "The Penn Manorial System and the Manors of Springetsbury and Maske," *Pennsylvania History* 10 (1943): 225–26.

[8]Pomfret, "First Purchasers," 148–52.

[9]Walter Klinefelter, "Surveyor General Thomas Holme's 'Map of the Improved Part of the Province of Pennsylvania,'" *Winterthur Portfolio* 6 (1970), 41–44.

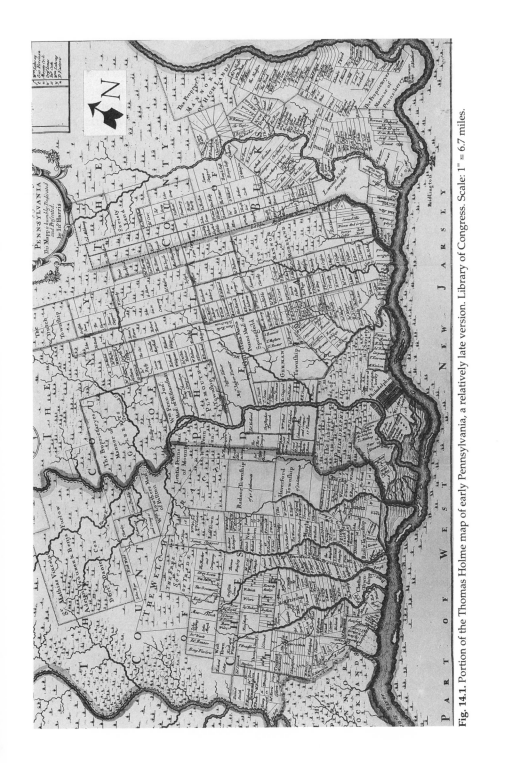

Fig. 14.1. Portion of the Thomas Holme map of early Pennsylvania, a relatively late version. Library of Congress. Scale: 1" = 6.7 miles.

sions and uncertainties. The subdivisions of some townships were not shown because some of the surveyors had not given Holme accurate and complete reports. Some land claims were in dispute. A few parcels were too small to depict. Even so, this map is testimony to careful land planning and management. Until he received the map, Penn had been deeply embarrassed by his lack of such concrete information about the colony he was trying to promote and build.

Holme's map was reprinted and copied with frequent revisions until at least around 1730. Even the latest of these maps of southeastern Pennsylvania show only a moderate number of changes from the original, including a few property subdivisions; as property ownership maps, they must more closely approximate conditions of 1687 than of 1730.

The Holme map records a ladder pattern of land division with property over sizable areas bounded by lines running in mutually perpendicular directions. Many of the smaller properties are narrow strips running between the long sides of the ladders; others are larger and elongated in the direction of the ladder. In other areas, especially near the Delaware River, the ladders are skewed and may be bounded by creeks. Klinefelter[10] suggests that these skewed strips were oriented with the boundaries of some of the holdings near the Delaware granted before Penn's time by Sweden or the Duke of York. Names of some of these earlier holders do appear on the map without exact indication of the boundaries of their smallholdings.

Two main parts of the map are dominated by the perpendicularity of the ladder pattern. These two areas are mostly separated by the Schuylkill River and meet one another at an angle of 31 degrees. Both may have drawn their general orientations from the Delaware and Schuylkill Rivers, as probably did the urban grid of Philadelphia, which had a yet different orientation. These two systems of directions in the rural surveys survive conspicuously in the present road patterns (fig. 14.2).[11]

Townships, which represented the community settlement pattern desired by Penn, provided the immediate frame for most of the land division. Many of the townships, which were not uniform in size and shape, are labeled on the Holme map with the same names they bear at present. Township boundaries are hardly visible on black and

[10]Ibid., 49–50.

[11]For example, on the Ambler and West Chester 7.5' topographic maps of the counties of Chester, Montgomery, and Bucks, as well as in the nonriverine boundaries of the City and County of Philadelphia.

N   0 ⌐——————————⌐ 1 Mile

Fig. 14.2. Rectangularity of the original survey of southeastern Pennsylvania surviving in Bucks County. USGS, 1968. Buckingham quadrangle.

white copies of the map, but they have been accentuated by heavy lines over the southwestern and eastern portions of the copy published in *Atlas of the Historical Geography of the United States*.[12]

Penn was pleased to note in 1685 that at least fifty townships had been laid out.[13] He had conceived the townships as including 5,000 acres each to be divided among at least ten families, and noted two ways of dividing them: "Our Townships lie square; generally the Village in the Center; the houses either opposite, or else opposite to the middle, betwixt two houses over the way, for near neighborhood. We have another Method, that tho the Village be in the Center, yet after a different manner. Five Hundred Acres are allotted for the Village, which, among ten families, comes to fifty acres each. This lies square, and on the outside of the square stand the houses, with their Fifty Acres running back [i.e., into the square] . . . [and on the outside] every man's 450 Acres of Land that makes up his Complement of 500." Two townships of the second design show clearly in Bucks County. New Town, the more conspicuous, had fifteen lots, one of which was labeled "Governers" for Penn under a frequently ignored plan to reserve a lot for him in every township. The suburban village of Newtown still has its grid oriented with the old central square, and five or six present-day roads so closely approximate the old radial property lines that we may assume they perpetuate the original survey (fig. 14.3). Plymouth Township in Philadelphia County was once planned with similar radial division. Its plan (ca. 1690) includes an elongated rectangle for the village in the center[14]— nothing to compare, however, with the four-mile by one-quarter-mile townstead allegedly laid out along the edge of the same township by a disgruntled surveyor.[15]

The first township plan described by Penn was more common. It was conceived as a square bisected by a road with strip holdings perpendicular to the road on each side, in a double ladder. The map shows several such townships. Concord in Chester County appears the most perfect example of the design on the Holme map. Upper and

---

[12]Charles O. Paullin and John K. Wright, eds., *Atlas of the Historical Geography of the United States* (Washington: Carnegie Institution of Washington and American Geographical Society of New York, 1932), plate 40.

[13]*A Further Account of the Province of Pennsylvania and Its Improvements*, in *Narratives of Early Pennsylvania, West New Jersey, and Delaware, 1630–1707*, ed. Albert Cook Myers (New York: Charles Scribner's Sons, 1912), 263.

[14]Reproduced in Lemon, 101.

[15]Klinefelter, 60.

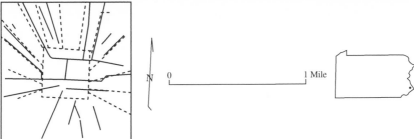

Fig. 14.3. Newtown, Bucks County, Pa. The solid lines in the diagram represent roads and field boundaries visible on the photograph, mostly those radiating from Newtown. The dashed lines show the land division of the Newtown township from the Holme map. The degree of coincidence between division lines on the Holme map and radial lines in the present landscape is considerable, especially considering the small scale of the Newtown representation on the Holme map. The relation between the central village square on the Holme map and the town of Newtown today is also evident. USGS, 1965. Lambertville and Langhorne quadrangles.

Nether Providence are less regular examples. Radnor Township shows no division other than the central road, but is noted as having forty settlements. Haverford shows no subdivision, but another map does show its thirty-two settlements arranged in a complicated resemblance to Penn's first plan.[16] Newlin Township, just south of the Brandywine River and not on the Holme map, is a later example with oblique lots as in the Providences.[17] Newton in Chester County (now Delaware County) combined the rectangular strip farms with a central rectangle probably intended as a village.

The largest tracts without divisions on the Holme map include manors assigned to the proprietor and members of his family, several large tracts sold for speculation or settlement, and the Liberty Lands of Philadelphia. Nine manors ranging from less than 2,000 to nearly 10,000 acres appear in the Pennsylvania portion of the map. Three lie on the Delaware River, and another, Rocklands, just across the present border in Delaware, was the largest of all these early manors. Five fronted on the Schuylkill, virtually blocking off that transportation way a few miles above Philadelphia. The Manor of Moreland was granted the president of the Free Society of Traders, a business organization of Quaker membership, which received a total of 20,000 acres and a monopoly on certain business ventures.[18] These, along with other large grants, must for some time have inhibited Penn's plan for dense settlement.

A number of the large tracts were purchased with the intent of settling particular groups. At least part of one of them was intended as a refuge for persecuted Huguenots. The Welsh Tract, which embraced upward of 30,000 acres, was the base for an elaborate scheme of settling companies of Welsh Quakers. Most of the companies of Welsh or their leaders purchased 5,000 acres, but had to accept their land in two parcels because of the universal preference for southeastern sites nearest Philadelphia. The Edward Jones and Company tract, which touched the Liberty Lands and the Schuylkill River, was the first of these tracts to be settled, with Haverford and Radnor Townships following.[19] German Township and the Dutch Township were other

[16]See maps in Charles H. Browning, *Welsh Settlement of Pennsylvania* (Philadelphia: William J. Campbell, 1912), 204, 232.

[17]Map from William C. Baldwin, *Brandywine Creek: A Pictorial History* (West Chester, Pa.: Author, 1977).

[18]Bronner, 62–63.

[19]Browning. Among the large grants in Delaware was another Welsh Tract of 30,000 acres, laid out in a rectangular ladder except as the compass needle was deflected by Iron Mountain (conversation with Edward F. Heite, Delaware Bureau of Archives and

tracts for settlement by national groups. William Penn had also offered to sell a tract to the Scottish group who finally settled in New Jersey.

Philadelphia was oddly conceived as "a green country town," 100 lots each of 100 acres, a house to occupy the middle of each lot.[20] Penn must have agreed with the modern author who wrote "For reasons, good or ill, owning land is the most effective way in which people keep their distance from others."[21] The 100 lots of Philadelphia would have matched 100 rural tracts of 5,000 acres each. But Pennsylvania's city needed space for artisans and tradesmen to serve the farmers in the fertile hinterland and denser settlement to facilitate commercial and social intercourse.

The city that was actually platted had little more than an eighth of the planned acreage, and yet, although a spectacular success, it was more than a century before Philadelphia filled that plat. The Liberty Lands adjoining the city were set aside to provide the rest of the town land that the purchasers of rural land had been promised. Thus many of them had to be satisfied with the "green country" alone. John Reed's 1774 property map[22] shows the Liberties divided into many longlots, some of them in ladder pattern, a manor, and even an area of eighty-acre gridded squares, some in turn subdivided.

The Holme map covers the division of 800,000 to 900,000 acres, about two-thirds of the area of the present counties of Bucks, Philadelphia, Montgomery, Delaware, and the part of Chester northeast of the Brandywine River. This "Old Rights" area proved to be as distinctive a pattern in Pennsylvania as it was in the colonies as a whole, for the regularity shown on the Holme map was not destined to spread with further settlement.

Records, April 1977). The modern tax map of the area preserves a number of parallel lines bounding properties as in the original divisions. The Baptist Meeting House of 1746 still stands on a property owned by Trustees of Welsh Tract Baptist Church and bisected by an interstate highway.

[20]Klinefelter, 47.

[21]Boyd Gibbons, *Wye Island* (Baltimore: Johns Hopkins University Press for Resources for the Future, 1977), 90.

[22]*Map of the City and Liberties of Philadelphia, with the Catalogue of Purchasers* (Philadelphia: 1774).

Later Colonial Land Division

Proprietary Manors

Penn was authorized by his charter to erect manors to be held by him or, assigned to others, of him.[23] Most of the Penns' tenth of the land went into these manors. There was little intention to operate the holdings as manors, such a social structure probably being incompatible with Quakerism and with Penn's plan to people the colony with landholding farmers. Rather the manors were speculative holdings, meant to yield later profits as real-estate values rose.[24]

The manors were staked out as the land was opened up. Earlier small claims that fell within manor boundaries continued to be recognized, but surveying of some manors was obstructed by squatters who had settled there first. Parcels were sold from the manors from time to time, and some land was rented. There seems to have been no intensive subdivision into leases. Some land sales or leases within no manor were still held as of the major manor in that county.[25]

Nearly eighty manors have been located on the Pennsylvania map (fig. 14.4). Several of these were reserved in the Old Rights area very early, and many others clustered within and just beyond the original counties. To the west developed the two largest manors, Springetsbury in York County with more than 64,000 acres and Maske in Adams County with more than 43,000. Manors in the southwest quarter of Pennsylvania were mostly small and widely scattered; one including the forks of the Ohio and other land south of the site of Pittsburgh was a clearly strategic choice. Two concentrations appear in the northeast. Those along the Susquehannah River were chosen to exploit the river corridor and river frontage, perhaps also to oppose the Susquehannah Company's entry. The concentration of mostly very small manors in the far northeast is harder to explain. At least some of them were mill sites. Most were on small streams rather than on the Delaware River. Again they may have been a protective response to the plans of the Susquehannah Company and the similar Delaware Company (although the latter never made permanent settlements). All the proprietary manors in Pennsylvania totaled about 600,000 acres.[26]

---

[23]Marshall Harris, 149–50, 153.

[24]Kain, 225–26.

[25]William Robert Shepherd, *History of Proprietary Government in Pennsylvania*, Studies in History, Economics, and Public Law, no. 6 (New York: Columbia University, 1896), 47.

[26]Kain, 240.

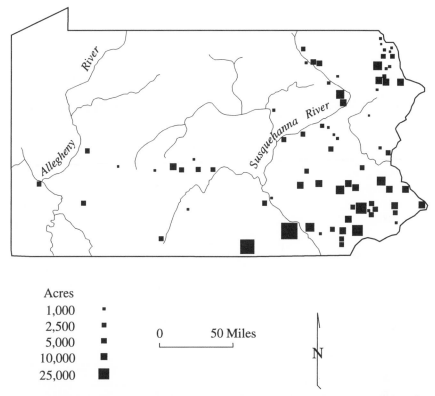

Acres
1,000
2,500
5,000
10,000
25,000

0   50 Miles

N

Fig. 14.4. Proprietary manors of Pennsylvania. The areal scale of the symbols is that of the map. Compiled from a list and maps in *Pennsylvania Archives*, ser. 3, and a list that accompanied *An Historical Map of Pennsylvania*, Pennsylvania Historical Society, 1875. A few manors, especially in the west, are located by county only.

At least half a dozen manors were also staked out in Delaware. Two of them, in Sussex County, were detached parts of Rocklands, which appeared on the Holme map. All Delaware manors identified belonged to Penn except one in the name of the Duke of York, possibly a present from Penn or the duke's reservation for himself.

At least ten present Pennsylvania townships bear the names of manors in their vicinities, and townships in Lancaster and Armstrong Counties are simply named "Manor." Examples of townships with manor names are Richland in Bucks County, Springetsbury in York County, Muncy in Lycoming County, and Cherry Hill in Indiana County. A small number of these townships have boundaries coinciding with the old manors.

Irregular Land Division

The townships of early Pennsylvania never developed the strong community coherence Penn had wanted. Townships on the New England model could hardly have grown in most of Pennsylvania, for not only was Quakerism not a highly structured movement,[27] but Quaker tolerance of others led to Pennsylvania's open door and more mixing of peoples. The lack of strongly organized townships may help explain the breakdown of regularity in Pennsylvania's land survey.

In any case the increasing immigration of peoples of diverse background brought pressures for land beyond what the surveyors could anticipate. Penn's agents' promises of land led many immigrants to move directly to the frontier, where, seeing the abundance of vacant land, they often squatted and soon claimed the land by virtue of the improvements they had made. Out of these conditions came the issuing of warrants for surveys and free choice of land for the settlers. Land purchasers were allowed an extra 6 percent for roads and barren land and 4 percent for surveying errors.[28]

Pennsylvania probably was opened up by squatters to a greater extent than any other colony. The government never succeeded in stemming these squatting claims, and actually encouraged them at times in order to protect frontiers. For example, Pennsylvania could not honestly collect the sale price from those settling in territory disputed with Maryland.[29] Squatter acreage was estimated at 100,000 as early as 1725. In 1735 a colony lottery for 100,000 acres of unclaimed land was announced; and, without the mediation of any drawing, many of the tickets apparently became titles to land already settled and improved.[30] Pennsylvania courts and ultimately a 1784 preemption law both supported claims by possession.

Lancaster, the first Pennsylvania county settled beyond the Old Rights area, shows variety in its surveys, but no significant tracts with as much regularity as the ladders of the Holme map. Many Lancaster County (civil) townships might almost have been in early Virginia for the lack of system in their land layout (figs. 14.5, 14.6), except that properties in these Pennsylvania areas were more usu-

[27]Joseph E. Illick, *Colonial Pennsylvania* (New York: Charles Scribner's Sons, 1976), 132.

[28]Shepherd, 55.

[29]Ford, 114–15; Shepherd, 49–50; John G. Stephenson III, "Land Office Business in Pennsylvania," *Villanova Law Review* 4 (1958–59): 184–85. Squatters could establish "inchoate titles" to 300 acres, but were still expected to purchase the land.

[30]Shepherd, 34.

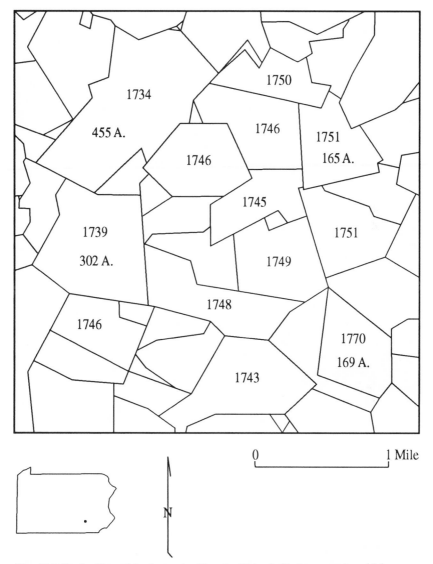

Fig. 14.5. Rapho Township, Lancaster County. Dates indicate warrants, which were usually followed promptly by survey. Two unusual lines along cardinal directions of the most northerly 1746 parcel form a right angle. By permission of the Pennsylvania Bureau of Land Records.

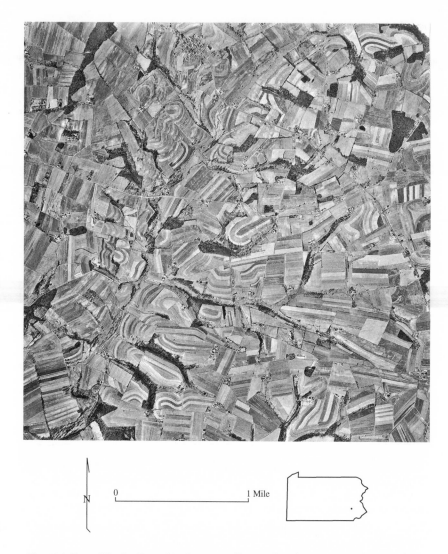

Fig. 14.6. Part of Rapho Township, Lancaster County, Pa., the same area shown in figure 14.5. The present-day fields evident in the photograph are, of course, smaller than the original grants. USGS, 1969. Manheim quadrangle.

ally compact and medium-sized. The county's Susquehannah River frontage was bordered by elongated parcels, irregular in length and width. Also frequent in Lancaster were rectangular and subrectangular systems that fell short of organization into grids or ladders.

The source of authority needed to produce regularity in some of the surveys is not always clear. At least in part it sprang from surveys of a few to several thousand acres for individuals, groups, or companies that exercised some control over the later subdivision into family farms. A report on four Lancaster County tracts shows two of them subdivided in mostly rectangular form, one largely in nonrectangular quadrangles, and one in irregular polygons.[31] One of these largely rectangular tracts comprised about 7,000 acres marked off in 1716 to help complete a 60,000-acre grant of 1699 to a "London Company." A land grant map of the German-settled Strasburg Township shows a possible response to terrain with a predominance of rectangularity in the more level north and west, smaller and less regular parcels in the slightly more hilly south and east.[32] Today's road systems line up with the old property lines in some of the rectangular areas. The state land grant map of Manor Township is crossed most of its width by a single even line that was probably the northern boundary of Conestoga Manor. Land division south of the line shows rectangularity such as might develop from selling off parts of the manor; division to the north shows irregularity that might more likely develop from independent exercise of warrants by settlers.

Irregular surveys also occurred in Delaware under Penn's administration, reflecting no great change from the Duke of York's time. A published land grant map along the Mispillion River separating Kent and Sussex Counties shows irregular surveys from both administrations, some orientation of parcels to streams, and one area of rectangular parcels apparently representing the subdivisions of a large earlier grant.[33] The median parcel ran about 550 acres in this mapped area, which included Penn's manor of Worminghurst, named for his home in England.

Irregular land division in Pennsylvania extends west and north from the original settlements through most of the areas settled before the Revolution. Many Virginia frontiersmen settled and claimed land in the southwestern corner of Pennsylvania, an area that fell within Virginia's early boundary line running indefinitely northwestward. Virginia land was cheap, and some Virginians came in

[31]H. Frank Eshleman, "Four Great Surveys in Lancaster County," *Journal of Lancaster County Historical Society* 28 (1924), 8–12.

[32]Marion Dexter Learned, *American Ethnographic Survey*, Conestoga Expedition, 1902 (New York: D. Appleton and Co. for University of Pennsylvania, 1911), opp. 20.

[33]E. Dallas Hitchens, *The Milford Delaware Area before 1776* (Milford, Del.: Author, 1976), 34–35.

with a number of military land rights.[34] When the boundary was settled in 1780, Pennsylvania promised to recognize Virginia claims except on land covered by prior Pennsylvania claims. More than a thousand Virginia claims, mainly from 1769 to 1774, were finally approved by Pennsylvania. Of the 200 entries in 1779 and 1780, the great majority were for the 400 acres then standard in Virginia.[35] One can hardly separate Virginia claims from Pennsylvania claims on the basis of property geometry. A sample in southwestern Pennsylvania, however, showed an average of 10.8 boundary courses per parcel against 7.8 in the smoother terrain of a Lancaster County sample. A late proprietary order for regular figures of four sides in property layout seems to have had little effect.

By the end of the colonial period the Penns had sold or granted about five million acres, leaving roughly five-sixths of Pennsylvania still to be divided. The Pennsylvania government took over the undivided land during the Revolution, and managed to collect something like half the back quitrents on the alienated land to help finance the war. The Penns were allowed to keep their manors, on which the interest of their heirs was finally liquidated only near the end of the nineteenth century. The Penns also received a payment from Pennsylvania of £130,000 (compare with the £16,000 debt canceled by the original royal grant) and an annuity of £4,000 from the British government, which was paid for about a hundred years.[36]

Land Division in the Susquehannah Company Settlement

The Susquehannah Company of Connecticut introduced an exotic element into the land system of northeastern Pennsylvania. The total area shaped by this New England land division was small, but the competition over nearly half a century between two peoples with differing land traditions in their differing cultures is of significance for our subject.

Connecticut's charter gave that colony a strip of land across the continent between the forty-first parallel and a line slightly north of the forty-second parallel (the present northern boundary of Penn-

---

[34]Solon J. Buck and Elizabeth Hawthorn Buck, *The Planting of Civilization in Western Pennsylvania* (Pittsburgh: University of Pittsburgh Press, 1939), 143–44.

[35]*Pennsylvania Archives*, ser. 3, vols. 2, 3: 507–17.

[36]Norman B. Wilkinson, *Land Policy and Speculation in Pennsylvania, 1779–1800* (New York: Arno Press, 1979), 1–5; Marshall Harris, 368.

sylvania). British conquest of Dutch New York abruptly cut Connecticut off on the west, and its western claims were largely forgotten. By the middle of the eighteenth century, however, Connecticut had granted its undisputed territory in townships, leaving no room for pioneer expansion and new land speculation.[37] In a reassertion of Connecticut's claim to its old charter territory, the Susquehannah Company was formed for sponsoring settlement on the Susquehanna River, and the company proceeded to buy a large tract of northern Pennsylvania from certain Indians of the area in a transaction of questioned validity.[38]

The first settlements by the Susquehannah Company were made in 1762,[39] and, during the next decade several followed, over the verbal and sometimes violent objections of the Pennsylvanians. Although the area was remote from Pennsylvania's government and beyond Pennsylvania's ecumene, it was nonetheless being probed by its pioneer settlers and speculators. The government of Connecticut finally gave the Susquehannah Company official backing by deliberately creating there in 1774 a new political unit with the status of a town bearing the suggestive name of Westmoreland,[40] an area about as large as Connecticut proper, then having about 2,000 inhabitants.[41] The Continental Congress later established a court to settle the disputed jurisdiction, and in 1782 Westmoreland was awarded to Pennsylvania.[42] But during the ensuing two decades it took to reach agreement on private ownership of the land, the Susquehannah Company poured more settlers ("half-share men") into the area and laid out a grid of townships reaching west far into the Allegheny River drainage.[43] A series of fights wherein New England settlers were several times driven off the land they had taken have been known as the Yankee-Pennamite Wars.[44]

[37]Daniels, *The Connecticut Town*, 30–33, 58.

[38]Julian Parks Boyd, *The Susquehannah Company: Connecticut's Experiment in Expansion*, Connecticut Tercentenary Commission, Pamphlet no. 34 (New Haven: Yale University Press, 1935), 11.

[39]Sydney George Fisher, *The Making of Pennsylvania* (Philadelphia: Lippincott, 1896), 246.

[40]Klein and Hoogenboom, 190.

[41]Boyd, 37.

[42]Ibid., 43. Although Connecticut's royal grant preceded Pennsylvania's, the king apparently held the prerogative of changing his mind.

[43]*The Susquehannah Company Papers*, 10 vols.; vols. 1–4, ed. Julian P. Boyd; vols. 5–10, ed. Robert J. Taylor (Ithaca, N.Y.: Cornell University Press for Wyoming Historical and Genealogical Society, 1930–71), 1: map in back pocket; 10: xxxiii and following.

[44]Fisher, 264–301, et passim.

The Susquehannah Company settled its people in towns, New England–style, typically assigning five-mile squares to fifty settlers and reserving an additional three shares for schools and churches,[45] much like the northwestern townships in Connecticut. The towns were often organized in Connecticut localities, whence their migrant members proceeded to the townships surveyed for them on the Susquehanna. The Seventeen Certified Towns along the Susquehanna River that went to the New England settlers in the final compromise on property claims amounted to 288,532 acres on issuance of 1,745 certificates.[46] Other towns that were settled after the 1782 decision, and the "pitches" or isolated farms, were not confirmed to the New Englanders. Pennsylvanians claiming land within the Seventeen Towns were given compensating parcels elsewhere.

The Connecticut towns in Pennsylvania varied in their layout, but typically had a bank of house lots and divisions comprised of equal strips side by side (fig. 14.7). Although house lots were unusual in new towns in New England itself in the eighteenth century, plans for compact villages on the Susquehanna may have been prompted by the hostile surroundings. The divisions of Wilkes-Barre land, for example, gave each settler a selection of house lot, farm lot, meadow or upland lot, and mountain lot,[47] distributed by lottery. The first division had distributed the farmland along the river. The second-division house lots were unusual in having been arranged in a 4 x 4 grid of oblong blocks, for which New Haven may have been the closest parallel in New England. The blocks were broken into six lots, each of a little more than three acres, often subdivided in their turn at an early date. The corners of the four blocks at the central intersection were cut off at angles of 45° to form an open square of a style more Pennsylvanian than New England.

Thus New England townships with their characteristic villages and strip divisions appeared late in northeastern Pennsylvania, and several grew into important urban communities, retaining the names given them by the New Englanders—Wilkes-Barre, Huntington, Kingston, Exeter, Hanover, Salem, Pittston, and others. The civil townships farther west, though mostly bounded today by lines square with the compass, do not perpetuate the grid laid out by the

---

[45]Boyd, 32–33.

[46]Ibid., 47–48; Fisher, 314–15.

[47]Boyd, 33. The upland and mountain lots both seem to be included in the long strips of the third division shown on the Pennsylvania Bureau of Land Records connected warrantee map of Wilkes-Barre Township and butting abruptly against the block divisions of adjoining Bear Creek Township.

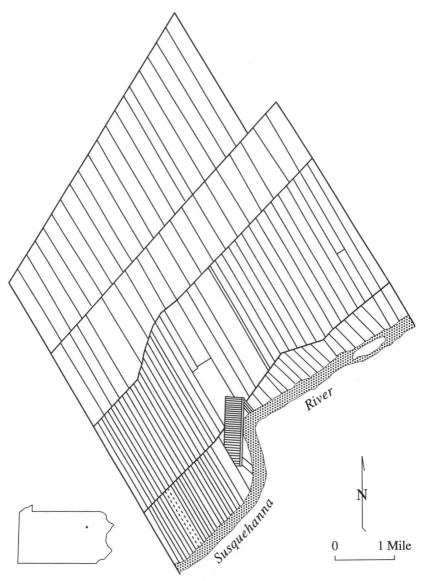

Fig. 14.7. Kingston Township, Luzerne County, on the Susquehanna River. A Susquehannah Company settlement, dating from 1769. Five-acre houselots comprised the first division, the lots along the river the second division, the tier of the longest lots the third division, and, farthest from the river, the Mountain Tier and Back Tier of the fourth division. A few lots of downtown Kingston today are oriented with the house lots, most, however, with the river. By permission of the Pennsylvania Bureau of Land Records.

Susquehannah Company, nor have they retained the names given them at that time. The Susquehannah Company, over its much shorter life, recapitulated much of Connecticut's changing settlement ways. Its early townships were pitched, divided, and assigned by lot under direction of associations of shareholder-settlers in parent Connecticut communities. Later, with more profit-minded shareholders, the company opened a land office in Pennsylvania that characteristically sold whole townships to individuals.[48]

The contest for the land between the Yankees and the Pennamites is sometimes adduced as a test of the governments, races, religions, educations, "and, above all, land systems" of the two groups.[49] And the (very limited) victory of the New Englanders is cited as evidence of the superiority of the New England system. There are really too many variables to attribute such a tenuous victory to a single condition. Pennsylvanians (and some settlers from New York and New Jersey also) sometimes did side with New Englanders and took New England land titles,[50] whether for reasons of expediency, for a greater chance to participate in their government, from disenchantment with land speculators, or for freedom from quitrents.[51] Even if successful for a time on the Susquehannah, the New England group settlement system persisted neither in New England itself nor to the west in competition with more individual action favored in other regions.

Pennsylvania Land after the Revolution

By 1780 the northern third of Pennsylvania and an even wider band in the northwest were still virtually unsettled by Europeans. Much other ungranted land remained in the southwest and the rugged country of the central mountains.

The state reopened its land office in 1784, and quickly offered land in different tracts on a variety of terms. Land west of the mountains and already given up by Indians was reduced in cost to about ten cents an acre with a limit of 400 acres per person. Land of the far north-

---

[48]*Susquehannah Company Papers* 1: xxxii–xxxvi. It appears to be the boundary of the whole township that was pitched rather than the subdivisions.

[49]Boyd, 48; he develops the argument at greater length in the introduction to vol. 1 of *The Susquehannah Company Papers*, xxiv, xxix, xxxii; see also Marshall Harris, 297–99.

[50]*Susquehannah Company Papers*, 1: xxxvi.

[51]In the last case the Pennsylvanian is enticed by an individualistic trait among the practices of the generally more community-minded New Englanders.

west about to be purchased from Indians was to be surveyed into lots of 200 to 500 acres and sold at auction without acreage limits. The enthusiasm for buying large tracts of the northwestern land at auction was soon quenched by a new state law setting the price in the region east of the Allegheny River at about eighty cents an acre,[52] with a limit of 1,000 acres.

Two large tracts in the west were set aside for soldiers. The Depreciation Lands were designed to compensate soldiers for the drop in the purchasing power of their wages. Land bounded by the Ohio and Allegheny Rivers on the south and an east-west line through the center of Butler County on the north was surveyed for this purpose into lots of 200 to 350 acres to be auctioned off in exchange for depreciation certificates. Less than half the land was sold by 1787, and the auctions were soon discontinued. The land brought a low price and probably went mostly to speculators who had bought up the soldiers' certificates. North of the Depreciation Lands the Donation Lands for bounties to military men were surveyed in ten separate tracts with lots of 200 to 500 acres (fig. 14.8). This land was distributed by lottery, soldiers being entitled to 200 to 2,000 acres, depending on rank. Three thousand soldiers eventually patented land here, but few of them actually settled in the area.[53]

After the needs for the soldiers' land were determined, a new law of 1792 reduced the prices on the remaining land. Land released by the Indians before 1784, which lay closest to settled areas and had been available longest, was offered at less than seven cents an acre. Other land east of the Allegheny River was priced at thirteen cents an acre, and the land west of the Allegheny at twenty cents an acre. These prices were more attractive, but land in the last category could be patented only if it was "cultivated, improved, and settled." Four hundred acres was the limit for an individual settler, but there was no limit for the purchaser who would subdivide his acquisition and settle a tenant or buyer on each 400 acres for five years.[54]

In this way land was opened up for both settlers in the west and speculators in Philadelphia. The rules governing land acquisition procedures were the subject of long contention on the land, in the legislature, and in the courts. Generally, western legislators supported squatters and other settlers and eastern representatives supported speculators. A provision of the law waived the requirement of set

---

[52]Buck and Buck, 205.
[53]Ibid., 205–6; Wilkinson, 30–31.
[54]Buck and Buck, 207.

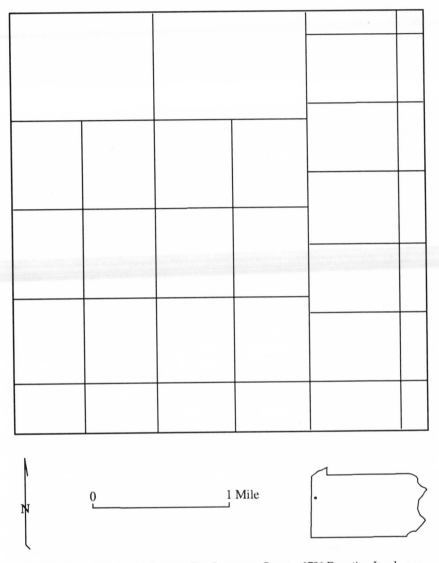

0   1 Mile

N

Fig. 14.8. Part of Neshannock Township, Lawrence County. 1786 Donation Lands surveyed into 200- and 500-acre lots for soldiers. The township also had one 250-acre lot that went to the widow of a private. By permission of the Pennsylvania Bureau of Land Records.

tlement if Indian hostility made it impossible. Speculators, supported by the Federalists, contended that the settlement requirement was permanently waived if hostilities intervened, while settlers and Republicans considered it only postponed. Different courts gave differing rulings, and in the end the individual settler and speculator often compromised. For example, a speculator could let a settler develop 100 acres and thereby validate the speculator's title to the remainder of 400 acres.[55]

The Philadelphia speculators included Robert Morris and his North American Land Company, John Nicholson and his Pennsylvania Population Company, Henry Drinker, and William Bingham. The Holland Land Company also invested heavily in Pennsylvania lands. The remote parts of Pennsylvania, like the remote parts of New York, were handled mostly by large speculators. In Pennsylvania, however, the speculators mostly obtained their holdings through certificates or warrants to relatively small tracts, originally issued to veterans or to real or dummy applicants. Usually these land jobbers did not gain large uninterrupted tracts comparable with those in New York, although John Nicholson, while state comptroller-general, was able to take nearly all the 202,000 acres of the Erie Triangle as well as an even larger area adjoining it. Typically, however, a Pennsylvania speculator would end up with smaller blocks of contiguous lots of 400, 1,000, or comparable acreages.

Grids of rectangular lots of sizes to which settlers would be entitled characterized both the military tracts and the lands open to the public. Most of the land in both types of areas passed through the hands of speculators before it was acquired by farmers. Some of the lots open to the public were distributed in a sequence that was determined by lottery, but that method did not prove popular and was abandoned. Since land offices were not located in the frontier areas themselves, speculators had the resources to know more about the land they acquired and resold than the would-be settler unless the latter had either squatted or paid a "discoverer" for first-hand information.[56]

The northwestern third of Pennsylvania, like the western half of New York, was divided mostly in rectangular land parcels. Rectangular surveys were not entirely limited to the area where they were dominant, as shown on figure 1.1. The land grant map of Dennison Township in Luzerne County, for example, shows a block of eight

[55]Ibid., 207–10.
[56]Wilkinson, 45–46, 257.

mostly rectangular tracts oblique to the cardinal directions surveyed in 1790 for the German Reformed Congregation. This block is overlaid by a larger one, square with the compass, comprising twenty-seven rectangles of about 400 acres each, mostly surveyed in 1792, twenty-four of which were finally patented to Robert Morris (fig. 14.9). These parcels were given names such as Jefferson, Derry, Norwich, Springfield, and Rover's Delight, probably for their promotional value in selling the tracts.

Most of the Pennsylvania speculators overextended their credit, among other questionable financial and promotional tactics. Only William Bingham is believed to have made major profits there. Their errors and stresses led to debtors' prison for Morris and Nicholson, to insanity for Nicholson and James Wilson.[57]

Summary of Land Division in the Middle Atlantic Region

All the middle colonies showed a confusing variety of land division procedures, and the plans and results in the different colonies showed little resemblance among them. None stayed long with any systematic plans, and their governments showed little control over the spontaneous practices that subsequently developed.

The first land plan in the middle colonies, for patroonships, was soon followed by additional plans for smaller farms and townships, all offered by a Dutch company primarily concerned with trade. Nor did British New York really ever bring a clear plan for its land development into focus. It followed with grants for all three of these Dutch settlement types, but found it expedient to put most of the land into large grants suggestive of the patroonships.

In New Jersey Berkeley and Carteret first planned to distribute most of the land by headrights in the manner most common in the South Atlantic colonies. Transfer of ownership to multiple shareholder proprietaries proved destructive of any general plan and left New Jersey land to be distributed in a variety of ways. Any order in the process was partly owing to sales competition among the many proprietors. The New Jersey government lacked any voice in the colony's land division that might have pulled the threads together.

Pennsylvania, by contrast, began with a controlled land survey that covered a much larger area than any initial organized survey in any other colony. The parcels of this survey were allocated to people

[57]Ibid., v, 221–54.

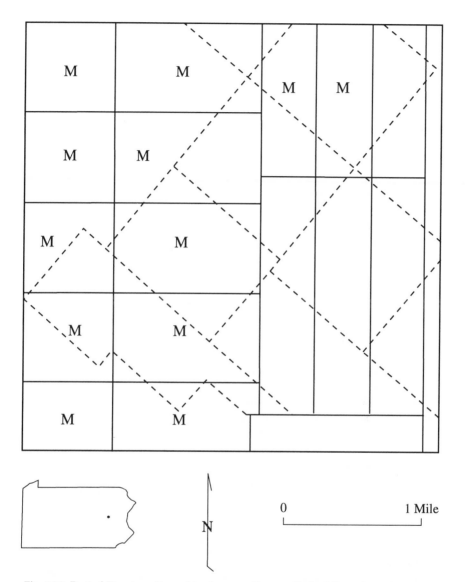

Fig. 14.9. Part of Dennison Township, Luzerne County. Dashed lines show the 1790 survey for the German Reformed Congregation. Solid lines show the later survey, mostly in 1792. M = parcels patented by Robert Morris in 1794, although the survey warrants had all been in other names. By permission of the Pennsylvania Bureau of Land Records.

who had bought their land in advance from Penn in England. As later farmers poured into Pennsylvania, there was not machinery in place to control their choice of land. Although the land was mostly to be sold rather than given out in headrights, squatting and indiscriminate location took over the process.

New York's patroonships and manors found limited development in other colonies. Patroonships had not lasted long in New Jersey and Delaware. Efforts to establish manors in New Jersey produced no more than a few tenanted estates. Manors in Pennsylvania and Delaware were sometimes divided into tenancies, but were mostly held for increasing land values, not operated as feudal baronies.

A few township settlements were founded in New York after the English conquest. Townships on the New England model succeeded in New Jersey and Pennsylvania only when actually settled by New Englanders. The townships laid out in the original survey of Pennsylvania were subdivided by the colony surveyors, and the civil townships later marked off as subdivisions of counties were subject to the "indiscriminate" choices of settlers; they lacked the governmental discretion of New England towns.

By the end of the Revolution, only New York and Pennsylvania among the middle states had any large unsettled areas remaining. Both states used part of their unassigned land to reward soldiers, and still larger areas in both states were acquired by major land speculators. The great tracts in New York were created in sales to speculators by New York and Massachusetts, whereas in Pennsylvania they were more commonly aggregated through purchase of individual rights and certificates. In both states a major part of the new land was laid out in rectangular grids oriented with the compass. Neither followed the new federal land survey, which was, however, approximated much more closely in New York than in Pennsylvania.

Land policies have been blamed with discouraging settlement in New York and in Pennsylvania both before and after the Revolution. New York's colonial land policies seem clearly to have retarded population growth in that colony. Pennsylvania's population, however, had a larger increase than any other colony between 1690 and 1750. Although Pennsylvania land prices were higher than in some of the royal colonies, terms of purchase were generous, quitrents were ineffective, and squatting was often tolerated.

Following the Revolution the complaint in both states was the way in which so much of the land went through the hands of speculators before it reached the farm settlers. In New York, of course, most of it was put in the hands of large holders before settlers ever had a chance at it. In Pennsylvania, the laws seemed to make most of it available to settlers, but, even so, those with rights to it frequently sold to land developers rather than settle it themselves. Pennsylvania population continued to grow, and New York took the lead after 1790. Both were, at the same time, also feeding people to the west.

Part V

Louisiana and Texas: Land Division Initiated under France and Spain

IN THE areas treated so far, land division was initiated under British auspices except for the early Dutch and Swedish periods in the middle colonies. The colonial periods in Louisiana and Texas fell largely under French and Spanish control as part of the roles of those countries on the coasts of the Gulf of Mexico and Atlantic Florida, in the Mississippi Valley, and in the Great Lakes area.

Spain's interest in what is now U.S. territory, all of which it originally claimed, came from its footholds to the south, in the Caribbean and Mexico. France's primary base lay to the north in what is now Canada. Both countries contested England's control of its Atlantic colonies, but had little success in displacing the relatively dense populations that developed there. French and Spanish dominion did extend over very large parts of the present United States, but their settlements were relatively small and scattered. The southern coast became the main meeting place of French and Spanish ambitions.

Spanish settlements in Florida, primarily at St. Augustine and Pensacola, provided a protective extension of activities in the West Indies. Farther west, the settlements from Texas to California were overland extensions of Mexico.

France's settlements in Atlantic Canada and the St. Lawrence were anchors for interior exploration, trade, and occasional settlement along the Great Lakes, Mississippi River, and other waterways. Its settlement of ports on the central Gulf Coast, however, was not simply a sequel to its discovery of the Mississippi mouth from the interior. These settlements depended also on the central location of the area, distant from Spanish bases to the east and west, and on important support from the French West Indies, primarily St. Domingue[1] (now Haiti).

European control of a major part of the present United States was radically realigned in 1763, following the French and Indian War. Britain acquired all the French and Spanish areas east of the Mississippi River except New Orleans (Isle of Orleans), while Spain acquired New Orleans and all the French area west of the Mississippi. Louisiana under Spain, as under France, drew its support from the West Indies rather than by way of its long land connection with Mexico.[2] In 1783 Spanish holdings expanded by annexation of East and West Florida; the United States completed control of West Florida in the War of 1812, and bought East Florida in 1821. Meanwhile Spain had regranted Louisiana to France, which had sold it to the United States. Later the revolts of Mexico and then of Texas, the annexation of Texas, the Mexican War, and finally the Gadsden Purchase ended Hispanic possession of territory in the present United States and drew the southern border of the United States in its present position. These changes of territory are summarized in table V.1.

Where the French divided land for agricultural purposes, they usually laid it out in long, narrow lots, side by side, often of even width and fronting on a river or road. The heritage of French longlots shows up on many modern topographic maps, examples including the vicinities of Cahokia, Illinois; Vincennes, Indiana; Detroit and Monroe, Michigan; and much of lowland Louisiana. The longlots shown on the maps were surveyed by official United States surveyors after holders of grants given by France and other countries proved their titles, and are likely more regular than they were in their original form. By the time the titles were proven, many of the lots granted farmers with French names had been sold to American settlers with British names.[3]

Spanish grants were more varied and lacked a signature as characteristic as the French longlots. A large portion of the Spanish and British grants in East and West Florida, as well as the Spanish grants in Missouri and Arkansas, went to American settlers relocating

[1]Donald W. Meinig, *The Shaping of America* (New Haven, Conn.: Yale University Press, 1986), 1: 200.

[2]Ibid., 283, 337. Cuba was the main political support for Louisiana under Spain, but St. Domingue continued cultural and economic support.

[3]Land grants made by other countries in territories later transferred to the United States, and accepted as legal by the United States, are listed in *American State Papers, class 8, Public Lands.*

TABLE V.1. Nations presiding over pre-U.S. land division, Gulf and Mississippi Valley

Florida East of Perdido River	Spain, 1565–1763
	England, 1763–83
	Spain, 1783–1821
Florida West of Perdido R. to Mississippi R.	France, 1701–63
(excluding Isle of Orleans)	England, 1763–83
N of 31°N (Natchez and surroundings)	Spain, 1783–95
S of 31°N	Spain, 1783–1810, 1813
Louisiana Territory (western Mississippi Valley and	France, 1712–63
Isle of Orleans)	Spain, 1763–1800
	France, 1800–1803
Eastern Mississippi Valley and Lower Lakes area	France, –1763
	England, 1763–83
Texas	Spain, 1715–1821
	Mexico, 1821–36
	Texas Republic, 1836–46

from other areas.[4] The irregular land division characteristic of the South Atlantic colonies often marked these American exclaves as anomalies, foreshadowing their annexation to the United States.

There was little resemblance in the land systems of Louisiana and Texas. Colonial Louisiana saw its natural levees progressively taken over by French longlots, which spread under the Spanish regime and even had some impact on the later American surveys. Texas, on the other hand, began with a variety of Spanish settlement patterns, followed with a period of mostly American settlers under specific Mexican land policies, but ultimately had most of its land divided under policies of the Republic and State of Texas that showed much more American than Mexican influence. Louisiana and Texas, however, each had examples of early land division considered more characteristic of the other. Insofar as these similarities are attributable to diffusion, the Spanish seem to have played the active role. From 1763 to 1800, Louisiana and Texas were both under Spanish rule, but even then the active cores of the two colonies were not in close contact.

[4]Some of the British grants in the Floridas were based on headrights as in other colonies. For the Natchez area, the Board of Trade favored township grants of 20,000 acres (Clinton N. Howard, *The British Development of West Florida, 1763–1769,* University of California Publications in History 34 [Berkeley: University of California, 1947], 8), a figure used in South Carolina and Georgia three decades earlier. The townships probably never materialized, but a number of land grants were for 20,000 acres. Howard, 80; D. Clayton James, *Antebellum Natchez* (Baton Rouge: Louisiana State University Press, 1968), 17.

15

Louisiana Land Division Patterns

LOUISIANA (fig. 15.1) displays a more distinctive set of land division patterns introduced under the flags of the respective nations that have governed it than any other state (fig. 15.2). The French longlots, the square leagues of the Spanish, the irregular subdivisions in the Florida parishes developing first under the British, and the American rectangular survey (covering about 85 percent of the state) give the land an unusual variety of regionalized textures easily distinguished from the air or from many kinds of maps.[1] That the patterns do not correspond exclusively with the national administrations indicated will be brought out in the discussion.

Laying Out Longlots

French Louisiana was administered as a royal colony during the periods 1699–1717 and 1731–63; private companies operated it from 1717 to 1731.[2] Spain and England later both treated parts of Louisiana as royal colonies. Permanent settlement occurred only in 1712. The early French stock settling around New Orleans have been identified as Creoles; later in the eighteenth century many refugees from French Acadia (Cajuns) made their way to the colony, settling to the west of New Orleans and also along a portion of the Mississippi bank upstream. German and Spanish colonists too concentrated along upstream banks. French culture, including land division patterns, prevailed, and the early non-French groups were mostly assimilated.[3] The French longlot system almost seems planned to fit the stream levees of southern Louisiana. These levees, sloping almost impercep-

---

[1]John W. Hall, "Louisiana Survey Systems: Their Antecedents, Distribution, and Characteristics" (Ph.D. diss., Louisiana State University, 1970).

[2]Ibid., 6–9.

[3]Helmut Blume, *The German Coast, During the Colonial Era, 1702–1803*, trans. Ellen C. Merrill (Destrehan, La.: German-Acadian Coast Historical and Genealogical Society, 1990; first published in German in 1956), 130–34.

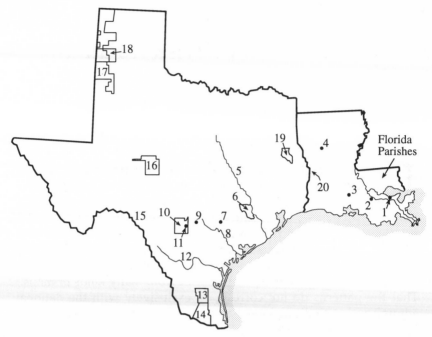

Fig. 15.1. Louisiana and Texas locations: 1. New Orleans 2. Point Houmas 3. Lafayette 4. Natchitoches 5. Brazos R. 6. Austin County 7. Gonzales 8. Guadalupe R. 9. San Antonio 10. Medina County 11. Castroville 12. Nueces R. 13. Brooks County 14. Hidalgo County 15. Rio Grande 16. Tom Green County 17. XIT Ranch 18. Deaf Smith County. 19. Nacogdoches County. 20. Sabine R.

tibly from the stream banks toward the backswamps of the floodplain, provided the only well-drained land in the realm. Longlots cut across the levees, giving each holder a proportional share of the lighter, better-drained soils near the river and the heavier, wetter lowland as well as access to fishing and stream transportation and to the roads that would run along the levees.

With their houses at the ends of the narrow lots, farm families lived close to their neighbors in a continuous line village that might develop central nodes with churches, schools, stores, and other services. The long dimensions of the lots facilitated drainage by gravity to the backswamps and permitted plowing furrows as long as the farmer might desire. Marking off the longlots was relatively simple: only the corners at the stream end and the directions of the sides leading toward the backswamp had to be fixed at first.[4]

[4]Hall, 66–67.

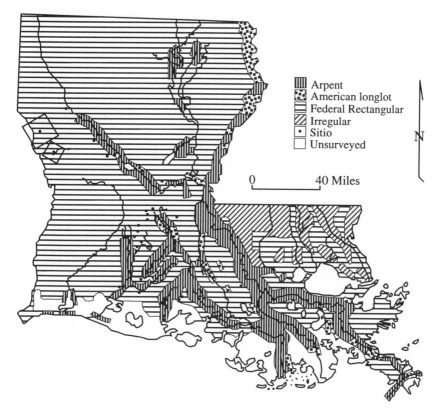

Arpent
American longlot
Federal Rectangular
Irregular
Sitio
Unsurveyed

N

0 _____ 40 Miles

Fig. 15.2. Louisiana land division patterns. Modified from figure 1 in John W. Hall, "Louisiana Survey Systems."

These graceful arrays of strips are sometimes described as the *arpent* system after the French linear measure, about 192 feet. The properties are typically a few arpents wide at the river and forty arpents deep (nearly a mile and a half).[5] The sides of the property were usually perpendicular to the waterway as it existed when the lots were laid out. Where waterways meander, sides tend to diverge on the outside of the bends and to converge on the inside. When several properties meet at the center of a meander neck, the pattern resembles an open fan, which may cover 180° of the circle. Inside sharp bends, the lots fronting on opposite stretches of the river may meet one another and close off property at a half-way line short of forty arpents (figs. 15.3 and 15.4).

[5]The depth of riverine longlots is more standardized in Louisiana than in Quebec.

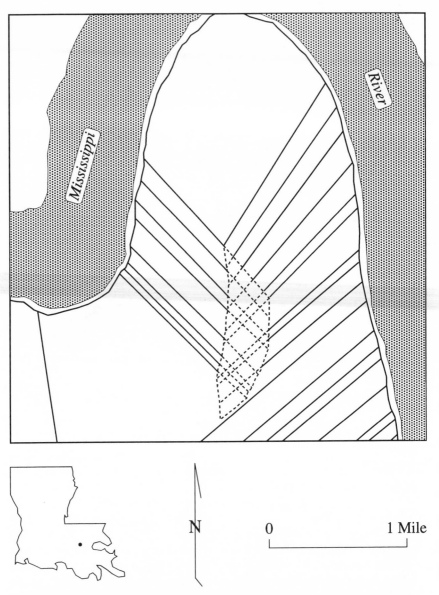

Fig. 15.3. Point Houmas on Mississippi River near Donaldsonville, La. Each of the small quadrangles marked off by dashed lines was assigned a section number. From 1843 township resurvey, filed in Louisiana State Land Office, as shown on USGS topographic quadrangles: Donaldsonville (north center) and Gonzales (south center).

Fig. 15.4. Point Houmas area, USGS, 1961.

The harmony and evenness of the arpent divisions neither landed in Louisiana full-blown nor sprang so from the soil of the levees. What is known about the beginnings of this distinctive land system in Louisiana hints that the longlots may not have been assumed from the beginning, and makes it clear that no standard depth had been anticipated for the lots and that the question of feudal holdings versus family farms had not been settled.

An edict of 1716 complained that many grants were larger than owners could cultivate, often being used only for cutting timber. These grants were to be reduced, and new grants were to be in the proportion of two to four arpents frontage by forty to sixty arpents depth. The grantees under this edict were to improve the land within two years and would not be free to sell it until it was two-thirds cultivated.[6] The Company of the West (later Company of the Indies) was given control of Louisiana in 1717. Its varied practices included distributing land as the settler chose it, as the company had laid it out ahead of time, and as large grants to nobility, who made little effort to settle them. After the French government took control again, it offered settlers assistance and holdings as wide as eight and ten arpents.[7]

In 1719 the company granted land in allodium and promised assistance to a Mr. de la Jonchère, who was to send fifty persons to Louisiana to establish a plantation "of four geometrical leagues in a square or otherwise figured."[8] A few other large grants were specified in leagues without hints regarding the shape they would take. In other cases only the river frontage was specified, in running arpents (*arpents courants*), hardly surprising considering the riverine nature of the settlements.[9]

Other irregular aspects of early Louisiana land division appeared in documents dealing with concessions made to Sieur de Bienville, governor of Louisiana for three separate periods, each of about ten years, between 1701 and 1743 (thus serving both royal and company regimes).[10] Bienville about 1719 granted himself two tracts, one of 213.5 arpents frontage on the north bank of the Mississippi just above early New Orleans, occupying most of the neck of land where the city's business center is now located; the other of 134 arpents on the opposite side of the river downstream from the city.[11] An old map[12]

---

[6] Henry P. Dart, ed. and trans., "The First Law Regulating Land Grants in French Colonial Louisiana," *Louisiana Historical Quarterly* 14 (1931): 346–48.

[7] Carolyn O. French, "Cadastral Patterns in Louisiana: A Colonial Legacy" (Ph.D. diss., Louisiana State University, 1978), 42–43. Raymond Herman Downs, "Public Lands and Private Claims in Louisiana, 1803–1820," (Ph.D. diss., Louisiana State University, 1960), 2–4, notes that some grantees had expected to collect quitrents on land sold to settlers; the 1716 edict called for mostly allodial ownership.

[8] Heloise H. Cruzat, trans., "Distribution of Land in Louisiana by the Company of the Indies: I. The Jonchère Concession," *Louisiana Historical Quarterly* 11 (1928): 554. The French league (*lieue*) was equated with about eighty arpents.

[9] E.g., "Documents Concerning Bienville's Lands in Louisiana, 1719–1737," supplemented with translations by Heloise H. Cruzat and historical comment by Henry P. Dart, *Louisiana Historical Quarterly* 10 (1927): 161.

[10] Ibid., 10 (1927): 5–24, 161–84, 364–80, 538–61; 11 (1928): 87–110, 209–32, 463–65.

[11] Ibid., 10: 8; 11: 229–30 (the depth of the concession is reported as forty arpents); 10: 372. The concession is confusingly reported in this document as about a league in

of Bienville's concessions (fig. 15.5) shows two different patterns in their division among more than thirty-five parties. The tract above New Orleans (fig. 15.1) approximates a pattern of lots perpendicular to the river and of forty arpents depth. Below New Orleans, however, most of the longlots are in a single block with parallel sides abutting the adjacent reach of the river at an angle of about 45°. Although the depth of the tract also approximated forty arpents, most of the lots, because of their angle to the river, were about fifty-five arpents long.

The longlot farms into which Bienville divided most of his two concessions ran from about three to twelve arpents frontage. He also reserved a domain of forty or more arpents in each concession for himself. The farms were sold to buyers who continued to owe Bienville annual quitrents characteristically entailing six or eight livres per arpent, anywhere up to twelve capons, and days of labor that might be as few as one or as many as twenty-four.[13] We may assume that the level of these feudal burdens varied inversely with the sale price and was also influenced by individual bargains.

Bienville was eventually called to account for his land acquisitions and threatened with their forfeiture. The 1716 edict of the crown had reserved the riverbanks below and above New Orleans for division into feudal holdings of only two or three arpents in order to settle a dense population on call to meet hostile threats to the city.[14] The company planned a similar division of that area into narrow lots with feudal tenure, but also, in keeping with its authority, granted many small strips elsewhere to settlers in allodium. Bienville himself held his land in allodial tenure, and had not subdivided it in lots as narrow as both the government and company wished. He was also accused of falsely representing his acquisitions as continuously flooded. In his defense he pointed to a large investment in draining the terrain.

After an investigation, the French Council of State decreed in 1728 that any allodial grants of more than twenty arpents frontage should be reduced to that width except insofar as their frontage had been cultivated to a depth of three arpents.[15] Exceptions were made

depth. This may go with one (also confusing) report of a French league as forty-two arpents, a measure not very different from the standard depth of longlots at forty arpents.

[12]Ibid., 10: 8.
[13]Ibid., 10: 540–61; 11: 87–110, 209–32.
[14]Ibid., 10: 164–5.
[15]Ibid., 10: 172.

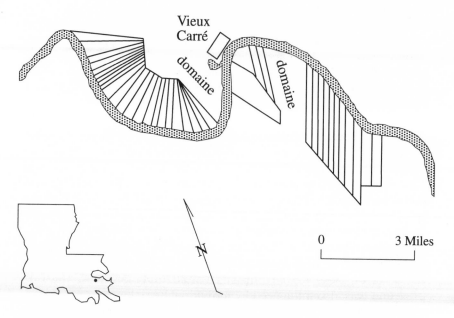

Vieux Carré

domaine

domaine

0 3 Miles

Fig. 15.5. Bienville survey, ca. 1719. The two banks of longlots run between the Mississippi River and a parallel line at a distance of forty arpents. The Vieux Carré is the original settlement of New Orleans. From an original map reproduced in *Louisiana Historical Quarterly* 10 (1927): 8.

for cattle grazers, but land not currently used was to be forfeited regardless of its frontage. These decrees threatened most, if not all of Bienville's holdings, but he seems to have later regained much of his property.[16]

Bienville's subdividing may have given an impetus to the standardization of forty arpents as the depth of longlots, but completion of the process evidently took more time. The company's 1717 plan for two- and three-arpent holdings actually specified lot depths of sixty arpents.[17] The edict of 1728 specified that lots should have depths of twenty to 100 arpents "according to their situation,"[18] probably recognizing the variability of widths of levees. In the same paragraph the edict granted the "ordinary depth" to those who had made good their claims by clearing their frontage. It also specified that owners should mark the "extent of their lands in breadth as well as in depth."

[16]Ibid., 10: 365–68.
[17]Ibid., 10: 164–65.
[18]Ibid., 10: 173.

The French left little firm record of their extensive longlot divisions. The Spanish adopted the French plan in the old settled areas of Louisiana, issued the earliest extant titles to the land, and expanded the longlot system with its arpent measures as new settlement spread along more water frontage.[19] Thus most of the French strips of today can be traced back archivally no further than to Spanish titles.

Spanish land laws in Louisiana of 1770 and 1798 indicate the achievement of much regularization in the decades since Bienville's period.[20] It would be hard to say how much of the standardization on the forty-arpent depth was owing to increasing French familiarity with the country and how much to Spanish bureaucracy. By 1770 new families in Louisiana were promised six or eight arpents to a depth of forty arpents, which was explained in terms of the need of cypress wood (from the swamps at the far edges of the levees), "as necessary as it is useful to the inhabitants." Governor Alexander O'Reilly reported to the king that a surveyor to mark off the lands was still an unfulfilled need in almost every district.[21] The 1798 laws provided an additional alternative of four arpents for the new settler.[22] Both sets of laws continued the French requirements of clearing the frontage and building levees, roads, drains, and fences and the restriction on sale before three years and meeting the ownership requirements. The laws provided that lots on points of land might be wider than normal (twelve arpents in 1770) to compensate for limitation on depth effected by convergence of the sides. The Spanish laws also provided for grants of square leagues in certain parishes not on the Mississippi.

The often unsurveyed longlots were finally fixed when American surveyors, laying out townships and sections, also bounded the preexisting private holdings, and gave them section numbers above thirty-six to distinguish them from the thirty-six standard sections.[23] The French at first resisted the American surveying in rectangles. For one thing they were not sure Americans were in Louisiana to stay. For another they could find no sense in laying off squares that bore no

[19] Hall, 34–36.

[20] "O'Reilly's Ordinance of 1770," *Louisiana Historical Quarterly* 10 (1927): 237–40; Francis P. Burns, "The Spanish Land Laws of Louisiana" *Louisiana Historical Quarterly* 11 (1928): 557–81.

[21] Ibid., 561.

[22] Ibid., 570.

[23] Ory Poret, "History of Land Titles in the State of Louisiana," *Publications of the Louisiana Historical Society*, ser. 2, 1 (1973): 25–42.

relation to the usable land and might not even have access to the streams. Soon the American surveyors gained authorization from Congress to survey the land along the streams in longlots of 160 acres that might better fit the *habitants'* perception of their land.[24] Standard dimensions for these lots were 58 x 465 rods, within a few feet of 5 x 40 arpents. The survey also filled in occasional second ranges of longlots in places where the French settlement was only one lot deep and where there was room for a second.

The arrays of longlots varied somewhat in accordance with their origins. Ranges of the original French strips are usually bounded by a continuous line marking the backs of the lots forty arpents from the stream border. In many cases the back line was beyond the cleared area, and had not actually been drawn before the survey. As Spanish settlement proceeded upstream, Spanish longlots were sometimes laid out on the upland away from the main river. These sometimes present ragged and discontinuous back lines,[25] apparently the result of determining lot lengths individually. Longlots created by the American surveyors were less likely to be perpendicular to the river bank and more likely to exhibit uniform width between parallel sides than the older French lots. They were often square with the compass and with the lines of the checkerboard survey. Although American surveyors did sometimes taper the lots to conform more closely with the river bends,[26] their designs were more suggestive of regular geometry than of the French arrays.

French inheritance customs called for dividing the properties among heirs. The logic of the longlots was honored by longitudinal division, making the new lots even narrower, but still forty arpents in length.[27] A property map of 1960 showed some lots too narrow to measure, but certainly not more than thirty feet wide at the river, and sometimes tapering to a point a mile and a half down the levee slope. A few strips shown in an inset are close to ten feet wide.[28] Such narrow strips could be agriculturally impractical if not for such practices as consolidation through leasing by sugar plantations.

From the beginning of settlement in Louisiana, land was granted and divided or aggregated in wide and narrow lots that served the needs of both plantations and family farms. It has often been the

---

[24]Hall, 55–58.
[25]French, 78, 82.
[26]Hall, 58–60.
[27]Ibid., 72
[28]*Ascension Parish, Louisiana, West Half,* Edgar Tobin Aerial Surveys, 1959–61.

case, over the whole period of European occupation, that the two types of holdings and economy lay interspersed.[29]

A curious product of the interaction of French settlers and American surveyors appears in figures 15.3 and 15.4, showing Point Houmas near Donaldsonville. Both sides of the point were claimed and settled, and farmers began clearing their strips from the edge of the river. Possibly an earlier course of the shore would explain the particular directions followed by the sets of longlots from the two sides. When the lots were originally assigned, there might even have been room for the forty-arpent lots reaching in from the two sides without any mutual overlap. When the American surveyors arrived, there was not ample room, but the strips had probably not been cleared to such a distance that any interference occurred. The surveyors found that extending the lots to their full forty arpents would create overlapping, as shown in figure 15.3. Although Spanish law had provided for terminating properties running from opposite shores at equal lengths in case of overlaps, the near right angle of intersection on Point Houmas may have seemed to complicate the process. Or perhaps the surveyors simply had no authorization for dealing with this case. Their action was to leave the decision for the future by extending all strips to the forty-arpent line and assigning each intersection jointly to the owners of the two strips crossing over it. The photograph (fig. 15.4) seems to tell us that the operators of property from the eastern side of the point have been more assiduous than those on the west in clearing their land toward the forty-arpent line, but more recent maps provided by the parish assessor's office and a letter from an owner in the area seem to say that ownership is still unsettled.

The longlots established cadastral patterns that have occasionally been adapted to new situations. Although the French laid out the Vieux Carré, or old quarter, of New Orleans in square blocks proper to a city, the upstream growth of the city led into a great fan of rural longlots (formerly Bienville's) fitted into the concavity of a river bend. Each pie-shaped sector bounded by converging boundaries (formerly canals and now streets) has its own grid orientation. The fan includes the central business district, the Garden District, and several suburbs, and shows up in the pattern of the city's wards.[30]

---

[29]Blume, 143–45.

[30]Peirce F. Lewis, *New Orleans: The Making of an Urban Landscape* (Cambridge, Mass.: Ballinger Publishing Co., 1976), 33, 42; Hall, 51–52, 67; Stanley D. Brunn, *Geography and Politics in America* (New York: Harper and Row, 1974), 137.

Audubon Park is bounded by the sides of one sector, and Tulane University mostly falls within a smaller angle in the narrower end of the same sector. The city of Natchitoches has a set of parallel, but irregularly spaced, downtown streets perpendicular to its river (formerly Red River, now Cane River) and deriving from earlier rural longlot boundaries. And streets in both upstream and downstream suburbs of the city of Lafayette get their direction from older strips bordering the Vermilion River.[31] Also short portions of narrow longlots are often cut off at the river end for house lots, and now may be owned independently of the farmed strip behind (fig. 15.6).

As their numbers grew, French farmers had no choice but to take newly surveyed upland not in the riverine habitat. Many took specially surveyed eighty-acre lots a half mile by a quarter, halves of quarter sections.[32] These eighty-acre rectangles as well as 160- and forty-acre squares have frequently been subdivided into narrow strips that range from four to twenty acres.

The American-surveyed longlots were sometimes in places such as the lower delta of the Mississippi that had not been settled previously because they offered little attraction for farming. American longlots occurred on more suitable land along the Mississippi in northern Louisiana in areas not previously settled by French, but an observer of about 1950 reported that no evidence of the longlot survey remained to be seen in the landscape.[33] Early plantations along the river had reflected the original division. Shifts in the course of the river, however, destroyed some of the original cadaster, left other longlot blocks miles from the river, and created new raw land of uncertain future. Depredations of the Civil War wiped out the physical installations. Lumbering communities had their turn at the land while the forests lasted. The economy around 1950 depended on large company holdings, sometimes in more than one tract, for cattle grazing, using old plantation cores as community centers. Some land no longer in use had been divided by the Farm Security Administration into 160-acre farms. Settlement had successively favored the stream bank, the railroad, and later the roads. Without the old French culture, there seemed no incentive to recreate the defunct longlot-riverbank farm ecology.

[31]Hall, 71.

[32]Ibid., 57.

[33]Fred Kniffen, principal investigator, *Cultural Survey of Louisiana*, reference section by Yvonne Phillips, Final Status Report N7 ONR 35606, 1951, P-3 to P-6.

Fig. 15.6. House on a short lot detached from a longlot, facing Bayou Lafourche, La.

Louisiana Land Systems Other than Longlots

West and northwest of the French areas, the Spanish introduced another type of land grant, called the *sitio* by Hall after Spanish colonial practice elsewhere.[34] These grants were usually square, often not oriented with the cardinal directions, and often a league on a side. The largest of the sitios shown on figure 15.2, one of which exceeded 200,000 acres, were in "neutral territory" west of the Mississippi drainage (which had never clearly belonged to France).[35]

A sitio grantee was expected to be able to put it to use; the applicant for a half-league grant needed 100 cattle, some horses and sheep, and two slaves. The sitio grants were unique to Spanish colonial culture and land use, but not so dominant as the riverine longlots among the French. Many sitio grants are conspicuous amid the uni-

[34]Hall, 98–111; idem, "Sitios in Northwestern Louisiana," *Journal of the North Louisiana Historical Association* 1, no. 3 (1970): 1–9.

[35]However, in 1795 Baron de Bastrop petitioned for and received from the governor a grant of twelve leagues square, on the order of a million acres, in northern Louisiana on the Ouachita River. The Bastrop grant, never consummated, figured in a great deal of litigation, and the claim to perhaps a third of it was eventually purchased by Aaron Burr for his "inland empire." Burns, 566–67.

form American survey patterns that later surrounded them. Their oblique boundaries are mostly visible from the air as roads and fence rows. Other sitio owners were given a section or sections of the American survey in lieu of their original grants.

Louisiana's Florida Parishes[36] contain a mixture of French, British, and Spanish royal grants, irregular American grants made to squatters, and later grants conforming with the official U.S. survey. A little less than half the total was taken up property by property, without prior survey, as were other colonial areas we have examined in Louisiana. Carolyn French's study of the area is probably the most comprehensive analysis of irregular land division of so large an area in the eastern half of the United States.[37]

Relatively few grants were made in the Florida Parishes during the French and British periods. The French grants were mostly long-lots along the Mississippi River. In the British and Spanish periods early settlers also sought the rivers and often laid out longlots along them. The Spanish administration was much more systematic about surveys, grants, and records than its predecessors. Various seating and planting requirements discouraged those who were not bona fide settlers or who would sell their grants without having made a serious effort to put them to use. As American settlers poured in after the Revolution, more and more of the grants were irregular in shape and more were entered by squatting than by application and approval. Spanish authorities encouraged Americans until they realized that American settlement weakened rather than strengthened Spain's hold on the land. After the cession of 1810 American authorities encouraged settlement, offering American squatters 640 acres, twice the size of most Spanish and British grants. These settlement grants were often finally surveyed in squares, as the land, because it had been unclaimed previously, could be laid out in the pattern of the U.S. survey.

Conclusion

No completely satisfactory explanation has been offered for the special association between French settlement and riverine longlots in North America. Longlots had been important in French agriculture,

---

[36]Formerly part of West Florida, comprising most of the area east of the Mississippi River and north of Lake Pontchartrain.

[37]See n. 7, above.

but not so as to mark France as the single European country most likely to lay out longlot colonies. The accident of France's appropriation of the two great river systems, providing terrain that could be effectively exploited by longlots, was probably critical.

In the case of the St. Lawrence, the initial grants of seigneuries did not hint of a longlot plan, but the grants of *rotures* to individual farmers quickly provided narrow river frontage with depths that might put much of a farm out of the farmer's reach. For practical reasons the depths of rotures were often limited to forty or so arpents, and widths often varied with the depth in a ratio of about 1:10. Where the strip of good land was wide enough, additional ranges of farms were often laid out behind the riverfront range. It seems that longlots were the expressed preference of the farmers rather than of the relatively passive seigneurs.[38] The French settlers came from many parts of France; there is no clear link to areas that might have provided a specific model for the longlot system that developed.[39]

The typical sites of longlots in Louisiana differed from those in Quebec in being levees between the river and the backswamp rather than more varied rolling upland and terraces above the river. These lowlands in Louisiana generally varied little in their arability along lines parallel to the streams, but showed regular changes from levee crest to backswamp. Laying boundaries perpendicular to streams produced many strips with nonparallel sides along the sinuous course of the Mississippi in contrast with the usually parallel sides of the properties in Quebec.[40] In neither colony was there a preordained plan for longlots perpendicular to the river. With probable, but perhaps not necessary, help of Quebec precedents, longlots evolved quickly in Louisiana, however, and forty arpents probably turned out to be the round measure that best fitted the terrain of the levees. That lot depths were more uniform in Louisiana is probably owing to postsettlement surveys imposed under Spain and the United States. The narrowness of the levees probably explains the lower frequency in Louisiana than in Quebec of multiple ranges of longlots. If physiographic convenience played a necessary role in implanting longlots in French North America, it did not prevent considerable uniformity in lot depths.

---

[38]Richard Colebrook Harris, *The Seigneurial System in Early Canada* (Madison: University of Wisconsin Press, 1966), 7–8, 115–36; Harris and John Warkentin, *Canada Before Confederation* (New York: Oxford University Press, 1974), 39–40.
[39]Harris and Warkentin, 19–20.
[40]Richard Harris, 119–20.

The French settlement patterns in lowland Louisiana were so well established that they came into considerable use in the Spanish, British, and American regimes that followed. The Spanish, in addition, introduced the sitio grants in western Louisiana, generally relatively large squares intended for upland farming or grazing.

American influence entered Louisiana in three distinct forms. Irregular holdings developed from either warrant systems or squatting under both Spanish and American regimes in the Florida Parishes. In due course the American rectangular land survey covered most of the state's area. But the older residents were actually able to persuade the U.S. Land Office to survey river borders into longlots in the only official systematic deviation from regular townships and sections on previously unsurveyed land that has come to my attention.

The French longlot system has exhibited a great deal of persistence. In Quebec it has been extended far beyond the river borders where it was first implanted. In Louisiana it governed the original layout of land along suitable stream systems, not only under the French, but also under later regimes. On the uplands it has been employed only as those accustomed to its logic have occasionally used it to subdivide lands laid out first in the rectangular pattern.

16

The Many Templates of Texas Land Division

TEXAS LAND division began under the systems sponsored by Spain and Mexico, but followed American patterns more closely immediately after Texan independence. About 15 percent of Texas was granted under Spain and Mexico.[1] The other 85 percent was distributed under the policies of the Republic and State of Texas. No part of this vast land was ever included in the United States public domain.

The disposal of Texas's land was directed by the needy commonwealth to reward soldiers, to bring money into the treasury, and to encourage immigration and internal development. The parcels and patterns into which the land was first divided reflected only in part the manner in which officials wanted Texas settled. Often the direct grants were simply blocks for speculation, subdivision, and resale. But the purposes for which the land was granted and the manner of its disposition usually showed some recognition of long-term public interest. Although many Texas officials and citizens have regretted the haste and the low prices that marked the disappearance of much of the public land, the prices of the land that was sold were probably in line with the market values at the time. If fraud and speculation figured in the land appropriation, they were probably not out of proportion to such behavior in many other areas we have examined.

Texas Land under Spain and Mexico

European dominion in Texas dates from 1716, when Spain established missions that were followed by presidios, farm and grazing settle-

[1]Thomas Lloyd Miller, *The Public Lands of Texas, 1519–1970* (Norman: University of Oklahoma Press, 1972), vii.

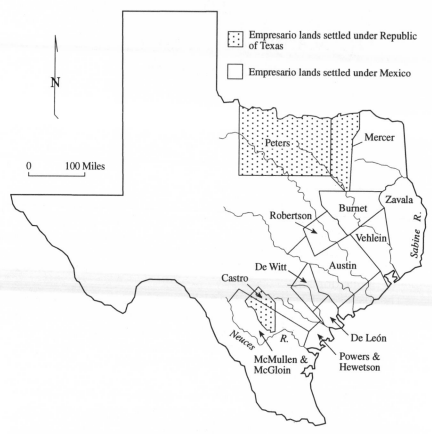

Fig. 16.1. Empresario colonies receiving appreciable settlement. The unshaded areas represent colonies of the Mexican period, the shaded areas those under the Texas Republic.

ments, and towns. Most of the first settlements, other than farm grants, were impermanent, and their land reverted to the crown. San Antonio, Goliad, and Nacogdoches were the only towns surviving at the end of Spanish rule in 1821. Miller estimates that ten million acres or more had been granted during the Spanish period.[2]

Texas proved a compatible habitat for certain aspects of Spanish land division, just as Louisiana did for the riverine longlots. Agricultural operations in Spain, with its relatively dry climates, included intensive, small irrigated farms as well as livestock enterprises that used large areas of land extensively. Texas proved similar to Spain,

[2]Ibid., 12.

not in its wet and dry seasons, but in its extensive subhumid and semiarid climates. These dry areas of Texas were crossed by a number of river valleys that provided fertile soils and water for irrigation. The great interfluvial plains were well suited for grazing, but often short on water for crop farming. Relatively small holdings for farming (both irrigated and nonirrigated) and large holdings for grazing characterized the land grants of Texas under both Spain and Mexico.

Although Spanish customs and traditions were important in early Texas land division, the administrative decisions governing grants were actually made in Texas, not subject to rigid colonial controls from Spain or Mexico. We have more record of regularity than of irregularity in the Spanish grants in Texas.

The sitio grants already discussed for Louisiana actually appeared earlier in Texas. The unit of land measure used by the Spanish was the square league (twenty-five million square *varas* or 4,428 acres).[3] A league was the standard *sitio de ganado mayor* for the raising of large stock, that is, cattle and horses.[4] A half-league grant (half a league on a side) could be made to an applicant with 100 head of cattle, some horses and sheep, and two slaves to tend them. Another source identifies a *sitio de ganado minor* as two-thirds of a league on each side.[5] Larger grazing grants often ran two, four, or more leagues. "One league to each wind" became a surveyor's description of a square four-league tract more or less oriented with the compass (as well as the title of the history of surveying in Texas just cited).

Longlots were also introduced into Texas in Spanish surveying, but in a variety of forms and without any specification in the laws. The first longlots were laid out in 1731 as irrigated plots or *suertes* for sixteen Canary Islanders who were the first civilian settlers at San Antonio.[6] The strips were about 290 feet wide (105 varas), and had lengths, varying with the distance between the two streams that bounded them, between a quarter mile and a mile (nine to thirty-five acres). The strips were a convenient means of giving all holders access to irrigation water drawn from a canal bisecting the strips.

[3]The vara is a somewhat variable measure reported as 33.33 inches in Texas. The term "league" will henceforth indicate the area of a square league unless otherwise indicated.

[4]Hall, 100–102.

[5]Sue Watkins, ed., *One League to Each Wind*, Historical Committee, Texas Surveyors Association (Austin: Von Boeckmann Jones, 1964), 8.

[6]Terry Jordan, "Antecedents of the Long-Lot in Texas," *Annals of the Association of American Geographers* 64 (1974): 71–74.

Suertes laid out elsewhere were usually more compact in shape, typically 200 x 400 varas (fifteen acres).

The riverine longlot idea was also applied to the great *porciónes* of nonirrigated land bordering the lower Rio Grande and its southern tributaries. The policy at the time of the survey in 1767 was to give original settlers two leagues of grazing land and twelve *caballerías* (400 acres) of cultivable land.[7] Later settlers were to receive the two leagues plus less cultivable land or none at all, depending on length of residence. Captains might receive twice the basic allowance. The river frontage bordering each longlot provided drinking water for livestock.[8] Irrigation rights are believed not to have been included.[9]

More than 300 of the great longlots were laid out along the Rio Grande in the 1760s. Most of those on the Texas side were 0.69 miles across, as wide as many of the suertes were long, and eleven to sixteen miles long, between one and two square leagues. The largest one, laid out in 1777, was five miles wide by seventeen miles long, containing well over ten leagues.

Settlement and division of the land of Texas lagged in the late eighteenth century and on until the beginning of the 1820s, when two events suddenly renewed settlement and turned Texas's destiny in new directions. The first event was the granting of a contract to Moses Austin to introduce American settlers, the second Mexico's gaining of independence. The effects of these events on Texas, however, depended on a longer-term trend, the westward advance of the American frontier.

The vision of Moses Austin, and the skillful management of him and his son and heir, Stephen Austin, gained them the credit for leading the American advance into Texas, but only with the aid of an unlikely coincidence. Moses Austin, with his credentials as a one-time Spanish subject in Missouri, went to San Antonio to present his colonization plan in 1820, but was ordered by the governor to leave immediately. On his way back to his room, however, Austin met Baron de Bastrop, a friend whom he had known much earlier in Louisiana and who had the ear of the governor. Austin's plan was soon approved as the only likely hope for settling Texas, but he died a few months later, leaving his son in charge of the project. While

---

[7]Milton Newton, "Certain Aspects of the Political History of Starr County, Texas" (M.A. thesis, Texas A and I University, 1964), 28.

[8]Betty Eakle Dobkins, *The Spanish Element in Texas Water Law* (Austin: University of Texas Press, 1959), 129.

[9]According to modern decisions of Texas courts (Jordan, "Antecedents of the Long-Lot," 74).

Stephen Austin was recruiting settlers and selecting his land, Texas passed from Spanish to Mexican sovereignty, and the fate of the colony again hung in the balance as Stephen in his turn had to spend a year in Mexico City before getting clear approval to go ahead with his plan.

The Austins' colonization schemes initiated the *empresario* method of land grants, which accounted for most of the settlement in Texas during the Mexican period. An empresario was given the authority to grant lands to settlers within an assigned tract and to receive in return a generous amount of premium land for himself if he settled the minimum number of families. Between two and three dozen empresario contracts were made, nearly filling the 150-mile-wide strip of coastal Texas between the Sabine and Nueces Rivers (fig. 16.1), with a few extending as fantasies over much of the rest of Texas. Some of the empresarios effected no settlement and others too little to fulfill their contracts and receive premium lands, but one author estimates that more families were settled than the total of the 9,248 specified in all the contracts.[10] Austin alone had settled more than 1,500 families, who are credited with more agricultural settlement activity in their first ten years than Europeans had carried out in all previous Texas history.[11] In the early 1840s the Republic of Texas was to have one more brief try with empresario grants.

The original Austin land distribution plan resembled an early colonial headright scheme with American land measures: 640 acres for a man, 320 for his wife, 160 for a child, and eighty for a slave.[12] The laws passed by Mexico and then its state of Coahuila and Texas, however, required Spanish measures for the empresario grants: a league of land for a family engaged in grazing, a *labor* (one million square varas, equal to 177 acres) for a family engaged in farming, and both for a family ready to pasture livestock and raise crops[13] (natu-

[10]Aldon Socrates Lang, *Financial History of the Public Lands in Texas* (1932; reprinted, New York: Arno Press, 1979), 96. The meager success of many empresarios makes it unlikely that they can have settled so many families on their tracts. Some settlers recruited by the empresarios, however, may have bought land from the state of Coahuila and Texas directly or established themselves as squatters.

[11]T. R. Fehrenbach, *Lone Star: A History of Texas and the Texans* (New York: Macmillan Co., 1968), 146.

[12]Eugene C. Barker, *The Life of Stephen F. Austin* (Nashville, Tenn.: Cokesbury Press, 1925), 39; idem, ed., *The Austin Papers*, in *Annual Report of the American Historical Association* (1919), 2: 818.

[13]Barker, *Life of Austin*, 73. After Austin's original grant, the grazing grant was reduced by the acreage in a *labor* so that the grazing and farming grants together comprised a league (Miller, 17).

rally, nearly all the settlers declared themselves both farmers and grazers). A single man was entitled to only a quarter or a third of the allowance of a family, but the deficiency could be made up on his marriage.[14] American immigration was stopped in 1830, and empresario contracts were abolished in 1834. The new idea was to settle Mexicans, for whom the land laws were already more liberal. Since very few Mexicans settled in Texas during the Mexican period, and the lavish grants made during the last two years of the Mexican period were not recognized by the Republic of Texas, the late changes in Mexican policies had little effect on the land.

Empresarios who met their contracts (usually a minimum of 100 families settled) were to receive premium lands at the rate of five leagues and five labores for each 100 families settled. Such quantities of Texas land were potentially valuable, of course, but hardly salable while their owners were still in the business of giving land away. Austin tried to cover his varied costs and sustain his current needs by charging settlers twelve and a half cents an acre for land granted them. Nearly half the sum would go to the government to cover mandatory fees for titles and surveys, but many of Austin's settlers considered the fee illegal and resisted payment. Even at Austin's rate, Texas land was far cheaper than land in the United States, but a league of Texas land meant a greater total commitment—in cash, commodities, and deferred payments—than that being made by most settlers in the United States.[15]

It is characteristic of Austin's careful management of his colony that, in view of the confusion which "still exists in Kentucky, Tennessee and many other states," he determined to have the lands surveyed "regularly and accurately" under his own direction rather than "to let each Settler run his lines as he pleased, and mark them or not."[16] Austin expected to define bounds clearly, obviate overlapping of claims, and guarantee titles to all settlers. No doubt he also hoped to gain control over the distribution of the better lands, maximize the marketable parcels, and keep the colony compact. Austin must have had to stand firm against many of the farmer settlers to protect his own survey. But a letter of 1823 to his assistant, Josiah Bell, suggests that he may not always have been rigid on the matter: "Decide before my arrival on the way you wish your land run, you

[14]Reuben McKitrick, *The Public Land System of Texas, 1823–1910* (1918; reprinted, New York: Arno Press, 1979), 31; Barker, *Life of Austin,* 138.

[15]Barker, *Life of Austin,* 109ff.

[16]*The Austin Papers,* 818–19.

may take it all in one tract the smallest quantity allowed is 1,000 yards square which may be increased without limit by myself and the commissioner. I presume you will want at least one League Square[;] agree on the division lines between your neighbors . . . I wish them to agree on their division lines themselves."[17]

Prominent features of the layout of Austin's colony were the leagues and labores of the settlers and Austin's capital town of San Felipe. He toyed with the idea of concentrating settlement on tracts of labores as residential farms along the Brazos River within fifteen or twenty miles of the town. Each settler could then "pick his league tract and have it surveyed elsewhere and it will be time enough if it is improved in two years."[18] We can guess that many settlers did not want their holdings so separated. The evidence suggests no concentration of settlement such as Austin planned. More details on the layout of Austin's colony are found in figures 16.2 and 16.3.

Adjoining Austin's colony on the southwest was the De Witt colony, considered to be the second most successful of the empresario colonies, although fewer than 200 families were settled there. Maps showing land taken up before 1832 reflect a riparian pattern of leagues and quarter leagues, not unlike the Austin colony,[19] but evidencing few, if any, separate labores, which may have been integral with the leagues (fig. 16.4). The holdings were usually as rectangular as possible with the one side formed by the Guadalupe River or one of its tributaries, somewhat elongated perpendicular to the stream, often sharing sides with adjoining holdings, varying in orientation with the general stream direction. By 1831 groups of holdings were almost continuous along the main streams, but the 80 percent of the territory that De Witt had not granted to colonists became public land again. A number of the holdings, including all those markedly larger than a league, had been granted directly by the government rather than by De Witt.

Both the Austin and De Witt colonies set aside four-league reserves fronting on rivers for their principal towns. The San Felipe Tract was more than three times as long as it was wide, while the Gonzales Tract in De Witt's colon,· was nearly square. The inner town of Gonzales consisted of a forty-nine-block square; the rest of the

[17]Ibid., 682–83.
[18]Ibid., 695.
[19]Ethel Zively Rather, "De Witt's Colony," *Quarterly of the Texas State Historical Association* 8 (1904): 95–191, map 1; Edward A. Lukes, *De Witt Colony of Texas* (Austin, Tex.: Pemberton Press, 1976), 88–93.

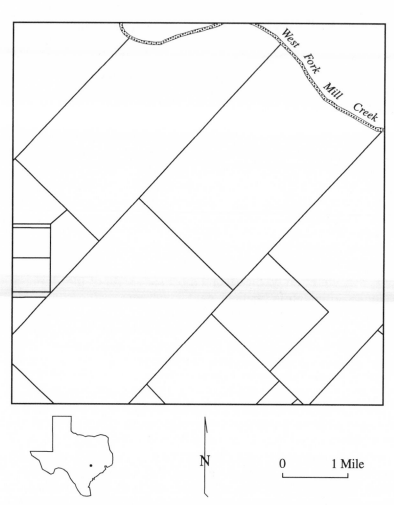

Fig. 16.2. Part of Austin County, Tex. The large lots were square leagues, some with creek frontage, granted by Stephen Austin. Industry (northeast) and New Ulm (northwest) quadrangles.

four-league tract comprised regular rectangular outlots of about ten acres. The western third of the outlots were square, the others being rectangles more than twice as long as wide. The town of San Felipe proper apparently had no such regular plan. The western half of its four leagues, however, was laid out in a grid of squares of about thirty-eight acres each.

The management provided by Austin and De Witt under the Mexican land laws produced more regularity in division of their land

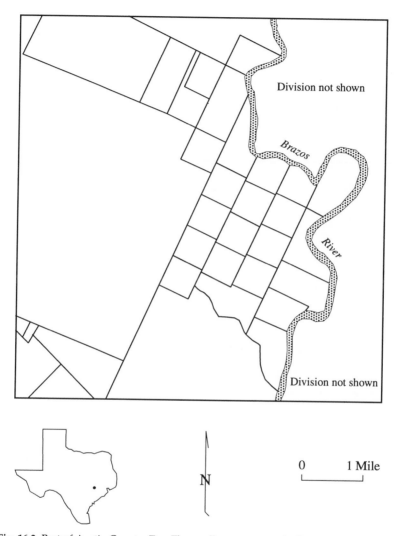

Fig. 16.3. Part of Austin County, Tex. The small squares near the Brazos River were labores. Seventeen longlot labores were just downstream on the opposite bank. The large parcel is the end of the five-league Mill Tract. Burleigh (northeast) and Sunnyside (northwest) quadrangles.

than would have been likely under indiscriminate location. Riparian sites were favored in both colonies, and strict geometric regularity was sought only within the town tracts. Since the empresario system lent itself to management of the survey, we may expect that some regularity showed up in other empresario colonies. In colonies

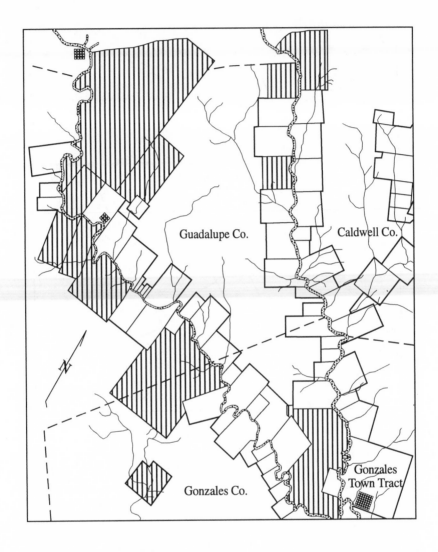

Guadalupe Co.

Caldwell Co.

Gonzales Co.

Gonzales Town Tract

0   10 Miles

Fig. 16.4. De Witt colony. The map represents most of the northern half of the area settled by De Witt. Most of the De Witt grants were either leagues or quarter leagues, the latter going to unmarried men. The vertically hatched lots, granted by the government rather than by De Witt, included the only lots larger than a league. Dates of entry into the colony do not correlate with the distance of grantees' lots from Gonzales. From Rather, "De Witt's Colony."

which the empresarios never really succeeded in organizing, however, any land grants may have been laid out at the whim of the grantee.

Rectilinearity in the empresario colonies may also have been influenced by laws of Coahuila-Texas. A law of 1824 provided for plotting parcels in squares unless the local situation required otherwise.[20] A subsequent law of 1832, rather late in the formation of the empresario colonies, provided that frontage on a stream or lake should not exceed a fourth of the depth.[21] The foregoing Coahuila-Texas policies were affirmed by the republic in 1837, although the water frontage rule was applied only to navigable water, where parcels should "front one half of the square on the water course."[22]

By the end of the Mexican regime about twenty-six million acres, 15 percent of the present state of Texas, were in private hands.[23] The Nueces River separated most of the Hispanic settlement to its south from the great Anglo-Texan area to its north. Settlement features of southeastern Texas show a marked orientation to the rivers.

Texas Land under the Republic

Texas moves toward independence quickly changed the land system. The provisional government immediately offered rewards in land to soldiers who would help to win those lands, "on spec" as it were. The first military bounty passed in 1835 abandoned Mexican units of measure with the promise of 640 acres to those who would serve in the army for two years. The policy was often modified, but always in similar units—1,280 acres, 320 acres, 160 acres.[24] A few months later the new constitution promised a first-class headright by March 1836 to everyone of European descent in Texas who had not received land from Mexico and had not failed in duty to Texas in the Revolution. The first-class headright, virtually having to match the Mexican standard, was a league and a labor for a married man, or a third as much for a single person. The Mexican requirement of living on the land was given up; the recipient need only mark it.

[20]H. P. N. Gammel, comp., *The Laws of Texas,* 10 vols. (Austin: Gammel Book Co., 1898), 1: 43.
[21]Ibid., 302.
[22]Ibid., 1412.
[23]McKitrick, 24.
[24]Miller, 45–46.

To encourage immigration and secure the newly won independence and the Indian frontiers, a second-class headright of 1,280 acres was offered to family heads who arrived in the nineteen months following March 1836, and a third-class headright for half that figure was passed in time to make immigration attractive during 1838 and 1839 (single men would receive half the family allotments). The second- and third-class headrights were conditioned on three years of residence in Texas and performance of the duties of citizenship. The fourth-class headright extended the offer two more years with the additional condition of cultivating ten acres of the land. These headrights, which offered more land than most settlers would have been able to buy in the United States,[25] may have put thirty million acres into private hands, more than all Spanish and Mexican grants and more than all direct transfers of public land to individuals by the later State of Texas. Military bounties and battle donations account for about 6,500,000 acres more.[26]

Homesteads and preemption claims also entered into the republic's land practices. A homestead law of 1841, far ahead of the homestead law in the United States, limited such homesteads to a twelve-mile strip on each side of a military road to run from the Red River to the Nueces. Heads of families would receive 640 acres on condition of living on the land and cultivating it for five years.[27] Texas's preemption law of 1845, four years after the preemption law in the United States, provided the exclusive right to purchase 320 acres at fifty cents an acre to one who had lived on the land for three years and made improvements. Preemption really elevated squatting to an officially approved manner of obtaining land.[28]

In one other effort to speed up immigration, the Republic of Texas initiated in 1841 a brief and unpopular revival of empresario land grants. Contractors were to have the land surveyed into sections (640 acres) for families and half sections for single men, alternate sections to be reserved as public property. To receive title, colonists must build houses on their property and cultivate fifteen acres. Empresarios would receive as premium land ten sections for every 100 colonists introduced, but could also receive up to half of each colonist's land in return for providing moving and settling expenses.[29]

[25]McKitrick, 40–41.

[26]Miller, 29–34.

[27]Ibid., 35.

[28]Ibid., 35–36.

[29]Ibid., 45–46. A change in the law in 1843 enabled the Peters Company to retain three-quarters of the acreage, but the company never pressed for the additional quar-

The last provision presumably explains how the first of the new empresario companies under W. S. Peters could receive about 1,088,000 acres to their colonists' 880,000, taking up less than a fifth of the huge tract including Dallas and lands lying to its north and west.[30] The Peters Company had actually done very little to help settle the colonists.[31] Its failure even to fulfill the requirement of surveying the land in advance of settlement led to more than a decade of uncertainty over land titles.[32] The company finally located its share of land in tracts marked off in the western part of the grant. Its scattered parcels comprised 3,400 squares of 320 acres each, which were distributed to stockholders at the rate of about 900 acres per share.[33] The spacing of roads and field boundaries at about seven-tenths of a mile still marks some of these anomalous grids of 320-acre squares.[34]

Of the other empresarios, the only one who received any premium lands was Henri Castro, a Frenchman, who settled perhaps 500 Europeans, largely Alsatians, on his lands mostly in two counties closely to the west and southwest of San Antonio. Because the riparian lands in Castro's tract were all taken up prior to his contract, most of his colonists were settled in three or four villages on riparian lands he had had to purchase in or near the northern edge of his tract. Here the settlers were assigned town lots and forty- or twenty-acre longlot farm plots adjoining the villages. Most of the main parcels laid out for the colonists in the interior of the tract proved to be suitable only for grazing, and many colonists kept their farming on their original plots,[35] but the oriented rectangularity of the section and half-section lots still shows on topographic maps.[36] Castro brought to Texas more than 2,000 colonists, for whom Texas granted 300,000 acres of land, but the majority of the colonists in fact settled elsewhere than on Castro's land.

Nearly 700,000 acres were granted colonists on another tract south of and overlapping the Peters tract, but the empresario, Charles F.

ter. Seymour V. Connor, *The Peters Colony of Texas* (Austin: Texas State Historical Association, 1959), 54–55, 87.

[30]Miller, 40, 41; Bobby D. Weaver, *Castro's Colony: Empresario Development in Texas, 1842–1865* (College Station: Texas A & M University Press, 1985), 11.

[31]Seymour Connor, 92.

[32]Ibid., 152–56.

[33]Ibid., 159, 161–62.

[34]E.g., True, Texas, USGS topographic sheet, 1:24000, 1964.

[35]Weaver, 50–55, 80–85, 109–23.

[36]E.g., Castroville, Texas, USGS topographic sheet, 1:24,000, 1964.

Mercer, held not to have fulfilled his contract, received no premium lands.[37] Another 1,750,000 acres were granted to some 7,000 German colonists settled in Texas by the Society for the Protection of German Emigrants to Texas, but they were unable to settle on the empresario tract bought for them because the tract, which lay beyond the frontier in an unsuitable area, had also been forfeited.[38] The few other Texan empresario tracts effected no colonization, but all the empresario tracts together resulted directly or indirectly in immigration of more than 15,000 colonists[39] and the granting of nearly 4,500,000 acres.[40] The American colonists Peters brought in settled on their separate farms, whereas the European colonists brought in by Castro and the Society for the Protection of German Emigrants focused, at least at first, on their villages and towns.[41]

Texas Land under the State

Texas's transition in 1845 from republic to state of the United States entailed no break in the continuity of its land system. The public lands continued to belong to Texas and to be at the disposal of its government. Alienation of land continued in close relation to population growth, but less directly than before. As part of the United States, Texas's need for more population was now less for security and more for developing its resources to increase prosperity and make the land, which many Texans had in surplus, more valuable.[42] Half of Texas was granted by the state to promote internal improvements. Although both the republic and the early state were desperately in need of funds, they could not sell much of the land while great quantities were being given away in promotional offerings.

Disposal of land in farm-size plots (eighty to 1,280 acres) was accomplished by sale of land scrip, preemption, homesteads, and veterans' bounties and donations. The republic had sold scrip for about a 1,300,000 acres to pay off some of the debts of the Revolution.[43] The state enacted a new scrip law in 1879, offering public land in fifty-

---

[37]Miller, 41.

[38]Ibid., 43; Terry G. Jordan, *German Seed in Texas Soil* (Austin: University of Texas Press, 1966), 45.

[39]Weaver, 138.

[40]Miller, 43.

[41]Weaver, 138.

[42]McKitrick, 41.

[43]Lang, 41.

four West Texas counties at fifty cents an acre; sales under the program, variously estimated at 1,600,000 to 3,300,000 acres,[44] dropped off sharply when the price was raised to two dollars. Texas's preemption and homestead laws extended through most of the statehood period so long as any land was left to settle. Although Texas had enacted a limited homestead law before the United States did, the Texas homestead conditions were closely parallel to the U.S. model after 1866. The homesteader in Texas, however, needed only three years to patent the title and was given greater protection against seizure for debt.[45] Preemption and homestead claims together are estimated at slightly under five million acres,[46] nearly all of it after statehood. Finally laws passed around 1880 resulted in the transfer of about three million acres of land to needy veterans of the Texas Revolution and of the Confederate army, mostly in parcels of 1,280 acres.

All other allocation of public lands by the State of Texas was dwarfed by the more than thirty million acres granted to railroads and the more than fifty million acres granted for the support of schools, the university, and other educational purposes.[47] The railroad lands and the public school lands were linked in a peculiar manner. Texas gave eight, sixteen, or twenty sections per mile to various railroads to encourage them to build, a policy that began with an abortive offer in 1836. The railroads were required to survey the lands they acquired, often not along their tracks, into a checkerboard pattern of mile squares in which the railroads would get the odd-numbered squares. After several railroad tracts had been surveyed, the even-numbered squares were turned over to the state public school fund, which was later by law guaranteed half of all remaining land in the state. Thus later railroad surveys were automatically divided between the railroad and the schools.[48]

Appropriation of land for the support of schools was an idea going all the way back to Spanish days in Texas.[49] The first systematic laws were passed in 1839 and 1840 to give each county four leagues of land, not necessarily in the same county, ultimately totaling more than four million acres, for school support. Later more than forty

[44]Miller, 62–65.

[45]McKitrick, 47–52.

[46]Ibid., 158.

[47]Ibid.

[48]Miller, 69–125.

[49]Frederick Eby, *Education in Texas: Source Materials,* University of Texas *Bulletin* no. 1824, Education Series no. 2 (April 25) (Austin: University of Texas, 1918), 5.

million acres were set aside for the state-administered permanent school fund. Both the county and state lands were variously leased and sold for the benefit of the respective school funds. Just as the state school lands were no longer part of the general public domain, the state school fund they fed was not part of the treasury's general fund. Laws controlling the sale of both county and state school lands, however, required preference to small farmers or grazers in specified numbers or fractions of sections. The school and university lands have provided great support to education.[50]

Other land grants for internal improvements included more than four million acres for improvement of navigation, half a million for digging irrigation ditches, and three million acres in the most unusual land deal of all, to build Texas's great red granite state capitol building. The constitution of 1876 set aside the huge tract of land in the western Panhandle for building the capitol.[51] In return for this land (on which they located the XIT ranch), a syndicate of both American and British interests contracted to meet the expenses of building the capitol, which came to $3,745,000.[52] The land exchanged for the capitol was currently valued at only fifty cents an acre, but many Texans think the state was too ready to part with it.

The public domain of Texas came to an end about the same time as the United States public domain. As with United States land too, Texas's efforts to get the land into the hands of those who would work it often ran afoul of the intercession of speculators who aggregated great quantities through buying up rights or land or through outright fraud. In 1898 the Texas land office, realizing that land was about to run out before the schools had received their promised half of it, refused to patent more land. When a man claiming a homestead filed suit, the court verified that the vacant land of Texas was gone. After a million and a half acres in excess grants to railroads were taken back, the school land was still short by 17,000 acres. The legislature then balanced the school fund by appropriating a dollar to replace each of those missing acres.[53]

[50]Lang, 123–31; Miller, 110, 192–94, 248.
[51]McKitrick, 78–79.
[52]J. Evetts Haley, *The XIT Ranch of Texas* (Norman: University of Oklahoma Press, 1953) (originally published 1929), 53–57.
[53]Miller, 114–15.

The Land Map of Texas

Texas's land mosaic was textured with tiles of sizes and shapes specified in a succession of laws mostly passed in the sixty years from 1821 to 1880. The square miles of the railroad lands and school lands covered extensive portions of west Texas. Otherwise the patterns changed frequently from place to place. We will use a few counties to sample the varied mosaic.[54]

Brooks and Hidalgo Counties in far southern Texas fall in the Hispanic-settled areas. In Hidalgo County the lower Rio Grande was bordered by the giant longlots mentioned above. In northern Hidalgo and in Brooks to its north, great rectangular tracts nearly square with the compass, mostly three to five leagues, but as large as fourteen leagues, lay beyond the single row of longlots.[55] La Encantada, San Rafael, Loma Blanca, and other tract names, as well as those of their grantees, were Spanish. The file numbers of these grants identify them as first-class headrights, probably Texan confirmation of older grants. Railroad surveys occupied some areas either not included in the early grants or subsequently given up. The odd-numbered railroad squares show the numbers of the scrip certificates used to claim them, perhaps after being forfeited by the railroad; the even-numbered school sections contain the names of their mostly Hispanic purchasers.

The modern property map of Brooks County shows a variety of changes.[56] Some of the large holdings are still large holdings. The great King Ranch is evidenced by several tracts in the name of R. J. Kleberg, Jr., as trustee, and by a 20,000-acre tract in the Mrs. H. M. King estate that reaches into the southeast corner of the county.[57] The King Ranch had begun in 1853 with the purchase of 15,500 acres for three hundred dollars.[58] With many subsequent purchases, sales,

---

[54]Texas is unique in having land grant maps for all its counties, prepared by its General Land Office. Each parcel is identified with a file number that indicates the legal basis for the grant.

[55]Another map of far southern Texas shows Spanish and Mexican land grants there "as of 1852" (Tom Lea, *The King Ranch,* 2 vols. [Boston: Little, Brown and Co., 1957], 1: 378–79). The latter map, retaining a few overlaps and showing several unclaimed areas, shows more rectangularity and compass orientation than typical of American-settled areas under Mexico. The largest grant shown is of the order of half a million acres.

[56]Maps of modern landownership in Texas counties have also been put together by private companies. These are also on file in the state's General Land Office.

[57]Reference to the Mrs. H. M. King estate seems to date the modern map to the period 1925–35. Lea, 2: 605.

[58]Ibid., 1: 104.

and divisions, the main ranch has frequently operated around a million acres.

A group of three tracts originally belonging to people with Garcia as last or middle name appears now subdivided into fifteen tracts about a league square each. The dominant name is now Jones, although Garcia has not disappeared. Other large tracts have been fragmented; the giant longlots of Hidalgo County have been almost microscopically divided into grids of citrus holdings (fig. 16.5) that lack river frontage even though they must have river water. Some of the railroad lands are still held as mile squares, others consolidated. An overlay of oil leases covers it all, many wells in evidence.

Austin County was Stephen Austin's base of operations. Its land grant map is dominated by rectangularity, most of it oriented with the rivers and the distant coast, but occasional orientations are outright discordant. Grids are generally absent. Forty or fifty tracts of a league each, mostly in the upper part of the county, were granted by Austin between 1824 and 1832 (fig. 16.2). Only five were square; the majority, bordering rivers, were about twice as long as wide. Austin himself had two of the leagues and an irregular tract of four or five leagues extending along a creek. About forty square labores were laid out in two irregular grids near the Brazos (fig. 16.3), but just across the Brazos in Waller County were seventeen longlot labores.[59] The town tract of San Felipe has already been mentioned. An almost rectangular five-league "Hacienda" or "Mill Tract" straddled Mill Creek as one of the first grants. Close to fifty square miles were later laid out in an imperfect grid for the Houston and Texas Central Railroad Company. The interstices in and around the grants mentioned were filled with a variety of headright and bounty grants.

The modern map of Austin County property preserves most of the original property lines, but shows a great deal of subdivision, mostly by new lines parallel to the sides of the original tracts. Division of property bordering streams sometimes produced more strips, and property straddling streams was sometimes divided along the stream. The huge Mill Tract was divided into hundreds of parcels, typically ranging from fifty to 200 acres, although some owners have groups of two or more contiguous parcels. Many of the railroad parcels remain whole. The San Felipe grid squares, a little small for farms, are mostly consolidated with a few others.

Tom Green County, 250 miles to the west and north, was mostly in railroad surveys, especially of the Houston and Texas Central (fig.

[59]Jordan, "Antecedents of the Long-Lot," 73.

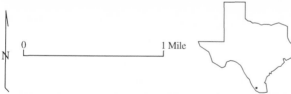

Fig. 16.5. Rio Grande Valley, Texas. The roads indicate the directions of early huge longlots. The intensively used squares are each about forty acres. The old longlots were designed for access to the Rio Grande. Today the river comes to the farms by way of canals. USGS, 1961. Donna (northwest) quadrangle.

16.6). The Concho River and its five tributaries, however, were almost continuously bordered with strips of about 200 acres laid out as third-class headrights in the names of either the German Emigra-

Fig. 16.6. Tom Green County. Longlots surveyed for German immigrants on North Concho River, and square miles of railroad survey. The heavy line is the boundary of a block of land surveyed for the Houston and Texas Central Railroad Co. Carlsbad (east center) and Mount Nebo (west center) quadrangles.

tion Company or of Germans presumably sponsored by it. Llano, San Saba, and Washington Counties each received a four-league grant of school land in Tom Green County. Today much of the pattern of strips and railroad sections has been obliterated by consolidation; subdivision, more common in the previous sample counties, is infrequent in Tom Green. The German strip farms along the rivers were probably unrealized. The German-born population of the county in 1880, 1890, or 1900 seems insufficient to have occupied even a tenth of the strips. Many purchasers of the railroad lands took several sections. Some of the Southern Pacific sections southeast of San Angelo, however, have been divided into two to six parcels.

Deaf Smith County, located in the western Panhandle, typifies the compass-oriented grid surveys of Texas's west. The eastern half of the county was surveyed in the mile square grid of the railroad grants, but the capitol lands of the western half were divided into league squares. Eventually the capitol lands were resurveyed into townships and ranges in the pattern of the U.S. Land Survey, with an adjustment of orientation of a degree or so. The roads and field boundaries of the much divided XIT Ranch today conform with the mile survey, leaving little if any trace of the original league division.

In Texas as a whole, land survey patterns have been grouped into four types: (1) irregular metes and bounds; (2) longlots; (3) irregular rectangular; (4) rigid rectangular (fig. 16.7).[60] The eastern half of Texas is predominantly irregular rectangular with orientation often paralleling the rivers, and the western half rigid rectangular with orientation to the cardinal directions. Most rivers in eastern Texas and a few in the west were lined with longlot systems. Areas characterized by irregular metes and bounds are small, scattered, and mostly in the eastern half, covering less than 2 percent of the area of the state.

The base for rectangular parcels was laid by the Spanish, continued by Mexico with support from the empresarios, and strengthened by ever more frequent use of the U.S. survey section as measure and model. The railroad and school checkerboards account for most of the rigid rectangular surveys. When the first parcels in an area were rectangular, the same orientation tended to be used for additional parcels as well as later subdivision of original parcels. Longlots along rivers were official policy from at least the Mexican period. The irregular metes and bounds surveys probably often mark the areas popular for squatters; the largest such area was in Nacogdoches County, which attracted woodland squatters from the U.S. South.

[60]L. Tuffly Ellis, Terry G. Jordan, and James R. Buchanan, *Cultural and Historical Maps of Texas from the Atlas of Texas* (Austin: University of Texas Bureau of Business Research, 1976), 15.

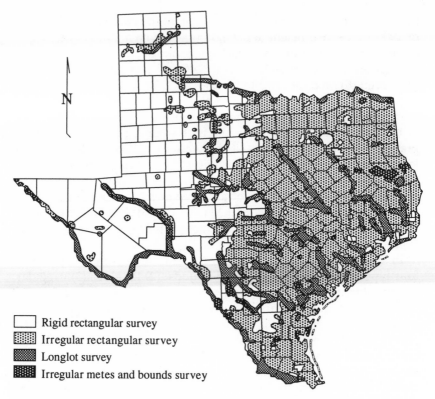

☐ Rigid rectangular survey
▨ Irregular rectangular survey
▰ Longlot survey
▰ Irregular metes and bounds survey

Fig. 16.7. Texas: Original Land Survey Types. From *Atlas of Texas* by Stanley Arbingast et al., by permission of the Bureau of Business Research, University of Texas at Austin, copyright 1976 by the Board of Regents, the University of Texas System, all rights reserved.

Summary

Up to the time Texas joined the United States, most of the land granted was intended for individuals. After that time only a small fraction of the land granted was intended to go directly to individuals. And even then much of the land intended for individuals in military bounties and donations, headright grants, and scrip sales was nonetheless aggregated by speculators before reaching the hands of small owners.

The Hispanic and Anglo-American regimes that successively controlled Texas were markedly contrasting in their policies of land grants to individuals. The Spanish and Mexicans with their grazing tradition offered very large tracts to those intending to raise animals. The Anglo-American governments of Texas following the Revolution phased out the huge grants quickly, although, for some years, they granted larger farms than were generally given out from U.S. public land. Many of these relatively large farms, however, were divided with surveyors, locators, or empresarios who helped the grantees settle.

The large Hispanic-type grants were almost entirely in the more humid eastern half of Texas; with notable exceptions they have tended over the years to be broken up into smaller farms. Contrarily, parcels granted to individuals in the drier western half of Texas, usually modest in size, have more often been consolidated into larger units. Although the great railroad and school tracts were mostly so checkerboarded as to limit individual parcels to 640 acres, the first individual purchasers often obtained several such sections.

Probably the largest grants of land made to individuals in Texas history went to Spanish and Mexican people. The magnitude of the larger grants is indicated by the eleven-league limit placed by Mexico on the total amount of land that could be held by one person. A few empresarios acquired larger quantities of land as premiums for settling colonists, but they were not permitted under Mexican law to retain these premium lands indefinitely. Holdings of the empresarios were often broken into many parcels, as leagues under the Mexicans and as sections and half sections under the republic. In all of Texas history, however, no single grant in one piece compared with

TABLE 16.1. Distribution of public land, by purpose of allotment, United States and Texas

Disposition of all public land	U.S. (%)	Texas (%)
Sales	16	3
Headrights, homesteads, preemptions	19	27
Military bounties and donations	5	7
Education	7	36
Railroads, canals, roads, and Capitol building	10	27
Swampland, mineral, timber grants	11	—
Miscellaneous	6	—
Reserves: forest, park, Indians	15	—
Still public domain	13	—

Sources: The data are modified from McKitrick, 158, and Hibbard, 570, with adjustments (primarily from Miller, passim) to make categories comparable. The figures and comparisons are very rough.

the three million acres of the Capitol Grant. The King Ranch, with all its acquisitions and connections, never approached such dimensions.

Although many United States public land practices were evident in Texas from shortly after Texas independence, the distribution of grants made for different purposes by Texas did not adhere closely to the collective proportions of such grants of United States public domain in other states (table 16.1).

Texas, at a competitive disadvantage, was not able to sell nearly as much of its land as the United States; the statement, however, applies particularly to the years before the Civil War, for in later years the United States was giving land away to individuals under the homestead and similar laws, whereas much Texas land was sold by railroads and school funds. Most of the land Texas gave to individuals was actually alienated under the policies of the republic. The United States did not compare with Texas at all in the proportions of its land given to railroads and set aside for support of education. The last four categories listed in table 16.1, totaling 45 percent of U.S. public land, did not appear significantly in Texas at all. Texas retained none of its public land except for support of education (and much of that only temporarily), and gave little special treatment to lands of particular physical quality.

Part VI

Perspective

17

Summary, Conclusion, Aftermath

THE LAND hunger that drew settlers to North America from Europe expressed a deep-seated territoriality on the part of Western folk to claim ownership of discrete parcels of land that they might perceive fondly and jealously as "home."[1] Basic aspects of human relations with the land support this territoriality: tending the land to tap its productivity often requires direct and continuous control over it as well as neighboring residence; a migratory way of life entails inconvenient costs in money, energy, and time.[2]

The settlers in North America faced the novelty of what they saw as a pristine and empty land waiting to be divided. The American Indians' holding of tribal lands in common simply did not meet the English colonists' ideas of individual ownership and title. This judgment was based not so much on the technicalities of English law, which were complicated enough, but rather on the perception that the Indians did not treat the land as if they owned it: "As for the Natiues in New England, they inclose no Land, neither haue any setled habytation, nor any tame Cattle to improue the Land by."[3]

The sponsors of colonies knew that assignment of land was a basic part of the process of getting their colonies in operation. Most, if not all, expected land to be assigned and platted on some systematic basis, and they expected this to be done under their own rules if not directly under their own control. With its variability and vast extent, land was too refractory a ware to control from across an ocean in the face of impatient settlers with direct access. Such control as was exerted shifted quickly to the colonies. The sponsors seldom even

[1]Edward W. Soja, *The Political Organization of Space*, Commission on College Geography Resource Paper no. 8 (Washington: Association of American Geographers, 1971), 9, 10.

[2]These conditions illustrate aspects of the dual material and spatial nature of land. C. Reinold Noyes, *The Institution of Property* (New York: Longmans, Green and Co., 1936), 395.

[3]*Winthrop Papers*, 5 vols. (Boston: Massachusetts Historical Society, 1931), 2: 141. (Not to be confused with *Winthrop Papers* in *Collections* of MHS.)

331

received the land grant maps they repeatedly ordered, which would at least have given them a sense of what was happening. In truth the colonies did well just to keep plats of individual properties. Holme's map of early Pennsylvania (fig. 14.1) is the one significant exception; in this case, most of the land had been sold in England before settlement, although the survey itself was worked out in the colony. The early plat of property around Savannah (fig. 8.5) was much less extensive. The platting of townships in New England was successful for the very reason that land distribution there had fallen to the local community in the absence of continuing overseas sponsorship.

Land appears to have been viewed as a marketable commodity from its first distribution in the colonies. Virginia promised and soon delivered land to both investors and settlers. There and in the other colonies except Georgia, land began to be sold and traded shortly after its distribution. Many early grantees of either great tracts or small farms held them in expectation of increasing value. As time went on, even newly granted land became more likely to be sold rather than given to its first owners.

For the most part the land survey patterns in the United States conformed with some simple principles. A regular geometric plan needs an authority with power to require that the plan be followed. Such authority may be governmental or stem from subdivision by the owner of a tract, often both. Geometric plans usually precede land distribution and settlement, for later imposition is troublesome, often to the point of being impractical. The efficiency of the geometric plan lies in the ease of its preliminary layout on the drawing board. The planner does not bother to find a separate rationale for each parcel in fitting it to the terrain and to the preference of the grantee. Geometric layouts may also facilitate description and location of the parcels and appeal to the esthetic senses of residents or planners. Only relatively small areas were laid out in grids or rectangular patterns during colonial days.

A chaotic arrangement of parcels is more likely to develop from independent choice of parcels by many persons. Individuals marking off land for themselves may have little concern for the overall ordering of holdings, and, in any case, could neither control nor predict the subsequent choices to be made by others. Efficiency for the individual is simply selection of the best land conforming with previous surveys and applicable rules. Leaving land selection to the individual is also an efficiency for a society with abundant land and limited resources to administer it. Most of the land in the colonies from New

York to Georgia was surveyed parcel by parcel, although the basis for entitlements varied considerably.

Some land patterns exhibit elements of geometric regularity, even though individually laid out. Sometimes they resemble arrays of the cells of an organism, parcels similar to one another and usually in harmonious, but not strictly regular, arrangement. Such organic replication may develop when individuals seeking sites are guided by strong community rules, traditions, or perceptions. The striking patterns that result, vivid in an aerial view, may even be unrecognized by their creators. The arrays of French strip holdings along Louisiana levees may be the closest American approach to such a design.

Limited regularity also occurs when the community plans its land with attention to local terrain or varying individual entitlements. New England townships often considered both in assigning land to their residents.

Sorting Out the Sources of American Land Division Practices

Colonial Land Division

Scholars have disagreed in their models of the origins of American culture, differing in the stress laid on (1) European traits selectively passing the filter of the Atlantic, as opposed to (2) novelties evolving by way of accommodation to frontier living conditions and a variety of American habitats.[4] So posed, the question emphasizes the European traits at the origin of the translocation and American novelties appearing at the destination. But it also hints at the processes occurring between, such as agencies of colony sponsorship and planning, utopian responses to the opportunity of a new start, communication of their experiences among the colonies, and feedback between colonies and mother countries. When their backgrounds are broken down in such terms, the cultures of the various colonial regions reflected most complicated mixes.[5] Our study offers an opportunity to examine the mix of sources in the land-taking systems, where much colonial cultural initiative resided.

Seen from Europe, the main land division geometries laid out on American soil were not radically novel. The irregular polygons of

[4]Robert D. Mitchell, "The Colonial Origins of Anglo-America," in *North America: The Historical Geography of a Changing Continent*, ed. Robert D. Mitchell and Paul A. Groves (Totowa, N.J.: Rowman and Littlefield, 1987), 93–94.

[5]Mitchell, "Colonial Origins," 118–19; idem, "American Origins," 404–6, 417.

most of the colonies reflected the newer European style of enclosure and dispersion of dwellings. New England towns reflected the layout of traditional medieval units (including open-field strips), and riverine arrays of longlots more likely reflected land reclamation projects. More regular land patterns characterized only relatively late developments on either continent. Schemes to begin settlement with regular division of the land, as in Carolina, Pennsylvania, and Georgia, were short-lived at best.

South of New York, indiscriminate location held sway for most of the land division. Such individual land choice had likely prevailed locally in the British past, but it can hardly have been an ongoing practice that was available for transfer to America in official plans or in the expectations of settlers. But the headrights that frequently accompanied indiscriminate location, although similarly not suitable for contemporary English usage, were implicit in the first plans for English settlement overseas and were officially decreed by the Virginia Company in the great charter of 1618. With land both promised and needed in a struggling colony that lacked both surveyors and the organization for distributing land in an orderly way, the colonists chose their own land, and indiscriminate location was never long headed off in the colonial South.

Headrights and indiscriminate location survived Virginia's transition to royal government. Headrights were written into the sponsors' plans for Maryland and later for Carolina. Indiscriminate location is more likely to have diffused directly from colony to colony than by way of colony sponsors; in any case it followed headrights in Maryland and Carolina as readily as it had in Virginia. The headright was written into Pennsylvania's land plan only for servants freed of their indentures, but indiscriminate location awaited only dissipation of the founder's initial control. Most land in Pennsylvania had to be purchased, but the claim to it was often staked by squatting, which probably initiated the most "indiscriminate" and insecure claims of all. New York's large estates seem on a map to be only a coarse-pattern case of indiscriminate location. Illegal as many estates were, they probably entailed more negotiation between officials and grantees than well fits what was meant by "indiscriminate." Likewise in the great private proprietaries of New Jersey, Virginia, and North Carolina, their owners' agents may have exercised some constraints on the shapes and locations of property they sold, but the results were nonetheless usually irregular. Finally, with the crumbling of trustee control in Georgia, indiscriminate location moved into the youngest colony.

Indiscriminate location seems unarguably to be a product of frontier living conditions. Headrights, to which it was often linked, however, were more a feature promulgated by colony sponsors. Land had been offered to recruit settlers on earlier frontiers, as in Ireland, and the formulas for granting it continued to be tested in successive colonies.

New England, in sharp contrast to colonies practicing indiscriminate location, offers a clear case of colonial land patterns following a familiar, even though obsolescent, English model in complex detail. The early New England township with its central common bordered by residence lots, open-farmed fields divided into strips, separate meadows, fragmented ownership, and undivided woods mirrored the ancestral manor or agricultural village. We have even seen that many details of individual township layouts were copied from the particular English home communities of their settlers.

Yet there appears to have been no preordained plan to lay out New England on this pattern, and the New England society that spun itself this habitat contrasted dramatically with its English predecessors. Both the Plymouth and Puritan settlements had planned single compact communities, but split up into smaller units as they faced the realities of their new circumstances. The township communities corresponded to the settlers' organization in church congregations, an occasional one of which moved from England as a single body. They found cohesion from participation in their church and local government rather than from a superimposed monopoly of landownership. The tenures under which residents of England and New England held their land were in corresponding contrast. Although the subsistence functions of the New England township's land paralleled those of its English model, the societies they supported were antithetical in both aims and structure.

Importantly, the manor pattern could be conveniently generated as the nascent New England community laid out its settlement on new ground. A compact residence area facilitated both protection and cooperation in the earliest pioneer stage. Surveying the land units before assigning them made for efficiency through selecting terrain suitable for the differing land uses, and proved manageable for the town organizations in their limited local domains. Successive divisions of the land occurred as the township residents became ready to cultivate new acreage and could be tailored to the changing number of residents and their entitlements.

The sources of New England land division seem to come mostly from the two ends of the transplantation process: old land patterns in

England on the one hand, decisions and experience in the New World on the other.

The townships, of course, changed as time went on. When communal open-field farming proved to be a hindrance to farm enterprise, farmers tended to take charge of their own parcels, preferably consolidating their holdings and moving their residences to their farms, effecting property patterns more like English enclosure. Division of new townships eventually became more commercial. Entire townships might be divided before settlement or even before the sale of lots, now in unitary farms of equal size and geometric arrangement, ignoring the variations in the terrain and the differences in status of potential buyers. The abiding constant, however, was the township as the unit of land division, settlement, and community.

We have seen townships as New England ideas diffuse to other colonies in at least three distinct ways. The most successful of these was within New England itself, where Massachusetts imparted its culture through varying roles of political dominance and migration (even by dissidents) to Connecticut, Rhode Island, New Hampshire, and Maine. Vermont in its turn was most influenced politically by New Hampshire and demographically by Connecticut.

New Englanders in migration to other regions transplanted townships when they arrived early enough to take over land before other practices were established. This happened on Long Island while at least part of it was governed by the Dutch, in New Jersey shortly after the Dutch left, and in northeastern Pennsylvania in the latter half of the eighteenth century. In New Netherland, Dutch and other Europeans followed the New Englanders in organizing a few townships, but in New Jersey and Pennsylvania the New England township system was limited to the settlements of New Englanders and not transferred significantly to other colonists.

At least a few sponsors of other colonies made efforts to establish township communities on the New England model. The planners of Carolina explicitly preferred its denser settlement and perceived development, and the last two colonies, Pennsylvania and Georgia, also planned settlement by townships. None of these plans met great success. Townships did not appear in Carolina until a new scheme launched several in the 1730s. Only a few of the small (about 5,000 acres) townships of Pennsylvania's first surveys were given any central focus in their property layout, and Pennsylvania's later political townships usually did not develop as close-knit communities. Some of the first townships of Georgia were laid out in rectangular designs, but townships played little role in Georgia's subsequent settlement and land division.

Longlots in the English colonies occurred most frequently in New England as part of that region's English inheritance and had a special use in dividing fertile intervale lands. In other colonies their use was largely for dividing frontage on navigable rivers. Such usage was specifically decreed by the proprietors of Carolina, but longlots were not widespread, general features in any of the colonies outside New England.

The frequent association of French settlement, river banks, and longlots was a unique North American development, depending on the novelty of their evolution on the St. Lawrence, the manner in which the French followed the continent's interior waterways, and their convenience for pioneer settlement. The river's edge was a very attractive place to begin settlement: transportation, the land safest from flood, the most workable soils, and access to fishing came together. A longlot could be defined by two monuments on the river bank indicating boundary directions. The narrow lots brought the residences close together in an extended village. As each strip was cleared from the river back, early activity remained close to home base. Proportionate division of the sequence of soils transverse to the river bank was a most equitable way to share the land.

The fashioning of longlots on the St. Lawrence had probably been the work of the *habitants*, the settlers. Official plans in Canada had favored a concentrated village settlement form,[6] and the landowning seigneurs, many absentee, seem to have provided little leadership in forming the cadastral geometry of their land. By comparison with the St. Lawrence, the levees of southern Louisiana presented narrower fringes of usable land between the rivers and swamps, were largely laid out in individual longlots without the presence of seigneuries, and developed longlots more quickly. Such directions for dividing the levees in longlots as came from France likely reflected feedback from the St. Lawrence or from what was already happening in Louisiana.

The Hispanic beginnings of Texas led to a variety of large holdings for grazing and smaller holdings for irrigated farming with few parallels in the more humid east-coast climates. The profusion of longlots along Texas rivers needs further investigation of specific sources. Jordan's attributing them to French influence from Louisiana is reasonable, but Texas was a different physical environment, and

[6]Richard Harris, *Seigneurial System*, 171–81.

discovery of a positive connection would be welcome. American patterns were adapted in Texas in novel ways, most notably the dedication of so much of the plentiful land to education.

The three major colonial land patterns—irregular polygons, townships, and longlots—grew in harmony with differing practices of land-taking. These practices had not been common or planned in the mother countries where the land was already taken, but developed in the colonies. Each of the three property patterns was generated in a unique manner by the early settlement practices that the colonists found convenient. The New England style changed most over time in order to reorganize the land for dispersed farms.

Geometric regularity lent itself to being the dream of a colony sponsor, but not a template the hard-pressed colonists could or would long continue. Only later was there time and organization to try out grids again. Then such planning came from the government of the nation, state, or township or from large landowners, people who could look ahead and view the landscape in the broad, or who just wanted to sell land. Several colonies had rules favoring compact shapes of parcels except on navigable streams, but, even when followed, they did not lead to regularity. Perhaps the scattering of square parcels in the early settlement of new areas in South Carolina and Georgia is the most noticeable evidence of adherence to such rules.

As for sizes of parcels, the sources of choices are varied. Most of the colonies developed a mixture of large- and smallholdings. This was the intent from the beginning in Virginia, where very early a single document provided for both headright claims of widely varying size and particular plantations. The sponsors of Maryland and Carolina provided for both large and small grants, and a similar mix was probably conceived for Pennsylvania and New Jersey. The policies of the Dutch West India Company permitted grants of small farms soon after patroonships were first envisioned for New Netherland. The vacant land of North America offered enticements not available in Western Europe for both landed nobility and for yeomen farmers.

Family farms were not merely included in the initial plans of most of the colonies. Their availability continued to be essential for attracting colonists. They were sought, whether through headright, township assignment, or purchase, by fresh immigrants as well as servants who had completed their indentures. They were, of course, encouraged by English government policy especially in royal colonies; and, in New England, the intentional nature of the communities supported smallholdings.

Large tracts were inherent in the interests of most colony sponsors, who included their own kind in their giant real-estate plans. Only Georgia was planned to be very different, and in New England the success of the communal colonies, although virtually implanted under the aegis of more conventional sponsors, led to township settlement on land earlier granted to several aristocratic proprietors. Large tracts gained their foothold under the concepts of the Virginia Company, implemented by promises to shareholders, headrights, and particular plantations. Manors were introduced by the settlement of Maryland under its charter and similarly fostered in later colonies. In colonial New York the idea of such large grants, not all technically manors, ran wild, almost to the exclusion of anything else, and largely on colony initiative in spite of contrary official orders from London.

The realization of profitable subtropical crops grown with slave labor paved the way for the Southern plantation and gave a new economic advantage to large estates. Such plantations evolved in the line of European enterprises in the tropics, usually finding their capital, management, and markets among Europeans. Tobacco, the first crop in our area leading to successful plantations, was a Virginia development soon drawing its botanical seed stock from West Indian colonies. Barbadian planters were intermediaries in the earliest establishment of plantations in South Carolina. Plantations might develop on older large estates, or result from new land grants, or consolidate smaller holdings. By 1700, there was a sizable net transfer of land from smallholdings to plantations.

Whereas the Southern plantation was an adaptation to regionally available subtropical climates, the French longlot pattern exploited local physical conditions. Minor adaptations to local terrain were, of course ubiquitous. Indiscriminate location itself was a way of responding to the local variability of the land.

Although the general ideas of property ownership and division were European, the specific forms they took were mostly adapted under frontier conditions by the authorities and the settlers in the colonies. Innovations for dividing the land in plans of colony sponsors often had short life expectancies. Exchange of ideas among different colonies on the basis of frontier experience played an important role in selection of cadastral patterns, usually favoring forms that were convenient to apply during the early settlement process.

Finally in 1774, the British government reasserted itself in an effort to regularize the loose and divergent land practices that had been permitted in the separate colonies for a century and a half. The new order required undivided land to be surveyed into lots of 100 to 1,000 acres to be marked, numbered, and auctioned at higher prices than the colonists had been paying.[7] Quitrents were to be raised to a half penny an acre (four and one-sixth shillings a hundred acres). Had this radical shift actually occurred, land division in the colonies would have been more uniform and regular, perhaps even rectangular. But the change came too late. It only added fuel to the flames of rebellion. "Raising the conditions of new Appropriations of Lands" was one of the complaints written into the Declaration of Independence.

Land Division in the Original Thirteen States

Following the Revolution, the states took over any unappropriated land within their boundaries that had belonged to the crown or proprietors. The only exception was New Jersey, where the two companies of proprietors still claim any land not previously alienated. The land not included in the original states became the public domain of the United States. The old colonies merely adjusted their divergent ways of dividing and distributing their land. The federal domain challenged the old regions of the new country to agree on some new, uniform, logical land policy. Although the colonial voice of potential buyers had wanted land cheap, their representatives in the new impecunious governments, as sellers, often raised the prices.

Colonial Land Practices and the U.S. Land Survey

As the Congress of the Confederation took up the land question in 1784, it could draw on the experience of New England with group settlements in presurveyed townships and that of the South with individual claims based on both grants and squatting.[8] Thomas Jefferson of Virginia and Hugh Williamson of North Carolina proposed a checkerboard based on a novel decimal system of measures, but encouraged buyers to pick out their land even before the survey. The plan was modified the next year with smaller square townships based on conventional measures.

[7]Ford, 84–85.

[8]The best account of the debate on the land question is in William D. Pattison, *Beginnings of the American Rectangular Land System, 1784–1800* (Chicago: University of Chicago Department of Geography Research Paper no. 50, 1957), 37–67, 82–96.

The contention over the land system between the New England and Southern delegates to the Congress boiled down to the manner of distributing the land. The inflexible grid of townships and sections, although novel to both groups, was reluctantly accepted because its order would facilitate surveying and selling the vast domain. The issues that slowed adoption of the land ordinance were those of individual settlement versus group settlement and individual choice of land versus orderly assignment. Southerners preferred that land be sold in the 640-acre sections, or better, half sections, with buyers free to choose their own lots and even to identify and settle on sites before survey. New Englanders preferred that the land be sold by townships of thirty-six sections in order to encourage community settlement. Whether by townships or sections, New Englanders wanted land to be sold in the numerical sequence of survey to guard against leapfrog settlement leaving the poor lands as empty gaps in the settlement fabric.

These contrasting attitudes are well expressed in correspondence among members of the Congress.[9] Selling land by townships "was adher'd to with great obstinacy by the Ea. [Eastern] men, and as firmly oppos'd by the Southern."[10] In New England views, "Virginia makes many difficulties, the eastern states are for actual survey, *and sale by Townships,* the Southern States for indiscriminate locations, etc.";[11] and "if adventurers should be permitted to ramble over that extensive country, and take up all the most valuable tracts, the best lands would be in a manner *given away;* and the settlers thus dispersed it will be impossible to govern: they will soon excite the resentments of the natives."[12] And in a Southern retort, "The New England delegates wish to sell the Continental land, rough as it runs . . . the Eastern people being amazingly attached to their own customs."[13]

William Grayson of Virginia, however, played the major role in bringing about the final compromise. Two weeks earlier he had written to Washington the arguments for the New England position:[14]

---

[9]Edmund C. Burnett, ed., *Letters of Members of the Continental Congress,* 8 vols. (Washington: Carnegie Institute of Washington, 1921–36), vol. 8 (only page numbers cited below).

[10]James Monroe to James Madison, ca. May 8, 1785, 115-17.

[11]Rufus King to Elbridge Gerry, April 26, 1785, 104.

[12]Timothy Pickering to Elbridge Gerry, March 1, 1785, in Octavius Pickering, *Life of Timothy Pickering,* 2 vols. (Boston: Little, Brown and Co., 1867), 1: 504–5.

[13]William Grayson to James Madison, May 1, 1785, 109–10.

[14]April 15, 1785, 95–97.

advance survey with reports on the land quality and sale at public auction, both designed to make land available to those living at a distance, and to provide "inducements to emigration which are derived from friendships, religion and relative connections." And a week after passage of the act he wrote with irony, "The Eastern people who before the Revolution never had an idea of any quantity of Earth above a hundred acres, were for selling in large tracts of 30,000 acres, while the Southern people who formerly could scarce bring their imaginations down so low as to comprehend the meaning of 100 acres of ground were for selling the whole territory in lots of a square mile."[15] Some Southerners saw disaster. "This formal and hitherto unheard of plan," predicted Richard Dobbs Spaight of North Carolina, could not be effected before the land was taken up spontaneously "by persons who have already and are daily crossing the Ohio."[16] And George Washington complained that "they do not know where to purchase, the lands are of so versatile a nature, that to the end of time they will not, by those who are acquainted therewith, be purchased either in Townships or by square miles."[17]

The final compromise, indeed, seemed to favor New England. The land would be surveyed before sale at auction, and it would be divided into townships. In the Seven Ranges in the hills of eastern Ohio, alternate townships were designated for sale entire, the others to be sold by 640-acre sections. Land in the Seven Ranges was slow to be surveyed and even slower to sell and be settled. Other areas were simply more attractive. Six hundred forty acres cost too much for any ordinary farmer, and represented more land than he could farm. Groups wishing to settle together might have managed whole townships, but in the end few, if any, full townships in the Seven Ranges were sold whole.[18] Settlement by townships seldom occurred elsewhere, even in areas settled by New Englanders.

Congress passed a new land act in 1796, making modifications to put the land survey in its final form, dividing half the townships into quarters and half into sections, and authorizing the first federal surveys after the Seven Ranges. Later changes gradually made it

[15]To James Madison, May 28, 1785, 129–30.

[16]To the Governor of North Carolina, June 5, 1785, 134–36.

[17]To William Grayson, August 22, 1785, in *The Writings of George Washington*, 39 vols., ed. John C. Fitzpatrick (Washington: U.S. Government Printing Office, 1931–34), 28: 232–34.

[18]Anthony M. Ford, "Land Distribution and Settlement in Eastern Ohio, with Special Reference to the First Two Ranges of the Lands of the Ohio River Survey, 1785–1820" (Ph.D. diss., University of London, n.d.) (copy in Columbus, Ohio, Public Library).

easier for the small farmer to acquire land, and made the land system even less what the New Englanders had sought. The minimum purchase was reduced to 320 acres in 1800, 160 in 1804, eighty in 1820, and forty in 1832.[19] The Preemption Act in 1841 was the final legalization of long-standing practices of possession by squatting and of leapfrogging to get the best land.[20]

With the climax of the changes in 1862, the Homestead Act provided 160 acres free to the settler who would live on the land five years, build a house, and initiate cultivation. The act came too late to be the major aid to settlers it would have been earlier, and, rather than the revolutionary change usually claimed, it was only a reprise of the colonial headright or New England land assignment, including seating and planting, but without any requirement of immigration or formal acceptance by the local community. The states of Georgia and Kentucky had both offered headrights earlier to any of their citizens without land.

In actual practice only a minor part of the public land was directly issued to the families who would live on it and farm it. The greater portion was amassed by speculators or railroads first. Nonetheless the survey remained the framework, and most of the land went into family farms.

Although largely novel, the U.S. Land Survey embraced some colonial features. Rectangularity had been sought in several of the colonies, although nowhere regularly employed until after the Revolution. The township was adopted from New England, where, in late colonial times, it often had or approximated a square shape six miles on a side. The square mile and its successsive halvings were rare lot sizes during the colonial period except in North Carolina, where 640 acres had become the standard grant in the middle of the eighteenth century.

Summary

Attracting settlers and getting the land in production were the immediate aims of colonial land distribution. Longer-range aims, depending on the colony, were to develop internal and external commerce, build communities, and produce profits. The choice of the

---

[19]Hildegard Binder Johnson, *Order upon the Land* (New York: Oxford University Press, 1976), 55–61.
[20]Ibid., 64.

land system to accomplish these aims was usually experimental, ad hoc, and dependent on who exercised the choices. If long-range plans were visionary, as in the cases of the Fundamental Constitutions, the Margravate of Azilia, the Georgia townships, and even Penn's plans for Pennsylvania, the actual decisions were usually local and aimed at more immediate welfare of the colony or the settlers.

Land Distribution and Economic Theories

The great common denominators of colonial and federal land disposal were the low cost at which land was usually available and the (at least ultimate) division of most of the land into family farms. Interestingly these relatively open land markets occurred under contrasting ideologies of British mercantilism and American democracy. Toward the end of the colonial period in the present United States, classical economists, beginning with Adam Smith, developed theories that seemed to endorse American land practices. American prosperity, they held, was explained largely by the abundance of cheap, fertile land.[21] Their position was challenged by Edward Gibbon Wakefield, whose later colonial settlement theories offer some perspective on our topic in their focus on the manner of disposing of land.

Wakefield's *A Letter from Sydney*,[22] although actually written in an English jail cell rather than in Australia, which he had never visited, attracted attention. Believing that a low sale price led to waste of both land and labor through sparse settlement, Wakefield advocated a land price "sufficient" to put all alienated land into cultivation and to keep available a supply of labor for agriculture and industry.[23] Proceeds from land sales would be used to bring in immigrant workers who would have to work a few years to save money to buy land before they could begin to farm on their own. Land would be filled up systematically, after new tracts were surveyed adjoining those already settled.[24]

---

[21]Donald Winch, *Classical Political Economy and Colonies* (Cambridge: Harvard University Press, 1965), 90–92.

[22]In *A Letter from Sydney, the Principal Town of Australasia; and Other Writings on Colonization by Edward Gibbon Wakefield* (London: J. M. Dent and Sons, 1929) (Everyman's Library), 5–106.

[23]Ibid., 99–102.

[24]Richard Charles Mills, *The Colonization of Australia (1829–42): The Wakefield Experiment in Empire Building* (1915; reprinted, London: Dawsons of Pall Mall, 1968), 102.

Many of the American colonies had struggled with the same problems of sparse settlement and shortage of labor that concerned Wakefield. They had even tried to use land policy to solve these problems. Most New England colonies kept control of their land in a manner close to Wakefield's goal, but without using the land price to do it or trying to maintain a landless group of laborers. In the case of New York, where the unused land was held off the market by being tied up in large estates, potential settlers often responded by going to other colonies where land was available. Wakefield's theory and influence drew on American experience, with most attention, however, to the early nineteenth century.

Wakefield participated in companies that sponsored colonies in South Australia and New Zealand, but was unhappy with the results of these settlements, laying the blame on their not following all aspects of his plan, particularly as to the uniform and sufficient land price.[25] All the colonies in Australia and New Zealand, however, were soon selling land to finance immigration as well as using other aspects of Wakefield's plan. In the end the Wakefieldians were no more able than the American sponsors to control all the conditions for the ideal development of a colony.

The priority and relative importance of North America among all of Britain's overseas colonies may seem to give it classical status among such colonies. That Wakefield's colonization proposals, promulgated nearly a century after the founding of the last American colony, could be called "the classical theory of colonization"[26] simply bespeaks the primitive and ad hoc state of the art of colonization in the seventeenth and eighteenth centuries. The colonies struggled with the problems Wakefield sought to avoid, and the role of cheap land in them was recognized, but they were hardly ready to try a comprehensive solution.

Conclusion

The diversity of land division behavior among the colonies enhanced the experimental nature of the land parceling in each colony. There was at least some chance for colonists to learn about what was being tried in other colonies. But the guiding force was the need for colonists, who found the prospect of obtaining land the most attrac-

[25]Ibid., 257, 289–90.
[26]Winch, 122.

tive of the economic incentives. Thus all colonial land systems, perhaps least in the case of New York, made land available to farmers.

Carl Sauer expressed the view that a most significant aspect of North America's development was its settlement by farmers. He was probably contrasting North America with economies elsewhere more devoted to plantation monocultures, grazing latifundia, mining, trading, hunting, or forestry. The cadastral corollary of settlement by farmers was division of the land into family holdings of twenty-five up to a few hundred acres, both a response to and an enticement for those who would work the land. The family farm was a clearly established value in the northern European countries that was transferred to North America.

The small farm that developed in these frontier areas of plentiful land was not only larger than its European prototypes but frequently larger than the demands of subsistence or even what all the labor of a single family could put to good use. Settlement was consequently sparse in new areas, but spread rapidly over the land. The likely costs were some prolongation of the period of frontier living conditions and a damaging view of the land as expendable and replaceable. Only inanimate power and farm machinery much later led family farms to grow greatly in size.

Laying out small farms never provided land for everyone, but it facilitated an important way of life and an expectation that underwrote the development of the United States. The building of property interests into the American Constitution had a broad base of support, serving more than the special interests of a small class.

The original division of the land in the United States was most importantly a starting point that gave a large part of the population a home base and the resources by which to live. From that starting point, under stable government, the land could be worked, improved, and traded in constant readjustment to changing circumstances on the part of individuals and of the society as a whole. The starting point of the land division seldom met the ideals of social planners, but gave many people more than their share and shorted many others or left them out entirely.[27] It did, however, provide for a broad enough ownership tradition among the population that land has been characteristically held and traded on a free market rather than monopolized. Insofar as the original division set the stage for subsequent adaptability, it has served the country's chosen political economy well.

[27]Chandler.

Although an ever smaller part of the population are living directly from the land, the affection for owning land is not confined to farmers. Much more than in gold, people from all walks of life find land an enduring form in which to store their wealth and watch it grow. Millions of properties play thousands of roles in the lives of people whose interests property boundaries separate.

Appendix A
Surveying and Property Boundaries

In 1618, probably before the first surveyor had reached Jamestown, the Virginia Company issued orders to the colony governor that the "Bounds and Metes" of all properties and territories be set out. The phrase "metes and bounds" is still in use to describe the laying out of irregular property surveys. Its original meaning, however, put in modern English words, seems to approximate "markers and boundaries."[1] Thus "metes and bounds" described the surveyor's way of defining a parcel of land, not the parcel itself or a mosaic of parcels. The method—laying out the boundaries and marking them on the land—was used alike for ad hoc surveys that were done one parcel at a time and for regular surveys of grids or strips that were made in advance of settlement. "Metes and bounds" has not been a well-chosen term for distinguishing irregular land surveys from the rectangular federal survey.

The boundary lines that were used to delimit and define grants of rural property were, with very minor exceptions, either straight lines or water bodies. Straight lines were the most common boundaries; most parcels are polygons bounded by three or more straight lines. The water boundaries were normally natural, streams or the edges of estuaries, bays, lakes, marshes, or oceans. Natural property boundaries virtually never follow divides or breaks in slope, soil, rock, or vegetation, except as a surveyor may approximate them with straight lines. The curved boundary of the Catskill estate in New York, which appears to have been arbitrarily located without

[1] Actually *mete* and *bound* have each carried the meanings of both boundary and marker: the geometric lines that limit a parcel of land *and* the physical evidence of those lines; *Oxford English Dictionary,* 13 vols. (Oxford: Oxford University Press, 1933), 1: 1021; 6: 389. "Boundaries and landmarks" is the modern equivalent suggested in Terry G. Jordan, "Division of the Land," in *This Remarkable Continent,* ed. John F. Rooney, Jr., Wilbur Zelinsky, and Dean R. Louder (College Station: Texas A & M University Press for Society for the North American Cultural Survey, 1982), 55.

regard to other natural or cultural features, is a rarity among all the land grant maps I have examined (fig. 11.2).[2]

Actually the straight line was the only boundary surveyors were well equipped to lay out. Points were related in the field by line-of-sight directions and distances between points measured with a surveyor's chain. Property surveys in England in the seventeenth century were commonly done with plane tables set up at a point or two within the property for sighting directions to corners and other points needing location.[3] Such surveys of "radiation" were ill suited to forested terrain or to very large grants. Most American surveying was done by *traverse,* that is, following the boundaries around the property and determining the length and direction of each *course* (a side of the polygon bounding the property).

Directions measured with a magnetic compass provided the basis for determining angles. Since compass needles are restless and devices for measuring angles were clumsy, the early colonial surveyors were unable to measure direction with precision. At first surveyors depended on the mariner's compass, reading directions as "northwest," "east southeast," or "east southeast by south." Since the mariner's compass had at most thirty-two points, directions could not be specified closer than about 6°.[4]

Distances were measured with the surveyor's chain, sixty-six feet long (four rods or poles), made up of 100 iron links. Many errors were possible in measuring. Tension on the chain tends to elongate the links, which may stretch from hard usage. Distances measured along slopes are greater than true horizontal distances, and the plot of a

---

[2]Parcels of land are often divided along curving roads. Since property was usually granted before roads were surveyed, however, roads seldom produced curved boundaries of original land grants. Some New England towns that laid out roads and lots together may have had greater numbers of curving property boundaries. Properties abutting on the boundaries of townships and counties may occasionally have taken on the curves separating those larger units. See also pp. 196–97.

[3]Hughes, 33; John Barry Love, "The Colonial Surveyor in Pennsylvania" (Ph.D. diss., University of Pennsylvania, 1970), 77–79.

[4]Samuel H. Yonge, "The Site of Old 'James Towne,' 1607–1698," *Virginia Magazine of History and Biography* 11 (1903–4): 257–76, 393–414, 12 (1904–5): 33–54, ref. 11: 406, found that only compass points were given in Virginia before 1644. After that azimuths were given to the nearest quarter point (intervals of about 2°45') and by 1656 occasionally to an eighth of a point. Degrees came into use by 1667, and some surveys recorded directions to the nearest quarter of a degree by 1683. Yonge suggests that more accurate measurements were made possible by introduction of the circumferentor. Practices varied widely, however. A Northern Neck survey used a sixteen-point compass as late as 1723.

circuit of courses so measured may not end close to the starting point. In measuring in woods, the chain must often have been bent around trees. And sometimes, in a later survey on the ground, "this ostensibly straight line becomes as crooked as a worm fence," following the actual course of the grantee "as he trudged through the woods, compass in hand and axeman in train, marking his boundary."[5]

Accurate calculation of area was beyond the mathematical knowledge of most early surveyors, even though straightforward trigonometric and graphic methods had been worked out.[6] Some surveyors tried to control area by giving simple shapes to their parcels. Others used such crude formulas as dividing the perimeter of a tract by four and squaring the result.[7] This formula works for a square, but underestimates the area of a circle by 21 percent and overestimates the area of a rectangle three times as long as wide by 33 percent. Probably because they were most immediately checked by the grantees who paid their fees, surveyors often enclosed more acreage than the warrants called for in order to avoid complaints. Colonies, recognizing the difficulty of precision, sometimes allowed overages; in Virginia it was 5 percent, and in Pennsylvania 4 percent plus an extra 6 percent for roads and barren land.[8]

Beyond the limitations of their equipment and knowledge, some surveyors were delinquent in attending to their duties. It was a common practice to omit the survey of the last course around a parcel, reporting simply completion of the traverse back to the beginning, thus losing an important check on the accuracy of the survey, that is, determining whether the courses as measured really would lead to a point close to the beginning. Some surveyors laid out only two sides of a parcel, leaving to the grantee the job of laying out other sides.[9] Still worse, surveyors sometimes produced records of surveys they had not made at all. Occasionally surveyors were bribed by their clients to misrepresent the parcel surveyed or to encroach on land properly belonging to others. With their knowledge of the land, surveyors were in a special position to let grantees know where good land might be found, or to take it for themselves.

The record of a survey is normally preserved in two ways: in a written record and in field markings left on the land. The written de-

---

[5]Montague, 65.

[6]Love, 69–70.

[7]A. W. Richeson, *English Land Measuring to 1800: Instruments and Practices* (Cambridge: MIT Press and Society for the History of Technology, 1966), 76.

[8]Shepherd , 55.

[9]Love, 68.

scriptions of colonial surveys normally followed the traverse around the parcel identifying the courses in order from a specified starting point, as in: beginning at a sycamore on Jug Creek, south 35° west 146 poles to corner with J. Parker, thence west 10° north 73 poles to pine tree. . . . The verbal description was usually accompanied by a plat or map, laying out the parcel to scale, specifying the courses, and showing trees identifying corners and other landmarks such as streams, hills, or vegetation boundaries.

Monumentation is the provision and marking of objects on the land for the purpose of preserving a survey. Identification of corners is most important, but markers along property lines are also helpful. Trees were favorite markers; they were usually identified by blazes that could be recognized years later. Trees marking corners were not necessarily at the precise corners, but were aids in finding the corners. Artificial monuments included stakes or piles of stones. Buried objects were better protected from removal; a charred stick, for example, will last for generations. The written record of the survey is often necessary for interpretation of the field markings, but the field markings take legal precedence in case of conflict.[10] Monumentation is subject to the depredations of time, and must be renewed from time to time or be lost.

As settlement in an area became more dense, new properties were more and more described in terms of the "buttings and boundings" with other properties rather than in terms of their landmarks and courses. When land is sold later, it is often identified only by its owner and the adjoining properties. Sometimes the lengths and bearings of boundaries are not restated after the original survey. Names of adjoining owners change, of course, but the continuity of folk history in a locality usually assures enough information to identify a property.

After a grantee's property was surveyed, he usually took the trouble to identify his corners and their markers. A new owner might go over the bounds with the previous owner, in order to preserve firsthand acquaintance with the boundaries. Likewise, an owner often traversed his boundaries with adjoining owners to confirm agreement on the boundaries or to settle disagreements. Such "processioning," "perambulation," or "beating the bounds" was required every few years in some colonies to refresh knowledge of the boundaries. Precinct or vestry officers known as processioners were appointed to be

[10]Juris Udris, "The Conveyancer and the Surveyor," *Surveying and Mapping* 29 (1969): 236.

sure the procedure was carried out.[11] In Virginia, boundaries processioned three times without disagreement could not afterward be called into question (unless, presumably, there was disagreement as to what had been agreed on). More generally, the agreement of two property owners on the location of their mutual boundary would take precedence over the actual original location. Even when plats and monuments are lost in an area, the network of property lines may still be recovered from the minds of owners and neighbors, from incidental marks in the landscape such as fences, and from the statement in a patent or deed.

Surveyors today are sometimes called on to reconstruct lines that are no longer marked and are unknown to owners of adjoining property. They may have to draw on a variety of knowledge and skills to do so. They may need to recognize the evidence of old structures that lay within or near a parcel. They may need to recognize species of corner trees and to know the chances of survival of each as well as to recognize plants that indicate old fence rows or fields or once-trampled paths. They must be aware of the working methods of earlier surveyors in their areas, especially as regards their reliability. They must know how magnetic directions have changed over the years (as much as 9° in the northeast), and know of local iron deposits that also influence the compass needle. Sometimes boundaries in forested mountain areas may never have been marked, but the surveyor may recover them by "bridging" from better known boundaries of parcels in adjoining valleys.[12]

[11]William H. Seiler, "Land Processioning in Colonial Virginia," *William and Mary Quarterly*, ser. 3, 6 (1949): 416–36.

[12]These comments on the surveyor's art draw from conversations with Roger Cordes of Atlanta and Francis Silver of Martinsburg, W.Va.; also Silver's articles in *Papers and Reports* from annual conventions of the West Virginia Association of Land Surveyors: "The Use of Land Grant Maps" (1976): 19–23; "The Need for the History of Surveyors in Your County" (1977): 35–38.

Appendix B
Land Grant Maps

Land grant maps comprise some of the most useful data for studying land division and provide most of the maps used to illustrate the present study. A land grant map shows the boundaries of all the original parcels of land that were laid out in a previously undivided area. The map or a supplementary list usually gives the name of each grantee, the date of the grant, the acreage, and sometimes names or numbers identifying the parcels. Ideally every point on the map should be included in one and only one grant, that is, the grants take up all the space on the map and do not overlap.

A land grant map thus summarizes the history of granting the land, shows the size and shape of each parcel, its relation to other parcels, and the patterns in the mosaic of parcels in the area. Land grant maps provide data for studying such matters as the size distribution of grants, the sequence of selection of sites, and changes in the size and shapes of new parcels with time. A land grant map normally does not represent property ownership as it was at any single time in the past, for early grants may have been divided, consolidated, or abandoned before later grants were even made.

Making a land grant map conform to the ideal mentioned above takes much effort, for early grants frequently overlapped, were separated by accidental gores or lacunae, and were abandoned and replaced later by new grants. If all parcels are plotted on the map as described in the grants, the viewer of the map gets a realistic and often confusing picture of the overlaps, gores, and regrants, sprinkled with a few surveyors' errors (figs. 7.4 and 8.2). Most of the land grant maps shown in this book, however, lack overlaps, gores, and regrants. The grants have been corrected to conform with boundaries after the adjudication of overlaps, absorption of gores, and elimination of abandoned grants that were later replaced. It is also possible that those who created land grant maps from the records took unstated liberties with grant boundaries in order to minimize the appearance of disorder.

Land grant maps have been prepared for only limited parts of the area of this study. Texas is the only state considered for which land grant maps are complete. The state General Land Office has prepared a map for each county, responding no doubt to interest in the state's abundant underground oil. The Pennsylvania Bureau of Land Records has drawn land warrant maps by townships, but only about a quarter of the counties have been mapped so far. When the Federal Survey divided such states as Louisiana and Florida into townships, their maps also showed the holdings of earlier settlement that survived all legal challenges. The U.S. Forest Service, in acquiring land for national forests, has made land grant maps as part of its title searches. Original land survey maps showing all parcels of property survive for many of the later New England townships, but are rare for very early ones. Elsewhere local land grant maps have occasionally been put together by genealogists, surveyors, or historians.

Appendix C
Size Distribution Samples of Land Grant Holdings from Selected Lists

The main source of data on parcel sizes are land grant records and rent rolls. Land grant records give the acreages of parcels granted over a period of time. Rent rolls give acreages of parcels held at a particular time. Rent rolls include parcels granted at a variety of previous times as they may have been modified, in the interim, by subdivision, consolidation, revision, or correction. Both land grant and rent roll records give statistics on individual parcels. They offer no measure of individuals' total holdings, for some persons received and held numerous separate parcels.

The land grant records used here are variously taken from indexes or other lists of land grants, published summaries of such lists, or land grant maps prepared from the primary records. Properties of sixteen acres and under are omitted.

Land grant distributions are frequently summarized by giving the median size or the average size of the grant. If all grants are listed in order of size, the median is the one that falls in the middle, half the grants being larger and half smaller. The average is the total acreage granted divided by the number of grants. The effect of very large parcels is usually to make the average larger than the median. One large parcel can have an appreciable effect on the average, but little or none on the median. The median is an indicator of the acreage received by the typical grantee. The average is more an indicator of what happened to the total acreage. Since some summaries give medians and some give averages, there are some difficulties in making comparisons. The 195 parcels of land in Virginia in 1625 (omitting three huge grants never really occupied) had a median of 100 acres and an average of 299. The disparity would not be the same in other parcel populations.

356

TABLE C.1. Percentage size distribution of land grants and holdings

Acreage:	16–32	32–64	64–128	128–256	256–512	512–1,024	1,024–2,048	2,048–4,096	4,096–8,192	8,192–16,384	16,384–
VIRGINIA											
James City Co. patents, 1624–38[a]	—	6	14	**35**	26	12	6	1			
Virginia Co. allotments in 1625[b]	—	12	**39**	27	9	6	3	3		1	1
James City County, 1650–62[c]	—	1	8	18	**35**	21	13	2	2		
James City County Rent Roll, 1704[d]	—	13	**25**	**25**	18	9	6	2	2		
Fairfax County, royal patents, 1651–79[e]	—	—	1	—	30	**38**	19	8	2	1	
Fairfax County, Northern Neck grants, 1729–40[f]	—	—	5	25	**36**	23	7	1	3		
Grants by two NN agents, 1690–92, 1713–14[g]	—	5	14	26	**27**	18	6	2	1		
Berkeley County (W. Va.) Northern Neck grants, 1750–75[h]	—	6	16	24	**44**	7	3				
Rent rolls 1704–05[i]	1	6	21	**31**	23	12	5	2	1		

Notes: Most frequent sizes are in bold. Percentages may not total 100 because of rounding.

[a]From index to James City County land patents, Virginia State Library and Archive.

[b]The list appears to include existing properties, including grants to boroughs, the university land, and two very large particular plantations. Compilations in Marshall Harris, 203, from data in Kingsbury, ed., 4: 551–59.

[c]Index to James City County land patents.

[d]Wertenbaker, 211–14.

[e]Beth Mitchell, 19–21.

[f]Ibid., 97–100.

[g]Huntington Library Manuscripts.

[h]Geertsema, indexes from Martinsburg and Tabler's Station 7.5′ quadrangles.

[i]Wertenbaker, 211–14.

(Table C.1 continued)

Acreage:	16–32	32–64	64–128	128–256	256–512	512–1,024	1,024–2,048	2,048–4,096	4,096–8,192	8,192–16,384	16,384–
MARYLAND											
St. Mary's County: pre–1660 grants on 1704 rent roll^j	—	11	29	21	13	13	9	1	1	1	
South side of Severn River, Anne Arundel County, 1658–ca. 1700^k	3	24	31	26	15	1					
Howard County, 1670–1729^l	—	3	19	29	27	14	5	2	1		
SOUTH CAROLINA											
Early warrants through 1672^m	6	7	34	21	20	5	4	1		1	
Northwestern Piedmont, 1734–84^n	—	3	27	43	17	9	1				
Purrysburg, 1735–45°	—	33	13	25	22	5	2				
N.C. grants in present S.C. (Tryon County), 1768–73^p	—	3	12	51	28	6					

^{j}Data furnished by Lois Green Carr, St. Mary's City Commission.

^{k}Dorsey "Original Land Grants of the South Side of Severn River," *Maryland Historical Magazine* 53 (1958): 397–400.

^{l}Dorsey, mimeo list of grants.

^{m}Salley and Olsberg.

^{n}Index to *Land Grant Maps*.

^{o}H.A.M. Smith "Purrysburg," 211–17.

^{p}Holcomb, 1–10.

(Table C.1 continued)

	Acreage:	16–32	32–64	64–128	128–256	256–512	512–1,024	1,024–2,048	2,048–4,096	4,096–8,192	8,192–16,384	16,384–
GEORGIA												
Landholders entering claims in 1754–55 for land previously acquired[q]		—	52	11	7	30						
St. George Parish, 1755–75[r]		—	2	34	39	21	3	1				
Wilkes County warrants for survey on Ceded Lands[s]		—	—	33	49	11	5	—	2			
Camden County, royal grants, 1760–75[t]		—	—	7	7	38	27	11	11			
Camden County, state grants, 1785–99[t]		—	4	5	24	26	19	8	8	5	1	
Camden County, state grants, 1800–49[t]		1	2	17	48	25	7					
PENNSYLVANIA												
First Purchasers (N = 590)[u]		—	—	2	17	39	21	6	2	10	1	1
Rapho Township, Lancaster Co. ca., 1735–1800[v]		11	17	24	39	7	2					

[q]Bryant.

[r]Ibid.

[s]Hitz, "Earliest Settlements," 274–80.

[t]Index to land grant map by James Fort King, 1918.

[u]Pomfret, "First Purchasers," 149–50. The 590 grants for which Pomfret reported acreages represent more than 80 percent of the total. Pomfret makes it clear that many of the other grants fell in the same acreage ranges. Half a dozen of the grants above 10,000 acres to institutions and speculators are not included.

[v]Pennsylvania Bureau of Land Records, connected warrantee maps for specified townships. Allowances for roads and error not included.

(*Table C.1 continued*)

Acreage:	16–32	32–64	64–128	128–256	256–512	512–1,024	1,024–2,048	2,048–4,096	4,096–8,192	8,192–16,384	16,384–
Donegal and East Lampeter Twps.											
Lancaster Co., eighteenth century[v]	—	—	11	38	**41**	8	3				
Kingston Township (warrants mostly early 1800s)[v]											
2nd Division	26	**64**	10								
3rd Division	6	31	**44**	15	4						
4th Division	—	2	10	**79**	10						
MAINE											
Freedom[w]	14	26	**55**	5	1						

[w]Land grant map of Freedom, Maine State Archives.

Appendix D
Geometric Analysis of Sample Properties

Six areas were selected for a comparative geometric analysis of their collective property configurations. Some were chosen because of distinctive characteristics, others lacking especially distinctive traits. The table below summarizes the results. In each case the area treated contained a contiguous group of properties with no unsurveyed enclaves within it. Some of the measures are affected by edge conditions that are likely to be least when the number of properties is greatest.

Numbers 4 and 6 show the high incidence of right angles to be expected. The higher than usual incidence of right angles in number 3 is the result of the very large number of angles per property; right angles were a very small proportion of all angles.

Number 3 stands out for its number of reentrant angles, nearly half of all the angles. Number 2, next highest in reentrant angles, probably got that measure from confusion in the early surveys rather than any deliberate decisions by the surveyors or grantees.

Points where four properties meet are rare even on the more rectangular surveys. Points where three properties meet should be a little more frequent where the number of properties is large. Their frequency range on the samples given involves a factor of nearly two.

Except for number 3, the average number of sides per property stays in the range of six to eight, probably typical of most uncontrolled surveys.

More than half the properties in each sample were relatively compact, with length less than three times the width. The properties of different shapes varied greatly from one sample to another.

361

TABLE D.1. Selected geometric characteristics of sample areas

	Number of properties	Average no. of right angles per property	Average no. of reentrant angles per property	Points where three or more properties meet, per property		Average number of sides per property
				3	4	
Martinsburg 7.5' quadrangle West Virginia[1]	43	0.8	1.2	1.4	0.1	6.7
Somerset County, Maryland[2]	147	1.5	1.9	1.2	.05	7.9
Howard County, Maryland[3]	29	2.1	15	1.4	—	39.8
Amelia Township, S.C.[4]	65	4.3	0.6	1.0	.01	7.0
Southern Union County area, S.C. Piedmont[5]	37	0.9	0.9	0.8	.05	6.8
Central Newberry County area, S.C. Piedmont[6]	43	3.4	0.8	1.0	.07	6.0

[1]Portion of land grant map by Geertsema, valley land without rugged relief.
[2]Map by Benson of Maryland Eastern Shore. Some properties elongated to reduce water frontage. Some complications are due to inconsistencies among surveys.
[3]Map by Dorsey. Many properties with a large number of sides have twisting patterns.
[4]Map by Bennett (fig. 8.7). Most property lines run northeast or northwest.
[5]*Land Grant Maps*, map 3. Typical maps in source, with some inconsistencies of boundaries.
[6]Ibid., map 6. Unusually large number of square properties.

(Table D.1 continued)

	Percentage of properties with a given number of sides							Percentage of properties with an approximate ratio, length to width									
	3	4	5	6	7	8	9	1/1	2/1	3/1	4/1	5/1	6/1	7/1	8/1	9/1	10/1
Martinsburg 7.5' quadrangle West Virginia	2	16	14	23	19	7	7	30	44	12	2	—	5	2	5		
Somerset County, Maryland	1	15	14	12	14	9	7	14	39	14	8	7	6	3	3	1	1
Howard County, Maryland	—	7	3	3	7	7	3	31	41	10	10	3					
Amelia Township, S.C.	5	57	9	12	5	11	—	65	17	9	5	2	3				
Southern Union County area, S.C. Piedmont	—	14	19	27	8	16	8	59	22	14	3	3					
Central Newberry County area, S.C. Piedmont	—	47	2	23	12	2	2	63	30	5	2						

Glossary

ADVERSE POSSESSION. Establishing the right to land by virtue of having been in possession of it for a stated period of time. Adverse possession and peaceful possession seem to differ only in what aspect of possession the law chooses to consider important.

ALLODIAL. Tenure of landownership free of feudal obligations and restrictions on alienation and inheritance. Essentially fee simple.

ANCIENT PLANTER. Early colonist in Virginia, residing there by about 1616.

BOUWERIE. Dutch term used in colonial New York for family-sized farms.

CADASTRAL. Pertaining to landownership or other land tenure.

COMMONER. A member of a New England town possessing rights to share in the division of the common land.

COPYHOLD. A feudal tenure under which the tenant held land on terms that depended on the custom of the manor. It lay between villeinage and outright ownership.

CORPORATE. Term used of some New England colonies in the special sense that they governed themselves under their own rules.

COURSE. A side of a polygon surveyed to enclose a parcel of land.

DEMESNE, DOMAINE. Part of a manor held directly by the lord, subject to being rented to tenants only for limited periods.

EMPRESARIO. In Spanish, but mostly Mexican, Texas, a contractor who undertook to recruit and plant settlers within a specified tract of land and who would receive land himself in proportion to the families settled.

ENCLOSURE. Arrangement of farm land of an individual or other entity in a single parcel under single management.

ENTAIL. Legal action that prevents division of an estate or inheritance under other than by a prescribed route such as male primogeniture.

ENTRY. Taking possession, crudely surveying, or other filing of an informal claim to vacant land.

FEE SIMPLE. Our common tenure of ownership of land free of constraints except those imposed by society.

FREE AND COMMON SOCAGE. A tenure of landownership comparable to fee simple except for the obligation of a quitrent.

FREEHOLDER. A commoner, New England. FREEHOLD generally signifies an inheritable interest in a property.

FREEMAN. A class of full citizenship in New England by virtue of an oath of loyalty to the colony.

GENERAL COURT. The governing body of a New England colony.

GORE. A narrow parcel of land left over between grants or townships.

HABITANT. Farming residents of French colonies in North America.

HEADRIGHT. Promise of a specified acreage of land for paying the passage of an immigrant (self or other), or later for simply being an inhabitant of a state who had not previously received such land.

HOLD OF, HOLD AS OF. Terms of feudal land tenure. In feudalism, only a king or other sovereign is conceived as owning land. Even freeholders, who have a right to sell their holdings, hold their land of the king or of a superior whose chain of tenure runs on to the king. "Of" in these phrases would be more clearly expressed in our present English by the word "under." At each step in the chain of holding, there was some kind of at least token obligation of the holder to the superior. Sometimes a person may hold "as of" a manor rather than directly of a lord. In this case, customs of the manor would define the holder's obligations, which were usually lighter than in the case of direct holding. Most of the American colony sponsors held the land as of the king's manor of East Greenwich.

HUNDRED. A subdivision of a county, similar to a township.

INDENTURE. A contract, especially for so many years' labor in return for passage to a colony.

INDISCRIMINATE LOCATION. A term developed during the colonial period for the process of land assignment by individual choice of location and bounds on any vacant land to the extent of the acreage entitlement. (It seems to be "indiscriminate" in the sense that the parcel is not arbitrarily laid out, say, in a regular grid in advance.)

INTERVALE. Term for alluvial land, mostly in New England.

LABOR. Mexican term for a farm-size parcel of 177 acres.

LADDER. Pattern of lots marked off by parallel lines running between a usually longer pair of parallel or subparallel lines.

LATIFUNDIUM. A large estate, much larger than a family farm, requiring proportionately more labor for similar uses.

LOCATOR. Person who scouts out frontier land for others for a share of the land or other reward.

LONGLOT. Lot in the shape of a long strip, often with the long sides parallel, often arrayed side by side with other longlots. For this study lots with lengths three or more times their widths are considered longlots.

MANOR. A medieval European style of latifundium, held by a feudal lord who had powers to hold courts, and whose relations with relatively permanent tenants and laborers were governed by custom.

METES AND BOUNDS. A term used to describe irregular property surveys laid out one at a time in the effective absence of land division plans that would produce a regular geometry (see Appendix A).

OPEN-FIELD. A farming system in which fields comprising strips of a number of owners or tenants are operated in some measure as cooperative units.

OUTLOT. One of the parcels laid off for farming outside a town when a town is laid off in city lots (inlots).

OUTLYER. A squatter claiming land and building on it with the intent of a quick sale and moving on.

PALATINE. Referring to the palace or holding the governmental powers of the palace.

PARTICULAR PLANTATION. A large land grant to one or more stockholders of the Virginia Company, virtually establishing a small, semi-independent colony.

PATENT. A finalized land grant from a sovereign power, as opposed to a transfer by deed from a nonsovereign person or entity. Patent in Carolina, however, meant an earlier stage in making the grant.

PATROONSHIP. A Dutch manor in New York, New Jersey, or Delaware, with a PATROON as its lord.

PEACEFUL POSSESSION. See ADVERSE POSSESSION.

PERPETUAL LEASE. A tenure on New York estates in which the occupant is treated as partly owner and partly tenant, holding a salable interest and also paying rent.

PITCH. The New England term for individual choice of vacant and unsurveyed land.

PLANTING. To take possession by planting crops or other use of the land. Seating and/or planting was required in most colonies for retaining land granted.

PLANTATION. General term for a new settlement. A colony. In New England an incipient township, not yet organized. A large agricultural estate with resident labor.

PREEMPTION. Right of a squatter to buy the land he had settled.

PROPRIETOR(S). Owner(s) of a large tract of land designed for further subdivision and distribution, ranging from a whole colony to a township.

QUARTER SALE. Feature of a perpetual lease whereby the landlord claimed a quarter (or other fraction) of the sale price if the tenant sold the property, also sometimes exacting the charge if the property passed by inheritance.

QUITRENT. An annual charge on land, replacing all earlier feudal obligations. Applied to land in free and common socage, but not in fee simple. A symbol of fealty.

RANGE. A tier or row of (long) lots between two parallel RANGE LINES, a ladder. Usage most common in New England. Tier of townships in the federal survey.

ROTURE. A concession of land, a farm, held by a habitant in Quebec, for which he paid a regular fee.

SEATING. Establishing residence on the land, usually by building a house. See PLANTING.

SEIGNEURIAL, SEIGNIORIAL. Pertaining to lordship of manorial holdings of varying status.

SELECTMAN. Member of elected governing board of a New England town.

SHOT. A ladder or range.

SITIO. Under Spain and Mexico, a relatively large grant of land for grazing.

SIZING. In New England, adjusting the size of a land entitlement for its quality.

SOCAGE. See FREE AND COMMON SOCAGE.

SQUAT. To settle on vacant land without authorization.

TAIL MALE. Land tenure permitting change of ownership only by male descent.

TOWNSHIP, TOWN. A sharply bounded community, ordinarily at least partly rural, entailing some organization of its citizens, the principal unit of local government in New England states. Town is used here to connote the people and organization, township to connote the land and area. Except in and near New England, town usually signifies a small city.

TITHING. Subdivision of a ward in the city of Savannah. Also church tax on land or its produce.

WARRANT. A document authorizing a surveyor to lay out vacant land for a settler or planter entitled to a specified acreage.

Table of Measures

(Many of these measures have varied with place and time. The table gives those that have been used in the text).

Linear

1 league = 3 miles = 4.83 kilometers
1 mile = 80 chains = 320 rods or poles = 5,280 feet = 1,609.6 meters
1 chain = 4 rods = 22 yards = 66 feet = 20.12 meters
1 rod = 5.5 yards = 16.5 feet = 5.029 meters
1 foot = .3048 meter
1 lieue (French league) = 80 arpents = 2.91 miles = 4.68 kilometers
1 arpent = 192 feet = 58.5 meters
1 legua (Spanish league) = 5,000 varas = 2.63 miles = 4.23 kilometers
1 vara in Texas = 2.78 feet = 33.33 inches = .847 meter

Areal

1 acre = 10 square chains = 160 square rods = 43,560 square feet = .4046 hectare = 4,046 square meters
1 square arpent = .846 acre = .342 hectare = 3,420 square meters
1 square lieue = 6,400 square arpents = 8.46 square miles = 5,416 acres = 21.91 square kilometers = 2,191 hectares
1 square legua = 25,000,000 square varas = 4,428 acres = 6.92 square miles = 17.91 square kilometers = 1,791 hectares
1 labor = 1,000,000 square varas = 177.1 acres = 71.65 hectares

Bibliography

Abernethy, Thomas Perkins. *Western Lands and the American Revolution.* New York: A. Appleton Century, 1937.

———. *From Frontier to Plantation in Tennessee.* 1932. Reprinted, University: University of Alabama Press, 1967.

"Abstract of Instructions to Sir Francis Wyatt, January 1638/9." *Virginia Magazine of History and Biography* 11 (1903–4): 54–57.

An Account Shewing the Progress of Georgia in America, written ca. 1740 by order of the Trustees, in Candler, comp., *The Colonial Records of the State of Georgia* 3: 373.

Ackerman, Robert K. *South Carolina Colonial Land Policies.* Columbia: University of South Carolina Press for South Carolina Tricentennial Commission, 1977.

Acrelius, Israel. *A History of New Sweden.* 1874. Reprinted, New York: Arno Press, 1972.

Adams, James Truslow. *History of the Town of Southampton.* Port Washington, N.Y.: Ira J. Friedman, 1962.

Agonito, Joseph. "St. Inigoes Manor: A Nineteenth Century Jesuit Plantation." *Maryland Historical Magazine* 72 (1977): 83–98.

Akagi, Roy H. *The Town Proprietors of the New England Colonies: A Study of Their Development, Organization, Activities, and Controversies, 1620–1770.* Philadelphia: University of Pennsylvania Press, 1924.

Allen, David Grayson. *In English Ways.* Chapel Hill: University of North Carolina Press for Institute of Early American History and Culture, 1981.

Allis, Frederick S., Jr., ed. "William Bingham's Maine Lands, 1790–1820," *Collections* (Colonial Society of Massachusetts) 36, 37 (1954).

American State Papers: Class 8: Public Lands. 8 vols. Washington: Gales and Seaton, 1832–61.

Anderson, Virginia DeJohn. *New England's Generation: The Great Migration and the Formation of Society and Culture in the Seventeenth Century.* Cambridge: Cambridge University Press, 1991.

Andrews, Charles M. *The River Towns of Connecticut.* Johns Hopkins University Studies in Historical and Political Science, ser. 7, nos. 7–9. Baltimore: Johns Hopkins, 1889.

———. *Our Earliest Colonial Settlements.* New York: New York University Press, 1933.

———. *The Colonial Period of American History.* 4 vols. New Haven, Conn.: Yale University Press, 1934–38.

Andrews, Matthew Page. *The Founding of Maryland.* Baltimore: Williams and Wilkins Co., 1933.

Andriot, John L. *Township Atlas of the United States.* McLean, Va.: Andriot Associates, 1979.

Archives of Maryland. 72 vols. Baltimore: Maryland Historical Society, 1883–1972.

Arnow, Harriette Simpson. *Seedtime on the Cumberland.* New York: Macmillan Co., 1960.

Atlas of the State of New York. 1829. Rev. ed., Ithaca, N.Y.: N. C. Burr, 1841.

Atwater, Edward E. *History of the Colony of New Haven to Its Absorption into Connecticut.* New Haven: Author, 1881.

Atwood, Stanley Bearce. *The Length and Breadth of Maine.* Maine Studies no. 96. Orono: University of Maine, 1973.

Bailey, Kenneth P. *The Ohio Company of Virginia and the Westward Movement, 1748–1792.* Glendale, Calif.: Arthur H. Clarke Co., 1939.

Baldwin, William C. *Brandywine Creek: A Pictorial History.* West Chester, Pa.: Author, 1977.

Bankoff, H. Arthur. "The Gravesend Project: Archaeology in Brooklyn." In *Brooklyn, U.S.A.: The Fourth Largest City in America,* edited by Rita Seiden Miller. New York: Brooklyn College Press, 1976, 61–68.

Barker, Eugene C. *The Life of Stephen F. Austin.* Nashville, Tenn.: Cokesbury Press, 1925.

———, ed. *The Austin Papers.* In *Annual Report of the American Historical Association* (1919), vol. 2.

Barnes, Viola Florence. "Land Tenure in English Colonial Charters of the Seventeenth Century." In *Essays in Colonial History Presented to Charles McLean Andrews by His Students.* New Haven: Yale University Press, 1931, 4–40.

Batchellor, Albert Stillman, ed. *State Papers of New Hampshire, Town Charters.* Vols. 24–29 (Concord: Edward N. Pearson, Public Printer, 1894–96).

Beatty, Richmond Croom. *William Byrd of Westover*. Boston: Houghton, Mifflin Co., 1932.

Beverley, Robert. *The History and Present State of Virginia*. 1705. Reprinted, Chapel Hill: University of North Carolina Press for Institute of Early American History and Culture, 1947.

Bien, Joseph R. *Atlas of the State of New York*. New York: J. Bien and Co., 1895.

Billington, Ray Allen. "The Origin of the Land Speculator as a Frontier Type." *Agricultural History* 19 (1945): 204–12.

Blume, Helmut. *The German Coast during the Colonial Era, 1702–1803*. Translated by Ellen C. Merrill. Destrehan, La.: German-Acadian Coast Historical and Genealogical Society, 1990. First published in 1956.

Bond, Beverley W., Jr. *The Quitrent System in the American Colonies*. New Haven: Yale University Press, 1919.

Bond, Henry. *Genealogies of the Families and Descendants of the Early Settlers of Watertown, Massachusetts*. Boston: Little Brown and Co., 1855.

Bonomi, Patricia U. *A Fractious People: Politics and Society in Colonial New York*. New York: Columbia University Press, 1971.

Bowen, Clarence Winthrop. *The History of Woodstock, Connecticut*. Norwood, Mass.: Author, 1926.

Boyd, Julian Parks. *The Susquehannah Company: Connecticut's Experiment in Expansion*. Connecticut Tercentenary Commission Pamphlet no. 34. New Haven: Yale University Press, 1935.

Bridenbaugh, Carl. *Myths and Realities: Societies of the Colonial South*. Baton Rouge: Louisiana State University Press, 1952.

_____. *Fat Mutton and Liberty of Conscience: Society in Rhode Island, 1636–1690*. Providence: Brown University Press, 1974.

Bronner, Edwin B. *William Penn's "Holy Experiment": The Founding of Pennsylvania, 1681–1701*. New York: Temple University Publications, 1962.

Brookes-Smith, Joan E., comp. *Master Index: Virginia Surveys and Grants, 1774–1791*. Frankfort: Kentucky Historical Society, 1976.

Brown, Alexander. *The Genesis of the United States*. 2 vols. Boston: Houghton, Mifflin and Co., 1890.

_____. *The First Republic in America*. New York: Russell and Russell, 1969.

Brown, Katherine M. "Freemanship in Puritan Massachusetts." *American Historical Review* 54 (1954): 865–83.

Brown, Robert E. and B. Katherine. *Virginia, 1705–1796: Democracy or Aristocracy?* East Lansing: Michigan State University Press, 1964.

Brown, Stuart E., Jr. *Virginia Baron: The Story of Thomas Sixth Lord Fairfax.* Berryville, Va.: Chesapeake Book Co., 1965.

Browning, Charles H., *Welsh Settlement of Pennsylvania.* Philadelphia: William J. Campbell, 1912.

Bruce, Philip Alexander. *Economic History of Virginia in the Seventeenth Century.* 2 vols. New York: Macmillan and Co., 1896.

Brunn, Stanley D. *Geography and Politics in America.* New York: Harper and Row, 1974.

Bryant, Pat. *Entry of Claims for Georgia Landholders, 1733–1755.* Atlanta: State Printing Office, 1975.

Buck, Solon J., and Elizabeth Hawthorn Buck. *The Planting of Civilization in Western Pennsylvania.* Pittsburgh: University of Pittsburgh Press, 1939.

Budke, George H. "The History of the Tappan Patent." *Rockland Record* 2 (1931–32): 35–50.

Bugg, James L., Jr. "The French Huguenot Frontier Settlement of Manakin Town." *Virginia Magazine of History and Biography* 61 (1953): 359–94.

Burnett, Edmund C., ed. *Letters of Members of the Continental Congress.* 8 vols. Washington: Carnegie Institute of Washington, 1921–36.

Burns, Francis P. "The Spanish Land Laws of Louisiana." *Louisiana Historical Quarterly* 11 (1928): 557–81.

Bushman, Richard L. *From Puritan to Yankee: Character and the Social Order in Connecticut, 1690–1765.* Cambridge: Harvard University Press, 1967.

Butterfield, L. H. "Judge William Cooper (1754–1809): A Sketch of His Character and Accomplishment." *New York History* 30 (1949): 385–408.

Byrd, William. *The Secret Diary of William Byrd of Westover, 1709–1712.* Edited by Louis B. Wright and Marion Tinling. Richmond, Va.: Dietz Press, 1941.

Cabell, Priscilla Harriss. *Turff and Twigg.* Vol. 1, *The French Lands.* Richmond, Va.: Author, 1988.

Cadle, Farris W. *Georgia Land Surveying History and Law.* Athens: University of Georgia Press, 1991.

Cadwalader, Mary H. "Charles Carroll of Carrollton: A Signer's Story." *Smithsonian* 6 (1975), no. 9: 64–70.

Cady, John Hutchins. *The Civic and Architectural Development of Providence.* Providence: Book Shop, 1957.

Calder, Isabel MacBeath. "The Earl of Stirling and the Colonization of Long Island." In *Essays in Colonial History Presented to Charles McLean Andrews by His Students.* New Haven: Yale University Press, 1931, 74–95.

Candler, Allen D., comp. *The Colonial Records of the State of Georgia.* 26 vols. Atlanta: Franklin Printing and Publishing Co., 1904–16.

Cannon, John. "Henry McCulloch and Henry McCulloh." *William and Mary Quarterly,* ser. 3, 15 (1958): 71–73.

Carr, Lois Green. "The Metropolis of Maryland: A Comment on Town Development along the Tobacco Coast." *Maryland Historical Magazine* 69 (1974): 124–45.

Carroll, Charles. "Extracts from Account and Letter Books of Dr. Charles Carroll, of Annapolis." *Maryland Historical Magazine* 26 (1931): 43–58.

Carstensen, Vernon, ed. *The Public Lands: Studies in the History of the Public Domain.* Madison: University of Wisconsin Press, 1968.

Chandler, Alfred N. *Land Title Origins: A Tale of Force and Fraud.* New York: Robert Schalkenbach Foundation, 1945.

Channing, Edward. *The Narragansett Planters.* Johns Hopkins University Studies in Historical and Political Science, ser. 4, no. 3. Baltimore: Johns Hopkins, 1886.

Chazanof, William. *Joseph Ellicott and the Holland Land Company.* Syracuse, N.Y.: Syracuse University Press, 1970.

Chernow, Barbara Ann. *Robert Morris, Land Speculator, 1790–1801.* New York: Arno Press, 1978.

Clark, Thomas D. *Kentucky: Land of Contrast.* New York: Harper and Row, 1968.

Clawson, Marion. *America's Land and Its Uses.* Baltimore: Johns Hopkins Press for Resources for the Future, 1972.

Colden, Cadwallader. "The State of the Lands in the Province of New York." In *Documentary History of the State of New York,* edited by Christopher Morgan, 1: 382–87.

_____. "Letters on Smith's History of New York." *Collections* (New York Historical Society) 1 (1868): 226–35.

_____. "Letters and Papers of Cadwallader Colden." *Collections* (New York Historical Society) 50–56 (1917–23).

Coleman, Kenneth. *Colonial Georgia.* New York: Charles Scribner's Sons, 1976.

_____. "Political Development in a Frontier State." In *A History of Georgia.* edited by Kenneth Coleman. Athens: University of Georgia Press, 1977, 89–104.

Committee of Dorchester Antiquarian and Historical Society. *History of the Town of Dorchester, Massachusetts.* Boston: Ebenezer Clapp, Jr., 1859.

Connor, R. D. W. *History of North Carolina.* Vol. 1. *The Colonial and Revolutionary Period, 1584–1783.* Chicago: Lewis Publishing Co., 1919.

Connor, Seymour V. *The Peters Colony of Texas.* Austin: Texas State Historical Association, 1959.

Cooper, William. *A Guide in the Wilderness, or the History of the First Settlements in the Western Counties of New York with Useful Instructions to Future Settlers.* Dublin: Gilbert and Hedges, 1810. Reprinted, Rochester: George P. Humphrey, 1897.

_____. Papers at the Stevens-German Library, Hartwick College, Oneonta, N.Y.

Corlew, Robert E. *Tennessee: A Short History.* Knoxville: University of Tennessee Press, 1981.

Coulter, E. Merton. *A Short History of Georgia.* Chapel Hill: University of North Carolina Press, 1933.

Couper, William. *History of the Shenandoah Valley.* 3 vols. New York: Lewis Historical Publishing Co., 1952.

Craven, Wesley Frank. *Dissolution of the Virginia Company.* 1932. Reprinted, Gloucester, Mass.: Peter Smith, 1964.

_____. *A History of the South.* Vol. 1. *The Southern Colonies in the Seventeenth Century, 1607–1689.* Baton Rouge: Louisiana State University Press and Littlefield Fund for Southern History at the University of Texas, 1949.

_____. *Red, White, and Black.* Charlottesville: University Press of Virginia, 1971.

Cruzat, Heloise H., trans. "Distribution of Land in Louisiana by the Company of the Indies: I. The Jonchère Concession." *Louisiana Historical Quarterly* 11 (1928): 553–56.

Curtis, Harold R. "Warwick Proprietors' Divisions." *Rhode Island Historical Society Collections* 20 (1927): 33–51.

Damon, Samuel C. *The History of Holden, Massachusetts.* Worcester: Wallace and Ripley, 1841.

Daniels, Bruce C. "Connecticut's Villages Become Mature Towns: The Complexity of Local Institutions, 1676 to 1776." *William and Mary Quarterly,* ser. 3, no. 34 (1977): 83–103.

_____. *The Connecticut Town: Growth and Development, 1635–1790.* Middletown, Conn.: Wesleyan University Press, 1979.

_____. *Dissent and Conformity on Narragansett Bay: The Colonial Rhode Island Town.* Middletown, Conn.: Wesleyan University Press, 1983.

Dart, Henry P., ed. and trans. "The First Law Regulating Land Grants in French Colonial Louisiana." *Louisiana Historical Quarterly* 14 (1931): 346–98.

Davis, Darrell Haug. *The Geography of the Jackson Purchase.* Frankfort: Kentucky Geological Survey, 1923.

Davis, Harold E. *The Fledgling Province: Social and Cultural Life in Colonial Georgia, 1733–1776.* Chapel Hill: University of North Carolina Press, 1976.

Davis, Richard Beale, ed. *William Fitzhugh and His Chesapeake World.* Chapel Hill: University of North Carolina Press for Virginia Historical Society, 1963.

Davis, William T. *Ancient Landmarks of Plymouth.* Boston: Damrell and Upham, 1899.

_____, ed. *Bradford's History of Plymouth Plantation.* New York: Charles Scribner's Sons, 1920.

Davisson, William I., and Dennis J. Dugan. "Land Precedents in Essex County, Massachusetts." *Essex Institute Historical Collections* 106 (1970): 252–76.

Delaware Department of State, Division of Historical and Cultural Affairs, Historic Preservation Section, *Delaware State Historic Preservation Plan,* ca. 1977.

Deming, Dorothy. *The Settlement of the Connecticut Towns.* Connecticut Tercentenary Commission Pamphlet no. 6. New Haven: Yale University Press, 1933.

Dickinson, Josiah. *The Fairfax Proprietary.* Front Royal, Va.: Warren Press, 1959.

Dobkins, Betty Eakle. *The Spanish Element in Texas Water Law.* Austin: University of Texas Press, 1959.

"Documents Concerning Bienville's Lands in Louisiana, 1719–1737." Supplemented with translations by Heloise H. Cruzat and historical comment by Henry P. Dart. *Louisiana Historical Quarterly* 10 (1927): 5–24, 161–84, 364–380, 538–61; 11 (1928): 87–110, 209–32, 463–65.

Dodson, Leonidas. *Alexander Spotswood.* Philadelphia: University of Pennsylvania Press, 1932.

Donnelly, Ralph H. "The Colonial Land Patent System in Maryland." *Surveying and Mapping* 40 (1980).

Dorsey, Caleb. "The Original Land Grants of Howard County, Maryland." *Maryland Historical Magazine* 64 (1969): 287–94.

Dowdey, Clifford. *The Great Plantation.* New York: Rinehart and Co., 1957.

Downs, Raymond Herman. "Public Lands and Private Claims in Louisiana, 1803–1820." Ph.D. diss., Louisiana State University, 1960.

Duke of York Record, 1646–1679. Original land titles in Delaware. Wilmington: Sunday Star Print by order of General Assembly of Delaware, 1903.

Earle, Carville. *The Evolution of a Tidewater Settlement System: All Hallows Parish, Maryland, 1650–1783.* Chicago: University of Chicago Department of Geography Research Paper no. 170, 1975.

Eaton, David W. *Historical Atlas of Westmoreland County, Virginia.* Richmond, Va.: Dietz Press, 1942.

Eby, Frederick. *Education in Texas: Source Materials.* University of Texas *Bulletin* no. 1824, Education Series no. 2. Austin: University of Texas, 1918.

Egleston, Melville. *The Land System of the New England Colonies.* Johns Hopkins University Studies in Historical and Political Science, ser. 4, nos. 11–12. Baltimore: Johns Hopkins, 1886.

Ekirch, A. Roger. *"Poor Carolina": Politics and Society in Colonial North Carolina, 1729–1776.* Chapel Hill: University of North Carolina Press, 1981.

Elliott, F. Andrew. "The Administration of the Public Lands in the Greenburg District of Louisiana, 1812–1852." M.A. thesis, Louisiana State University, 1961.

Ellis, David Maldwyn. *Landlords and Farmers in the Hudson-Mohawk Region, 1790–1850.* Ithaca: Cornell University Press, 1946.

Ellis, L. Tuffly, Terry G. Jordan, and James R. Buchanan. *Cultural and Historical Maps of Texas from the Atlas of Texas.* Austin: University of Texas Bureau of Business Research, 1976.

Elting, Irving. *Dutch Village Communities on the Hudson River.* Johns Hopkins University Studies in Historical and Political Science, ser. 4, no. 1. Baltimore: Johns Hopkins, 1886.

Engerrand, Steven. "The Evolution of Landholding Patterns on the Georgia Piedmont, 1805–1830." *Southeastern Geographer* 15 (1975): 73–80.

Eshleman, H. Frank. "Four Great Surveys in Lancaster County." *Journal of Lancaster County Historical Society* 28 (1924): 8–12.

"Essays in the Social and Economic History of Vermont," *Collections of the Vermont Historical Society* 5 (1943).

Evans, Paul D. "The Pulteney Purchase." *Proceedings of the New York State Historical Association* 20 (1922): 83–104.

Fausz, J. Frederick. "Patterns of Settlement in the James River Basin, 1607–1642." M.A. thesis, William and Mary College, 1971.

Federal Writers' Project, Savannah Unit. A series of articles in *Georgia Historical Quarterly*, vols. 22–27 (1938–43), deals with development of plantations in the Savannah area.

_____. "Plantation Development in Chatham County." *Georgia Historical Quarterly* 22 (1938): 303–30.

_____. "Mulberry Grove in Colonial Times." *Georgia Historical Quarterly* 23 (1939): 238–52, 315–36.

_____. "Whitehall Plantation." *Georgia Historical Quarterly* 25 (1941): 343–63; 26 (1942): 40–64, 128–55.

Fehrenbach, T. R. *Lone Star: A History of Texas and the Texans.* New York: Macmillan Co., 1968.

"First Land Grants in Maryland: A Note on All the Warrants for the Granting of Land in Maryland." *Maryland Historical Magazine* 3 (1908): 158–69.

Fisher, Sydney George. *The Making of Pennsylvania.* Philadelphia: Lippincott, 1896.

Force, Peter, comp. *Tracts and Other Papers Relating Principally to the Origin, Settlement, and Progress of the Colonies in North America.* 1836. Reprinted in 4 vols., New York: Peter Smith, 1947, 1: no. 6.

Ford, Amelia Clewley. *Colonial Precedents of Our National Land System as It Existed in 1800.* Bulletin of the University of Wisconsin, no. 352. Madison: University of Wisconsin, 1910.

Ford, Anthony M. "Land Distribution and Settlement in Eastern Ohio with Special Reference to the First Two Ranges of the Ohio River Survey, 1785–1820." Ph.D. diss., University of London, n.d.

Foster, Theodore G., transcriber. "The Minutes of the Westconnaug Purchase." *Rhode Island Historical Society Collections* 25 (1932): 121–28; 26 (1933): 26–36, 94–98; 27 (1934): 24–32, 57–61, 127–28.

Foster, William E. *Town Government in Rhode Island.* Johns Hopkins University Studies in Historical and Political Science, ser. 4, no. 2. Baltimore: Johns Hopkins, 1886.

Fox, Dixon R. *Yankees and Yorkers.* Port Washington, N.Y.: Ira J. Friedman, 1963. First published in 1940.

Fox, Edith. *Land Speculation in the Mohawk Country.* Cornell Studies in American History, Literature, and Folklore III. Ithaca: Cornell University Press, 1949.

Frantz, Joe B., and Mike Cox. *Lure of the Land: Texas County Maps and the History of Settlement.* College Station: Texas A & M University Press for Texas General Land Office, 1988.

Freeman, Douglas Southall. *George Washington.* 7 vols. New York: Charles Scribner's Sons, 1948–57.

French, Carolyn O. "Cadastral Patterns in Louisiana: A Colonial Legacy." Ph.D. diss., Louisiana State University, 1978.

Fries, Adelaide L., and J. Edwin Hendricks, eds.; Stuart Thurman Wright, comp. *Forsyth: The History of a County on the March.* 1949. Rev. ed., Chapel Hill: University of North Carolina Press, 1976.

Fries, Adelaide L., et al., eds. *Records of the Moravians in North Carolina.* 11 vols. Publications of the North Carolina Historical Commission. Raleigh: Edwards and Broughton, Printers, 1922–69.

Friis, Herman. "A Series of Population Maps of the Colonies and the United States, 1625–1790." *Geographical Review* 30 (1940): 463–70.

Fry, William Henry. *New Hampshire as a Royal Province.* Studies in History, Economics, and Public Law 19, no. 2. New York: Columbia University, 1908.

Gammel, H. P. N., comp. *The Laws of Texas.* 10 vols. Austin, Tex.: Gammel Book Co., 1898.

Garvan, Anthony N. B. *Architecture and Town Planning in Colonial Connecticut.* New Haven: Yale University Press, 1951.

Garvin, James L. "The Range Township in Eighteenth-Century New Hampshire." In *New England Prospect: Maps, Place Names, and the Historical Landscape,* edited by Peter Benes. Proceedings of the Dublin Seminar for New England Folklife, 1980. Boston: Boston University, 1980, 47–68.

Gentry, Daphne S. *Virginia Land Office Inventory.* Richmond: Virginia State Library, 1976.

Gibbons, Boyd. *Wye Island.* Baltimore: Johns Hopkins University Press for Resources for the Future, 1977.

Giles, Bascom. *History and Disposition of Texas Public Domain.* Austin: State of Texas, 1942.

Gouger, James Blaine III. "Agricultural Change in the Northern Neck of Virginia, 1700–1860." Ph.D. diss., University of Florida, 1976.

Gould, Clarence P. *The Land System in Maryland, 1720–1765.* Johns Hopkins University Studies in Historical and Political Science, ser. 31, no. 1. Baltimore: Johns Hopkins, 1913.

Grant, Charles S. *Democracy in the Connecticut Frontier Town of Kent.* New York: Columbia University Press, 1961.

Green, E. R. R. "Queensborough Township: Scotch-Irish Emigration and the Expansion of Georgia, 1763–1776." *William and Mary Quarterly,* ser. 3, 17 (1960): 183–99.

Greven, Philip J., Jr. *Four Generations: Population, Land, and Family in Colonial Andover, Massachusetts.* Ithaca: Cornell University Press, 1970.

Hakluyt, Richard. *The Principal Navigations, Voyages, Traffiques, and Discoveries of the English Nation.* 12 vols. Glasgow: James MacLehose Sons, 1904. First published in 1589.

Haley, J. Evetts. *The XIT Ranch of Texas.* Norman: University of Oklahoma Press, 1953. First published in 1929.

Hall, John W. "Louisiana Survey Systems: Their Antecedents, Distribution, and Characteristics." Ph.D. diss., Louisiana State University, 1970.

———. "Sitios in Northwestern Louisiana." *Journal of the North Louisiana Historical Association* 1, no. 3 (1970): 1–9.

Haller, William, Jr. *The Puritan Frontier: Town-Planting in New England Colonial Development, 1630–1660.* New York: AMS Press, 1968.

Hamilton, Edward Pierce. *A History of Milton.* Milton, Mass.: Milton Historical Society, 1957.

Hammon, Neal O. "The Fincastle Surveyors in the Bluegrass, 1774." *Register of the Kentucky Historical Society* 70 (1972): 277–94.

———. "The Fincastle Surveyors at the Falls of the Ohio." *Filson Club Historical Quarterly* 47 (1973): 14–28.

———. "Captain Harrod's Company, 1774: A Reappraisal." *Register of the Kentucky Historical Society* 72 (1974): 224–42.

———. "Land Acquisition on the Kentucky Frontier." *Register of the Kentucky Historical Society* 78 (1980): 297–321.

Hamor, Ralph. *A True Discourse of the Present State of Virginia.* 1615. Reprinted, Richmond: Virginia State Library, 1957.

Harley, Robert Bruce. "The Land System in Colonial Maryland." Ph.D. diss., University of Iowa, 1948.

Harris, Marshall. *Origin of the Land Tenure System in the United States.* 1953. Reprinted, Westport, Conn.: Greenwood Press, 1970.

Harris, Richard Colebrook. *The Seigneurial System in Early Canada.* Madison: University of Wisconsin Press, 1966.

Harris, Richard Colebrook, and John Warkentin. *Canada Before Confederation.* New York: Oxford University Press, 1974.

Harrison, Fairfax. "The Northern Neck Maps of 1737–1747." *William and Mary Quarterly,* ser. 2, 4 (1924): 1–15.

_____. *Virginia Land Grants.* Richmond: Old Dominion Press, 1925.

_____. *Landmarks of Old Prince William.* Berryville, Va.: Chesapeake Book Co., 1964.

Hart, John Fraser. *The Look of the Land.* Englewood Cliffs, N.J.: Prentice-Hall, 1975.

_____. "Land Use Change in a Piedmont County." *Annals of the Association of American Geographers* 70 (1980): 492–527.

Hartsook, Elizabeth, and Gust Skordas. *Land Office and Prerogative Court Records of Early Maryland.* Annapolis: Hall of Records Commission, State of Maryland, 1946.

Hartwell, Henry, James Blair, and Edward Chilton. *The Present State of Virginia, and the College.* 1727. New ed., Williamsburg: Colonial Williamsburg, 1940.

Hatch, Charles E., Jr. *The First Seventeen Years, 1607–1624.* Williamsburg: Virginia 350th Anniversary Celebration Corporation, pamphlet no. 6, 1957.

Heite, Louise B. "Appoquinimink: A Delaware Frontier Village." Delaware Historic Preservation Section, 1972. Manuscript.

Hening, William Walker, ed. *The Statutes at Large: Being a Collection of All the Laws of Virginia from the First Session of the Legislature.* 13 vols. New York: Editor, 1823.

Hibbard, Benjamin Horace. *A History of the Public Land Policies.* Madison: University of Wisconsin Press, 1965.

Hienton, Louise Joyner. *Prince Georges Heritage: Sidelights on the Early History of Prince Georges County from 1696–1800.* Baltimore: Garamond Pridemark Press, 1972.

Higgins, Ruth L. *Expansion in New York.* Ohio State University Studies, Graduate School Series, Contributions in History and Political Science, no. 14. Columbus: Ohio State University, 1931.

Hilliard, Sam B. "An Introduction to Land Survey Systems in the Southeast." *West Georgia College Studies in the Social Sciences* 12 (June 1973): 1–15.

_____. "Headright Grants and Surveying in Northeastern Georgia." *Geographical Review* 72 (1982): 416–29.

Hitchens, E. Dallas. *The Milford Delaware Area before 1776.* Milford, Del.: Author, 1976.

Hitz, Alex M. "Georgia Bounty Land Grants." *Georgia Historical Quarterly* 38 (1954): 337–48.

_____. "The Earliest Settlements in Wilkes County." *Georgia Historical Quarterly* 40 (1956): 260–80.

_____. "The Wrightsborough Quaker Town and Township in Georgia." *Bulletin of Friends Historical Association* 46 (1957): 10–22.

Holcomb, Brent. *North Carolina Land Grants in South Carolina.* Vol. 1. *Tryon County, 1768–1773.* Clinton, S.C.: Author, 1975.

Holder, Gerald L. "The Eighteenth Century Landscape in Northeast Georgia." *Pioneer America* 13, no. 1 (March 1981): 39–48.

Howard, Clifton. *The British Development of West Florida, 1763–1769.* University of California Publications in History 34. Berkeley: University of California, 1947.

Hudson, Charles. *History of the Town of Marlborough.* Boston: T. R. Marvin and Son, 1862.

Hughes, Sarah. *Surveyors and Statesmen: Land Measuring in Colonial Virginia.* Richmond: Virginia Surveyors Foundation, and Virginia Association of Surveyors, 1979.

Huntting, Isaac. *History of the Little Nine Partners of North East Precinct and Pine Plains.* Amenia, N.Y.: C. Walsh and Co., 1897.

Illick, Joseph E. *Colonial Pennsylvania.* New York: Charles Scribner's Sons, 1976.

Isaac, Erich, "Kent Island": Part I—"The Period of Settlement"; Part II—"Settlement and Land Holding under the Proprietary"; Part III—Kent Fort Manor," *Maryland Historical Magazine* 52 (1957): 93–119, 210–32.

James, Alfred P. *The Ohio Company: Its Inner History.* Pittsburgh: University of Pittsburgh Press, 1959.

James, Bartlett B. *The Labadist Colony in Maryland.* Johns Hopkins University Studies in Historical and Political Science, ser. 17, no. 6. Baltimore: Johns Hopkins, 1899.

James, D. Clayton. *Antebellum Natchez.* Baton Rouge: Louisiana State University Press, 1968.

Jameson, J. Franklin, ed. *Narratives of New Netherland, 1609–1664.* New York: Charles Scribner's Sons, 1909.

Jillson, Willard Rouse. *The Kentucky Land Grants.* Louisville, Ky.: Standard Printing Co., 1925.

Johnson, Amandus. *The Swedish Settlements on the Delaware.* 2 vols. Philadelphia: University of Pennsylvania, 1911.

Johnson, Hildegard Binder. "Rational and Ecological Aspects of the Quarter Section." *Geographical Review* 47 (1957): 330–48.

_____. *Order upon the Land.* New York: Oxford University Press, 1976.

Johnson, John. *Old Maryland Manors.* Johns Hopkins University Studies in Historical and Political Science, ser. 1, no. 7. Baltimore: Johns Hopkins, 1883.

Jones, Charles C., Jr. *The Dead Towns of Georgia.* Savannah: Savannah Morning News Steam Printing House, 1878.

Jones, Theodore F. *Land Ownership in Brookline from the First Settlement.* With genealogical additions by Charles F. White. Publication no. 5 of the Brookline Historical Society. Brookline, Mass.: Riverdale Press, 1923.

Jordan, Terry G. *German Seed in Texas Soil.* Austin: University of Texas Press, 1966.

_____. "Antecedents of the Long-Lot in Texas." *Annals of the Association of American Geographers* 64 (1974): 70–86.

_____."Land Survey Patterns in Texas." In *Man, Culture, and Settlement,* edited by Robert C. Eidt, Kashi N. Singh, and Rana P. B. Singh. National Geographic Society of India Publication, no. 17. New Delhi: Kalyani Publishers, 1977.

_____. "Division of the Land." In *This Remarkable Continent,* edited by John F. Rooney, Jr., Wilbur Zelinsky, and Dean R. Louder. College Station: Texas A & M University Press for Society for the North American Cultural Survey, 1982, 54–70.

Journal of the Senate of the State of Georgia. November and December 1832.

Kain, Roger J. P., and Elizabeth Baigent. *The Cadastral Map in the Service of the State.* Chicago: University of Chicago Press, 1992.

Kain, William H. "The Penn Manorial System and the Manors of Springetsbury and Maske." *Pennsylvania History* 10 (1943): 225–42.

Kammen, Michael. *Colonial New York.* New York: Charles Scribner's Sons, 1975.

Kelley, Joseph J., Jr. *Pennsylvania: The Colonial Years, 1681–1776.* Garden City, N.Y.: Doubleday and Co., 1980.

Kershaw, Gordon E. *The Kennebeck Proprietors, 1749–1775.* Portland: Maine Historical Society, 1975.

Keys, Alice Maplesden. *Cadwallader Colden.* New York: AMS Press, 1967.

Kilty, John. *The Land-Holder's Assistant and Land-Office Guide.* Baltimore: G. Dobbin and Murphy, 1809.

Kim, Sung Bok. *Landlord and Tenant in Colonial New York.* Chapel Hill: University of North Carolina Press for Institute of Early American History and Culture, 1978.

Kingsbury, Susan M., ed. *Records of the Virginia Company*. 4 vols. Washington: Government Printing Office, 1906–35.

Klein, Philip S., and Ari Hoogenboom. *A History of Pennsylvania*. University Park: Pennsylvania State University Press, 1980.

Klinefelter, Walter. "Surveyor General Thomas Holme's 'Map of the Improved Part of the Province of Pennsylvania.'" *Winterthur Portfolio* 6 (1970), 41–74.

Kniffen, Fred, principal investigator. *Cultural Survey of Louisiana*. Reference section by Yvonne Phillips. Final status Report N7 ONR 35606, 1951.

Knipmeyer, William. "Settlement Succession in Eastern French Louisiana." Ph.D. diss., Louisiana State University, 1956.

Kross, Jessica. *The Evolution of an American Town: Newtown, New York, 1642–1775*. Philadelphia: Temple University Press, 1983.

La Potin, Armand Shelby. *The Minisink Patent*. New York: Arno Press, 1979.

Labaree, Leonard W. *The Early Development of a Town as Shown in Its Land Records*. Connecticut Tercentenary Commission Publication no. 13. New Haven: Yale University Press, 1933.

Land Grant Maps. Union, S.C.: Union County Historical Foundation, 1976.

Landesman, Alter F. *A History of New Lots, Brooklyn*. Port Washington, N.Y.: Kennikat Press, 1977.

Landsman, Ned C. *Scotland and Its First American Colony, 1683–1765*. Princeton: Princeton University Press, 1985.

Lang, Aldon Socrates. *Financial History of the Public Lands in Texas*. 1932. Reprinted, New York: Arno Press, 1979.

Langdon, George D., Jr. *Pilgrim Colony*. New Haven: Yale University Press, 1966.

Langston, Anthony. "Anthony Langston on Towns, and Corporations; and on the Manufacture of Iron." *William and Mary Quarterly*, ser. 2, 1 (1921): 100–106.

Lea, Tom. *The King Ranch*. 2 vols. Boston: Little, Brown and Co., 1957.

Learned, Marion Dexter. *American Ethnographic Survey*. Conestoga Expedition, 1902. New York: D. Appleton and Co. for University of Pennsylvania, 1911.

Leder, Lawrence H., *Robert Livingston (1654–1728) and the Politics of Colonial New York*. Chapel Hill: University of North Carolina Press for Institute of Early American History and Culture, 1961.

Lee, Lawrence. *The Lower Cape Fear in Colonial Days.* Chapel Hill: University of North Carolina Press, 1965.

Leete, Charles H. "The St. Lawrence Ten Towns." *Quarterly Journal of the New York State Historical Association* 10 (1929): 318–27.

Lefler, Hugh Talmadge, and Albert Ray Newsome. *North Carolina.* Chapel Hill: University of North Carolina Press, 1954.

Lemon, James T. *The Best Poor Man's Country.* Baltimore: Johns Hopkins Press, 1972.

Lester, William Stewart. *The Transylvania Colony.* Spencer, Ind.: Samuel R. Guard and Co., 1935.

Lewis, Peirce F. *New Orleans: The Making of an Urban Landscape.* Cambridge, Mass.: Ballinger Publishing Co., 1976.

Lockridge, Kenneth A. "Land, Population, and the Evolution of New England Society, 1630–1790." *Past and Present* 39 (1968): 62–80.

———. *A New England Town: The First Hundred Years.* New York: W. W. Norton and Co., 1970.

Love, John Barry. "The Colonial Surveyor in Pennsylvania." Ph.D. diss., University of Pennsylvania, 1970.

Lukes, Edward A. *De Witt Colony of Texas.* Austin, Tex.: Pemberton Press, 1976.

MacLear, Anne Bush. *Early New England Towns: A Comparative Study of Their Development.* Studies in History, Economics, and Public Law 29, no. 1. New York: Columbia University, 1908.

Mark, Irving. *Agrarian Conflicts in Colonial New York.* New York: Columbia University Press, 1940.

Marschner, Francis J. *Land Use and Its Patterns in the United States.* Agriculture Handbook no. 153. Washington: USDA, 1959.

———. *Boundaries and Records: Eastern Territory of Early Settlement with Historical Notes on the Cadaster.* Washington: USDA, 1960.

Marshall, Bernice. *Colonial Hempstead.* Port Washington, N.Y.: Ira J. Friedman, 1962.

Martin, John Frederick. *Profits in the Wilderness: Entrepreneurship and the Founding of New England Towns in the Seventeenth Century.* Chapel Hill: University of North Carolina Press for the Institute of Early American History and Culture, 1991.

McCain, James Ross. *Georgia as a Proprietary Province: The Execution of a Trust.* Boston: Richard C. Badger, 1917.

McKitrick, Reuben. *The Public Land System of Texas, 1823–1910.* 1918. Reprinted, New York: Arno Press, 1979.

McLendon, S. G. *History of the Public Domain of Georgia.* Atlanta: Foote and Davies Co., 1924.

McLoughlin, William G. *Rhode Island*. New York: W. W. Norton Co., 1978.

Meeks, Harold A. *Time and Change in Vermont: A Human Geography*. Chester, Conn: Globe Pequot Press, 1986.

Meinig, Donald W. "The Colonial Period, 1609–1775." In *Geography of New York State*, edited by John H. Thompson. Syracuse: Syracuse University Press, 1966, 121–39.

———. "Geography of Expansion." In *Geography of New York State*, edited by John H. Thompson. Syracuse: Syracuse University Press, 1966, 140–71.

———. *Imperial Texas*. Austin: University of Texas Press, 1969.

———. *The Shaping of America*. Vol. 1. *Atlantic America, 1492–1800*. New Haven: Yale University Press, 1986.

Menard, Russell R. "Economy and Society in Early Maryland." Ph.D. diss, University of Iowa, 1965.

Mereness, Newton D. *Maryland as a Proprietary Province*. 1901. Reprinted, Cos Cob, Conn.: John E. Edwards, 1968.

Meriwether, Robert L. *The Expansion of South Carolina, 1729–1765*. Kingsport, Tenn.: Southern Publishers, 1940.

Merrens, Harry Roy. *Colonial North Carolina in the Eighteenth Century*. Chapel Hill: University of North Carolina Press, 1964.

Miller, Thomas Lloyd. *The Public Lands of Texas, 1519–1970*. Norman: University of Oklahoma Press, 1972.

Mills, Richard Charles. *The Colonization of Australia (1829–42): The Wakefield Experiment in Empire Building*. 1915. Reprinted, London: Dawsons of Pall Mall, 1968.

Mitchell, Beth. *Beginning at a White Oak . . . : Patents and Northern Neck Grants of Fairfax County, Virginia*. Fairfax: Fairfax County, 1977.

Mitchell, Robert D. "Content and Context: Tidewater Characteristics in the Early Shenandoah Valley." *Maryland Historian* 5 (1974): 79–92.

———. *Commercialism and Frontier: Perspectives on the Early Shenandoah Valley*. Charlottesville: University of Virginia Press, 1977.

———. "American Origins and Regional Institutions: The Seventeenth Century Chesapeake." *Annals of the Association of American Geographers* 73 (1983): 404–20.

———. "The Colonial Origins of Anglo-America." In *North America: The Historical Geography of a Changing Continent*, edited by Robert D. Mitchell and Paul A. Groves. Totowa, N.J.: Rowman and Littlefield, 1987, 93–120.

Montague, Ludwell. "Landholdings in Ware Neck, 1642–1860." *Virginia Magazine of History and Biography* 60 (1952): 64–88.

Montgomery, Sir Robert, and Colonel John Barnwell. *The Most Delightful Golden Isles.* 1717. Reprinted, Atlanta, Ga.: Cherokee Publishing Co., 1969.

Morgan, Christopher, ed. *The Documentary History of the State of New York.* 4 vols. Albany: State Printer, 1949–51.

Morris, Gerald E., ed. *The Maine Bicentennial Atlas: An Historical Survey.* Portland: Maine Historical Society, 1976.

Morton, Richard L. *Colonial Virginia.* 2 vols. Chapel Hill: University of North Carolina Press, 1960.

Munroe, John A. *Colonial Delaware.* Millwood, N.Y.: KTO Press, 1978.

Myers, Albert Cook, ed. *Narratives of Early Pennsylvania, West New Jersey, and Delaware, 1630–1707.* New York: Charles Scribner's Sons, 1912.

Newman, Harry Wright. *Seigniory in Early Maryland.* Washington: Descendants of the Lords of the Maryland Manors, 1949.

_____. *The Flowering of the Maryland Palatinate.* Washington: Author, 1961.

Newton, Milton. "Certain Aspects of the Political History of Starr County, Texas." M.A. thesis, Texas A and I University, 1964.

Nicholls, Michael L. "Origins of the Virginia Southside, 1703–1753: A Social and Economic Study." Ph.D. diss., College of William and Mary, 1972.

Nissenson, S. G. *The Patroon's Domain.* New York: Columbia University Press, 1937.

Noyes, C. Reinold. *The Institution of Property.* New York: Longmans, Green and Co., 1936.

Nugent, Nell Marian. *Cavaliers and Pioneers.* Richmond, Va.: Dietz Printing Co., 1934.

O'Donnell, Thomas F., ed. Introduction to Adriaen Van Der Donk, *A Description of the New Netherlands,* trans. Jeremiah Johnson. Syracuse, N.Y.: Syracuse University Press, 1968.

O'Hara, Anne M. "The Loyal Land Company of Virginia." M.A. thesis, Columbia University, ca. 1954.

Old South Leaflets. Boston: Directors of the Old South Work, n.d., no. 172.

"O'Reilly's Ordinance of 1770." Reprinted from translation by Gustavus Schmidt, 1841. *Louisiana Historical Quarterly* 10 (1927): 237–40.

O'Toole, Dennis A. "Democratic Balance: Ideals of Community in Early Portsmouth." *Rhode Island History* 32 (1973): 3–17.

Owings, Donnell MacClure. "Private Manors: An Edited List." *Maryland Historical Magazine* 33 (1938): 307–44.

Park, Orville. "The History of Georgia in the Eighteenth Century." *Report of the Thirty-Eighth Annual Session of the Georgia Bar Association* (1921): 154–296.

Pattison, William D. *Beginnings of the American Rectangular Land System, 1784–1800*. Chicago: University of Chicago Department of Geography Research Paper no. 50, 1957.

Paullin, Charles O., and John K. Wright, eds., *Atlas of the Historical Geography of the United States*. Washington: Carnegie Institution of Washington and American Geographical Society of New York, 1932.

Payne, C. Frederick, "A Geographic Analysis of Responses to the 1805 Lottery Lands in Wayne County, Georgia." 1970. Manuscript on file in Georgia Surveyor-General Department.

Pennsylvania Archives. Ser. 3, vols. 2, 3.

Pett-Conklin, Linda Marie. "Cadastral Surveying in Colonial South Carolina: A Historical Geography." Ph.D. diss., Louisiana State University, 1986.

Phillips, Ulrich Bonnell. *Life and Labor in the Old South*. Boston: Little, Brown and Co., 1930.

Pickering, Timothy. Letter to Elbridge Gerry, March 1, 1785. In Octavius Pickering, *Life of Timothy Pickering*. 2 vols. Boston: Little, Brown and Co., 1867, 1: 504–5.

Pomfret, John E. "The First Purchasers of Pennsylvania." *Pennsylvania Magazine of History and Biography* 80 (1956): 137–63.

———. *The Province of West New Jersey*. Princeton: Princeton University Press, 1956.

———. *The Province of East New Jersey*. Princeton: Princeton University Press, 1962.

———. *The New Jersey Proprietors and Their Lands, 1664–1776*. New Jersey Historical Series, vol. 9. Princeton: D. Van Nostrand Co., 1964.

Pool, William C. *A Historical Atlas of Texas*. Austin: Encino Press, 1975.

Poret, Ory. "History of Land Titles in the State of Louisiana." *Publications of the Louisiana Historical Society*, ser. 2, 1 (1973): 25–42.

Potash, P. Jeffrey. *Vermont's Burned-Over District: Patterns of Community Development and Religious Activity, 1761–1850*. Brooklyn N.Y.: Carlson Publishing, 1991.

Powell, Sumner Chilton. *Puritan Village: The Formation of a New England Town.* Middletown, Conn.: Wesleyan University Press, 1963.

Raper, Arthur F. *Tenants of the Almighty.* New York: Macmillan Co., 1943.

Rather, Ethel Zively. "De Witt's Colony." *Quarterly of the Texas State Historical Association* 8 (1904): 95–191.

Rayback, Robert, ed. *Richards Atlas of New York State.* Phoenix, N.Y.: Frank E. Richards, 1957–59.

Reeder, Faye Bartlett. "The Evolution of the Virginia Land Grant System in the Eighteenth Century." Ph.D. diss., Ohio State University, 1937.

The Report of the Superintendent of the Coast and Geodetic Survey. 1895. 54th Congress, 1st Session, Senate Document no. 25. Washington: Government Printing Office, 1896.

Reps, John W. *The Making of Urban America.* Princeton: Princeton University Press, 1965.

Rice, Otis K. *The Allegheny Frontier: West Virginia Beginnings, 1730–1830.* Lexington: University of Kentucky Press, 1970.

Richeson, A. W. *English Land Measuring to 1800: Instruments and Practices.* Cambridge: MIT Press and Society for the History of Technology, 1966.

Richman, Irving Berdine. *Rhode Island: Its Making and Its Meaning.* New York: G. P. Putnam's Sons, 1908.

Richmond, Henry I. "The Plat of Little Compton" *Rhode Island Historical Society Collections* 21 (1928): 93–94.

Rife, Clarence White. "Land Tenure in New Netherland." In *Essays in Colonial History Presented to Charles McLean Andrews by His Students.* New Haven: Yale University Press, 1931, 41–73.

Riker, James. *Revised History of Harlem.* New York: New Harlem Publishing Co., 1904.

Rivers, W. J. *A Sketch of the History of South Carolina to the Close of the Proprietary Government.* Charleston: McCarter and Co., 1856.

Robertson, William. "An Account of the Manner of Taking up and Patenting of Land in Her Majesty's Colony and Dominion of Virginia with Reasons Humbly Offered for Continuance Thereof." *William and Mary Quarterly,* ser. 2, 3 (1923): 137–42.

Rutman, Darrett B. *Winthrop's Boston: Portrait of a Puritan Town, 1630–1649.* Chapel Hill: University of North Carolina Press for Institute of Early American History and Culture, 1965.

_____. *Husbandmen of Plymouth: Farms and Villages in the Old Colony, 1620–1692.* Boston: Beacon Press for Plimouth Plantation, 1967.

Rutman, Darrett B., and Anita Rutman. *A Place in Time: Middlesex County, Virginia, 1650–1750.* New York: Norton, 1986.

Sakolski, A. M. *The Great American Land Bubble.* New York: Harper and Brothers, 1932.

Salley, A. S., Jr., ed. *Warrants for Lands in South Carolina, 1672–1711.* 1910–15. Revised with introduction by Nicholas Olsberg, Columbia: University of South Carolina Press for South Carolina Department of Archives and History, 1973.

Sanders, William L., ed. *The Colonial Records of North Carolina.* 10 vols. Raleigh, N.C.: State Printer, 1886. Reprinted, New York: AMS Press, 1968.

Scharf, John Thomas. *History of Maryland.* 2 vols. Baltimore: John P. Piet, 1879.

Schenck, Elizabeth Hubbell. *History of Fairfield.* Vol. 1. New York: Author, 1889.

Scofield, Edna. "The Origin of Settlement Patterns in Rural New England." *Geographical Review* 28 (1938): 652–63.

Sears, Joan Niles. *The First One Hundred Years of Town Planning in Georgia.* Atlanta: Cherokee Publishing Co., 1979.

Seiler, William H. "Land Processioning in Colonial Virginia." *William and Mary Quarterly,* ser. 3, 6 (1949): 416–36.

Sergeant, Thomas. *View of the Land Laws of Pennsylvania.* Philadelphia: James Kay, Jun., and Brother, 1838.

Shepherd, William Robert. *History of Proprietary Government in Pennsylvania.* Studies in History, Economics, and Public Law no. 6. New York: Columbia University, 1896.

Sherman, Richard P. *Robert Johnson: Proprietary and Royal Governor of South Carolina.* Columbia: University of South Carolina Press, 1966.

Sherwood, Jeannette B. "The Military Tract." *Proceedings of the New York State Historical Association* 24 (1926): 169–79.

Shurtleff, Nathaniel B., ed. *Records of the Governor and Company of the Massachusetts Bay in New England.* 5 vols. Boston: Press of William White, Printer to the Commonwealth, 1853.

Simmons, Richard C. "Freemanship in Early Massachusetts: Some Suggestions and a Case Study." *William and Mary Quarterly,* ser. 3, no. 19 (1962): 422–28.

Sirmans, Eugene. *Colonial South Carolina: A Political History, 1663–1763.* Chapel Hill: University of North Carolina Press, 1966.

Smith, David C. "Maine and Its Public Domain: Land Disposal on the Northeastern Frontier." In *A History of Maine,* edited by Ronald Banks. Dubuque, Ia.: Kendall/Hunt Publishing Co., 1969, 192–98.

Smith, Ellen Hart. *Charles Carroll of Carrollton.* Cambridge: Harvard University Press, 1942.

Smith, Henry A. M. "The Colleton Family in South Carolina." *South Carolina Historical and Genealogical Magazine* 1 (1900): 325–41.

_____."Purrysburgh." *South Carolina Historical and Genealogical Magazine* 10 (1909): 187–219.

_____. "The Baronies of South Carolina," series of articles in the *South Carolina Historical and Genealogical Magazine:* "I: Ashley," 11 (1910): 75–91; "II: Fairlawn," 11: 193–202; "III: Cypress," 12 (1911): 5–13; "IV: Wadboo," 12: 43–54; "V: Seewee," 12: 109–17; "VI: Winyah" and "VII: Wiskinboo," 13 (1912): 3–20; "VIII: Boone's," 13: 71–83; "IX: Oketee or Devil's Elbow," 13: 119–75; "X: Hobcaw," 14 (1913): 61–80; "XI: Raphoe," "XII: Tomotley," and "XIII: Malling," 15 (1914): 3–17; "XIV: Ashepoo," 15: 63–72; "XV: Landgrave Ketelby's," 15: 149–65; "XVI: Quenby and the Eastern Branch of Cooper River," 18 (1917): 3–36.

_____. "Charleston and Charleston Neck." *South Carolina Historical and Genealogical Magazine* 19 (1918): 3–76.

_____. "The Ashley River: Its Seats and Settlements," *South Carolina Historical and Genealogical Magazine* 20 (1919): 1–51, 75–122.

_____."The Upper Ashley and the Mutations of Families." *South Carolina Historical and Genealogical Magazine* 20 (1919): 151–98.

Soja, Edward W. *The Political Organization of Space.* Commission on College Geography Resource Paper no. 8. Washington: Association of American Geographers, 1971.

Spalding, Phinizy. *Oglethorpe in America.* Chicago: University of Chicago Press, 1977.

Starrett, Paul. "Appraisal: The Creek Nation—Lands in Southern Georgia and Southeastern Alabama." Before the Indian Claims Commission, Docket no. 21, n.d., on file in Georgia Surveyor-General Department.

Stephenson, John G. III. "Land Office Business in Pennsylvania." *Villanova Law Review* 4 (1958–59), 175–97.

Stitt, W. Robinson, Jr. *Mother Earth: Land Grants in Virginia, 1607–99.* Williamsburg: Virginia 350th Anniversary Celebration Corporation, 1957, pamphlet no. 12.

Stiverson, Gregory A. *Poverty in a Land of Plenty.* Baltimore: Johns Hopkins Press, 1977.

Stokes, I. N. Phelps. *The Iconography of Manhattan Island.* 6 vols. New York: Arno Press, 1967. First published in 1915.

The Susquehannah Company Papers. 10 vols. Vols. 1–4, ed. Julian P. Boyd; vols. 5–10, ed. Robert J. Taylor. Ithaca: Cornell University Press for Wyoming Historical and Genealogical Society, 1930–71.

Sutherland, James Franklin. *Some Original Land Grant Surveys along Green River in Lincoln and Casey Counties (1781–1836).* Casey County, Ky: Casey County Bicentennial Committee, 1975.

T. "The Mode of Acquiring Land in Virginia in Early Times." *Virginia Historical Register* 2 (1849): 190–94. (This article signed "T" has been attributed to Virginia lawyer and governor Littleton Waller Tazewell.)

Tatter, Henry W. *The Preferential Treatment of the Actual Settler in the Primary Distribution of the Vacant Land in the United States to 1841.* New York: Arno Press, 1979.

Taylor, Alan. *Liberty Men and Great Proprietors.* Chapel Hill: University of North Carolina Press for Institute of Early American History and Culture, 1990.

Taylor, Paul S. *Georgia Plan: 1732–1752.* Berkeley: Institute of Business and Economic Research, University of California, 1972.

Thrower, Norman J. W. *Original Survey and Land Subdivision: A Comparative Study of the Form and Effect of Contrasting Cadastral Surveys.* Chicago: Rand McNally and Co. for Association of American Geographers.

Todd, John R., and Francis M. Hutson. *Prince William's Parish and Plantations.* Richmond: Garrett and Massie, 1935.

Udris, Juris. "The Conveyancer and the Surveyor." *Surveying and Mapping* 29 (1969): 235–38.

Vanderhill, Burke G., and Frank J. Unger, "Georgia's Crenelated County Boundaries," *West Georgia College Studies in the Social Sciences* 16 (1977): 59–72.

_____. "The Georgia-Florida Land Boundary," *West Georgia College Studies in the Social Sciences* 18 (1979): 59–73.

Voorhis, Manning Curlee, "The Land Grant Policy of Colonial Virginia, 1607–1644," Ph.D. diss., University of Virginia, 1940.

_____. "Crown versus Council in Virginia Land Policy," *William and Mary Quarterly*, ser. 3, 3 (1946): 499–514.

Wacker, Peter O. *Land and People: A Cultural Geography of Prein-dustrial New Jersey: Origins and Settlement Patterns.* New Brunswick: Rutgers University Press, 1975.

Wagner, Philip L. "Cultural Landscapes and Regions: Aspects of Communication." *Geoscience and Man* 5 (1974): 133–42.

Wakefield, Edward Gibbon. *A Letter from Sydney, the Principal Town of Australasia; and Other Writings on Colonization by Edward Gibbon Wakefield.* London: J. M. Dent and Sons (Everyman's Library), 1929.

Wallace, William H. "Some Aspects of Colonial Settlement in New Hampshire." *Proceedings of the New England–St. Lawrence Valley Geographical Society* 7 (1977): 16–23.

_____. "Compact Rural Settlement in Colonial New Hampshire." 1979. Manuscript.

_____. "Colonial Land Survey, 'Centre Squares,' and Reality in New Hampshire: The Masonian Grants, 1748–1754." 1980. Manuscript.

_____. "Lines on the Granite Hills: Rectangular Land Survey in Colonial New Hampshire." 1981. Manuscript.

_____. "The Mark of the Past upon the Land: Colonial Land Survey and Territorial Organization as an Element in the Contemporary Landscape of New Hampshire." 1983. Manuscript.

Wallach, Bret. "Logging in Maine's Empty Quarter." *Annals of the Association of American Geographers* 70 (1980), 542–52.

Washington, George. Letter to William Grayson, August 22, 1785. In *The Writings of George Washington,* edited by John C. Fitzpatrick, 39 vols. Washington: U.S. Government Printing Office, 1931–34, 28: 232–34.

Watkins, Sue, ed. *One League to Each Wind.* Historical Committee, Texas Surveyors Association. Austin: Von Boeckmann Jones, 1964.

Weaver, Bobby D. *Castro's Colony: Empresario Development in Texas, 1842–1865.* College Station: Texas A & M University Press, 1985.

Wertenbaker, Thomas J. *The Planters of Colonial Virginia.* Princeton: Princeton University Press, 1922.

Wheeler, George. "Richard Penn's Manor of Andolhea." *Pennsylvania Magazine of Biography and History* 58 (1934): 193–212.

White, C. Albert. *A History of the Rectangular Survey System.* Washington: USDI Bureau of Land Management, 1983.

Wilkinson, Norman B. *Land Policy and Speculation in Pennsylvania, 1779–1800.* New York: Arno Press, 1979.

Wilstach, Paul. *Mount Vernon.* Garden City, N.Y.: Doubleday, Page, and Co., 1916.

Winch, Donald. *Classical Political Economy and Colonies.* Cambridge: Harvard University Press, 1965.

Winthrop Papers. 5 vols. Boston: Massachusetts Historical Society, 1931.

Wood, Joseph Sutherland. "The Origin of the New England Village." Ph.D. diss., Pennsylvania State University, 1978.

Wood, William. *New England's Prospect.* Amherst: University of Massachusetts Press, 1977. Originally published 1634.

Woodward, Florence May. *The Town Proprietors in Vermont.* Studies in History, Economics, and Public Law no. 418. New York: Columbia University Press, 1936.

Wright, Henry Burt. *The Settlement and Story of Oakham, Massachusetts.* New Haven: H. B. Wright and E. D. Harvey, 1947.

Wyckoff, William. *The Developer's Frontier: The Making of the Western New York Landscape.* New Haven: Yale University Press, 1988.

Wykoff, V. J. "The Sizes of Plantations in Seventeenth-Century Maryland." *Maryland Historical Magazine* 32 (1937): 331–39.

Yonge, Samuel H. "The Site of Old 'James Towne,' 1607–1698." *Virginia Magazine of History and Biography* 11 (1903–4): 257–76, 393–414; 12 (1904–5): 33–54.

Index

Local place names are indexed under "localities."

397

The University of Chicago
GEOGRAPHY RESEARCH PAPERS

Titles in Print